Writing in Our Time
Canada's Radical Poetries in English
(1957–2003)

Writing in Our Time

Canada's Radical Poetries in English
(1957–2003)

Pauline Butling and *Susan Rudy*

Wilfrid Laurier University Press

This book has been published with the help of a grant from the Canadian Federation for the Humanities and Social Sciences, through the Aid to Scholarly Publications Programme, using funds provided by the Social Sciences and Humanities Research Council of Canada. We acknowledge the support of the Canada Council for the Arts for our publishing program. We acknowledge the financial support of the Government of Canada through the Book Publishing Industry Development Program for our publishing activities. We acknowledge the Government of Ontario through the Ontario Media Development Corporation's Ontario Book Initiative.

Library and Archives Canada Cataloguing in Publication

Butling, Pauline
    Writing in our time : Canada's radical poetries in English (1957–2003) / Pauline Butling and Susan Rudy.

Includes bibliographical references and index.
ISBN 978-0-88920-430-0

    1. Experimental poetry, Canadian (English)—History and criticism. 2. Canadian poetry (English)—20th century—History and criticism. 3. Avant-garde (Aesthetics). I. Rudy, Susan, 1961–   II. Title.

PS8155.B88 2005   C811'.540911   C2005-900692-7

© 2005 Wilfrid Laurier University Press
Waterloo, Ontario, Canada
www.wlupress.wlu.ca

Cover and text design by P.J. Woodland. Cover image: Roy K. Kiyooka (Canadian: 1926–1994). *Barometer no. 2,* 1964. Polymer on canvas, 246.4 x 175.3 cm. Art Gallery of Ontario, Toronto. Gift from the McLean Foundation, 1964. © Estate of Roy K. Kiyooka.

Every reasonable effort has been made to acquire permission for copyright material used in this text, and to acknowledge all such indebtedness accurately. Any errors and omissions called to the publisher's attention will be corrected in future printings.

Printed in Canada

The only thing that is different from one time to another is what is seen and what is seen depends upon how everybody is doing everything.

—Gertrude Stein

Contents

Contents

List of Illustrations

Pauline Butling and *Susan Rudy*

● *Writing in Our Time: Canada's Radical Poetries in English* provides both historiographic and critical introductions to poetry that has been variously described as radical, experimental, oppositional, avant-garde, open-form, alternative, or interventionist. We chose the adjective "radical" because its general definition—"tending or disposed to make extreme changes in existing views, habits, conditions, or institutions" (*Webster's*)—encompasses political, social, and aesthetic activities. The radical poetries in this study all enact "extreme changes." In the chapters that follow we discuss aspects of the *Tish* poetics, concrete and sound poetry, deconstructive poetics, and poetry inflected by race, gender, class, and sexuality. Such poetries have in common a compositional process that emphasizes the construction rather than the reflection of self and world—the production of meaning over its consumption. We also note that the social meaning of radicality has changed dramatically in response to identity politics and the global imperatives of the 1980s and '90s. We chose our title to emphasize that shift: *Writing in Our Time* refers to both an event held in 1979 and to *our* time (the turn of the twenty-first century). In 1979, the series of seven benefit readings for West Coast literary presses referred to as "Writing in Our Time" featured a predominantly white and male group of poets linked through three interconnected tracks. One started in western Canada with the *Tish* poets and extended into other sites of experimental poetics in locations across Canada. (These poets included George Bowering, Fred Wah, Frank Davey, Roy Kiyooka, Lionel Kearns, Brian Fawcett, Eli Mandel, Daphne Marlatt, Steven Scobie, Douglas Barbour, Victor Coleman, Dennis Lee, D.G. Jones, and Robert Kroetsch). The sound and concrete poets from Vancouver and Toronto formed a second track, associated with *Blew-Ointment* magazine in Vancouver and *grOnk/Ganglia* publications in Toronto (Victor Coleman, Steve McCaffery, bpNichol, Gerry Gilbert, and bill bissett). A third group included American poets associated with Beat and Black Mountain poetics, all of whom had influenced the Canadian scene. They were Robert Creeley, Diane di Prima, Allen Ginsberg, Robert Duncan, Edward Dorn, Lawrence Ferlinghetti, Ann Waldman, and Michael McClure. At the edge of this relatively homogeneous group, however, disturbances were brewing. Feminist initiatives were well underway with *Fireweed, cv2, Room of One's Own,* Women's Press, and Press Gang; and Japanese Canadian redress, Black power movements, and First Nations activism in Canada and the USA were successfully foregrounding social justice issues. So despite the celebratory, even self-congratulatory atmosphere of "Writing in Our Time," it proved to be the last time that such a homogenous gathering would go unquestioned. A major concern of this book is to note that shift and to redefine the social meaning of the radical accordingly.

The book is divided into two parts that follow this shift, with a chronology of nodes in an alternatives poetics network at the start of each section. Each chronology provides historical grounding for the discussions of poetics while also emphasizing that radical poetries are always intertwined with material and social contexts. Part 1 covers 1957–1979; Part 2 covers 1980–2003. Chapter 1, "(Re)Defining Radical Poetics," offers a historiography of the radical; critiques the linearity, implicit elitism, and gender bias in the discourses of avant-gardism; and posits an expanded discourse of radicality where innovation refers to the introduction of new subjects as well as new forms. Chapter 2 locates radical poetics within rhizomatic formations that are sustained by community-based poetry readings, grassroots publishers, "working ground magazines" (Duncan "Letter" 63), cultural nationalism, and even the commodification of dissent. The remaining five chapters cover aspects of *Tish*, bpNichol, Nicole Brossard (in English), George Bowering, Fred Wah, and Robert Kroetsch in that order. For the 1980–2003 period, we discuss later work by poets from the 1960s in chapters on Daphne Marlatt's *Salvage*, Robert Kroetsch's *The Hornbooks of Rita K*, and Robin Blaser's later "Image Nations" poems. Work by the younger generation is discussed in chapters on Erin Mouré, Claire Harris, Lisa Robertson, Jeff Derksen, and a section on Rita Wong in chapter 16. Chapter 16 also returns to the topic of historical/social contexts with a discussion of the crucial role of editorial activism in expanding discursive and material sites for marginalized subjects.

We make no claim to comprehensiveness in the selection of poets, nor in the topics discussed: there are too many of both to be addressed in a single book. Nor do we offer a definitive periodization of radical poetics. Our choice of specific texts developed in response to events, such as conferences that caught our interest, or to contingencies, such as a reading that excited us, or a book that peaked our curiosity. Also, in discussing the texts, we responded to the urgencies in the text, rather than following a predetermined agenda. That is, we were also writing in *our* time.

In the critical essays, we discuss both formal and social radicality. Micro-compositional strategies that destabilize semantic, syntactic, phonic, spatial, social, and ideological systems and open the poem to social critique and intervention are discussed in detail. Writing practices such as unconventional punctuation, interrupted syntax, variable subject positions, repetition, fragmentation, and disjunction, we suggest, make the poem a kinetic site for interventions in and rearticulations of "meaning." At the macro level, we examine the poets' explorations of the intersections of self and history, ideology, language, and the social text. These writers show us once again, like so many before them, the cultural utility of radical poetries: they offer habitation for difference.

More than ten years in the making, the book went through many changes: we stumbled frequently as we grappled with the shifting political/literary ground of the 1990s and the challenges of collaborative work. Practical matters proved to be the most difficult: to find time when we were both free, for instance. We managed weekly meetings for only a couple of months during the whole project; we had sabbaticals in different years; we both had other projects at various (and usually different) times. It helped that we had decided to write separately from the start, believing that the book would have greater range if we wrote from our different generational and professional experiences. Susan Rudy went to graduate school in the 1980s, Pauline Butling in the 1960s; we both lived in Calgary: Susan is a professor at the University of Calgary, Pauline has recently retired from the Alberta College of Art and Design. Pauline's interest in radical poetics started with personal friendships and later extended into her professional life; Susan's developed in reverse order. Susan's formation as a feminist took place in the late 1980s; Pauline's a decade earlier. However, we found common ground in our shared feminist politics, a love of poetry, and a desire to share those interests with others in print form (and we wear the same size of shoes!). Our different backgrounds meant that we could respond to each other's work as an outside reader more than as a co-writer. In fact, our interaction as readers was the most gratifying aspect of working together. We learned a tremendous amount from each other as we talked endlessly about who, when, where, what, why, how, and so what? We went through at least three titles, several epigraphs, and many rearrangements of the material. When we decided to include a chronology, the book began to come together. Here was a material grid that could structure the parts without collapsing the book's necessary disjunctions, without becoming reductive or invoking closure. Now, finally, we pass this writing in *our* time to you. Let the reading begin.

Acknowledgements

● We could not have completed this project without the intellectual engagement and emotional support provided by our extended family of spouses, daughters, friends, colleagues, students, and writers in Calgary and elsewhere.

The research for this book included interviewing some two dozen contemporary Canadian poets about their poetry, poetics, and histories. Special thanks go to them for being so generous with their time and for sharing their knowledge and experience with us: Marie Annharte Baker, derek beaulieu, Ayanna Black, Dionne Brand, Di Brandt, Stephen Cain, Victor Coleman, Jeff Derksen, Robert Kroetsch, Nicole Markotić, Daphne Marlatt, Ashok Mathur, Suzette Mayr, Steve McCaffery, Erin Mouré, Lisa Robertson, Lola Lemire Tostevin, Fred Wah, and Darren Wershler-Henry. For more general but equally generous conversation over the years, we thank Jeannette Armstrong, Caroline Bergvall, Nicole Brossard, Barbara Crow, Frank Davey, Lynette Hunter, Roy Miki, Miriam Nichols, Jeanne Perreault, Mary Polito, and the late Eli Mandel, bpNichol, and Bronwen Wallace.

We thank the following editors and conference organizers for providing opportunities to develop papers that served as a basis for some of the chapters in this book: W.H. New, editor of *Inside the Poem: Essays and Poems in Honour of Donald Stephens*; Charles Watts and Edward Byrne, editors of *The Recovery of the Public World: Essays on Poetics in Honour of Robin Blaser*; the Israel Association for Canadian Studies and Danielle Schaub, editor of *Mapping Canadian Cultural Space: Essays on Canadian Literature*; Frank Davey and *Open Letter* magazine, especially the issues on *Wanting It Otherwise* and *Poetry of the 1960s*; Lynette Hunter and Marta Dvorak who co-organized, with Susan Rudy, the Leeds conference "Women and Texts: Languages, Technologies, Communities"; Burton Hatlen, who organized "The Opening of the Field: A Conference on North American Poetry in the 1960s" at the University of Maine; Romana Huk, editor of *Assembling Alternatives: Reading Postmodern Poetries Transnationally*; and Charly Bouchara and Patricia Godbout, translators at *Ellipse: Oeuvres en traduction/Writers in Translation*.

The work of several graduate student research assistants must be acknowledged, particularly derek beaulieu, Susan Holbrook, Cindy

McMann, Jason Wiens, and B.J. Wray from the University of Calgary; Stephen Morton, University of Leeds; and Anne-Marie Wheeler, Oxford University. We thank each of them for their diligence and enthusiastic support for the project.

We gratefully acknowledge the generous support of the Social Sciences and Humanities Research Council of Canada, the Killam Foundation, the Centre for Women's Studies and Gender Relations at the University of British Columbia, the Centre for Research and Teaching on Women at McGill University, as well as our own institutions, the University of Calgary and the Alberta College of Art and Design.

Parts of the following sections of this book have been published previously, often in considerably different form:

Chapter 5 (an early version) presented at the McGill Centre for Research and Teaching on Women, 5 March 2002.

Chapter 6 (several pages) in Danielle Schaub, ed., *Mapping Canadian Cultural Space: Essays on Canadian Literature* (Jerusalem: Magnes, 2000) 18–36.

Chapter 7 (an earlier version) at the University of Maine Opening of the Field conference organized by Burton Hatlen.

Chapter 8 (a few pages) in *Open Letter* 9.5–6 (1996): 75–92.

Chapter 9 in *Women's Studies International Forum* 25.2 (2002): 225–34.

Chapter 10 (an early version) in *Essays on Canadian Writing* 60 (Winter 1996): 78–99.

Chapter 11 in Charles Watts and Edward Byrne, eds., *The Recovery of the Public World: Essays on Poetics in Honour of Robin Blaser* (Burnaby, BC: Talonbooks, 1999) 36–49.

Chapter 12 in W.H. New, ed., *Inside the Poem: Essays and Poems in Honour of Donald Stephens* (Toronto: Oxford, 1992) 167–73.

Chapter 13 (a few pages) in Romana Huk, ed., *Assembling Alternatives: Reading Postmodern Poetries Transnationally* (Middletown, CT: Wesleyan, 2003) 284–98.

Chapter 14 (an early version) in a French translation by Charly Bouchara and Patricia Godbout, *Ellipse: Oeuvres en traduction/Writers in Translation* 53 (1995): 54–71.

The authors wish to thank the following writers for permission to quote from their publications: Robin Blaser, Nicole Brossard, George Bowering, Jeff Derksen, Robert Kroetsch, Daphne Marlatt, Erin Mouré, Lisa Robertson, Fred Wah, Phyllis Webb, and the estate of bpNichol. The images from the Writing in Our Time and Women and Words conferences appear courtesy of the Contemporary Literature Collection, W.A.C. Bennett Library, Special Collections and Rare Books Division, Simon Fraser University; the cover image is from *Colour: An Issue* courtesy of *West Coast Line*. Thanks as well to Goose Lane Editions for permission to quote extensively from Claire Harris's *Drawing Down a Daughter*. Finally we thank our indexer and editor, Jacqueline Larson, for her impeccable work and enthusiastic support through the final stages of the book.

■

From the Canada Council to Writing in Our Time

● The little magazines, small presses, conferences, festivals, and other discursive/material sites that supported poetic experimentation in Canada between 1957 and 1979 are documented here. A second chronology for the period 1979–2003 follows in Part 2. Small presses and magazines that have not published poetry and/or have existed for less than two years are not included. Unless otherwise indicated, quotations of magazine editorial positions are taken from the first issue of the magazine. Descriptions of small presses are from the presses' publicity materials, usually on their websites. A brief list of contributors, titles, and/or participants is given with most entries in order to suggest the range of writers and the community interconnections at a given site, with particular attention to the poets who are associated with radical writing communities.

A note on accuracy: exact dates and precise information are often difficult to come by in the ephemeral world of little magazines and small presses. Whenever possible, we took our information from the physical objects rather than from the Internet (which proved to be inaccurate more often than not). Our main sources were the Special Collections at the University of Calgary Library, the Contemporary Literature Collection at Simon Fraser University, and the personal library of Pauline Butling and Fred Wah. We also consulted present and past editors of presses and magazines whenever possible. We thank them for their help. General references that we consulted were A.A. Bronson, *From Sea to Shining Sea*; Holly Melanson, *Literary Presses in Canada, 1975–1985*; Barry McKinnon, *BC Poets and Print*; David McKnight, *New Wave Canada*; Ken Norris, *The Little Magazine in Canada*; *The Oxford Companion to Canadian Literature* (2nd ed.); and Grace Tratt, *Checklist of Canadian Small Presses*. Internet sources include the Canadian Magazine Publishers' Association <http://www.cmpa.ca> (July 2000) and the Literary Press Group <http://www.lpg.ca> (December 2000).

1957 **The Canada Council** was established to "foster and promote the study and enjoyment of, and the production of works in the arts, humanities, and social sciences" (Bronson 24).

Combustion (Toronto, last issue, 1960). "A review of modern poetry." Edited by Raymond Souster. Featured both Canadian and American writers. The latter included Robert Creeley, Robert Duncan, Gary Snyder, and Louis Zukofsky.

1

The Contact Poetry Readings (Toronto, ended in 1962). Organized by Raymond Souster. Sponsored by Contact Press (1952–66), which was founded by Raymond Souster and Louis Dudek and published books by many of the experimental young poets including Eli Mandel, Milton Acorn, George Bowering, and Margaret Atwood. The Contact Poetry Readings provided a public forum for many young poets in the Toronto area.

Delta (Montreal, last issue 1966). Edited, printed, and published by Louis Dudek. "Delta is primarily a local affair: it is a poetry magazine for Canada with a job to do here." Featured young poets from central Canada, together with Dudek's own poems, essays, and reviews. *Delta* 19 (October 1962) focused on the *TISH* writers and other Vancouver poets.

1960   *Alphabet* (London, ON, last issue 1971). Edited by James Reaney. "A semi-annual devoted to the Iconography of the Imagination." Each issue was devoted to a particular myth or archetypal image. Contributors included many experimental young writers and artists including James Reaney, bpNichol, Jack Chambers, Margaret Atwood, Colleen Thibadeau, Greg Curnoe, George Bowering, and bill bissett.

Bohemian Embassy (Toronto). Opened June 1960 as a non-profit literary coffeehouse devoted to the development of literature and music. In 1963 Victor Coleman and Don Black began to host a Tuesday evening reading series. Coleman broadened the scope to include multimedia happenings. Poets who read included Gwendolyn MacEwen, Al Purdy, Margaret Atwood, Fred Wah, and bpNichol.

Evidence (Toronto, last issue 1967). Editors Alan Bevan, Kenneth Wells, Kenneth Craig. "The title of this magazine suggests its purpose. It is hoped its contents will reveal evidence of a search for new ideas and their expression." Published poets from central Canada (Al Purdy, Seymour Mayne, James Reaney, etc.) together with West Coast poets George Bowering, Daphne Buckle [Marlatt], Frank Davey, and Lionel Kearns.

The New American Poetry, 1945–1960 (New York: Grove, 1960). Edited by Donald M. Allen. Made available the work of many of the innovative American poets, including the beats, the Black Mountain poets, and the New York School. Also included important statements on poetics by Charles Olson ("Projective Verse") and Allen Ginsberg ("Notes for *Howl*"). Reprinted 1999.

1961   *TISH: A Poetry Newsletter* (Vancouver, last issue 1969). "*TISH* is the result of and proof of a movement which we ... feel is shared by other people as well as ourselves. Its poets are always obsessed with the possibilities of sound, and anxious to explore it meaningfully in relation to their position in the world: their 'stance in circumstance.'" (Davey, "Editorial," *TISH* 1). Editors for the first phase (*TISH* 1–19, 1961–63) were Frank Davey, George Bowering, David Dawson, Jamie Reid, and Fred Wah (first phase rpt. as *TISH* 1–19. Edited by Frank Davey. Vancouver: Talonbooks, 1975). Second phase, *TISH* 20–24 (Oct. 1963–May 1964), edited by David Dawson, Daphne Buckle [Marlatt], Dave Cull, Gladys Hindmarch, Peter Auxier, and Dan McLeod. Three more editorial groups kept the magazine going from 1964 to 1969 with various editorial combinations of Dan McLeod, Gladys Hindmarch, David Dawson, Peter Auxier, and others (*TISH* 25–30); Dan McLeod and Peter Auxier edited *TISH* 31–40. Editors for *TISH* 41–43, "d" [44] and "e" [45] included Brad Robinson, Colin Stewart, Dan McLeod, Stan Persky, and Karen Tallman. *TISH* featured the work of its editors, other Vancouver poets, and poetry by like-minded writers from Eastern Canada and the USA.

1963 *blewointment* **magazine** (Vancouver, last issue 1978). Edited by bill bissett. Others actively involved with the magazine included Martina Clinton, Maxine Gadd, Judith Copithorne, and Lance Farrell. Produced five volumes to 1968, followed by unnumbered "speshuls" such as "Oil Slick Speshul" (1971) and "End of th World Speshul Anthology" (1978). Featured Vancouver experimental poets and artists (especially those doing concrete poetry), together with Eastern Canadian poets such as Colleen Thibadeau, bpNichol, Dennis Lee, and Margaret Atwood. Established Blew Ointment Press in 1967 (see 1967).

Periwinkle Press (Vancouver, 1963–65). Founded by Takao Tanabe. Published only five titles: *Elephants, Mothers and Others* (1963) by John Newlove, *Kyoto Airs* (1964) by Roy Kiyooka, *Four Poems* (1963) by Robin Matthews, *White Lunch* (1964) by Gerry Gilbert, and *Naked Poems* (1965) by Phyllis Webb.

The Vancouver Poetry Conference. A University of British Columbia Summer School poetry course (24 July–16 August), it consisted of a three-week, intensive creative writing course (English 410, 3 credits), together with an evening, non-credit course in contemporary poetry, offered through the Extension Department. Organized by Warren Tallman and Robert Creeley, English 410 consisted of morning lectures and afternoon workshops while the non-credit course consisted of three evening readings per week. Writing-workshop leaders were Charles Olson, Allen Ginsberg, and Robert Creeley, with Margaret Avison, Denise Levertov, and Robert Duncan contributing. About one third of the forty-eight registered students were from Vancouver. Students from Eastern Canada and the USA included Roy MacSkimming, Clark Coolidge, John Keys, and Drummond Hadley. Many more attended unofficially.

1964 *Imago* (Calgary, London, and Montreal, last issue 1974). Edited by George Bowering. "It is intended ... for the long poem, the series or set, the

IMAGO
(seventeen)

Figure 1. Front cover of *Imago* 17 (1970).

sequence, swathes from giant work in progress, long life pains eased into print." Every third issue is a book-length collection. Contributors included Victor Coleman, Gladys Hindmarch, Daphne Marlatt, Stan Persky, Fred Wah, Michael McClure, and Ian Hamilton Finlay. Also published a chapbook series, Beaver Cosmos Folios.

Island (Toronto, last issue 1966). Edited by Victor Coleman. Contributors include Ron English, Gerry Gilbert, bpNichol, and Phyllis Webb. Continued as *IS.* in 1966. (See 1966).

1965   **Coach House Press** (Toronto, dissolved in 1996). Founded by Stan Bevington (printer) and Dennis Reid (art historian/designer), with editorial direction from Wayne Clifford and Victor Coleman (1966 to 1975). After 1975 an editorial board ran the press. Board members included Frank Davey, bpNichol, David Young, David McFadden, Michael Ondaatje,

Linda Davey, Christopher Dewdney, and Sarah Sheard. In 1967, with the publication of bpNichol's *Journeying & the Returns* (the fourth book published by CHP), the characteristic CHP combination of imaginative book design and innovative content was achieved (Dennis Reid 25). Coach House Press was arguably the single most important publisher of experimental poetics during the 1970s and '80s. Their twenty-year catalogue (1965–85) lists 385 titles, 134 of which were poetry books. CHP also published a Quebec translation series, which introduced the work of Nicole Brossard and others to English-Canadian readers.

Ganglia Press (Toronto 1965–80). Founded by David Aylward and bpNichol. Produced *Ganglia* magazine (1965–67) and grOnk publications (see 1967). Invited "manuscripts concerned with concrete sound kinetic and related borderblur poetry." Contributors included bill bissett, Victor Coleman, d.a. levy, and Ian Hamilton Finlay.

The Open Letter (Victoria). Edited by Frank Davey. "*The Open Letter* is an attempt to combine within the pages of a periodical the features of both a symposium and a debate. The subject will be poetry and its medium, language." Associate editors at its inception were George Bowering, David Dawson, and Fred Wah. Title changed to *Open Letter* as of Second Series, no. 1 (1971–72). The subtitle "A Canadian Journal of Writing and Theory" was added beginning with the Seventh Series, no. 1 (Spring 1988). Recent contributing editors include bpNichol, Fred Wah, Barbara Godard, Terry Goldie, Steve McCaffery, Lola Lemire Tostevin, and Smaro Kamboureli. Has also had numerous guest editors. Focuses on current poetics and cultural critique. Has published numerous conference proceedings and special topic issues (on Warren Tallman, Louis Dudek, Steve McCaffery, Bronwen Wallace, and others).

Weed/Flower Press (Kitchener and Toronto, 1965–73). Edited by Nelson Ball with graphics by Barbara Caruso. Moved to Toronto in 1967. Titles included books by bill bissett, George Bowering, bpNichol (*The True Eventual Story of Billy the Kid*), Victor Coleman, Nelson Ball, and David McFadden. Also published two periodicals, *Weed* nos. 1–12 (see 1966) and *Hyphid* nos. 1–4.

1966 **Iron** (Simon Fraser University, Burnaby [1966]–78). Series 1 (to May 1973), edited by Brian Fawcett and Hank Suijs; subsequent contributing and guest editors include Colin Stewart, Neap Hoover, Alben Gouldan, and Brett Enemark. "*Iron* will try to run a narrow course between the pedantic, the artsy-craftsy and cultural therapy, that is, between premature or artificial ejaculation." *Iron* II (1975–78) co-edited by Sharon Fawcett [Thesen] and Brett Enemark: "this series promises to continue playing with form ... *Iron*'s function we believe, as core, metal of earth, of this age—is to compose each issue into a fusion of many contemporary voices, one voice, other & working from outside in at history." Contributors include Robin Blaser, Gladys Hindmarch, Fred Wah, Susan McCaslin, Daphne Marlatt, Sharon Fawcett [Thesen], and Stan Persky.

IS. (pronounced eyes) (Toronto, last issue 1974). Edited by Victor Coleman. "Dedicated to the Occasional Poem." Continuation of *Island* magazine (see 1964). Subtitle dropped after Issue 1. Contributors included bill bissett, Ron Caplan, Frank Davey, Joy Kogawa, Tom Raworth, Gerry Gilbert, bpNichol, Michael Ondaatje, Judith Copithorne, Paulette Jiles, Maxine Gadd, P.K. Page, Daphne Marlatt.

New Wave Canada: The New Explosion in Canadian Poetry (Toronto: Contact Press, 1966). Edited by Raymond Souster with "crucial assistance (unacknowledged) from Victor Coleman" (Miki, "remains," *Meanwhile* 490). "I contend in all seriousness that within the covers of this anthology is the most exciting, germinative poetry written by young Canadians in the last 100 years of this country's literary history" (Souster, "About," *New Wave Canada*, 5). Contributors include Daphne Buckle [Marlatt], Victor Coleman, Gerry Gilbert, Lakshmi Gill, David McFadden, bpNichol, Michael Ondaatje, and Fred Wah. This was Contact Press's last publication.

Weed (Kitchener, last issue 1967). Edited by Nelson Ball. Contributors include bill bissett, George Bowering, bpNichol, Victor Coleman. Published by Weed/Flower Press (see 1965).

West Coast Review: A Tri-Annual Magazine of the Arts (Simon Fraser University, Burnaby, last issue 1989). Edited by Fred Candelaria (1966–86) and Harvey de Roo (1986–89). In 1990 merged with *Line* (see 1983) to form *West Coast Line* (see 1990). Published Earle Birney, Pat Lowther, Lionel Kearns, and many other BC poets. *West Coast Review* 12.2 (1977) was the book *New: West Coast: A Collection of 72 Contemporary British Columbia Poets*, edited by Fred Candelaria.

1967   **Blew Ointment Press** (Vancouver, 1967–83). Founded by bill bissett as an offshoot of *blewointment* magazine. Published numerous books by Vancouver's experimental poets. The press was sold in 1983 (see Nightwood Editions, 1983).

grOnk publications (Toronto 1967–80). Edited by David W. Harris, bpNichol, and rah smith. Published both Canadian and European "borderblur" poets. Contributors include bill bissett, Victor Coleman, d.a. levy, Ian Hamilton Finlay. Ganglia Press and grOnk publications became the core of the concrete and visual poetry movement in Canada.

House of Anansi Press (Toronto). Founded by Dennis Lee and David Godfrey. Founded to publish and promote Canadian writers. Poetry titles

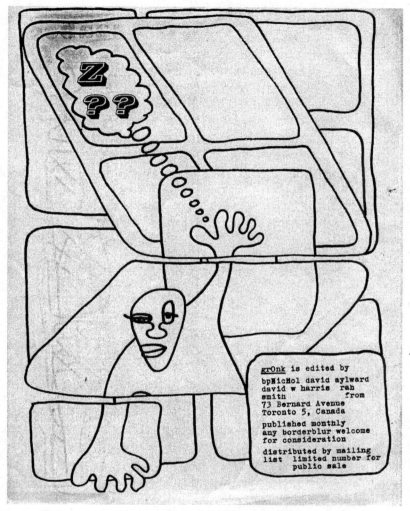

Figure 2. Announcement of *grOnk* publications; graphic by bpNichol.

include books by Christopher Dewdney, Dennis Cooley, and Erin Mouré. In 1988, the press was sold by owner Ann Wall to Stoddart publishing. Erin Mouré's *Furious* was the last book published before the changeover. Has continued to publish some poetry titles, including books by Mouré, Darren Wershler-Henry, and Monty Reid.

The Malahat Review (University of Victoria). Editors John Peter (to 1971) and Robin Skelton (to 1982); Constance Rooke 1982–92; Derk Wynand, 1992–98; Marlene Cookshaw (1998–present). Under Rooke's editorship, the magazine devoted three issues to "The West Coast Renaissance" (nos. 45, 50, and 60).

The Pacific Nation (Vancouver, last issue 1969). Edited by Robin Blaser. "I wish to put together an imaginary nation. It is my belief that no other nation is possible.... Images of our cities and of our politics must join our poetry." Contributors include Robin Blaser, Jack Spicer, Charles Olson, ·Gladys Hindmarch, and Stan Persky.

Poets: Here Now and Then. CBC television (30 April–23 July 1967). A series of thirteen half-hour programs on Canadian poets written, organized, and hosted by Phyllis Webb. Those profiled include bill bissett, George Bowering, Louis Dudek, Roy Kiyooka, and bpNichol.

Talonbooks (Vancouver). Founded by David Robinson from *Talon* magazine (Vancouver, last issue 1968. Edited by Jim Brown and David Robinson). Became Talonbooks in 1967. Talonbooks initially had a combined imprint with Very Stone House Press (formed by Patrick Lane, Seymour Mayne, Jim Brown, and bill bissett in 1965). In 1974, Karl Siegler became Talonbooks' owner/editor/manager. The press has published numerous poetry books including *Selected Poems* by bill bissett, Daphne Marlatt, Frank Davey, bpNichol, and Fred Wah in 1980; Phyllis Webb's *Selected Poems: The Vision Tree* in 1982; and *Pacific Windows: The Collected Poems of Roy K. Kiyooka* in 1997. Other poetry titles include books by those listed above together with younger writers such as Jeff Derksen, rob mclennan, and Adeena Karasick.

1969 ***Georgia Straight Writing Supplement*** (Vancouver, 1969–72). Editors Stan Persky and Dennis Wheeler. "What we're up to: simply, to publish writing. As a literary problem we think that this form ends the bind of the 'little magazine' with its esoteric coterie of writers and readers. As a political problem we want to serve a notion like: the mind of the community, of the imagination of the place, Vancouver" (Persky and Wheeler, no. 2, 39).

1970 **The Four Horsemen** (Toronto). Sound poetry ensemble made up of bpNichol, Steve McCaffery, Paul Dutton, and Rafael Barreto-Rivera. Performed at numerous, venues in Canada and at international sound poetry festivals.

Press Gang (Vancouver, 1970–2002). Began as a print shop that printed pamphlets and posters for leftist and counterculture groups in Vancouver. Became an all-women collective in 1974 and began publishing feminist and lesbian books in 1975. In the 1990s also published First Nations, Asian, and other progressive writers in Canada. Poetry titles include books by Betsy Warland, Joanne Arnott, Beth Jankola, and Rita Wong.

1971 **A Space** (Nicholas Street, Toronto). An artist-run centre for the presentation of experimental work in performance, poetry, and video. When Victor Coleman became executive director in 1975, it became a site of numerous poetry readings.

Open Space (Victoria). Founded by Gene Miller as an interdisciplinary venue. Sponsored numerous literary cabarets.

1972   *BC Monthly* (Vancouver). Edited and produced by Gerry Gilbert. Appears sporadically, with an emphasis on current work by West Coast poets, including Gilbert's own poetry.

Caledonia Writing Series (Prince George). Published by Barry McKinnon. Established to provide a non-commercial press in Prince George to promote local and British Columbia writing. Published Barry McKinnon, Pierre Coupey, Brian Fawcett, and others. (McKinnon, "The Caledonian Writing Series: A Chronicle" 2–17).

The Capilano Review (Capilano College, North Vancouver). Founding editor, Pierre Coupey. Edited and published by students and faculty of Capilano College. Poetry editors include Daphne Marlatt (1973–76) and Sharon Thesen (1976–89). General editors include Dorothy Jantzen and Sharon Thesen (2002–current). Published many young Vancouver writers and visual artists along with other Canadian experimental writers. Early issues include poetry by Earle Birney, George Bowering, Gerry Gilbert, Susan Musgrave, John Newlove, Andrew Suknaski, Andreii Voznesensky, Tom Wayman, and Phyllis Webb and visual work by bill bissett and David UU as well as fiction, photography, and reviews. Published numerous feature issues, including issues on George Bowering, Victor Coleman, Brian Fawcett, Daphne Marlatt, Michael Ondaatje, Gathie Falk, Roy Kiyooka, and sound poetry.

Island: Vancouver Island's Quarterly Review of Poetry and Fiction (Lantzville, last issue 1987). Nos. 1–16 edited by John Marshall, no. 17 by Angela Hryniuk. Contributing editors: Stephen Guppy (7), Daphne Marlatt (7–16), Lorraine Martiniuk, and Angela Hryniuk (15–16). Also published a chapbook series: *here and there* by Daphne Marlatt and *Owner's Manual* by Fred Wah in 1981, *Tin Roof* by Michael Ondaatje and *Sunday Water* by Phyllis Webb in 1982.

Repository (Seven Persons, AB, 1972–74 and Prince George 1974–77). Editors include John Harris and Bob Atkinson. Also published titles under Repository Press, including books by John Pass, Barry McKinnon, and Andrew Suknaski.

Véhicule Gallery (Montreal). An artist-run centre (primarily anglophone) that became an important venue for performance art, experimental music, poetry, and video. Writers associated with the gallery include Stephen Morrissey, Pat Walsh, André Farkas, Ken Norris, and Claudia Lapp.

Véhicule Press (Montreal). Founded by Simon Dardick. Began as part of Véhicule Art Gallery, to publish posters, newsletters, and programs. In 1973, the literary press was established under the direction of Guy Lavoie and others. From 1975 to 1981 it became part of the *Coopérative d'Imprimerie Véhicule*—Quebec's only co-operatively owned printing and publishing company. The press continued after the co-op dissolved under Simon and Nancy Marrelli. Began its Signal Poetry Series in 1981, edited by Nancy Marrelli, Anne Dardick, Rosemary Dardick, Simon Dardick, and Michael Harris.

Women's Press (Toronto). Emerged out of "Discussion Collective No. 6," a group of Toronto women. In the beginning the press was non-hierarchical and decisions were made collectively; it was avowedly anti-capitalist and nationalist in addition to being feminist. In the late 1980s its focus shifted somewhat to publish more writers of colour. Has published Makeda Silvera, Beth Brant, M. Nourbese Philip, Lillian Allen, Betsy Warland, Lydia Kwa, and Cherrie Moranga.

1973   ***Grain*** (Regina). Published by the Saskatchewan Writers' Guild. Editors have included Anne Szumigalski, Ken Mitchell, and Caroline Heath. Included both "new writers and writers of international recognition. How are they selected? By writing stories that are stories, and poems that are poems (a craft not nearly as easy as it sounds)." Contributors include Douglas Barbour, Dennis Cooley, Kristjana Gunnars, Robert Kroetsch, and John Newlove.

Oolichan Books (Lantzville). Founded and edited by Ron Smith. The name "is taken from the small fish which was so necessary for nutrition and light in First Nations cultures. The candlefish was also a valuable commodity on the trade routes where stories and news were broadcast in the oral tradition." Poetry titles include books by Daphne Marlatt, Robert Kroetsch, George Stanley, Sharon Thesen, Lionel Kearns, and E.F. Dyck.

Toronto Research Group (Toronto). Steve McCaffery and bpNichol began publishing a series of "Reports" on their investigations into psychoanalytic and poststructuralist theory and its applications to poetic practice. Their reports were performed at various locations and published in *Open Letter* when bpNichol became a contributing editor.

The Western Front (Vancouver). An interdisciplinary, artist-run centre that became an important venue for performance art, video, new music, and experimental writing. Poetry readings have been a constant feature at the Front, including a series of some fifty readings organized by Gerry Gilbert, Dwight Gardener, and Mary Beth Knechtel over a three-year period in the mid–1970s.

1975   **Brick/Nairn Books** (London, ON). Began as Nairn books, edited by Stan Dragland. Don McKay became an editor and co-publisher in 1977; Truus

Dragland and Jean McKay also helped with editing and production. Became Brick books in 1981 "to foster interesting, ambitious, and compelling work by Canadian poets, both new and established." Publishes six poetry titles per year, including books by Margaret Avison, Robert Kroetsch, Jan Zwicky, Hilary Clark, and Stan Dragland.

Clouds 'n' Water Gallery/Off Centre Centre (Calgary). An exhibition space for alternative art forms, it became an important venue for poetry readings, experimental theatre, new music, and dance in the late 1970s and '80s, under the direction of Calgary multimedia artist Don Mabie. Has changed locations several times and was renamed the Off Centre Centre in 1980, and The New Gallery in 1985.

Coteau Books (Regina). Founded by four poets: Gary Hyland, Robert Currie, Barbara Sapergia, and Geoffrey Ursell in order "to publish the best work by new western Canadian voices." Three of the first four books Coteau published were poetry; it published the first anthology of Saskatchewan poetry, *Number One Northern* in 1978 and a follow-up anthology, *A Sudden Radiance*, in 1987 (co-published with Thunder Creek Publishing Co-operative). Poetry titles include books by John Newlove, Andrew Suknaski, Louise Halfe, Kristjana Gunnars, Patrick Lane, Anne Szumigalski, and Dennis Cooley.

Contemporary Verse II (Winnipeg). Established and edited (1977–78) by Dorothy Livesay, who was one of the founders of the original *Contemporary Verse* (Victoria, 1941–52). "The poetry we want to praise and to print must have the authority of experience and action from all levels of society: the deprived, the enslaved, the sheltered, the brainwashed.... It must spring from all ethnic (and immigrant) sources, whose roots will nourish us.... And especially from all parts of the country we would like to explore the true feelings of women." From 1978–1985, there were several guest editors and special issues (Special Alberta Poetry Issue, Special British Columbia Poetry Issue, and Poetry from the Kootenays). In 1985, the magazine was redesigned and the editorial structure changed to a feminist collective (see *Contemporary Verse II* 1985).

Dandelion (Calgary 1975–99). Began as *The Dandelion Rag*, a biweekly publication of the Dandelion Gallery and Workshop (also established in 1975), which listed local art activities. Became a literary magazine in the summer of 1975 with an emphasis on publishing local writers. Founding editors were Edna Alford, Joan Clark, and Velma Foster. Subsequent editors included Alberta poets Robert Hilles, Claire Harris, and Ian Adam. Contributors included Douglas Barbour, Dennis Cooley, Kristjana Gunnars, Robert Hilles, Erin Mouré, M. Nourbese Philip, Monty Reid, Anne Szumigalski, George Elliott Clarke, Yasmin Ladha, and Robert Kroetsch. The demise of *Dandelion* was announced with its twenty-fifth anniversary edition (25:2,

1999) but it was resuscitated almost immediately as *dANDelion* (26:1, spring 2000) (see 1999).

Matrix (Lennoxville and Montreal). Founded by Phil Lanthier, Michael Benazon, Jan Draper, Marjorie Retzleff, Nigel Spenser, and Debbie Seed at Champlain College, Lennoxville. Moved to John Abbott College in Montreal, under Linda Leith and Kenneth Radu, in 1988. Various faculty and students from the creative writing department at Concordia University have edited and designed it since 1995. (Allen, "Editorial" *Matrix* 55). Publishes art, essays, fiction, and poetry from English-speaking writers and artists, mainly from central Canada but also includes work from other parts of the country. Recent poetry contributors include Lisa Robertson, Ryan Knighton, Ken Norris, Stephanie Bolster, and Tim Bowling.

Owen Sound performance group (Toronto). Brian Dedora, Michael Dean, David Penhale, Steven [Ross] Smith, and Richard Truhlar. Performed privately in 1975, first public performance was in 1976 at Fat Albert's Coffee House on Bloor Street in Toronto.

Porcupine's Quill (Erin Mills). Started as a production arm of Dave Godfrey's Press Porcepic. In 1975 became an independent press. Founded and still owned and operated by Tim and Elke Inkster in Erin Mills, Ontario. Published a number of poetry titles in its early years by young authors whom Tim Inkster knew from his student days at the University of Toronto. In the 1980s, the press shifted its emphasis to prose fiction. Recent poetry publications include Margaret Avison's *Always Now* and John Newlove's *Apology for Absence.*

Red Deer College Press (Red Deer). Founded by Gary Botting. Dennis Johnson became editor in 1981. Renamed Red Deer Press when it moved to the University of Calgary in 1999. In the late 1980s and early '90s, the press published Writing West Poetry Editions, a series that included Douglas Barbour, Monty Reid, Anne Szumigalski, Daphne Marlatt, Stephen Scobie, and Susan Holbrook. Nicole Markotić was poetry editor from 1998 to 2004. Titles under her editorship included books by Jonathon Wilke, Ian Samuels, and Susan Holbrook.

Room of One's Own: A Feminist Journal of Literature and Criticism (Vancouver). Founding editors, The Growing Room Collective (Laurie Bagley, Lora Lippert, Gayla Reid, Gail van Varseveld). "*Room of One's Own* will serve as a forum in which women can share and express their unique perspectives on themselves, each other, and the world." Publishes a range of traditional and experimental women writers.

Turnstone Press (Winnipeg). Founded by John Beaver, Dennis Cooley, and Robert Enright. David Arnason was peripherally involved at the start and later on became an official editor. "We were determined to publish poets from the prairies. We'd all grown up in a world that told us poetry was by definition written elsewhere, and that's where its worth was decided too" (Cooley email). Publishes several poetry books every year, including books by Patrick Friesen, Robert Kroetsch, Di Brandt, Kristjana Gunnars, Andrew Suknaski, Jan Horner, Fred Wah, Lydia Kwa, Janice Williamson, and Roy Miki.

1976 **NMFG [No Money from the Government]** (Vancouver, last issue 1979). Edited by Gordon Lockhead [Brian Fawcett]. "NMFG is a newsletter of poetry published without much pretence for the information of writers, painters, musicians & kindred. It has the political and cosmical purpose of making the west coast & specifically Vancouver a better place to work & live." Produced by Gerry Gilbert, Stan Persky, and Brian Fawcett. The majority of issues were distributed through a mailing list. Contributors included the editors and other West Coast poets together with some from other parts of Canada.

1977 **Periodics: A Magazine Devoted to Prose** (Vancouver, last issue 1981). Editors Daphne Marlatt and Paul de Barros. Contributors include Kathy Acker, Chris Dewdney, Gerry Gilbert, Roy Kiyooka, David McFadden, Anne Szumigalski, Fred Wah, Robert Kroetsch, Lyn Hejinian, Roy Kiyooka, Steve McCaffery, and Charles Bernstein.

Ragweed Press (Charlottetown). Founded by Harry Baglole. Established "for the purpose of publishing literary fiction, poetry and non-fiction from Atlantic Canada." Poetry titles include books by M. Nourbese Philip, Milton Acorn, and Fred Cogswell.

1978 **ECW Press** (Toronto). Founded by Jack David and Robert Lecker. Began as an extension of the journal *Essays on Canadian Writing*. Published more than fifty poetry titles to date, including books by Clint Burnham, Nancy Shaw, Catriona Strang, Karen Mac Cormack, Stuart Ross, Nelson Ball, Steve McCaffery, damian lopes, and Jacqueline Turner.

Fireweed (Toronto). Founding Editorial collective: Gay Allison, Lynne Fernie, Hilda Kirkwood, and Charlene Sheard. Devoted to stimulating dialogue, knowledge, and creativity among women. Recent editorial collectives include Tonia Bryan, Ritz Chow, and Aviva Rubin. Contributors include Dionne Brand, Erin Mouré, Kate Braid, Lillian Allen, Cécile Cloutier, Joanne Arnott, Louise Bak, Kam Sein Yee, and Neesha Dosanjh.

International Festival of Sound Poetry (Toronto). Eleventh Annual Festival organized by Steve McCaffery, Sean O'Huigin, and Steven Ross Smith. An annual event that began in Sweden in 1968, this was the first time the festival was held in North America. Performers came from eight countries. Noted for "the prominence given to collective and group performance: the simultaneous work of Jackson MacLow, the multi-voice pieces of Jerome

Rothenberg, the two British groups Konkrete Canticle and JGJGJGJG, the two Canadian groups Owen Sound and The Four Horsemen, and the American collective Co-Accident" (McCaffery, "International Festival" [19]).

Mercury Press (Stratford). Founded by Glynn Davies as Aya Press. Became Mercury Press, run by Donald and Beverly Daurio in Stratford. As Aya Press, published bpNichol, Steve McCaffery, and Arnold Itwaru. As Mercury Press published Sally Ito, M. Nourbese Philip, Gerry Shikatani, damian lopes, Nelson Ball, Paul Dutton, Di Brandt, Steven [Ross] Smith, bpNichol, and others.

Room 3o2 (Toronto/Ottawa). Founded by jwcurry, *Room 3o2* publishes curry's countless imprints including the magazines *Industrial Sabotage* and *Spudburn* and the leaflet series *Curved H&z* and *1cent.* curry uses a variety of publishing methods, including mimeograph, photocopy, holograph, silkscreen, and rubber stamp.

School of Writing at David Thompson University Centre (Nelson, September 1978–Spring 1984). The centre offered diplomas (in conjunction with Selkirk College) in writing, theatre, visual arts, and music; and bachelor degrees (in conjunction with the University of Victoria) in creative writing/English, fine arts, and education. The provincial government closed the centre in 1984. Founder and director (until 1982) of the writing program was Fred Wah; faculty included Tom Wayman, Colin Browne (director 1982–84), David McFadden, Paulette Jiles, and John Newlove. Students included Jeff Derksen, Angela Hryniuk, Calvin Wharton, Caroline Woodward, and Gary Whitehead. Following the DTUC closure, the Kootenay School of Writing was formed as a non-profit society in 1984 in Nelson and Vancouver (see 1984).

Underwhich Editions (Toronto). Founded by Michael Dean, Brian Dedora, Paul Dutton, Steve McCaffery, bpNichol, John Riddell, Steven [Ross] Smith, and Richard Truhlar. Later editors included jwcurry, Bev Daurio, Karl Jirgens, and Lucas Mulder for short periods. Paul Dutton and Steven [Ross] Smith have been the editors since the mid 1990s. Produced visual poetry, chapbooks, and audiocassettes such as *Sleepwalkers* by Richard Truhlar and Steven [Ross] Smith; *Beyond the Range* (Underwhich Audiographic no. 4, 1980); and *Sign Langage*, (Underwhich Audiographic no. 14, 1985).

Writers in Dialogue. (Toronto). A series of readings featuring American and Canadian women writers. Initiated by Marie Prins, Toronto Women's Bookstore, and Betsy Warland, Women's Writing Collective: "to demonstrate the similarities and differences of experience for women writing and publishing in the two countries" and to promote "a feminist dialogue on women and writing" (Lockey 9). The first in 1978 featured May Sarton and

Audrey Thomas; the second in 1980 featured Margaret Atwood and Marge Piercy; the third in 1981 featured Adrienne Rich and Nicole Brossard.

1979 **Writing in Our Time.** (Vancouver, 1979). A series of seven readings and panel discussions organized by Warren Tallman, Annette Hurtig, Jenny Boshier, and others under the auspices of the Vancouver Poetry Centre as a benefit for West Coast literary presses, particularly bill bissett's Blew Ointment Press. Featured Canada's pre-eminent avant-garde writers, including Steve McCaffery, bpNichol, bill bissett, Gerry Gilbert, Victor Coleman, George Bowering, Frank Davey, Fred Wah, Daphne Marlatt, Stephen Scobie, Douglas Barbour, Colleen Thibadeau, Dennis Lee, D.G. Jones, Eli Mandel, and Robert Kroetsch. Also included USA writers Robert Creeley, Lawrence Ferlinghetti, Robert Duncan, Diane di Prima, Allen Ginsberg, Ann Waldman, and Michael McClure.

■

Pauline Butling

● Aesthetic radicality throughout the twentieth century has mostly been defined by the discourses of avant-gardism.[1] Radical poets are described as cutting edge, ahead of the pack, forward-looking, on the attack, pushing the edges, leading the way in the discovery and conquest of the "new." Because of their advanced position (ahead of the social and economic mainstream), they must also create their own means of production. In 1912, when Ezra Pound, H.D., and Richard Aldington shook up the British/North American poetry world with the "Imagist Manifesto" (Pound, "Retrospect" 619) calling for a radically new, minimalist, free-verse poetry, they and others also simultaneously started writer-run little magazines to publish this new work (e.g., *Blast, Vortex, Poetry*, etc.). Likewise dadaists Hugo Ball, Tristan Tzara, and Hans Arp, who introduced their innovative sound poetry in 1916, simultaneously invented the venues for their work, such as the Cabaret Voltaire in Zurich. Throughout the twentieth century, experimental literary communities everywhere have taken on the task of making the necessary magazines, presses, and performance venues needed to present their work.

English-speaking Canadian poets joined this international avant-garde movement when F. R. Scott and A.J.M. Smith launched *The McGill Fortnightly Review* in 1925 to publish the new Canadian modernist/imagist poetry and when Dorothy Livesay, Raymond Knister, Smith, Scott, and others started publishing their imagist poems. The Anglo-Canadian avant-garde continued during the 1940s and '50s through an assortment of little magazines (*Preview, First Statement, Contemporary Verse, Combustion,* and *Delta*) and small presses (Contact Press, McGill New Poets series, etc.). In the 1960s, the countercultural social movements together with the new poetics from the USA and Britain (Beat poetry, projective verse, sound poetry, deep image poetry) brought new energy and direction to the Canadian and international avant-garde, as evidenced in many magazines and small presses established in the 1960s.[2]

From these founding moments onward, "avant-garde" has referred to both a social position—ahead of the mainstream—and to a subject position—that of adventurous, forward-looking individuals. These have continued to be the defining terms of radicality in the second half of the twentieth century, despite changes in the social meaning of the radical in the face of increasingly porous political, social, and aesthetic categories. From Raymond Souster's introduction to *New Wave Canada* (1966), to Richard Kostelanetz's *Dictionary of the Avant-Gardes* (2000), and including feminist studies such as Susan Suleiman's *Subversive Intent: Gender Politics, and the Avant-Garde* (1990), the concept of one group leading the way in a forward advance has been pervasive. For example, Souster praises the radical young poets of the 1960s in avant-garde terms: "this is Canadian poetry after one hundred years of our history, at last vigorous and very sure of where it is going" (n.p.). Kostelanetz cites "initial unacceptability" as one of his major selection criteria (preface to *Dictionary of the Avant-Gardes* xiii). Even American poet Hank Lazer's critical study of *Opposing Poetries* (1996)—a title which seems to intentionally avoid the term avant-garde in order to broaden the notion of what constitutes oppositional writing—is subtitled *The Cultural Politics of Avant-Garde American Poetry.*

One reason for its persistence is that, despite its outsider socioeconomic position, the avant-garde exists within the dominant ideology in that it enacts the progressive narratives of modernism/capitalism. All the strands of avant-gardism, as Charles Jencks notes—whether art as social critique, art for art's sake, or art as anti-art—are defined as a progressive advance: "All the avant-gardes of the past believed that humanity was going somewhere, and it was their joy and duty to discover the new land and see that people arrived there on time" (224). Indeed, their very existence is based on the "annihilation of the fixed, the valued, the already achieved" (Jencks 220). Further, the concept of an avant-garde fits with capitalist economic agendas. To cite Jencks again: "the avant-garde which drives Modernism forward directly reflects the dynamism of capitalism, its new waves of destruction and construction" (222).[3]

Its link to hegemonic narratives perhaps explains why the idea of the avant-garde persists as the basis for defining aesthetic innovation even as late twentieth-century literary radicality is often signified as much by class, gender, sexuality, and race-based critiques of power relations as by "new" forms and countercultural positioning. And as poets, cultural critics, and others have increasingly questioned the very notion of progress in light of failures on many fronts and/or because the "new" has become the rule rather than the exception. Consider, for example, the technological acceleration of the "new" to the point where "novelty is no longer particularly ground-breaking, since newness has itself become nothing more than an upgrade to the software of ideology" (Bök and Wershler-Henry 109).[4] Also, as writers and readers alike accept their complicity and interconnectivity, the claim to a "pure" countercultural or adversarial position becomes untenable.

Late twentieth-century radicality is more accurately characterized, I suggest, as a wide-ranging, historiographic project to reconfigure existing domains, reterritorialize colonized spaces, and recuperate suppressed histories. In military terms, it's more like a guerilla action. Taking Dominick LaCapra's definition of historiography as "the study of social meaning as historically constituted" (46), I reposition radicality within a history of community activism, little magazine and small press production, and within "enabling fictions of place, politics and poetics" (Davidson, *San Francisco* 10).[5] This last category includes a history of diverse local narratives of emergence (as opposed to a single line of avant-gardism), together with an account of nationalist institutions and agendas that have supported those local sites. The new radicality includes, but is not limited to, the traditional qualities of youthful rebellion, formal invention, and individual adventurousness. Also, the material sites remain similar—poetry readings, little magazines, small presses, and alternative performance venues continue to be the mainstays of experimental poetics in late twentieth-century English Canada—but the subject position includes minoritized figures (women, writers of colour, or explicitly lesbian or gay poets), and the social formation is rhizomatic.[6] As we suggest in the title of our chronology, literary radicality in the second half of the twentieth century is best characterized as multiple "nodes in an alternative poetics network," rather than as a single line with one group out in front.

This model not only embraces diversity but also avoids the implicit elitism that lies at the heart of the notion of an avant-garde. Like the specially trained military group to which the "vanguard" originally referred—"the foremost part of an army or fleet advancing or ready to do so" (*Concise Oxford*)—the literary avant-garde is seen as an elite group of "pioneers or innovators in any art in a particular period" (*Concise Oxford*). This assumption that one set of aesthetic practices is superior to all others, that one group represents "the newest radical alternative seeking to render all conflicting modes of representation obsolete" (Jim Collins 96) favours young, white, able-bodied, male subjects who are expected to be out in front, discovering the "new." The gender bias, however, is effectively concealed by the claim that *formal* innovations and countercultural positioning alone signify radical aesthetic practices. Richard Kostelanetz, for instance (arguably the foremost authority on the international avant-garde), insists that his membership criteria are objective: "My basic measures of avant-garde work," he declares, "are esthetic innovation and initial unacceptability" (preface, *Dictionary of the Avant-Gardes* xiii). Yet those who meet his criteria just happen to be overwhelmingly white and male. Can they be "naturally" more inventive? In a 1970s article on "The New Poetries," Kostelanetz explicitly excludes "'black poetry,' 'women poets,'" and any number of other "author-determined or content-determined rubrics" from the avant-garde. To claim avant-garde status for these groups, he argues, is a "debasement of critical language, mostly in the interest of exploiting the prestige of the avant-garde, without delivering the goods" and further that this "regrettably obscures the emergence of genuinely new poetries" (18).

Kostelanetz does have a point in that "author-determined or content-determined" subjects don't fit his definition. But his reason for excluding them begs the question. He should ask why not? That question might have led him to what USA black poet Erica Hunt calls the "political question of for whom new meaning is produced" (204).[7] The answer: if new meaning is produced for the cultural fathers, as it is in the Oedipal historiography of avant-gardism, then of course minoritized subjects don't belong.[8] The flaw is in Kostelanetz's definition in the first place and in his assumptions about subject position.

For a feminist or racialized subject who exists as the Other that affirms the potency of the dominant, radicality begins with first claiming subjectivity. As Rosi Braidotti puts it, they "must first gain access to a place of enunciation" (*Patterns* 122).[9] Since such subjects are not at the starting line, they can't be first off the mark. Their radicality lies as much in demanding to be heard, to which the fathers might very well turn a deaf ear. In LaCapra's terms, they have to reconstitute themselves historically. As Nicole Brossard argues, "if we talk in terms of feminist transgression, it is more complicated because the goal is not to make trouble for the sake of it, but to change the law and the authority to which it refers" ("The Aerial Letter" 59). And further: "Those who have never been able to speak the reality of their perceptions, those for whom the conquest of personal emotional territory has been precluded politically and patriarchally, will grasp that identity is simultaneously a quest for and conquest of meaning" ("The Aerial Letter" 67). Those who set out "to change the law" in their "quest for and conquest of meaning" have to change the social formations that relegate them to dependent or outsider positions.

"Re" poetics: "again, against ... anew, backward"

One common feature of the discourses that have developed in what Brossard called the "quest for and conquest of meaning" is the prefix "re": *re*defining, *re*writing, *re*claiming, *re*articulating, *re*inventing, *re*territorializing, and *re*formulating are some ways to change historical constructions and social positionings. Fred Wah usefully defines a "re poetics" as "the re-reading and re-writing strategies generated in the ethnic and feminist rejections of assimilation, the bargaining for a position of the potent in the reterritorialization of inherited literary forms and language" ("Poetics of the Potent," *Faking It* 203). *Re* posits lateral, spiral, and/or reverse movements rather than the single line and forward thrust of avant-gardism. *Re* disarticulates the forward imperative (as in disconnecting the links between cars on a train) and *re*articulates by jumping the tracks and hitching up trains that have been sitting idle or are rusting away on abandoned tracks. Not to be confused with the reactionary, neo-conservative political agendas, or the equally conservative nostalgia that informs retro-cultural productions, a *re* poetics involves *re*writing cultural scripts and *re*configuring literary/social formations. The goal is to *change*, not conserve, past and present constructions.

Any number of poems could be cited as examples of such historiographic reconstructions. Dionne Brand, for instance, in a sequence of poems from *Primitive Offensive*, describes herself as "a palaeontologist ... an archaeologist ... a papyrologist ... a geopolitical scientist" who works with shards, skeletons, bits of ancient scripts to find "any evidence of me." At the same time, she takes apart the oppressive, racist histories that contain her and reconstructs an alternative history, pieced together from fragments:

> a bit of image
> a motion close to sound
> a sound imaged on my retina
> resembling sound.
> a sound seen out of the corner of my eye
> a motion heard on my inner ear
> ("Canto III" 30)

Note that Brand's historical reclamation work is not simply a "documentary realism" aimed at authenticating a forgotten history.[10] Her goal is also to transform the present moment by reconfiguring the racialized subject as active and present. Similarly, Claire Harris notes that "in her poetry she works to *reverse* customary connotations and meanings" rather than simply uncover the past (Sanders 12, my italics). Rita Wong also constructs an alternative history to reconfigure the present moment, in her case a Chinese-Canadian history. The poet tracks a genetic lifeline into the past: "centuries of strong mothers bred me / blood crossing ocean & mountains / my cells shout history" ("pandora street," *monkeypuzzle* 43). But history is a double-edged sword. Its meanings ricochet back and continue to oppress the speaker, even as she rewrites it: "i can't bear the weight of history & i can't not bear it" ("ricochet" 26).

Marie Annharte Baker likewise writes of a double-edged relationship with history. In her comic satiric poem "Coyote Columbus Cafe," Baker takes shots at the historical erasure of Native people while also both mocking and affirming the need to rewrite that history:

> I always forget to mention
> we were too good way back when
> to be real people before discovery
>
> when I'm having an Indian taco day
> I discover it's just about too late
> not to educate the oppressor
> but am I ever good at doing it
>
> my tiny whiny coyote heart
> thump de thump thump thump
> kicking on the inside
> to get outside to howl
>
> how does a coyote girl get
> a tale outta her mouth?
> (Armstrong & Grauer 75–76)

Such historical reconstructions are not limited to racialized writers. In a series of poems by Jeff Derksen titled "Excursives," the tourist/narrator parodies Ezra Pound's dictum to *make it new* with the comment "I make it *old* here"(*Dwell* 32).[11] Further on he explains:

> Older because our oppression is
> ongoing. Today, the voice of the marketplace is Rod
> Stewart. Cauliflowers the size of a *fútbol*, he says: later
> their colour is described as "blancissimo." Tourists

> become social structures realized architecturally. Yet,
> in January, these empty structures move around—
>> a neocolonial hermit crab?
> (*Dwell* 33)

The oppressions enacted through colonialism are ongoing: in the above excerpt, for instance, an American voice rules the marketplace, tourism exploits the local economy. Derksen's tourist/observer is both complicit with and critical of the oppressions, is commoditized himself (as a tourist) yet is also a consumer of tourist commodities. Much of the poem exposes the irony of those contradictions, as in the following lines: "Parasite and place. A mackerel, figs, dried apricots and almonds, turnips, chorizo, three postcards, and a cultural dialogue that cancels all cultures" (*Dwell* 34). But the poem offers more than ironic self-awareness. Derksen "make[s] it *old* here" with a disjunctive language that functions as a wedge against the certainties of the "modern." Derksen, like Wong, Brand, Baker, and Harris, thematizes the problems of oppression, exclusion, and containment as well as disarticulates some tropes and codes that perpetuate those conditions.

Any number of group activities—from the Japanese-Canadian redress movement to the founding of magazines, presses, readings, conferences, and festivals that foreground new subjects—could also be cited as examples of historiographic reconstructions that helped change the face of the radical. Many of these will be discussed in more detail in subsequent chapters. Here I describe three such events. The first, Writing in Our Time (1979) represents both a high point and also the beginning of the end of a unified avant-garde in English-speaking Canada. The second, Women and Words/Les Femmes et Les Mots (1983), just four years after Writing in Our Time, shows a burgeoning feminist poetics. Some ten years later, Writing Thru Race (1994) in turn brought writers of colour and First Nations writers to the forefront.

Writing in Our Time
(Vancouver 1979)

A series of seven readings and panel discussion held throughout the year, the events featured many of Canada's pre-eminent avant-garde writers, including George Bowering, Frank Davey, Fred Wah, Daphne Marlatt, Roy Kiyooka, bill bissett, bpNichol, Steve McCaffery, Eli Mandel, Dennis Lee, Michael Ondaatje, Margaret Atwood, Colleen Thibadeau, and Victor Cole-

Figure 3. Warren Tallman at Writing in Our Time, Vancouver, 1979. Photograph courtesy of Simon Fraser University, Contemporary Literature Collection.

man; together with American luminaries such as Robert Creeley, Diane di Prima, Lawrence Ferlinghetti, Ann Waldman, Allen Ginsberg, and Michael McClure. Despite the national and international successes of these poets in mid-career (Talonbooks, for instance, published *Selected Poems* by Bowering, Davey, Wah, Marlatt, bissett, and Nichol the following year), the atmosphere was countercultural. The first reading, billed as "an evening of sound poetry" with performances by bill bissett, Victor Coleman, bpNichol, and Steve McCaffery, set the high-energy, celebratory tone of the series. Organized by Warren Tallman, Annette Hurtig, Jenny Boshier, and others under the auspices of the Vancouver Poetry Centre, the events drew audiences of as many as eight hundred. *Maclean's* magazine quotes Steve McCaffery saying (with reference to the opening reading) "it was the largest reading I've ever been to in Canada, not to mention one of the most boisterous ever" (Fournier 20d). Ostensibly a fundraiser for bill bissett's *Blew Ointment* magazine and press, the series also celebrated the cumulative successes of the North American, male-dominated avant-garde. (The handful of women included in the program had begun their careers in association with that group.)[12] Some discord surrounded the event: Phyllis Webb refused to attend; Dorothy Livesay protested Tallman's cultural imperialism.[13] But for the time being, at least at this event, critical voices were largely subsumed by the predominantly male ethos.

Women and Words/les femmes et les mots
(Vancouver 1983)

Just four years later, however, Women and Words/les femmes et les mots (a weekend conference), put women on stage, front and centre.[14] Definitely a watershed event, it represented the culmination of more than a decade of feminist activism on many fronts. It also inspired many more ongoing activities.[15] The Vancouver literary/academic community was startled and in some cases outraged by this women-centred gathering.

Daphne Marlatt, Nicole Brossard, Gail Scott, France Théoret, Louky Bersianik, and others presented their radical feminist texts. Jeannette Armstrong, Lillian Allen, Makeda Silvera, and Beth Brant spoke of their experiences of double colonization, as women writers and writers of colour. Barbara Godard, Lorraine Weir, Shirley Neuman, and Louise Forsyth, together with Quebecois feminist theorists Louise Cotnoir, France Théoret, and others, applied feminist critical theory to various

Figure 4. Daphne Marlatt and Louise Cotnoir at the Women and Words Conference, Vancouver (1983). Photograph courtesy of Simon Fraser University, Contemporary Literature Collection.

issues and texts. Others talked about women's theatre, women's presses, women's activism. Clearly "new meaning is [being] produced" (Hunt 204) for the mostly female conference audience, not the cultural fathers. Another significant departure from male avant-garde practices was that the venue was mainstream. The conference organizers chose the university as the site of resistance rather than the more typical countercultural, alternative venues. If your "goal is not to make trouble for the sake of it, but to change the law and the authority to which it refers" (Brossard, "The Aerial Letter" 67) then what better place to begin than at one of the major sites of "law and authority."

Writing Thru Race
(Vancouver 1994)

Writing Thru Race, a conference for First Nations writers and writers of colour organized by the Racial Minorities Committee of The Writers' Union of Canada, was a similarly groundbreaking event. Some two hundred writers of colour and First Nations writers attended the conference; audiences for the gala evening readings (open to the general public) numbered between four and five hundred (Miki, "Writing Thru Race: Chair's Report" 7). On opening night, Lenore Keeshig-Tobias captured the polemical reach of the event: she invited everyone to close their eyes, breathe deeply, and reflect on the promise of the moment. Then Dionne Brand, Daniel David Moses, and Lillian Allen read from their work, "mesmeriz-

Figure 5. Mark Nakada, Lillian Allen, Larissa Lai, and Roy Miki at the Writing Thru Race Conference, Vancouver (1994). Photograph courtesy of Roy Miki.

ing the audience as they did so" (Tator 93). Daytime plenary sessions addressed the hotly debated issues of access to publishing and appropriation of voice, together with strategies for coalition building and editing/publishing interventions. As with Women and Words/les femmes et les mots some ten years previous, the atmosphere was festive, celebratory, even polemical. Makeda Silvera, speaking in a session on publishing, paused to celebrate a moment of solidarity: "As everyone rose, and held hands, there was an audible sigh, a collective let-down, as if the worst was indeed over. And it was" (Conference Report, appendices, Tator 93). Indeed, this conference was a benchmark event, marking the culmination of more than a decade of literary/social activism aimed at redressing systemic racism and, for the first time, bringing together writers of colour and First Nations writers to talk about shared concerns. Like Women and Words, it also generated ongoing editing and publishing initiatives (see chapter 16).

By the 1980s and '90s then, radicality could no longer be adequately described within the discourse of avant-gardism. The "new" as often as not critiques the privileged subject formations and grand narratives of progress that lie at the heart of avant-gardism. The cultural utility of the radical now lies in recuperating the *old* and reconstituting the *now* into rhizomatic formations that embrace difference. Its social effects include knocking the dominant off their pedestals (including the white men who have dominated the paradigm of the radical), if not shaking the whole edifice. When women take possession of words, when writers write through a racialized history, when minoritized subjects begin to speak, the effects extend well beyond the realm of formal innovation.

Notes

1 See Charles Jencks's essay "The Post-Avant-Garde" for a very useful outline of the various discourses of avant-gardism and the historical complexities covered by this term (Jenks 215–24).

2 See the 1960s entries in the chronology for the names of the English Canadian avant-garde little magazines and small presses of that decade.

3 A further reason for our reluctance to give up the notion of "advance" is perhaps, as Jim Collins suggests, based on our "nostalgia for the Paradise Lost of the homogenous culture, and the Marxists'/avant-gardists' ability to stand in opposition to it, making easy, yet absolute value judgments—rather like a countercultural Salvation Army beating its moralistic drum about the wickedness of the dominant culture" (99).

4 This remark is made by Christian Bök in dialogue with Darren Wershler-Henry. Wershler-Henry responds by noting "that puts us in an impossible position… because we can no longer 'make it new' because that was what the modernists did. Making it new is old" (Bök 109–10).

5 In LaCapra's analysis, this is only one strand among several new trends in historiography. However, it is the most relevant to my argument because it relates to intellectual history. LaCapra's full list of the "prominent trends" is as follows: "an inclination to rely on a social definition of context as an explanatory matrix; a shift toward an interest in popular culture; a reconceptualization of culture in terms of collective discourses, mentalities, world views, and even 'languages'; a redefinition of intellectual history as the study of social meaning as historically constituted; and an archivally based documentary realism that treats artifacts as quarries for facts in the reconstitution of societies and cultures of the past" (*History and Criticism* 46).

6 The presence of gay male subjects is not new. Avant-garde groups have included many gay men, from Rimbaud to Roland Barthes, suggesting that male privilege overrides sexual orientation. However the explicit celebration of male homosexual experience is relatively new.

7 Hunt's statement is worth quoting in full: "One troubling aspect of privileging language as the primary site to torque new meaning and possibility is that it is severed from the political question of for whom new meaning is produced" ("Notes" 204).

8 For an excellent critique of Oedipal historiography, see Katherine Kearns, *Psychoanalysis, Historiography, and Feminist Theory* (9–10).

9 See also Nancy K. Miller's *Subject to Change: Reading Feminist Writing*.

10 See LaCapra in note 5 above.

11 See also Miriam Nichols's discussion of this shift from the new to the old in her article "A/Politics of Contemporary Anglo-Canadian Poetries."

12 I don't mean to suggest that the women were simply falling into line. In fact most of them were involved in feminist work by that time. My point is rather that the dominant ethos was male.

13 Warren Tallman notes: "complaints about the invasion by American poets who take up places at the readings which might better be occupied by BC poets" in the *Vancouver Poetry Centre Newsletter*. Tallman dismisses these complaints as pure xenophobia, calling them "a timorous, querulous, islanded outcry" ("'Some Consistent Quality of Intelligent Love': Open Letter to Phyllis Webb" 2).

14 In terms of numbers alone it was a huge success. The conference "brought together over 1,000 anglophone and francophone women involved in traditional and alternative forms of literary activity" (Dybikowski et al. 9). See chapter 9 for more discussion of this event.

15 In the editorial statement for the first issue by the feminist collective of *Contemporary Verse II*, for instance, the editors explain that "*Women and Words* focused our frustrations and our energies and we began to think seriously about forming an editorial collective" (Banting et al. 4).

■

Poetry, Publishing, Politics, and Communities

Pauline Butling

● Like the image of multiple nodes and tendrils of plant rhizomes—
think of potatoes, peanuts, irises, buttercups, or crab grass—adopted by
Gilles Deleuze and Felix Guatarri to describe the postmodern discursive
field, the radical poetics field since 1960 has increasingly become a network
of multiple, asymmetrical, interconnected nodes. With more than one
line, and more than one site of intervention, the generative energy is local-
ized and mobile. In both the plant rhizome and the literary networks, the
nodes are where the action is, where the growth occurs. At the same time,
nodes are interconnected via tendrils that circulate nutrients throughout
the network. In this chapter, I outline some of the constitutive vectors of
radical literary nodes together with their sustaining networks. Specifically,
I consider the centrifugal function of locally identified publishers, confer-
ences, and festivals; the community-building role of poetry readings; the
importance of "working ground" magazines in providing discursive/mate-
rial sites for new subjectivities and formal experiments; and the complex
relationship of radical poetics to the cultural nationalism (i.e., Canada
Council funding) that partially sustains it.

I particularly like the rhizome model because it avoids the extremes of
an isolated or xenophobic localism often found in decentred models, or the
ahistorical pluralism implied in liberalism and/or multiculturalism (as in
the ubiquitous United Colors of Benetton images, for instance, of happy,
multiracial groups holding hands across racial and cultural divides where
economic inequality and systemic exploitation magically disappear). The
rhizome posits a dynamic interconnectivity together with the possibility of
intervention because nodes are critically active sites that can "intersect
roots and sometimes merge with them," or "cut roots and make new con-
nections" (Deleuze and Guatarri 13). Nodes can tendril into the political/
social body with a disruptive and/or transformative criticality. In place of
the single line of avant-gardism, the rhizome metaphorizes a fertile matrix
of provisional, critically active positions. As such, it also usefully works
against the nationalist "line" which collapses multidirectional activities
into a homogenous Canadian literary family complete with a genealogy of
mothers, fathers, and rebellious or derivative sons and (mostly) dutiful
daughters. It also emphasizes the potential for social effects in the image of
growing and overspilling, or intersecting and merging. To cite Deleuze
and Guatarri:

unlike trees or their roots, the rhizome connects any point to any
other point.... The rhizome is reducible neither to the One nor the mul-
tiple.... It is composed not of units but of dimensions, or rather direc-
tions in motion. It has neither beginning nor end, but always a middle
(*milieu*) from which it grows and which it overspills. (21)

A parallel notion of a kinetic "middle" that generates radiating, interactive
networks first showed up in the radical poetics of the 1950s and '60s. Pro-
jective verse, Deep Image poetry, Beat poetry, etc. were all connected to new
epistemologies that emphasized interconnectivity. Drawing from such
diverse fields as particle physics, Gestalt psychology, structural linguistics,
anthropology, Zen Buddhism, or Heraclitean philosophy, writers in the
1950s and '60s called for nothing less than a paradigmatic shift at both the
macro and micro levels. Charles Olson, for instance, begins his highly
influential "Projective Verse" essay with a call for a change in the "stance
toward reality outside the poem" (394) because projective verse calls for
changes that are "beyond, and larger than, the technical" (386).[1] Specifically,
Olson emphasizes decentring the self and opening the poem to dynamic,
"natural" processes:

> Objectism is the getting rid of the lyrical interference of the individ-
> ual as ego, of the "subject" and his soul, that peculiar presumption by
> which western man has interposed himself between what he is as a crea-
> ture of nature ... and those other creations of nature which we may, with
> no derogation, call objects. (395)

Similarly, Robert Duncan, in an essay on "Ideas of the Meaning of Form"
published in *Kulchur* magazine in 1961 speaks of the "world of thought and
feeling in which we may participate but not dominate, where we are used
by things even as we use them" (91) and of "a vision of life where informa-
tion and intelligence invade us, where we are part of the creative process,
not its goal" (101). Or Allen Ginsberg declares "Mind is shapely, Art is
shapely" (415) in "Notes for *Howl* and Other Poems" urging the poet to trust
the interconnections between the internal processes of thought and feel-
ing and the external act of writing the poem.

In the Canadian context, poetic experimentation likewise turned to
field models with the *Tish* poets' emphasis on "composition by field"
(Olson, "Projective Verse" 387) and in the Canadian/international exper-
iments in sound and visual poetics. In sound poetry, for instance, the
poem is produced within a gestalt of social, psychological, emotional, and
phonic energies. Although the particularities of various locals make for

diverse practices, all the different experiments share an interest in kinetic, interactive, epistemological models. As a corollary, the new poetries often went hand in hand with social/political liberation movements. The pursuit of sexual freedom, psychogenic freedom, liberation from middle-class values, from hierarchical systems, along with gay liberation, women's liberation, etc. were often intertwined with radical poetics as poets enacted various "locals" against the homogenizing, controlling power of the dominant.[2]

Experiments in poetic form were also often characterized as liberatory. One well-known example was *Translating Translating Apollinaire*, a playful, fluid, rhizomatic project initiated by bpNichol in the 1970s that disrupted notions of meaning and authorship. An open-ended collaborative project, the first publication included Nichol's own "translations" as well as those by seven other writers, including Dick Higgins, Steve McCaffery, Richard Truhlar, Douglas Barbour, and Cavan McCarthy. In place of translation as the transmission of meaning from one language to another, they invented other modes, such as Nichol's "sound translation" (6), or his "walking east along the northern boundary looking south" (10), or Steve McCaffery's "stereo translation" (25), or Hart Broudy's "alchemical translation" (39). bpNichol and Steve McCaffery's collaborative publications as the Toronto Research Group are another example of a combined political/social/aesthetic project (see chap. 4).[3] The popularity of the renga as a collaborative form is yet another. In *Linked Alive*, a title which itself posits a polymorphous body, Ayanna Black, Dôre Michelut, Anne-Marie Alonzo, Charles Douglas, Paul Savoie, and Lee Maracle produce an intertwined body of poems by a circular writing process.[4] Finally, the development of the Canadian long poem as the preferred form for much experimental poetry in English-speaking Canada over the past three decades can also be linked to a liberatory model in the sense that its fluid, disjunctive, and often playful seriality continuously intercepts narrative systems and lyric closures.[5]

Changes in the social positioning of the radical to sites that facilitate diverse modes of intervention were linked to changes in the material conditions of cultural production as much as to new epistemologies and liberatory social movements. The 1970s saw the reorganization of Canadian literary publishing into a rhizomatic, countrywide network of regional presses and grassroots magazines that linked literary production to local narratives of resistance and emergence. This replaced the former, centralized publishing system that revolved around nationalist agendas and was concentrated in central Canada.[6] Frank Davey notes the transformative role of this decentred publishing network in supporting diversity and regionalism in the introduction to his 1974 publication, *From There to Here: A Guide to English Canadian Literature since 1960*. The technological shift to micro-production, he suggests, facilitated an ideological shift to a "restructured world of diminished central authority and amplified individuals and counter-structures" (15). That is, "the decentralisation made possible by portable, inexpensive, electric or electronic equipment has meant that a multiplicity of alternative aesthetic systems, or even value systems, can co-exist without any one of them needing to gain total domination to survive" (13–14).

Beginning with the founding of Coach House Press in 1965 and Talonbooks, Blew Ointment, grOnk, and House of Anansi presses in 1967, a virtual tidal wave of publishing swept across the country over the next two decades. In 1966–67 alone, seven little magazines were established. Nineteen-seventy-five was another benchmark year with four new regional presses starting up: Turnstone in Manitoba, Red Deer in Alberta, Brick/Nairn in southern Ontario, and Coteau in Saskatchewan. This grassroots publishing movement was often geographically based, as for example with the prairie-identified presses—Turnstone (Winnipeg), Thistledown (Saskatoon), Coteau (Regina), or NeWest (Edmonton), or the prairie-identified magazines *Grain, Prairie Fire,* and *Dandelion*. But the "local" often signified social formations as well as geographic locations. There were women-identified magazines such as cv2 (1975), *Fireweed* (1978), and *Tessera* (1984) and women-identified presses: Press Gang (1970), The Women's Press (1972), and Sister Vision Press (1985). Other local sites included Theytus Books (1980) to publish First Nations writing, Pemmican (1980) for Métis, Williams Wallace (1980) for writers of colour and tsar (1981) for South Asian.

Research Sites

The diversification of literary publishing into local nodes produced a systemic change that created the conditions whereby "new" subjects could emerge, at least insofar as the kinetics of the rhizomatic and the nodal work against centrist, exclusionary systems. However, not all such nodes supported experimental work. Within that rhizomatic network, literary activities can be further categorized in a tripartite structure that was suggested by bpNichol in a 1974 interview. Nichol describes three broad areas of literary activity—popularizing, synthesizing, and researching—all of which, he insists, are necessary in a vibrant literary culture, and all of which occur simultaneously, not just in the trickle-down formation suggested by avant-gardism (interview with Pierre Coupey et al. 338).[7] These categories can be applied to both oral events (readings, performances, workshops, festivals, and conferences) and to publications.

In the popularizing category of *oral* events are summer festivals such as the Milton Acorn Summer Festival in Charlottetown, PEI; the Festival of Words in Moose Jaw, Saskatchewan; the Erin Mills Writers Festival in Ontario; and the Sechelt Writers' Festival in BC. The high profile, showcase-style literary festivals in Toronto (the International Festival of Authors), Calgary (Wordfest), and Vancouver (Writers' Festival) also fit into this category as do the many book launches and readings that feature established writers. For the most part, these events celebrate writers who have received a stamp of approval—the ubiquitous prize-winning authors who crisscross the country on promotional tours. Such popularizing events serve to broaden literary audiences, increase book sales, and introduce new writers to the general reading public—all of which are essential to a vital literary culture.

At the other end of the spectrum from showcase-style readings, launches, and festivals are those that feature what Nichol calls "research"; that is, investigative, experimental writing. Normally a term reserved for scientific endeavours, the notion of "research" in the arts brings a welcome legitimacy to creative work that is often dismissed as wacky and self-indulgent, if not irrelevant and just plain silly. The scientists' laboratory is replicated in the literary communities that provide material space and discursive contexts for poetics "research." Such communities provide a space where poets can work together to explore new ideas and forms, assert "new" subject formations, and investigate alternative histories.

Important *oral* research sites of the past two decades include conferences such as Women and Words/Les femmes et les mots in Vancouver in 1983;[8] The New Poetics Colloquium, and Split Shift: A Colloquium on the New Work Writing in 1985 and 1986 respectively;[9] Telling It: Women and Language across Cultures in 1988;[10] or Writing Thru Race in 1994.[11] All of these events were groundbreaking: the first all-women conference, the first gathering of Language writers[12] in Canada, the first conference on work writing, the first conference to address the intersections of gender, race, and sexuality, and the first conference of First Nations writers and writers of colour. Also in this category are literary festivals that disturb the social/literary norms, festivals such as the eleventh International Festival of Sound Poetry in Toronto in 1978, organized by Steve McCaffery, Sean O'Huigin, and Steven Ross Smith. This was the first time the festival was held in North America; it was also the first time a significant body of collaborative performance poetry was presented. Another crucial literary "research" site was the Third International Feminist Book Fair in 1988 in Montreal, organized by Nicole Brossard. It was "an event of historic importance" because it "established a space where crucial questions about women's relationship to language could be raised" (Nelson and Weil 3). All of these events of course also had synthesizing, popularizing, even canonizing effects in that they helped to legitimate new subjectivities and oppositional poetics. But they were first and foremost community-based events that supported and affirmed political/social/poetic investigations and interventions.

The Poetry Reading: Poetry and/in Communities

Big conferences happen only once a decade or so. Equally important in the category of oral events that support "research" are the poetry readings that feature experimental, unknown, and/or marginalized writers. The venues range from bookstores, libraries, university or college classrooms, and high-school auditoriums, to galleries, bars, or women's centres, but the "research" readings share several features. Writers usually organize them, they have a core audience (with a high percentage of poets in that audience), they feature like-minded poets (who have similar poetic and/ or political/social agendas) and the readings themselves are part of an ongoing dialogue within an identifiable community. The readings offer a place to try things out, to get feedback, take a chance, have some fun, drink some wine and beer, and talk about poetics and politics. They also offer a form of publication for work-in-process, work that often may not appear in print until several years later.

Perhaps most important, poetry readings—together with the events described here—help build a supportive, core community. When writers and readers get together to listen to and discuss current work, to plan events, to argue about poetics in editorial meetings, or to write grant applications and publicize events, they develop a group identity and a context for an ongoing dialogue. Eventually such sites may, as Michael Davidson points out in his study of the poetry communities of *The San Francisco Renaissance*, appear cliquish and intolerant from the outside. But for those on the inside, they can be highly enabling. As Charles Bernstein explains: "what appears to be dogmatic and hermeneutic ... must simultaneously be understood as an effective oppositional strategy that allows the needed social space for poetry to be created" ("Optimism" 166).

This phenomenon of the poetry reading as a cultural/social nexus for community formation is by no means a recent one, as Maria Damon explains in an excellent article analyzing public readings as "foundational community events" (335).[13] Ranging "from the legendary 'contest of bards' in pre-literate Great Britain; to contemporary gatherings of Ethiopian intelligentsia"; to the reading as "public harangue" in Jewish culture that "combined religious and civic directives"; to the Homeric, and rap, or other Afro-American oral poetry traditions, the public reading has a long history of providing a social space for subversive activities. However, such traditions have been largely overlooked in recent literary/social history, Damon continues, first because oral cultures "became print-based, [and] the concept of a static text authored by one individual—text as private property for private consumption—came to have more prestige and to command more formal respect than the oral" (336). Another factor is the modernist bias against oral poetry, that "one 'covers up' the 'weakness' of a poem ... by a performance style; public reading is the surface that must be brushed aside for a more weighty 'expert' assessment of the work's 'true,' i.e., 'deep' value" (336). Nevertheless, Damon concludes, public readings have continued to be effective oppositional, community-building sites. Certainly, poetry readings in English-speaking Canada have often supported subversive, investigative, and community-building activities.

To take Vancouver as an example: from the jazz clubs, coffee houses, university and Vancouver Art School readings of the 1960s to the performance events at Intermedia from 1967–1973;[14] to the many readings at The Western Front since its inception in 1973; to the Writing in Our Time series in 1979; to the many bookstore readings throughout the 1980s and 1990s (at Octopus East, R2B2, Women in Print, for instance, where the audience jams into small spaces); to the thirty to sixty events per year sponsored by the Vancouver section of the Kootenay School of Writing since its founding in 1984; to the 1990s phenomenon of readings in local bars, poetry readings have been a major constitutive vector of Vancouver's radical literary culture. They have helped provide the aforementioned "needed social space for poetry to be created" (Bernstein) and as such have played a crucial role in community formation.

One inevitably wonders, as Peter Culley does in his analysis of "avant-garde" readings at Vancouver's Western Front, what accounts for the continuing success of the poetry reading as a cultural/social nexus: "why ... on any given Vancouver evening, do groups of people travel various distances, often in the rain, to hear writers read aloud from their work? Work that often enough does not offer the simple comforts of either lyrical or narrative flow?" (190). In answering his question, Culley echoes Olson's reification of voice in "Projective Verse" where he declares that "breath allows *all* the speech-force of language back in" (Olson 391). Culley suggests that listening to a text (as opposed to reading it on the page) makes "the point of convergence for writer and listener ... the centrality of *voice*" (192) and voice, in turn, is a more suitable medium for "disclosing levels of meaning and patterns of usage over which the eye might have hesitated and stumbled" (191). Certainly, Vancouver audiences (myself included)[15] have consistently demonstrated a "willingness ... to allow the voice and bearing of a reader to contribute to the terms of his or her reception and to allow the detail of that reception to form the basis of judgement" (Culley 193).[16] Also the social context of the reading in itself makes for a more receptive audience. Shared excitement, group laughter, or even group silence (attentiveness) creates a receptive critical mass that raises everyone's awareness.

Julia Kristeva's explanation of the linguistic *chora* can help to account for the community-building role of the public reading. While Kristeva's analysis of the *chora* relates to the formation of the subject in language, not to the effects of oral poetry on an audience, her description of the linguistic *chora* as "an essentially mobile and extremely provisional articulation constituted by movements and their ephemeral states" (*Revolution* 26) describes key aspects of a poetry reading. The ephemeral nature of orality creates a fluid, provisional relationship: "the *chora* precedes and underlies figuration and thus specularization, and is analogous only to vocal or kinetic rhythm" (*Revolution* 25–26). In arguing for restoring "gestural and vocal play ... on the level of the socialized body" (26) Kristeva foregrounds a kinetic matrix of "provisional articulations" within which the subject (and the poem) is mobilized. The kinetics of the poetry reading undermine both the specular, detached viewer and the stable, self-expressive writer. Destabilized subject/object relations, in turn, create a fluid space where figuration (of self, of meaning, of subject/object relations) remains "mobile" and "provisional" (26). The audience finds multiple points of entry to the text. The "in-your-face" and "in-your-ear" nature of the reading makes the work accessible, especially for "difficult" poetry and/or poetry that introduces "new" subjectivities.

In Kristeva's terms, it is the kinetics of the reading that makes for an interactive, reader/listener relationship. Or in Culley's account, the listening experience is essentially phenomenological. Consciousness finds meaning and form in the world by intermingling with it through the sensory and cognitive registers that include the body. Culley's view is similar to Roland Barthes's notion of reading as a potentially rhapsodic encounter with "the language lined with flesh, a text where we can hear the grain of the throat, the patina of consonants, the voluptuousness of vowels, a whole carnal stereophony, the articulation of the body, of the tongue, not that of meaning, of language" (*Pleasure of the Text* 66–67). In all of these different accounts of readings, and in other analyses of reading effects, the relevant point for my argument here is that in the public reading, poems become linguistic and social *events*, rather than cultural objects designed for silent contemplation by the connoisseur or messages to decode by an individual in a private sanctuary. As such, the public reading contributes to a cultural/social nexus that strenghthens communities and creates a receptive environment for experimental work.[17]

"Working Ground" Magazines and Presses

"Small press" by definition exists in a network of collaborative and connected work that stands in opposition to the mainstream of capitalist publishing.   Clint Burnham,
Allegories of Publishing

Small press is a process, an activity, a performance. It constitutes itself in play—in a range of activities that are not confined to the printed page.   Daniel Jones,
"Toward a Theory of Small Press"

Equally crucial in nurturing radical literary activities are the community-based, writer-run magazines and presses of the past few decades. Like the oral venues described here, they also have a range of agendas and effects. At one end of the spectrum are the popularizing literary newspapers designed for a general audience (*Poetry Canada Review, Prairie Books Now, BC Bookworld*, etc). Mainstream magazines that propose to be arbiters of "good" writing include *The Malahat Review, Canadian Poetry Magazine, The Fiddlehead, The Tamarack Review*, and *Prairie Fire*. At the other end are magazines that offer what poet Robert Duncan called a "working ground" for experimentation and investigation ("Letter" 63). It is these "working ground" sites that concern me here. In differentiating the "working ground" magazine from the "show-window" magazine, Duncan emphasizes the generative function of the former. Working-ground magazines focus on work in process, rather than on work that has already received a stamp of approval. In Duncan's words, this is work that is "unestablished in the Good." Duncan is here cautioning the young editor of *Measure* magazine, John Wieners, against using the magazine as simply a "show window" based on current taste and judgement:

> if the new writers USE the magazine to work out their part of the process, if it is a working ground; then the maximum use for us all will be there. If you use them—presenting what you feel shows the process— then it will be limited to that showing—it will be the show-window, as all magazines tend to be, and not the working ground. ("Letter to John Wieners" 63)

Duncan differentiates magazines on the basis of their purpose rather than their appearance, a distinction that I find more useful than the more commonly used distinction between the "literary periodical" and the "little magazine," adopted by Ken Norris in *The Little Magazine in Canada* from Thrall and Hibbard's 1960 publication, *A Handbook to Literature*. Norris's two categories, "literary periodicals" and "little magazines," are based on differences in appearance (glossy versus cheap production values). Certainly cheap production was the norm in the 1960s and '70s for "little magazines"—*TiSH, blewointment, Mountain, Island, grOnk, Ganglia*, or NMFG, for example, were all mimeographed or printed on an offset press. But by the 1970s and '80s, with the help of electronic publishing technology and government subsidies, they all began to *look* pretty much the same.

Yet even a cursory glance at the editorial positions stated in the promotional blurbs in the 1993 issue of *Canadian Magazines for Everyone* shows differences in purpose—that is, between "working ground" and "show-window" magazines. The latter are recognized by their value-based selection criteria. Despite a professed interest in "new" writing, the final selection criteria are value-based: "*Dandelion* has been combining the traditional and innovative ... since 1975. Both emerging and established writers are featured. *The only criterion is excellence*" (30). *The Fiddlehead* likewise claims an editorial openness "by printing fiction and poetry from everywhere" but again "*the sole criterion [is] excellence*" (32). *Grain* publishes "*the finest* new writing and visual art" (32). *PRISM International* declares "whether it's writing from Calgary or Kuala Lumpur, you'll find *the best* in *PRISM International*" (36, my emphasis throughout).[18] These magazines commoditize and showcase the "good" and thus, despite claims to "newness," may tend to exclude experimental work because, in Duncan's words, it is often "unestablished in the good." Duncan's assumption here is that "good" usually reflects normative tastes and values. As Gertrude Stein so wisely observed to Picasso, an art object becomes "beautiful" only with repetition. I would hasten to add that of course "beauty" and "goodness" do not exist only in commoditized forms. Ann Lauterback says it well: "Beauty does not have to be housed only and always in commodity's gaze, nor does it have to be relegated to the past (conclusion, canon, monument)" (600).

Some magazines do indeed provide more of a working ground than a show window. Their self-definitions range from formally innovative to socially interventionist, but they all emphasize openness and work in process. *The Capilano Review* claims "we're still challenging readers with our innovative approach to words and images, and finding new ways to explore the meaning of art. Grocery lists?? Sixteen studies of the Letter H?? Yup" (*Canadian Magazine* 29). In a similar vein, *Writing* magazine defines itself, via a statement of Charles Bernstein's, as "advocating a poetics that is not adjudicating, not authoritative for all other poetry, not legislating rules for composition. But rather a poetics that is both topical and socially invested; in short poetic, not normative" (40). *Fireweed* also emphasizes a working ground—specifically for feminist work—in the magazine's epigraph, which appears on the title page in every issue: "fire-weed *n*: a hardy perennial so called because it is the first growth to reappear in fire-scarred areas; a troublesome weed which spreads like wildfire invading clearings, bombsites, waste land and other disturbed areas."

Numerous magazines founded in the 1980s and '90s continue to focus on work-in-process, to offer a working ground rather than a show window.[19] In 1980s Toronto, alternative publishing sites flourished when, as Clint Burnham explains, "two marginalizations attack[ed] the ramparts simultaneously (Introduction 5)." There were publishing ventures launched by poet/editors Daniel Jones, Stuart Ross, Clint Burnham, jwcurry and other young white men, as well as magazines such as *The Toronto South Asian Review* that developed from an ethnic base, to produce a burgeoning small press culture.[20] The former includes Stuart Ross's Streetcar Editions and jwcurrie's *1 cent* publications. The Toronto Small Press Book Fair, an annual event started by Nick Power and Stuart Ross in 1987, and Desh Pardesh, an annual conference/festival of diasporic South Asian art and culture that began in 1989, celebrated and supported this culture. There was even a "zine" devoted to information *about* the small press scene: *Mondo Hunka-mooga*, (1982–current) founded by Stuart Ross, which provides a small press and magazine directory, reviews of small press books, and interviews with editors in a lively, street-smart language and format. On a similar note, *hole* magazine (Ottawa 1990–1996), founded to "intersect innovative form with cultural critique and theory," devoted the first issue to a survey of the editorial positions of other poetry magazines (Cabri). A mix of identity politics, formal experimentation, and cultural critique continued to inform magazines of the 1990s, but always within an investigative/ oppositional, rather than a gatekeeping role. *Absinthe* (Calgary 1991–1998) invited exploration of diverse subjects and forms, especially in its special topic issues on First Nations writing, life writing, lesbian writing, and so forth.[21] In Vancouver, *Rice Paper* was founded in 1994 to facilitate "networking and information exchange among writers and artists from a common Pacific Rim heritage" (editorial, 5.1 [1999]). *filling Station* (Calgary 1994–current) offered "a stop between … fixed points on a map," a place to gas-up, talk a bit, get some nourishment. *The Queen Street Quarterly* (Toronto 1996–current), subtitled a "Forum for the Contemporary Canadian Arts," added camouflage to the list of working-ground processes. Founded by Suzanne Zelazo, an undergraduate at the University of Toronto, its glossy look was an intentional disguise. The editors disturbed the field of glossy magazines by publishing innovative writing in an upscale format: "sending a Trojan horse into Chapters" is how literary editor Stephen Cain described it (personal interview). While these magazines certainly diverge in their goals, they all support exploration and experimentation across a range of registers, including "subject-determined and author determined" ones (Kostelanetz, "New Poetries" 18).

A particularly clear statement of working ground magazines' goals appears in the fifth anniversary issue of *filling Station* (Spring 1999) in the "editorial mapping" provided by editors Courtney Thompson and derek beaulieu. First they reiterate the magazine's openness via the metaphor of the filling station: it is a meeting point that is "*between* … fixed points on the map." Then they reaffirm the magazine's commitment to editorial openness:

> *filling Station* has attempted to be a space in which different travellers may find one another…through the years, the intersections served by this stop have increased in number and destination as the lines between communities continue to prove themselves elastic. The blurring of the map under coffee rings and the creases of repeated foldings obscure the geography, reminding us that navigation of creative spaces is a process only tentatively mapped and that strict definition keeps us on a road that may be too narrow for our passage. (n.p.)

All such magazines exist to encourage dialogue, to support risk-taking, to generate argument and debate, and to foreground work in process. To repeat Charles Bernstein's statement, they support "a poetics that is both topical and socially invested; in short poetic, not normative" (*Canadian Magazines for Everyone* 40). Community-based and themselves always in process, they have sustained the social/material/discursive nexus that enables radicality.

The Canada Council

Although the proliferation of working ground presses, magazines, readings, festivals, and the like that have flourished in English-speaking Canada for the past several decades has repositioned radicality within local, diverse, and community-based narratives of emergence, opposition, and intervention, that's not the whole story. Curiously, this alternative network has also been sustained by the centripetal, homogenizing narratives of the nation. The link between culture (including oppositional culture) and the nation was emphatically articulated in the historic Massey Commission *Report* of 1951.[22] The *Report* recommended establishing such cultural institutions as the National Library (which was established in 1953) and the Canada Council for the Encouragement of the Arts, Letters, Humanities and Social Sciences (accomplished in 1957). The link between culture and nation has been officially reaffirmed on several subsequent occasions, including the centennial celebrations in 1967; the *Reports* of the Royal Commission on Bilingualism and Biculturalism (1967–1970); the White Paper of 1971, which proposed an official policy of multiculturalism within a bilingual framework (Trudeau); the Applebaum-Hébert *Report on the State of the Arts in Canada* in 1982 (Federal);[23] and the Canadian Multiculturalism Act of 1988, which legislated official multiculturalism. The link between culture and nation is clear in these documents, as indeed it has continued to be in the 1990s' attempts to protect cultural programs (not always successfully) against the impact of the Free Trade Agreement of 1989 and its successor, the North American Free Trade Agreement (NAFTA) of 1994.

It is no accident that we begin our "chronology of nodes in an alternative poetics network" in 1957, with the founding of the Canada Council. Federal subsidies have certainly played a role in sustaining poetics networks. Obviously the prizes, public reading programs, writers-in-residence programs, and grants to publishers, magazines, and individuals have provided invaluable financial support for both communities and individuals.

Less obvious are the benefits derived from Canada's peculiar combination of nationalism and modernism. To prove to the world that the nation has shed its colonial past and achieved mature nation status (a nationalist goal), the government supports experimental, "avant-garde" art (a modernist goal).[24] The Canada Council has thus regularly supported innovative, experimental, separatist, independent, even anarchic work as much as mainstream cultural production—work that often bites the hand that feeds it. Jon Kertzer summarizes this contradictory relationship:

> Nationalism and literature have long been eager but fractious allies. If nation building is a triumph of imagination ... so is nation deconstructing.... Literature makes the nation both possible and impossible, imaginable and intolerable.... On the one hand, the nation owes its very "life" to literature ... literature exposes the national life as unjust, and even monstrous, because it has the paradoxical ability to criticize the ideology in which it is immersed and by which it is compromised. (12)

As well, even as the nation supports oppositional culture, it also co-opts (and thereby normalizes) the work of radical writers to its nationalist goals. Openly antinationalist writers, such as Dionne Brand, Claire Harris, or Jeannette Armstrong, for instance, are supported on both national and international reading tours as representatively Canadian. Under the banner of multiculturalism, the nation foregrounds writers of colour. Their presence in the national narrative supposedly attests to Canada's tolerance. As Smaro Kamboureli explains, the Multiculturalism Act "defines the ethnic subject by normalizing it," by stressing "those elements of its subjecthood that conform to 'Canadianness'" ("Technology of Ethnicity" 211). Official multiculturalism, like official biculturalism that preceded it, provides codes of containment. Daniel Jones takes an even more critical view, suggesting that official multiculturalism does more than normalize and contain oppositional positions. It also functions as an "ideological camouflage." That is, "the state promotes indigenous cultural production to conceal the reality of transnational capitalism and vested interests in the continued growth of production and consumption of mass culture" ("Towards a Theory" 23).

The fact that opposition has itself become commodified also contributes to the normalization of difference. As early as the 1970s, with the advent of a "consumer unbound" who replicates the freewheeling lifestyle of Beat culture in his endless pursuit of pleasure, the "counter cultural ideal of resistance" entered mainstream culture in commodified forms:

one hardly has to go to a poetry reading to see the counter cultural idea acted out. Its frenzied ecstasies have long since become an official aesthetic of consumer society, a monotheme of mass as well as adversarial culture. Turn on the TV and there it is instantly: the unending drama of consumer unbound and in search of an ever-heightened good time. (Frank 32–33)

Whatever the explanation, it's clear that government support for the arts has produced an increasingly symbiotic relationship between small press and magazine networks and mainstream institutions. The oppositional networks need the government subsidies to survive and the nation needs their products to provide self-definition and international credibility. The structural challenges and contradictory ideologies in this position are obvious. Culture must be autonomous and oppositional to be modernist, but it must also serve the nation. The solution, in part, is a structural sleight of hand, that of an arms-length relationship between government and its cultural institutions. Now you see it, now you don't: the federal government formulates general policy but leaves implementation and interpretation to the cultural institutions and to independent peer juries. Because awards and grants are based on recommendations from peer juries, the system allows for critiques of the nation.

However, not everyone jumped on the subsidy bandwagon. Some poets/editors adopted a marxist position, claiming that the money comes with too many ideological strings attached. The 1970s magazine NMFG exemplifies this position.[25] The title, an acronym for No Money From the Government, emphatically positioned the magazine outside the realm of government "contamination." The Toronto small press scene of the 1980s also prided itself on its independence: "the most vibrant new poets in Toronto began, and still work, in the messy, self-controlled venues of small press publishing, a world where Canada Council grants are notable by their absense" (Burnham et al., introduction, *Toronto Since Then* [*Part 1*] 1). *filling Station* magazine has also managed to survive without Canada Council funds (though it does receive some Alberta arts funding). A call for submissions for its tenth anniversary issue makes a point of celebrating that independence: the issue will "commemorate our longevity and our success as one of the few independent literary magazines in Calgary, and in Canada for that matter" (email from Natalie Simpson).

Those that do partake of federal funding find the relationship fraught with problems. For women writers and writers of colour, a major problem has been jury bias. The so-called "peer" juries were, for many years, almost exclusively composed of mainstream subjects. Research such as Sharon Nelson's study of gender bias in juries in the 1970s and '80s shows a direct correlation between the gender of the jurors and the gender of the award winners and grant recipients ("Bemused, Branded, and Belittled"). Similarly, in the early 1990s the racial minorities committee of the Writers Union of Canada demanded that juries include more writers of colour to redress a racial bias in prizes and grants.

An equally troublesome issue—one that confronts publishers every year when they apply for their block grants—lies in the varying interpretations of the council's mandate. Publishers have to second guess a given jury's interpretation of the council's general guidelines. Robert Lecker explains: "the Council encourages publishers to become interpretive agents" but they are successful "only insofar as they succeed in replicating the Council's own interpretations" (446). Lecker continues:

> This process of replication places publishers in the position of collectively mimicking the hermeneutic activities of a central interpretive body. Such a process is perfectly in keeping with the way in which institutions usually work: they preserve themselves by encouraging the replication of their self-defining values. (446)

A related problem shows up at the more mundane level of the supposedly innocuous procedural rules that magazines and small presses must follow to qualify for grants. Many editors rail against the market-oriented, corporate ideology that underlies these rules. For magazines, the rules dictate size, distribution, and frequency of production, which often do not fit local variables. To publish the requisite four issues per year, for instance, may mean adding filler that doesn't fit with the magazine's goals, or may stretch the volunteer resources beyond their limits. Also when success is judged by numerical outcomes (number of subscribers, number of issues per year, number of years of production, etc.), playing the numbers game necessarily becomes a priority. For magazines, the need to increase subscribers may dictate editorial choices. For small presses, the rules about the number of titles that have to be produced per year, the acceptable size of books (minimum of forty-eight pages, which excludes chapbooks but provides an exception for children's books), and numerous other stipulations based on numbers, also shapes editorial policy.

Nevertheless, many writers, artists, editors, and publishers still attest to the Canada Council's crucial role in supporting cultural production, including oppositional and experimental work. Here are three testimonials. Robert Lecker (editor of *Essays on Canadian Writing* and publisher/editor of ECW press) claims that "no other agency has done more to foster the growth of a national literature and to assist in the business of cultural production ... the council has managed to support a very broad range of books, from all parts of the country, encompassing conventional and ex-centric forms" (446). A.A. Bronson (performance artist) describes how the "establishment of the Canada Council has had an effect on the cultural life of the country at every level beyond anyone's expectations. Its ability to adapt to artists' needs and to support new forms is legendary in the visual arts" (24). Karl Siegler, editor-owner of Talonbooks, referring to the period from 1965 to 1995, has this to say:

> In the intervening thirty years, we did, in fact, create a vibrant, post-colonial Canadian literature and culture of our own.... And how did we do that? The way all struggles of liberation, the re-inscription of the self and the other, are carried out. Through sweat equity, and a great deal of help from our colonial government which, throughout the 1960s, 1970s, and, at least at the level of lip-service, even the 1980s, said it wanted to be as independent as its foot soldiers on the front lines wanted to be. (2)[26]

Notwithstanding the fraught relationships between the nation and the oppositional communities that it supports, it has helped sustain diverse sites of poetic innovation and social intervention in English-speaking Canada for the past forty years or so.

The "radical"—as both a discursive term and material site—has thus retained its social value of offering habitation to difference and/or opposition, even though difference itself has, to some extent, become normalized under the twin banners of multiculturalism and globalization. I am skeptical enough to suspect that the success of alternative poetics during the past four decades (like the success of the avant-garde earlier in the century) means that it is complicit with dominant narratives. For instance, does the emphasis on localism and diversity that has been so important in establishing new subjects also serve the nationalism and globalism that it exists to criticize? Have we normalized diversity to the point where social change seems unnecessary? On the other hand, in the words of African-American poet Erica Hunt: "Oppositional culture is both a wedge against domination, opening free space, and an object/material, absorbed by dominant culture" (203). I am optimistic enough to believe that in the case of oppositional culture, the parts that "wedge" remain stronger than the whole that absorbs.

Notes

1 The essay was first published in 1950 and more widely circulated via Donald Allen's *The New American Poetry* anthology published in 1960.

2 The notion of "network consciousness" for instance, a popular 1960s counterculture concept formulated by the fluxus artists and adapted to the Canadian literary field via Michael Morris and others at Vancouver's Western Front, refers to a kinetic interconnectivity, to "a critical point of investigation,... the fertile matrix of contestatory cultural politics" (Sava 24). The Mail Art project that began in the 1960s and continues to this day (Stake/Mabie) is one example of a rhizomatic network consciousness in action. Writers and visual artists exchanged postcard art in a "fluid, playful, rhizomatic transmission of ideas through the postal system" (Sava 25). The formation of the Association of National Non-profit, Artist-run Centres (ANNPAC) in 1976 is another example of an organizational enactment of network consciousness.

3 See McCaffery and Nichol's *Rational Geomancy*, a collection of their collaborations.

4 "A renga is a group of haiku-like verses linked in any one of several special ways. It is usually written by two or more poets who take turns writing the verses.... Each verse may launch us in a new direction, providing the next poet with a new puzzle to solve.... The result is a constantly changing mosaic which discourages development of a logical, sequential narrative." < http://members.tripod.com/~ theWORDshop/renga.htm >

5 For examples of this form, see *The Long Poem Anthology*, edited by Michael Ondaatje (1979), *The New Long Poem Anthology*, edited by Sharon Thesen (1991), and *The New Long Poem Anthology: Second Edition*, edited by Sharon Thesen (2001). See also *Long Liners Conference Issue* of *Open Letter* and Smaro Kamboureli's *On the Edge of Genre: The Contemporary Canadian Long Poem* for critical discussions of this form. Specific long poems are discussed in chapter 8 (Robert Kroetsch's *The Hornbooks of Rita K*) and chapter 11 (Robin Blaser's *Image Nation*) of this book.

6 In the 1950s, for instance, Ryerson, Macmillan, and McClelland and Stewart did virtually all of the literary publishing. Even the small presses were centralized, with Contact Press in Toronto and Delta in Montreal. The only major exception was the *Fiddlehead* Poetry Series in Fredericton, New Brunswick.

7 Regarding the choice of the term "research," Stephen Scobie quotes from an unpublished interview with Nichol: "I tend to avoid the word 'experimental,' because it's become a rather loaded term. I use the term 'research,' which is a more neutral term" (Scobie, *bpNichol* 13).

8 See Dybikowski et al., *In the Feminine: Women and Words/Les Femmes et les mots: Conference Proceedings* 1983.

9 The New Poetics Colloquium and Split Shift were organized by the Vancouver Kootenay School of Writing collective for the purpose of exploring two diverse experimental nodes: language writing and work writing. The New Poetics Colloquium took place at the Emily Carr Institute of Art and Design on Granville Island and featured the US Language writers (Charles Bernstein, Bruce Andrews, Barrett Watten, Bob Perlman, Ron Silliman, Carla Harryman, Lyn Hejinian, and

Susan Howe) together with Canadians Steve McCaffery, Fred Wah, bpNichol, Sharon Thesen, Gerry Gilbert, Robin Blaser, and others. Split Shift focused on Canadian and American work writing. It was held at the Trout Lake Community Centre in East Vancouver. Note the change in site from Vancouver's trendy Granville Island to a community centre in the working-class area of east Vancouver.

10 See Lee et al. (eds.), *Telling It: Women and Language across Cultures.*

11 For an analysis of this conference, see *Challenging Racism in the Arts: Case Studies of Controversy and Conflict* by Carol Tator, Frances Henry, and Winston Mattis. See also my discussion in chapter 16 of this book.

12 We have followed the custom of capitalizing the word "Language" when referring to a poetics that emerged in the USA and Canada in the 1970s. Michael Davidson, in the entry on "Language poetry" in *The New Princeton Encyclopedia of Poetry and Poetics*, explains: "experimentation in new forms of prose, collaboration, proceduralism, and collage have diminished the role of the lyric subject" and defamiliarization strategies such as the use of "sentence fragments, false apposition, and enjambment displaces any unified narrative, creating a constantly changing semantic environment" (675–76).

13 For further analysis of the role of the poetry reading, see Peter Middleton's "The Contemporary Poetry Reading."

14 For more information on Intermedia, see Nancy Shaw, "Expanded Consciousness and Company Types."

15 See chapter 9 ("Who Is She?") for an account of my own involvement with various literary communities.

16 Regarding the role of speech in poetry, see also Ron Silliman's article "Who Speaks? Ventriloquism and the Self in the Poetry Reading."

17 These effects are not limited to readings of experimental work, but they are perhaps more significant for such work because they help to make the work more available. The reading is often the only site where such work can be presented because print publication comes only after a degree of acceptability has been achieved via the community-based readings.

18 All these editorial statements are taken from the 1993 publication of *Canadian Magazines for Everyone.*

19 See chronology for details.

20 For more information about the Toronto scene, see the introductions by Burnham et al., and Burnham to two issues of *Open Letter: Toronto since Then* published in 1994.

21 See, for instance, "HypheNation: A Mixed Race Issue," *Absinthe* 9.2 (1996); "sista-speak: a collection of poetry and prose written and compiled by Aboriginal women and women of colour," *Absinthe* 8.1-2 (1995); or "Women Writing Lives," *Absinthe* 10.2 (1998).

22 The full title is the *Report of the Royal Commission on National Development in the Arts, Letters, and Sciences.* The report is usually referred to as the Massey Commission Report, after its chair, Vincent Massey. Here are some key statements from the report: "We are now spending millions to maintain a national independence which would be nothing but an empty shell without a vigorous and distinctive cul-

tural life" and "Canadian achievement in every field depends mainly on the quality of the Canadian mind and spirit. This quality is determined by what Canadians think, and think about; by the books they read, the pictures they see and the programmes they hear. These things ... we believe to lie at the roots of our life as a nation" (cited in Pacey, 495–96).

23 The committee that produced the report was officially called the Federal Cultural Policy Review Committee, but it is usually referred to as the Applebaum-Hébert Report, named after its two chairs. The committee produced both a *Summary of Briefs and Hearings* in 1981 and a *Report* in 1982.

24 I am drawing from an excellent article on Canada's nationalism/modernism by Jody Berland, "Nationalism and the Modernist Legacy: Dialogues with Innis."

25 *NMFG*, a magazine started by Brian Fawcett in 1976, at first stood for No Money From the Government. During its three-year run, it acquired some forty-two additional meanings. See Brian Fawcett, "Interview with Barry McKinnon" (34) and the 1976 entry in the chronology.

26 Siegler is alluding here to the impact of NAFTA on federal government cultural policy and the Canadian publishing industry. For instance, he notes that in 1995, Paul Martin, "having quietly decided to 'reclassify' what publishers create as 'industrial products' rather than 'cultural products,' cut the federal subsidies available to Canadian owned publishers ... by fifty-five percent.... No other cultural or educational sector, institution or industry was cut anywhere near as deeply as Canadian publishers" (n.p.).

■

Pauline Butling

> It is certain that the direction of change depends on the state
> of the system of possibilities...that is offered by history
> and that determines what is possible and impossible at a
> given moment.... But it is no less certain that it also depends
> on the interests... that orient agents—as a function of their
> position vis-à-vis the dominant pole or the dominated pole
> of the field—towards the most secure and established pos-
> sibilities, towards the newest possibilities among those which
> are already socially constituted, or even towards possibili-
> ties that must be created for the first time.
>
> Pierre Bourdieu,
> The Field of Cultural Production

> And the only
> position from which he can (with accuracy) write
> is the one (physical/psychological/physiological)
> IN WHICH <u>HE</u> IS STANDING
>
> Frank Davey, "The Problem of Margins"[1]

● One of the main socio/historical sites for the development of radical poetics in English Canada in the 1960s was the magazine *TISH: A Poetry Newsletter, Vancouver*. The first issue of the magazine appeared in September 1961, following a year or so of much talk about poetry and poetics by a group of student writers, young professors, and other literary aficionados at the University of British Columbia (UBC). But the genesis of *TISH* goes back to 1958 when several would-be writers arrived in Vancouver.[2] By the late 1950s, a community of student writers had formed, including Frank Davey, George Bowering, Fred Wah, Jamie Reid, and David Dawson, who became the founding editors of the magazine. Others who were active in the group, though not officially editors, included Lionel Kearns, Daphne Buckle [Marlatt], Gladys Hindmarch, and Robert Hogg. (The latter two also published a couple of issues of a companion fiction magazine called *Motion*). The first editorial group published nineteen issues in less than two years, more or less keeping to their goal of providing a monthly poetry newsletter.[3]

What drew the *TISH* poets together was not just that they all wanted to write. They also shared a class-consciousness, or at least an outsider experience, in that most of them came from working-class, and/or non-urban families.[4] They had arrived at UBC in Vancouver on the wave of a post-war economic boom that brought an influx of students from working-class and lower middle-class families into Canadian universities. Most of the *TISH* poets were the first members of their families to attend university. They shared an impulse to defy and to invade the establishment, a need to carve out a more inclusive cultural space. However, they are best known for their formal innovations (based on their association with Black Mountain poetics) rather than for their class and community-based politics. They are credited with introducing an anti-lyric, speech-based, processual, open-form poetics combined with a historicized approach to the local. This poetics has since developed into a major strand of English Canadian poetry. But the importance of class and geo-political positions in developing this poetics has been largely ignored. My focus here will thus be to analyze the connections between their poetics and their geopolitics as well as to examine their "position *vis-à-vis* the dominant pole" (Bourdieu 183).

Despite the influx of working-class, non-urban students at UBC in the post-war years, pre-war class hierarchies still prevailed. The "dominant pole" (i.e., the student government, the fraternities, and sororities) came mainly from the Vancouver upper middle class, had a city-bred sophistication, and moved easily into (and felt entitled to) the available positions of power and privilege. The UBC hierarchies, in turn, reproduced those in Canadian society in which the upper middle-class elite of central Canada dominated the nation. While the *TISH* poets were investigating "the problem of [poetic] margins" in order to develop an open-form poetics (*TISH* 3 and 4), they were also directly experiencing the problems of negotiating life on the social margins at the university. Their resulting class-based anger helped propel them toward an oppositional poetry and poetics. As Frank Davey comments, in an interview with Irene Niechoda and Tim Hunter:

> I think we felt marginalized in a number of ways, having come from a small town. Marginalized by being Canadian in North America; marginalized by being from the West Coast and British Columbian, in the Canadian context; marginalized by becoming more and more interested in language rather than in content, which was the dominant esthetic. That sense of being marginalized, and the anger that that aroused in us, was I think a very important source of the abrasive energy. (92–93)

They identified themselves as outsiders, positioned at a considerable distance from the "the dominant pole," in terms of both geographic location and social position. This outsider position proved empowering, however, because it spurred them to look elsewhere for support, encouragement, and inspiration. Luckily for them, the "system of possibilities … offered by history" (Bourdieu 183) at that historical moment included Black Mountain and Beat poetics and various counter-dominant social liberation movements.

Black Mountain poetics arrived in Vancouver via Robert Duncan, who came to Vancouver several times to visit Warren and Ellen Tallman, beginning in 1959 when he gave an informal reading and talk in the Tallmans' basement; via *The New American Poetry*, which Warren Tallman put on his reading list for his Studies in English Poetry class at UBC in 1960–61; and via Robert Creeley, who read at the UBC Arts Festival in 1961 and then taught English and creative writing there for a year (1961–62). This new poetics so intrigued the young student poets at UBC that they started a weekly discussion group that met throughout the spring and summer of 1961 to try to figure it out.[5] Toward the end of the summer, the group invited Robert Duncan to give a series of lectures in Vancouver on this new poetics. At a final gathering of the group, which Duncan attended, the plans for a magazine were formulated.[6] Further connections with Black Mountain poetics developed during the 1963 summer poetry workshop through Charles Olson, Allen Ginsberg, Denise Levertov, Margaret Avison, Robert Creeley, and Robert Duncan (the course instructors), and the many other poets who attended.[7]

Olson's challenge to the hegemony of the personal lyric and to Western humanism in general, especially its Platonic mind/body divisions that "placed language at the beck and call of the life of ideas" (Kalaidjian 69) struck a receptive chord in the young writers in Vancouver who were themselves beginning to contest the dominance of the modernist/humanist tradition in the Canadian cultural field.[8] Olson's directive to write about where you are reinforced their desire for a locally based poetry and poetics. As Eli Mandel notes, when they launched *Tish*, a "major impetus" was to publish "writing that emerged out of *their* place." They were "poets who understood that they were writing out of a particular place, places like Abbotsford, like Vancouver and so on, and they were not poets of American poetics; they were poets of Vancouver" ("Talking West" 29). Mandel usefully emphasizes the geopolitics that underscored their poetics. Their project was as much to establish Vancouver as a legitimate cultural site as to develop an open-form poetics. Robert Creeley and Robert Duncan also affirmed the local and communal function of *Tish* in their commentaries written to mark the completion of the first year (twelve issues) of publication. Robert Duncan is "excited" by the collective energy of the group: "I recognize everywhere an operating intelligence that is beyond the individual poets" ("For the Novices" 255). Creeley writes: "No matter what becomes of it, art is local, local to a place and to a person, or group of persons.... It happens somewhere, not everywhere. When it does so happen everywhere, it has become a consequence of taste purely, a vogue or fashion" ("Why Bother" 251).

Another empowering discourse in what Pierre Bourdieu calls the "available system of possibilities ... offered by history" (183) was the liberatory rhetoric of the emerging 1950s/1960s Beat culture which crossed class boundaries to bring diverse people together in a resistance to mainstream values. News of this movement was everywhere. In Montreal, Milton Acorn had declared himself the poet of the vernacular, the people's poet; Leonard Cohen had started singing his poems. Lionel Kearns returned to UBC in 1959 after a year in Quebec with news of the vibrant Montreal scene. In 1960s Vancouver, bill bissett, Roy Kiyooka, Maxine Gadd, Lance Farrell, John Newlove, Judith Copithorne, Al Neil, Gerry Gilbert, and others began performing their poems throughout the city at coffee houses such as The Advance Mattress and The Black Spot,[9] at the Vancouver School of Art (organized by the writer/artist Roy Kiyooka who was an instructor there), and at UBC.

From the USA came news of Allen Ginsberg's first reading of "Howl" in 1955, a riotous night described by Jack Kerouac as "the night of the birth of the San Francisco Poetry Renaissance."[10] News of these events travelled to Vancouver via the underground telegraph of Beat culture and/or via young American intellectuals who came to teach in Canadian universities in the late 1950s and 1960s.[11] Numerous San Francisco writers also came to Vancouver throughout the 1960s to give readings, including Robert Duncan, Allen Ginsberg, Lawrence Ferlinghetti, Jack Spicer, and Philip Whalen. At the Cellar Jazz Club, Vancouver jazz pianist Al Neil collaborated with Kenneth Patchen and other poets in poetry/jazz performances.[12] bill bissett's poem about his entry into Beat culture in 1957 encapsulates this liberatory narrative:

> three uv us wer leeving
> home from halifax   copees uv allen ginsbergs
> howl n yr on th road in th front n back pockits
> uv   my breething mind

> i wantid to leev western civilizaysyun   yr
> buddhist north amerikana jazz soulscape   n my
> frend as my travelling guides
>
> n my need to live free
> ("untitled poem" n.p.)

The liberatory impulse took a somewhat different direction for the *TISH* writers. They chose not so much communal living, mind-altering drugs, political action via sit-ins, be-ins, or the vagabond, on-the-road escape from middle-class conformity (although they were peripherally involved in all of these activities). They chose instead to stay in one place and "liberate" that literary/social space, to make room for a different kind of poetry and a different kind of poet. They had grown up listening to jazz (and in the case of Hindmarch, Wah, and Kearns, playing in high-school jazz bands), learning to jive, and absorbing the countercultural ideals of personal liberation; now they wanted to write an equally embodied, free-form, and "natural" poetry. Several liberation anecdotes from *TISH* lore demonstrate its importance to their project. Frank Davey, George Bowering, and Fred Wah, for instance, tell stories of escapades to "liberate" paper and postage stamps for the magazine from the UBC English department and from the student society offices at Brock Hall. In Beat culture, the Establishment was always the enemy, which made taking what one needed from them morally (if not legally) acceptable. It was not theft but liberation in the sense that you were enacting a salutary disregard for established authorities and institutions.

The Brock Hall heist was especially important to the developing *TISH* narrative of liberation in that the writers had to crawl through the office window to get the paper. The story became highly symbolic of their ability to invade institutional inner sanctuaries. Another story, of "liberating" paper from the UBC bookstore (with the help of poet John Newlove who was working there), is narrated as a hit-and-run heist, successfully executed by innocent, picaresque poets. The stories thematize the success of the underprivileged, and their ability to outwit and/or invade the Establishment. My own copy of the *New American Poetry* is inscribed "from Lucky Luciano" because Fred Wah "liberated" it for me from the UBC bookstore. The irreverent title of the magazine (*TISH* is a phonetic inversion of *shit*) can also be read within a liberatory narrative, as a kind of nose-thumbing gesture toward the genteel literary establishment that prevailed in early 1960s English Canada.

The newsletter itself had a working-class, back alley feel to it. It was cheaply produced, first on a mimeograph machine and then on a second-hand, offset press. The editors did all the production work. It was either given away to local writers or mailed to subscribers with a two-cent stamp. ("This magazine is not for sale," they declared on the cover page). All the typing and printing was done in the graduate student office shared by Frank Davey, George Bowering, and the now well-known scholar/critic W.H. New. That office, in turn, became a hub for daily socializing among the *Tish* editors and other graduate students and thus provided an alternative physical/social space, even as the magazine was establishing an alternative discursive/cultural space. The fact that the graduate student offices were in temporary buildings (two former science-lab trailers) set apart from the other campus buildings perhaps also contributed to the formation of this defiant, outsider, literary community by physically differentiating them from the main campus buildings. In any case, the community thrived in this outsider location.

They also thrived because they hooked up with the underground literary and Beat culture of the time: the newsletter-style magazines such as *The Floating Bear*, edited by LeRoi Jones [Amiri Baraka] and Diane di Prima in New York City; Louis Dudek's *Delta* from Montreal; Raymond Souster's *Combustion* in Toronto; David McFadden's *Mountain* from Hamilton; and Seymour Mayne's *Cataract* from Montreal. The *Tish* editors were in touch with Jones [Baraka] and di Prima from the start (prompted by Robert Duncan's suggestion) and received immediate support and encouragement for their own project of establishing a locally based magazine to publish the poetry "news."

The editorial policies of *Tish* further demonstrate their democratizing goals. *Tish* would publish mostly local poets (signalled by its subtitle *A Poetry Newsletter, Vancouver*).[13] The magazine also had a democratic editorial structure: poems had to get a "majority vote among the editors ... including poems by the editors" (Davey, introduction, *Tish* 1–19: 7). As such, it was the first of many editorial collectives that have since become a common feature of Canadian little magazines and presses. Moreover, their speech-based poetics were articulated within democratizing discourses.[14] Against the official verse culture of 1950s Canada that defined poetry as an elitist, *object d'art* for private contemplation, they offered a return to an oral poetic tradition that would return poetry to its populist and community-based roots.[15]

In light of these social/historical positions, the *TISH* editors' discussion of "the problem of margins," while ostensibly referring only to the margins on the page, takes on social/political resonance.[16] Wah declares: "No one gives a damn about you, the one, but you the intermingler, and becoming bigger by this, are more important" ("Editorial, A Sound Direction" 51). "Intermingling" here refers mainly to an anti-lyric poetic practice, but "becoming bigger ... more important" also implies a social project. When Davey and Wah discuss the technicalities of margins, Davey links the poet's open stance in the poem to a more fluid social context: "The margin is the indicator of the poet's location/stance/locus (for reception) in the universe" ("The Problem" 65). Instead of the stable left-hand margin, which provides a single point of departure for a unitary "I," Davey suggests variable margins because they more accurately represent a socially inflected self: "margins shift in location as the LOCUS [/] as the physical/ psychological/ physiological [/] reality of the *poet moves*" ("The Problem" 66, my emphasis).[17]

The complexities of how margins *construct* the poet are of course not taken up by the *TISH* poets until the 1980s when the discourses of identity politics becomes available, but linking "locus of line" and "locus of poet" (Davey, "The Problem" 66) implies an incipient politicized notion of subjectivity. It would seem that, in Bourdieu's terms, the "directions of change" (183) chosen by the *TISH* poets, such as decentred subjectivity and variable margins, are linked to their political goals of undermining class hierarchies, and challenging central Canada's literary dominance. Their class-based anger provided the necessary "abrasive energy," the liberatory rhetoric of the Beats added ideological momentum, the new American poetics provided a new toolbox, and the underground networks provided legitimation and support. All of this enabled them to move "toward the newest possibilities among those which are already socially constituted, or even towards possibilities that must be created for the first time" (Bourdieu 183). Such innovations include articulating "place" as a complex cultural and historical formation and democratizing the Canadian literary field by legitimating alternative discursive/geopolitical positions.[18]

But that's not the whole story. If we follow the *TISH* group into the 1970s, we discover that within ten years from the start of the magazine, they had all published at least a couple of books, had acquired significant cultural capital as the exemplars of cutting-edge, radical poetics in English Canada, and most had jobs teaching at universities or colleges. I don't think this rapid shift from margin to centre can be fully explained by the capacity of the nationalist cultural agenda to quickly absorb all forms of cultural production or by the trend toward commoditization of dissent that I discussed in chapter 2, or even by the fact that jobs were relatively plentiful in the 1970s.

Their success also relates to their relatively high level of social capital as young, white, able-bodied, men.[19] As such, they were in fact quite close to the "dominant pole" despite their claim to outsider status. In the case of young white men, gender trumps social and economic position. Their lack of money and power is temporary. They are the inheritors of the patrimony and thus will "naturally" move quickly into positions of power and influence. Their proximity to the centre also meant that they unwittingly perpetuated the "legitimate symbolic violence" by which the patrimony maintains itself.[20] That is, despite the innovative nature of their poetics and their democratizing social goals (based on their geographic and social positions), the subject that they were liberating was a mainstream male subject. Like their counterparts in the USA, they "developed their poetics within a group ethos of male solidarity and sodality" (Davidson, "Compulsory" 198).[21] This male ethos can be seen in an editorial by Jamie Reid who claims that the poem "lives in the verb, in the naked verb. Don't be an amateur, but be a master of bombs. Pay exquisite attention to what you are doing or you go off half-cocked" (Davey, *TISH* 1–19: 71). The gendered metaphors in this editorial statement enact an unconscious male privilege. The *TISH* poets were committed to opening up new possibilities, but only in relation to geographic and class-based exclusions.

Even the women, mixed race, and bisexual writers associated with the group enacted the dominant male ethos and in so doing participated in a violence against themselves as well as in the group violence against other outsider positions. It would take many years, for instance, for Daphne Marlatt to unravel her own acts of self-censorship and be able to articulate lesbian/feminist possibilities, or for Fred Wah to explore his personal/ social history as a racialized subject.[22] Angela Bowering aptly describes the confusion for a female subject in such a milieu in a fictionalized memoir that she wrote many years later with her husband George Bowering and two other members of the 1960s UBC literary community, David Bromige and Mike Matthews:

> She doesn't like the character they've drawn for her and doesn't seem
> to know how to invent one.... She isn't the Snow Queen, the Compul-

sive Lecturer, or Goldilocks, or the Killer of Little Joy Boys, but how can she wade her way through this morass of male bonhomie to anything that seems remotely authentic?... What's upsetting is that she's beginning not to like them much—all that bafflegab about their little oolicans, measured in fractions of yards, comparisoning off each others' personae. All that trumpeting, disappearing into their own stories—the ones they make up and the ones that have been made up for them. (*Piccolo Mondo* 112)

What to make of all this? Yes, the economic underclass position of the *Tish* poets, along with their geopolitical location as "provincial" (at the western edge of Canada and also from small towns) distanced them from the "dominant pole" and provided the "abrasive energy" that propelled them toward an oppositional politics and poetics. At the same time, their social capital as young white men gave them considerable power and stature and led to the fairly rapid legitimation of their work. Indeed as young white men, their very radicality increased their social capital (in spite of their working-class origins) because opposition and rebellion are desirable attributes in young men, a necessary ingredient in their classic Oedipal overthrow of the fathers, which leads, in turn, to their taking their rightful place among the powerful. "Radical" is a position of power *within* a patrilineal genealogy, which explains why its legitimating cachet has been mainly reserved for white male subjects. "Radical" feminists, for instance, are characterized as too aggressive, hysterical, or out of control. "Radical" racialized subjects are also characterized negatively, as too militant, aggressive, irrational, extreme (i.e., disturbing the normative).[23] These discursive variables suggest that the "radical" is a site of power and as such is both a contested *and* a protected site.

All of this leads me to a somewhat polemical conclusion: in order to articulate the "radical" as a position of power that includes non-mainstream subjects, we need to identify more pathways to that power and also to challenge some of the protective barriers erected by those who have a vested interest in maintaining its exclusivity. That such change is possible is perhaps demonstrated by the success of the *Tish* poets in claiming a space for a class-based politics and poetics within the discourse of the radical. As the current tidal waves of global capitalism destabilize race-based boundaries (in much the same way that the post-war economic boom destabilized class boundaries), perhaps the definition of the radical can be further democratized. The position can then sustain its cultural utility, which is, ultimately, that it offers habitation to difference.

Notes

1 I am quoting from the original publication in *TISH* 3 (14 November 1961). Davey changes this line slightly in the reprint (*TISH* 1–19). He deletes the underscore of HE and puts the whole phrase in bold: "IN WHICH HE IS STANDING" (65).

2 They met in creative writing classes (taught by Tony Friedsen, Earle Birney, and later on Robert Creeley); in a biweekly off-campus writers' workshop advised by Friedsen; in Warren Tallman's Studies in English Poetry course; and at various literary events, including the annual UBC Festival of Contemporary Arts which featured some of the most experimental contemporary artists of the time, such as Merce Cunningham, John Cage, Robert Creeley, and Robert Duncan. The idea of starting a magazine apparently began when Fred Wah went to see his high-school friend Lionel Kearns (they had both played in a jazz band in Nelson, BC) and said "let's start a poetry magazine so that we can read each others' work." Kearns said, "we should talk to my friend George Bowering." Bowering said "we need to talk to Frank Davey." And Davey said, "let's go see Warren Tallman." Tallman said, "you don't know enough yet, let's form a summer study group." At the last meeting of the study group, which Robert Duncan attended, the plans for the magazine were formulated. See Brad Robinson's conversation with Gladys Hindmarch for more details of this genesis ("Before *TISH*").

3 This is the first phase of *TISH*, from 1961 to 1963 (*TISH* 1–19). In September 1963, after Davey, Wah, and Bowering left Vancouver to continue graduate studies elsewhere, the second phase began (*TISH* 20–24), with David Dawson (the only one remaining from the first group), Daphne Buckle [Marlatt], Peter Auxier, David Cull, Gladys Hindmarch, and Dan McLeod forming the editorial group. Three more editorial groups kept the magazine going from 1964 to 1969 with Dan McLeod as the managing editor. McLeod later went on to start *The Georgia Straight* newspaper. The notion of a local poetry newsletter continued on into *The Georgia Straight Writing Supplement* (1969–1972), edited by Stan Persky and Dennis Wheeler and into Gerry Gilbert's *BC Monthly* (started in 1972), or NMFG (1976–79) edited by Gordon Lockhead [Brian Fawcett].

4 Frank Davey and Robert Hogg were from Abbotsford, Lionel Kearns and Fred Wah from Nelson, Gladys Hindmarch from Ladysmith and George Bowering from Oliver, BC. Those who were from Vancouver came from other outsider positions: David Dawson was from the working-class suburb of Burnaby; Jamie Reid was raised by a single mother; Daphne Marlatt was a cultural hybrid, having recently emigrated from Penang via England.

5 I should add that I was part of this study group, having signed up for Warren Tallman's Studies in English Poetry class in 1960–61 and through that class, met the group of students, poets, and young faculty members who became known as the *TISH* group.

6 The group had met Duncan when he read at the UBC Festival of Contemporary Arts in the winter of 1961. Some had met him during his first visit to Vancouver in 1959. They were intrigued, not only by his poetry but also by his vast knowledge of modern and contemporary poetry and poetics. Ellen Tallman was instrumental in getting Duncan to come to Vancouver because she had known him when she

was a student at Mills College in Oakland. The Tallmans offered to host him and the group chipped in ten dollars each to cover the cost of return bus fare. Duncan spoke for three evenings in a row, for roughly three hours each session. Audio tape recordings of Duncan's lectures are available in the Contemporary Literature Collection, Simon Fraser University.

7 For more information about the course, see the chronology entry and my discussion in chapter 9.

8 For an excellent discussion of Olson's various literary and ideological interventions, see the rest of Kalaidjian's essay, "Mapping Historical Breaches: The Maximus Poems of Charles Olson" in *Languages of Liberation.*

9 This group formed what Maxine Gadd calls a "tribal culture" based on "the idea ... [that] groups of people doing things, instead of doing things as individuals, was fun" (172); those group activities in turn forged tribal bonds: "the Advance Mattress coffeehouse was a place where we'd all read. bill bissett would do chants and Judith Copithorne would read and Pat Lowther ... and Roy Lowther read there and the tribe was formed, right there and at the Mandan Ghetto [a communal house in Kitsilano] and be-ins" (Gadd 174).

10 The full description (from Kerouac's *The Dharma Bums*) is as follows: "Anyway I followed the whole gang of howling poets to the reading at Gallery Six that night, which was, among other important things, the night of the birth of the San Francisco Poetry Renaissance. Everyone was there. It was a mad night. And I was the one who got things jumping by going around collecting dimes and quarters from the rather stiff audience standing around in the gallery and coming back with three huge gallon jugs of California Burgundy and getting them all pissed so that by eleven o'clock when Alvah Goldbook [Allen Ginsberg] was reading his, wailing his poem "Wail" [*Howl*] drunk with arms outspread everybody was yelling "Go! Go! Go!" (like a jam session) and old Rheinhold Cacoethes [Kenneth Rexroth] the father of the Frisco poetry scene was wiping his tears in gladness" (19).

11 Americans such as Ellen and Warren Tallman, for example. Ellen had met Robert Duncan, Robin Blaser, and Jack Spicer at Anarchist Society meetings in Berkeley in the 1950s. Ellen was a student at Mills College, Oakland, and then the University of California, Berkeley, and a friend of Marthe and Kenneth Rexroth. She later introduced Warren to the San Francisco poets.

12 See *Front 7* for more information on Al Neil's role in the Vancouver jazz and counterculture scene.

13 The subtitle changed from "A Magazine of Poetry" to "A Poetry Newsletter" with issue 4.

14 "Poems In *TISH* Are Intended for Reading Aloud" they declared in the first issue, and the first few editorials all stress voice, sound, and orality: "A Sound Direction" is the title of Fred Wah's editorial (*TISH* 3); Jamie Reid begins an editorial in *TISH* 4 with the directive to "listen to the sound of it" (71).

15 For further discussion of this tradition, see Peter Middleton's very thorough article "The Contemporary Poetry Reading" (275–84) and Maria Damon's "Was that 'Different,' 'Dissident' or 'Dissonant'?" (324–41).

16 Davey, "The Problem of Margins" and Wah, "Margins into Lines: A Relationship."

17 Davey is of course echoing Charles Olson's "Projective Verse" essay where Olson calls for changes in "the stance toward reality outside a poem as well as a new stance towards the reality of a poem itself" ("Projective Verse" 386).

18 See for instance, Daphne Marlatt's *Vancouver Poems* and *Steveston*; Fred Wah's *Earth, Among*, and *Pictograms from the Interior of* BC; George Bowering's *George: Vancouver, Rocky Mountain Foot*, and *Genève*; Frank Davey's *The Clallam*; and Gladys Hindmarch's *The Watery Part of the World*.

19 The two women in the group were equally successful in getting teaching jobs and getting published, perhaps in part because of the cultural capital they acquired by association with a male-dominated group.

20 The term comes from Pierre Bourdieu who explains: "If the relations which make the cultural field into a field of ... position-taking only reveal their meaning and function in the light of the relations among cultural subjects who are holding specific positions in this field, it is because intellectual or artistic position-taking are also always semi-conscious strategies in a game in which the conquest of cultural legitimacy and of the concomitant power of legitimate symbolic violence is at stake" (137).

21 I am quoting from an article by Michael Davidson on gender bias in the poetics of Charles Olson and Jack Spicer. Davidson argues that "the attempt to go beyond the artisinal poetics of high modernism often replicates phallic ideals of power, energy, and virtuosity" ("Compulsory" 190) and further that "while women were often absent from the centers of artistic and intellectual life in general in the 1950s, their absence in these groups [Olson and Spicer's] was a structural necessity for the liberation of a new, male subject" ("Compulsory" 198).

22 See especially Marlatt's *Salvage* and Wah's *Diamond Grill*. See chapters 7 and 12 for more discussion of these texts.

23 See, for instance, Roy Miki's critique of the discursive positions around the Writing Thru Race conference in Vancouver in 1994, especially his critique of the word "controversy" (Miki, "Re-Siting Writing Thru Race").

■

"The Play of a Value and the Value of Play"

Pauline Butling

● Another important node in the radical poetics networks that began in 1960s English Canada was the *grOnk/Ganglia* and *blewointment* nexus.[1] Made up of both print (magazines, broadsides, chapbooks) and oral events (readings and performances), these sites supported concrete poetry, sound poetry, interdisciplinary performance work, and, more broadly, the project of deconstruction that dominated 1970s experimental poetics.[2] From bill bissett's phonetic spellings, visual poems, and shamanistic chants; bpNichol's playful desconstructions of letters, sounds, words, forms, histories, ideas, and ideologies; the Toronto Research Group's parodies of literary forms; to the Four Horsemen and other sound poetry groups' wacky performances (such as the Horsemen's spoof on Derridean deconstruction, which consisted of "deconstructing" eggs by dropping them from the top of a ladder), these writers introduced a salutary irreverence for established systems of all kinds. As such, they were part of a wide-ranging literary/political project in the 1970s that aimed to "dismantle first principles embedded in systems of meaning" and "to show them to be products of particular systems" (Godard, "Stucturalism/Post-Structuralism" 44).[3] Propelled by a passionate critique of the entrenched hierarchies and deadening conformity in post-war culture, they found endlessly inventive ways to expose "the play of a value" and to explore the generative "value of play" (McCaffery and Nichol, "Intro: The Open Ladder Essay" 227).

Like the TISH group discussed in the previous chapter, these communities positioned themselves emphatically outside mainstream culture and within the liberatory rhetoric of Beat culture, albeit in a more extreme version; for many of them the lifestyle was as radical as their poetics. They lived communally and/or on welfare; they were not university-based (although most were university educated); many openly smoked pot and wore hippie attire.[4] Yet like the TISH poets, some concrete and sound poets became well known within a decade. For example, bpNichol won the Governor General's Award for poetry (shared with Michael Ondaatje) in 1970. The outcry over the award going to Nichol's "obscene" books (especially his irreverent *The True Eventual Story of Billy the Kid*) added to his fame.[5] Bissett also became famous later in the decade as one of the bad boys of Canadian poetry when parliamentarians declared his work obscene.[6] As with the TISH poets, these writers' mainstream status partially came from their cultural capital as rebellious young men.

However, here I am less concerned with how "rebellious" such writers were, or what Pierre Bourdieu would call their external "positioning *vis-à-vis* the dominant pole" (183); instead I focus on the internal dynamism of these nodes, on the "excess" energy generated from within by a gift economy. Taking bpNichol as an exemplary figure, I show how a gift economy—an economy characterized by surplus, excess, and continuous dispersal—is enacted in Nichol's "excessive" editing, publishing, performing, and various other activities that helped generate and sustain sites for his own and others' artistic risk-taking and social interventions. I conclude that deconstructive poetics had an impact on Canadian intellectual life and political/social thought, not so much by the trickle-down process posited by avant-gardism as by its capacity to grow and overspill in a gift economy.

In material terms, a gift economy is one that produces surplus or excess goods rather than (or in addition to) tidily packaged, marketable commodities. Typically many of the products are given away. From Frank Davey's declaration in *Tish* 1 that "it will give … to its readers FREELY" (Davey, *Tish* 1–19, 13) to Nichol's habit of handing out armloads of *grOnk* publications to anyone and everyone, to bissett's similarly ubiquitous gifts of books, paintings, magazines, and the like, to Coach House Press's warehouse freebies, not to mention the thousands of hours of volunteer labour that went into producing these products, a gift economy thrives on the dispersal rather than the accumulation of material goods. "Expenditures" are made without expectation of return, investment is made in the *processes* as much as the product, and giving rather than accumulating goods signifies wealth. The individual takes pride in his/her contributions to the community as much as (or more so than) his/her material successes.

In the 1970s and '80s, the concept of a gift economy was often explained by an analogy to the Kwakiutl (as they were called then), Haida, and other northwest coast First Nations' practices associated with potlatch.[7] A potlatch is a giant gift-giving party where the host virtually impoverishes himself. Cultural capital (acquired by gifting) replaces economic capital as the determiner of social status. Steve McCaffery suggests a parallel to the Kwakiutl gift economy in his benchmark essay "Writing as a General Economy." McCaffery likens deconstructive poetic practices to a gift economy in that "a linguistic space in which meanings splinter into moving fields of plurality" parallels the Kwakiutl or Haida potlatch ceremonies where wealth is not hoarded but constantly redistributed or thrown away (221).[8] We might now question the analogy because it ignores the difference in social contexts and effects—the purpose of excessive giving in potlach is to achieve status and prestige for the individual and economic levelling for the group. In deconstructive poetics as well as in little magazine and small press publishing, the primary intention of dispersal is not to achieve status, nor is there a question of economic levelling, since there is no expectation of profit. However, the adventurousness of writers and the volunteerism of small-press editors and publishers certainly contributes to their status in the community.[9] As Darren Wershler-Henry explains, there's no denying the ego boost that comes with the territory. "After you've donated copious amounts of your time and energy to a project, the rush of energy and inspiration that results from your burgeoning reputation is something that science fiction fans refer to as 'egoboo' (short for *egoboost*)" (*Free* 12). Whatever the arguments for or against the analogy, the potlatch concept did circulate in literary discourse in the 1970s and thus helped to articulate the alternative exchange values of a gift economy.

Lewis Hyde's *The Gift: Imagination and the Erotic Life of Property*, published in 1975, also contributed to the discourse about gift economies. Hyde emphasizes that cultural rather than economic capital determines status:

> Every culture offers its citizens an image of what it is to be a man or woman of substance. There have been times and places in which a person came into his or her social being through the dispersal of his gifts, the "big man" or "big woman" being that one through whom the most gifts flowed. The mythology of a market society reverses the picture; getting rather than giving is the mark of a substantial persona, and the hero is "self-possessed," "self made." (xiii)

In Hyde's view, a gift economy still operates in the contemporary arts, not only in terms of the gift exchange of material products but also in terms of the non-material "economy of the creative spirit" which values "the inner gift that we accept as the object of our labor, and the outer gift that has become a vehicle of culture."[10] This is "the gift we long for, the gift that, when it comes, speaks commandingly to the soul and irresistibly moves us" (xvii).

Hyde's definition certainly has parallels in Nichol's life-long project, which he described in his first book in 1967, as "finding as many entrances and exits as possible from the self (language/communication exits) in order to form as many entrances as possible for the other"; "the other" Nichol continues, "is emerging as the necessary prerequisite for dialogues with the self that clarify the soul & heart and deepen the ability to love, I place myself there, with them, […] who seek to reach themselves and the other thru the poem by as many exits and entrances as are possible" ("statement," 18). Here, as in all Nichol's life and work, his interest in the materiality of language together with its many modes of communication and dispersal ("language/communication exits") was always linked to an interest in the spiritual ("entrances for the other"). How this project plays out in Nichol's writing is beyond the scope of this chapter; I focus instead on Nichol's life-long efforts to generate as many material/discursive entrances and exits as possible through his work as editor, publisher, performer, theorist, and all-round community builder.[11]

Throughout his life, as Frank Davey notes in a posthumous tribute, Nichol enacted a "continuing commitment to minority literary productions, small presses, young authors, regionally marginalized writers and women's writing together with his mistrust of the authoritative, canonical and hegemonic" ("Editorial Changes" 5). Appropriately, one of the last works Nichol completed before his death is titled *Gifts* (the *Martyrology Book*[s] *7 &*, published posthumously in 1990). In the second poem of this book, the letter "i" in the word family is highlighted as it dances through different formations of the word:

> the dance goes
> on goes
> on
>
>   fam-ily
>   fami-ly
>   fam-ily
>   fami-ly
>   fam-i-ly
>
>   -i-ly
>
>   -i-
>
>   -i-
> ("read, dear" *Gifts* [15])

The "i" is mobile and provisional; the self continually disperses within family and community. Certainly that is how Nichol's literary life played out.

Concrete Poetry

Nichol's first efforts to generate community networks and publishing outlets for creative risk-taking focused on concrete and sound poetry.[12] The Canadian concrete and sound poetry movements began in Vancouver with the poets associated with *blewointment* magazine (1963–78) and Press (1967–83). They included bill bissett and Martina Clinton (the magazine's founders), Gerry Gilbert, Pierre Coupey, Lance Farrell, Maxine Gadd, and Judith Copithorne. Nichol's interest in concrete poetry began with his discovery of past and present networks of visual and sound poetry. In Vancouver in the early 1960s, he heard bill bissett read, met the writers associated with the short-lived *Adder* magazine (James Alexander and Arnie Shives), met David Phillips, and also discovered Gertrude Stein, Kenneth Patchen, and the dadaists.[13] When he moved to Toronto in 1964, he was dismayed that no one had heard of the Vancouver sound and concrete poets. James Reaney had occasionally included some concrete poems in his magazine *Alphabet* in the early 1960s, but there was nothing else in central Canada. Thus began Nichol's publishing/community-building activities. He persuaded David Aylward to join him in starting *Ganglia* magazine and press (1965–67). This was followed by *grOnk* publications (1967–1980), with David Aylward, rah smith, David Harris (aka David UU), Barbara Caruso, Nelson Ball, and others. Nichol's purpose was to build a community, starting with bringing the Vancouver poets to the attention of Toronto writers (the fourth issue of *Ganglia*, for instance, was a book by bissett—*We Sleep inside Each Other All*). At the same time, he called for submissions from anyone and everyone "concerned with concrete/kinetic and related borderblur poetry" (front cover, *Ganglia* no. 1).

The very title *Ganglia* posits a kinetic network: the plural of ganglion, it refers to "a mass of nerve tissue containing nerve cells external to the brain or spinal column" (*Webster's*). *Ganglia* and *grOnk* became legendary in Canadian publishing for achieving just such a lively critical mass.[14] In material terms, the sheer number of publications made concrete poetry a highly visible form (sixty-four issues of *grOnk* were produced in a little over ten years) while the innovative publishing formats—including poems on cards, handbills, in envelopes, in boxes, as well as on the more conventional letter-size page—made each issue an exciting event. The *grOnk* critical mass also included international sound and concrete poets, beginning with one of those serendipitous connections that so often characterize the growth of literary communities.[15] In the mid-1960s Nichol had sent some of his own concrete poems to George Bowering for consideration in Bowering's *Imago* because Bowering had published the Scottish concrete poet Ian Hamilton Finlay in the first issue of *Imago*. Although Bowering turned down Nichol's poems, he sent him names and addresses of poets in Britain who were doing concrete, including Cavan McCarthy at *Tlaloc* magazine. Nichol got in touch and the next year McCarthy featured a group of Canadian concrete poets in *Tlaloc*, including Nichol, Gerry Gilbert, Lionel Kearns, and bill bissett (McCarthy, *Tlaloc* 10, 1966). Nichol also published his early concrete work in England in the book *Konfessions of an Elizabethan Fan Dancer* (1967).

There were immediate benefits for Nichol himself, as he explains: "from 1965–1967 it was really vital that I have that European–South American connection because it was really the only place from which I got feedback and input that propelled me on" (interview with Norris 250). *Ganglia* publications also provided the impetus for many others as well. Caroline Bayard explains:

> The merits of *grOnk/Ganglia* were considerable. First of all they provided a sense of community for the avant-garde: a forum where events, readings, exhibitions, and listings were modestly and unassumingly offered in the small, uncapitalized letters of Nichol's mimeo-sheet newsletter.... Secondly, by devoting either entire or partial issues to developments in other parts of the world, they put Canadian experimenters in touch with what was going on in Germany, Czechoslovakia, Brazil, Japan, and France. (108)

A gift economy is evident not only in Nichol's prodigious output but also in the fact that he literally gave away many of the *Ganglia* and *grOnk* publications, albeit partially for practical reasons—"the amount of energy you put into accounts wasn't worth the money you got back for it, so I decided I might as well publish it as news and as a giveaway" (interview with Norris 244)—but also because his primary goal was dispersal. He wanted to get the news out, get as many poets as possible into print, and reach as many readers as possible. *Ganglia* was essentially "a free information service to an audience of about 250 people" (Nichol, introduction, *Ganglia Press Index*, [5]). The resulting network of loosely interconnected individuals and groups typifies the social organization of a gift economy.[16]

Sound Poetry and the Four Horsemen Ensemble

Nichol began doing sound poems in the 1960s by extending the word play in his concrete poems into performances so that he "could just let emotions out" (interview with Bowering 18).[17].Hearing bill bissett and Michael McClure read in Vancouver in the early 1960s gave him some initial directions.[18] He found McClure's beast language of grunts, cries, and howls in *Ghost Tantras* especially intriguing. From there he went on to discover the sound/concrete poets in Britain, the most important being Bob Cobbing. Nichol describes his excitement: "Wow, here was this stuff, I was into it, it was happening someplace else, it sort of blew my mind open. I didn't think anybody had done it since the Dadaists had kicked the bucket in the '20s" (interview with Norris 247). Here, as with concrete, Nichol credits both the historical and contemporary "gifts" with getting him started: "I knew *somebody* had done *something*, I wasn't quite sure what exactly they'd done, but the sense was that if some guys could get up there and kick out the jams why shouldn't I do it? That gave me the encouragement. So it's one of those things, you start doing something and then you start to track down all the other writers you've heard rumours about who are doing it" (interview with Norris 248–49). Nichol's later tribute to the dadaists in "Dada Lama," a sound poem dedicated to Hugo Ball, acknowledges this debt. The title positions Ball as both the spiritual guru (the Dalai Lama) and genealogical father (Dada) of the concrete and sound poetry movements (*An H in the Heart* 33).

As with concrete, Nichol not only explored sound poetry on his own but also worked hard to support its production by others. On the publishing front, for example, he included sound poetry scores in *grOnk*. When *grOnk* ended, he joined forces with Michael Dean, Brian Dedora, Paul Dutton, Steve McCaffery, John Riddell, Steven (Ross) Smith, and Richard Truhlar to establish Underwhich Editions, a small press that published mainly visual texts and sound poetry audio tapes. On the production/performance front, Nichol also worked both individually and collectively. When Nichol and Steve McCaffery met in 1969, they began to perform as a duo. The next year, they joined Paul Dutton and Rafael Barreto-Rivera to form the Four Horsemen. The Horsemen generated a stir immediately for both their innovative performances and their social critique. They hummed, chanted, roared, executed incredible articulatory gymnastics, and performed complex rhythmic patterns as they deconstructed and played with concepts and values. Performing in venues ranging from small

Figure 6. The Four Horsemen: Steve McCaffery, Rafael Barreto-Rivera, Paul Dutton, and bpNichol performing at David Thompson University Centre, Nelson (1982).

community centres to school auditoriums, and the new performance spaces that were established in the 1970s for interdisciplinary work, they crossed disciplinary boundaries to reach a wide audience. Indeed, these centres, such as A Space in Toronto (1971); Intermedia (1966–79) and The Western Front (1973) in Vancouver; Véhicule Gallery in Montreal (1972–79), or the Clouds 'n' Water Gallery in Calgary (1975) did for sound poetry what grOnk/Ganglia and Blew Ointment did for concrete.[19] They offered a public venue and supportive environment for play and experimentation, a place to try things out and get feedback, to "publish" the current news.

The Four Horsemen also quickly made international contacts, performing at International Sound Poetry Festivals in Cleveland, Ohio, in 1975 (with Jean François Lyotard in the audience) and Toronto in 1978; at the Dada Festival at the Western Front in Vancouver in 1978; and at several sound poetry festivals in Europe, including Amsterdam in 1981. As well, Nichol got in touch with other Canadian sound/performance poets, including Toronto Dub poets Lillian Allen and Clifton Joseph, the Toronto sound performance group Owen Sound, Toronto performance poets such as Gerry Shikatani and Brian Dedora, and the Edmonton duo of Stephen Scobie and Douglas Barbour.[20] Again we see a gift economy at work in the form of "investment" in the processes (as much as products), in the "excessive" production and continuous dispersal. By the mid-1970s, concrete and sound poetry were flourishing in English Canada in a vibrant alternative network sustained by a gift economy of little magazines, small presses, and multimedia centres, with the rhizomatic figure of bpNichol inter-twined with most if not all of the activities.

Coach House Press and Open Letter

Nichol's editing and production networks extended into two other sites that were also central to the broader deconstructive project of what Barbara Godard called "dismantling first principles" ("Structuralism" 44). The first was Coach House Press, which began in 1965. Nichol became involved with the press in 1966 when he helped with the production of *bp*, a box/ book of his work that included a small book, *Journeying & the returns,* a flip poem titled *Wild Thing,* an envelope containing visual poetry, a single sheet "statement," and a recording of some of his sound poems.[21] From that point on, Nichol, along with editor Victor Coleman and printer Stan Bev-ington, helped develop the press into arguably the most important small press of the next two decades.

Coach House Press published far more poetry titles than any other press, many of them by unknown and highly experimental writers. Nichol played a major role in that development. Victor Coleman, the mainstay of CHP for many years (along with Stan Bevington), credits Nichol with ener-gizing the press with his "open mind, ... fund of knowledge about interna-tional Concrete poetry and fringe-publishing, and ... aggressive desire to produce" (29). In the second phase of the press, which began in 1975 with the formation of an editorial board (including Nichol, Frank Davey, Michael Ondaatje, David Young, and Stan Bevington), Nichol continued to provide leadership—Coleman calls it "spirit maintenance" (34)—as well as much of the practical, time-consuming work of editing and producing books. From 1975 on, he edited as many as four or five poetry books per year, many of which were first books and/or books by writers who might not oth-erwise have made it into print.[22]

As if Coach House Press, *grOnk*, and Underwhich were not enough, in 1972 Nichol joined the editorial board of *Open Letter* where he again expended "excessive" time and energy in support of creative risk-taking and poetics "research." Frank Davey gave Nichol "a section in each issue of *Open Letter* in which I could do whatever I wanted" ("a contributed edi-torial" 5) and Nichol proceeded to contribute his own articles and interviews and cajole or encourage others to do likewise.[23] With characteristic excess, he began by launching, with Steve McCaffery, the Toronto Research Group Reports in the spring of 1973.[24] Over the next ten years, they published close to a dozen reports in *Open Letter* under three general headings: translation, narrative, and "the language of the performance of language." As well, he and Davey met often to talk about general directions of *Open Letter* and plan special issues. Special issues included the "no tay syun" [*sic*] series, for instance, a series of invaluable discussions of the line (Bowering, "The End of the Line"), the sentence (Marlatt, "The Measure of the Sentence"), the new prosody (Nichol and Davey, "The Prosody of Open Verse"), the letter (Nichol, "The Pata of Letter Feet") and the book (Nichol and Davey, "The Book as a Unit of Composition").[25] Nichol's energetic participation in *Open Letter*, as both editor and writer, helped establish the theoretical framework and the discursive terms for many forms of experimental writing of the 1970s and '80s.

Also, it is largely through the TRG reports that the political project of deconstructive poetics was articulated.[26] Nichol and McCaffery challenged logocentrism and commoditization; they critiqued established forms, values, and meanings via exuberant performances of fragmentation and dispersal; and they applied poststructuralist and psychoanalytic theory to poetics to expose underlying socio/cultural assumptions. The first TRG report, a "Report on Translation," begins with a proposition: "Let us see what is to be gained from a break with the one-dimensional view of translation. What we will present are possibilities, probes, alternate directives" (27).[27] Their second report, a project on narrative, included "The book as Machine," "The Search for Non-Narrative Prose," and "Narry-A-Tiff," a comic-book-style presentation of some issues that arise in collaborative work. This last title also shows the playfulness of much of their research. The third report, on "The Language of the Performance of Language," included sixteen performance essays (many with punning, playfully deconstructive titles) in which they explore assumptions about language.[28] "Erasa" plays with the traditional concept of the page as a *tabula rasa* and parodies the trendy postmodern notion of erasure. "The Macro-Roni Project" (243) and "Too Soon Sausserne" (245) parody some effects of fragmentation and disjunction. "The Body: Disembodied" (255) problematizes the naturalized body. Throughout all the TRG reports, the many puns, repetitions, reversals, exaggerations, parodies, and other deconstructive devices serve to destabilize, fragment, and open out other possibilities for reconstructing meaning, form, and value.

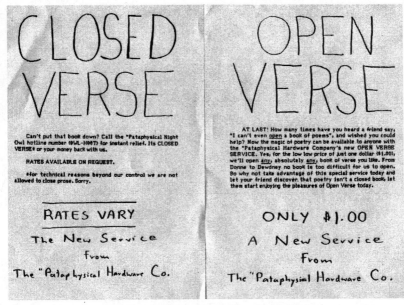

Figure 7. "Closed Verse / Open Verse" by bpNichol.

Nichol's deconstructive playfulness also shows up in his invention of the "Pataphysical Hardware Co., an offshoot of the TRG in which Nichol produced various "tools" to use in developing a Canadian "Pataphysics, defined as "the science of the perpetually open" (TRG, "Introduction" 7).[29] One such "tool" was a handbill offering to "open" or close any verse, a comic/satiric spoof on the 1970s obsession with open forms:

> At last! How many times have you heard a friend say, "I can't even open a book of poems," and wished you could help? Now the magic of poetry can be available to anyone with the "Pataphysical Hardware Company's new OPEN VERSE SERVICE. Yes, for the low low price of just one dollar ($1.00), we'll open *any*, absolutely *any*, book of verse you like. From Donne to Dewdney no book is too difficult for us to open. So why not take advantage of this special service today and let your friend discover that poetry isn't a closed book, let them start enjoying the pleasures of Open Verse today. (handbill)

Barbara Godard's comments that I cited earlier are worth repeating here in their entirety for the way she aptly summarizes "the political bite," not only of Nichol's work but also of most of the 1970s experimental poetics:

> If Nichol's deconstruction is aesthetic, since the poem turns inward on itself, deconstructing its own history and its own basic materials, this does not mean that Canadian deconstruction has lost the political bite characteristic of its European roots. On the contrary, the contemporary popularity of deconstruction in this country is attributable to deconstruction's project to dismantle first principles embedded in systems of meaning to show them to be products of particular systems, rather than what supports the system from without. ("Stucturalism/ Post-Structuralism" 43–44)

Appropriately, this deconstructive project was largely enacted within a gift economy. How better to deconstruct the hegemonic than by enacting an alternative economy as well as undermining its values? Nichol's editing, publishing, and performance work took place almost exclusively within the alternative production networks; his first goal was the expenditure and dispersal of goods, services, and ideas, not their accumulation or commodification. His life was a continual potlatch in which "wealth" was constantly redistributed or thrown away—his "fame" based on that continuous dispersal.

As in potlach, the effects also percolate beyond the initial act of dispersal. The gifts continue to circulate and have an impact on others who come upon them. Daphne Marlatt, for instance, describes Nichol as "a figure of permission" who provided tools that she could adapt for her feminist investigations of non-linear prose in the 1980s.[30] Writers of colour, such as Ashok Mathur and Marie Annharte Baker, likewise found invaluable tools (not to mention enthusiastic support) for their explorations of race poetics.[31] George Bowering describes this role in his introduction to a posthumously published Nichol *Reader*:

> bpNichol was a preternaturally generous human being, giving of himself and his talent to a whole world of writers and other people. Commentators often bring up Lewis Hyse's [Hyde] idea of the gift economy when they are discussing Nichol's writing and teaching and editing. He gave his time and he (gave his) art to a thousand younger and older poets, and he gave his writing to a network of little magazines and small literary presses in the poetry diaspora. In a sense it is an unNicholesque thing to do, this making of a book of Barrie's writing to be published by a major publisher. (*An H in the Heart* xiii)

Critics such as Carolyn Bayard also note broader social effects. Citing Juri Lotman, Bayard explains that "the elements that a culture rejects from its own description as extra-systemic will be seen to be essential to that culture as the source of its future development" (113). She links the deconstructive poetics of the 1970s to the social/political critique that emerged in the 1980s of "the unequal exchange between centre and margin" and the recognition of a "plurality of factors, ethnic, social, institutional, and cultural in defining the relationship of centre to periphery" (113–14). I would also link deconstructive poetics and its numerous poet/critic/theorist practitioners to the seismic shifts in critical discourse, in particular the emerging popularity of critical theory in Canadian colleges and universities in the 1980s, which also supported experimental poetics.[32]

John Moss certainly identifies a crucial social role for writer/theorists of the 1980s in changing the intellectual climate of the 1980s. In his introduction to *Future Indicative: Literary Theory and Canadian Literature*, the conference proceedings for a symposium held at the University of Ottawa in 1986, Moss begins with the claim that the symposium demonstrated a "flourishing diversity in the critical thought in this country"(1). Moss credits the work of poet/theorists such as Robert Kroetsch and George Bowering, along with that of academic theorists such as Linda Hutcheon, Barbara Godard, Terry Goldie, and Shirley Neuman, with "deconstructing the box in which we have tried to contain our culture" (3). Shifting away from the coming-of-age narrative of the previous decades (30), these poets and critics established poetry (and criticism too) as a legitimate "intellectual activity" (3).[33]

Linda Hutcheon similarly finds the intellectual and theoretical range of the Ottawa conference exemplary; in her remarks at the final conference panel, she claims that the writer/theorists of the 1970s and '80s show us "the social and ideological functions of both language and literature" ("Present Tense" 242). Whether or not one shares Moss's optimism that the anti-intellectualism in English Canadian literature and criticism had disappeared by the mid-1980s, his point is well taken. The fact that this conference could occur at all in 1986, or that a mainstream publisher would publish Hutcheon's *The Canadian Postmodern* in 1988 (Oxford University Press) is itself largely due to the deconstructive theory/practice work of the poet/theorists of the 1970s. Once again, the initial acts of dispersal spill and extend into other contexts and communities.

When Nichol died in 1988, many of the networks that he was personally involved with began to unravel. Obviously his death meant the end of the Four Horsemen, although not the end of sound poetry. Current practitioners include Steven Ross Smith, Penn Kemp, Paul Dutton, Douglas Barbour, Stephen Scobie, and Christian Bök. Smith and Dutton have also kept Underwhich Editions going. *Open Letter* has remained a vital magazine, after a period of readjustment to Nichol's absence. Coach House Press shut down in 1995. Possibly Nichol's death accelerated its demise, but Frank Davey dates "the beginnings of an End" of the press as 1984 or 1985 with the changes that were made in editorial policy and direction that he and Nichol argued against as early as 1984 (Davey, "Beginnings of an End" 41–44). Would the combined efforts of Nichol and Davey have been able to stay the course of the press against the pervasive corporatism of the 1990s? Possibly not.

A reductive and narrowing trend was already in motion in the literary field by the mid 1980s, as indicated by Gary Geddes's decision, in 1985, to cut the section on concrete poetry from the third edition of *20th Century Poetry & Poetics*.[34] As he puts it,

> I have lost some of the innocence and catholicity that once made me smile favourably on poetic fashions that I now regard as interesting but of limited significance. Imagists, Beats, Black Mountain poets, and Concrete poets have all had their say.... However, the poetic groups and movements of this century now seem less important than the brilliance and performance of their best practitioners. (xvi)

Geddes's explanation reflects an emerging conservatism of the late 1980s that continued into the 1990s. He privileges individual taste and individual performance over community activity and historical context. His message is that if concrete poetry doesn't fit with current "taste" (i.e., the normative) and/or it can't be commoditized as *individual* production, forget it.

Nonetheless, concrete and sound poetry continue to attract readers, listeners, and practitioners, Geddes's dismissal notwithstanding.[35] In fact, the gift economy has taken on new life with the advent of the free economy of cyberspace, as in peer-to-peer sharing and other freeware as well as numerous poetics sites. Young writer/editors still provide excessive gifts of their time, energy, and material goods within a gift economy that values surplus, as opposed to the restricted economy of capitalism, which values products. No doubt this is a necessary condition of little magazines and small presses since they have little hope of success in capitalist terms. However bpNichol's production work represents an exemplary version of this model. Pivotal in his own time, and an inspiration to many who came after him, "bpNichol" extended beyond the borders of his individual body to become intertwined in/with language, responsive to time, place, and history, and grounded in family, friends, and communities. Always firing on all circuits and continually undermining fixed positions, Nichol enacted in his life and his writing an exemplary excess.

Notes

1 The phrase in my title comes from McCaffery and Nichol, "Intro: The Open Ladder Essay" (227). See Caroline Bayard's *The New Poetics in Canada and Quebec* for a detailed history of this formation.

2 I follow bpNichol in using the term "concrete" but whether the term should be "concrete" or "visual" poetry has been much debated. See, for instance, Darren Wershler-Henry's comments in "A New Medium Immediately."

3 This project involved others besides those doing concrete and sound poetry, such as Robert Kroetsch, Daphne Marlatt, Chris Dewdney, Roy Kiyooka, Gerry Shikatani, George Bowering, Stephen Scobie, Roy Kiyooka, Dennis Cooley, and Douglas Barbour.

4 Some literary communes were the York Street commune in Vancouver (where New Star Books was founded), which included Stan Persky, Lanny Beckman, Gladys Hindmarch, and Brian DeBeck; the Mandan Ghetto, also in the Kitsilano area of Vancouver, where many of the poets associated with *blewointment* magazine and press lived (Maxine Gadd, bill bissett, Martina Clinton, and others); and Therafields, a rural Ontario co-operative and alternative therapy centre where bpNichol lived and worked for several years as a lay therapist.

5 Members of Parliament protested the award going to such a "trashy" book. For details, see Jack David, "A Published Autopopography."

6 In 1978, some MPs from the province of British Columbia demanded (unsuccessfully) that Canada Council funding be withdrawn from bill bissett's Blew Ointment Press and from Talonbooks because they had published bissett's "obscene" books. Characterizing bissett's work as "sex, filth, smut, dirt," they invited "concerned citizens and moral leaders in our communities" to write protest letters to the Canada Council ("BC poet faces critics"). See also Wachtel "Why bp into CC Won't Go."

7 They are now called Kwakwaka'wakw.

8 McCaffery explains further: "In Kwakiutl communities televisions are thrown into the sea, precious objects broken and their parts distributed in order to catalyze the circulation ... to increase the momentum of the giving. Accumulation is unthinkable in potlatch beyond its provisional power to permit an immediate distribution" ("Writing as a General Economy" 220). McCaffery draws his information on potlatch from the French anthropologist Marcel Mauss's *The Gift: Forms and Functions of Exchange in Archaic Societies.* For a contemporary view of potlach and gift economies, see Wershler-Henry, *Free.*

9 Think of Karl Siegler, Victor Coleman, Stan Bevington, Dennis Lee, Dennis Cooley, David Arnasson, Dorothy Livesay, Lenore Keeshig-Tobias, Jeannette Armstrong, Nicole Brossard, Roy Miki, Daphne Marlatt, Sharon Thesen, and many more who are well known for their work as editors and publishers. McCaffery also admits that there are "limits to ... the analogy ("Writing" n.19, 219).

10 Hyde does not dichotomize gift exchange and market exchange totally. Gifts can also be commodities and vice versa. His concern is rather to develop an analysis of gift economies as such.

11 For discussions of Nichol's poetics, see *Tracing the Paths: Reading ≠ Writing The Martyrology* (ed. Roy Miki), *Read the Way He Writes: A Festschrift for bpNichol*, Douglas Barbour's *bpNichol and His Works*, or Stephen Scobie's *bpNichol: What History Teaches*.

12 Although I refer to sound and concrete together here, sound poetry is discussed separately later in the chapter.

13 See Nichol's interview with Ken Norris for further details.

14 There were six issues of *Ganglia* (1965–1967); *grOnk* doubled as both magazine and press, with sixty-four issues of the magazine, and twenty-four issues featuring the work of one writer (Nichol, introduction, *Ganglia Press Index*, 3–5).

15 For detailed information on the international concrete and sound poetry movements and Nichol's connection to them, see Stephen Scobie, *bpNichol: What History Teaches* (30–43 and 55–57). See also Caroline Bayard's *The New Poetics in Canada and Quebec: From Concretism to Post-Modernism*. For a detailed account of the history of sound poetry, see Steve McCaffery's "Voice in Extremis."

16 As Hyde explains, gift economies typically have a "decentralized cohesiveness" (xiv).

17 Audio recordings of the Four Horsemen include *CaNADAda* and *Live in the West*. Audio recordings of Nichol's sound poetry include *bpNichol* and *Ear Rational*. For video tape recordings of the Four Horsemen, see Ron Mann's *Poetry in Motion* and Michael Ondaatje's *Sons of Captain Poetry*. See also the CD *Carnivocal* (Barbour and Scobie) for a selection of Canada's major sound poets.

18 For Nichol's account of bissett and McClure's influences, see Nichol's interview with Ken Norris (248) and Nichol's "Introduction to *The Last Blew Ointment Anthology Volume 2*" (417).

19 See the chronology for details about these venues.

20 At a conference honouring bpNichol ten years after his death, Lillian Allen publicly thanked Nichol for his support for the Toronto dub poets. ("On the H Orizon: bpNichol after Ten," a *West Coast Line* event at Emily Carr College of Art and Design, Vancouver, 25–26 September 1998). Also, rumour has it that Nichol successfully fought to get the names of Lillian Allen and Clifton Joseph on the approved list for Canada Council Readings. Owen Sound members were Michael Dean, David Penhale, Steven [Ross] Smith, and Richard Truhlar and originally also Brian Dedora. The group performed privately in 1975 and had their first public performance in February 1976, at Fat Albert's coffee house on Bloor Street West in Toronto (email to Pauline Butling from Stephen Ross Smith).

21 See Nichol's essay "Primary Days: Housed with the Coach at the Press, 1965–1967" for his account of making this book (425–26).

22 When the editorial board was established in 1975, each member had complete freedom to select two titles per year. Nichol often edited more than his allotted two titles, as some editors would do less in a given year. In fact, according to Frank Davey, Nichol and Davey edited "more than half of the Coach House titles" between 1975 and 1983 or '84 ("Beginnings of an End" 41).

23 Davey's act of giving Nichol carte blanche is an ironic reversal of Davey's initial negative response to Nichol's work. Eight years earlier, Davey had rejected some of Nichol's concrete poems for *The Open Letter* because he found them "irrelevant to what I know as poetry" ("Dear Fred, David, George, others" 3).

24 For a detailed description and critique of the TRG projects, see Peter Jaeger, *ABC of Reading TRG*.

25 The notation issues were *Open Letter* Fifth Series, no. 2, 3, 7, and Sixth Series, no. 1.

26 The TRG were by no means the only ones doing theoretical work in the 1970s but they were arguably the most productive and energetic.

27 All quotes from TRG reports are from the more widely available book publication of the TRG reports, *Rational Geomancy* which McCaffery completed after Nichol's death, rather than from the original *Open Letter* publications.

28 McCaffery explains that "this third report was presented in its entirety as a performance Studio Gallery Nine, Toronto, 27 March 1982" ("Research Report 3: The Language of the Performance of Language," *Rational Geomancy* 225).

29 In keeping with the notion of "the science of the perpetually open," the term is always written with only one quotation mark, as "Pataphysics. The TRG explains: "If "Pataphysics [always written with an open quote] is the 'science of imaginary solutions' and the source of answers to questions never to be posed, then "Pataphysics ... will be the 'literature of all imaginary sciences.' As such it will constitute the "patasignificant advance of a field of non-signification, moving us closer to (and hence by the transcendental law of the "patadox further away from) its origin(s). Hence the Science of the never-ending, never commencing discourse" (Introduction, *Open Letter: Canadian "Pataphysics*. Edited by the Toronto Research Group. 4.6–7 (Winter 1980–81) 7.

30 Marlatt's comments were made when she was a panel member at On the H Orizon: bpNichol after Ten, a *West Coast Line* event at Emily Carr Institute of Art and Design, Vancouver, 25–26 September 1998.

31 Marie Baker worked with Nichol directly at the Red Deer College summer writing and publishing workshops. See "I make sense of my world through writing," interview with Pauline Butling, in *Poets Talk*, University of Alberta Press.

32 Think of Eli Mandel, Barbara Godard, and Frank Davey at York University along with the many sessional creative writing instructors there (including bpNichol); Robert Kroetsch, David Arnasson, and Dennis Cooley at the University of Manitoba; Douglas Barbour and Stephen Scobie at the University of Alberta (prior to Scobie moving to the University of Victoria); Robin Blaser, George Bowering, and Roy Miki at Simon Fraser University; Fred Wah, and Colin Browne at David Thompson University Centre in Nelson, BC.

33 Moss describes the conference in dramatic terms, as a group intervention. In his narrative, Robert Kroetsch and George Bowering were the "bookends" of the program; a performance by the Four Horsemen punctuated the middle, while papers by Linda Hutcheon, Barbara Godard, Shirley Neuman, Terry Goldie, and others fleshed out the middle. Bringing these people together, Moss claims, confirms the seismic shift in English Canadian literary theory and criticism away from the nationalist fervor of the 1960s to the diversity of the 1980s (3).

34 Ironically Geddes gave concrete poetry its first mainstream recognition by including it in the first (1969) and second (1973) editions of the same anthology. He removed it from the third edition (1985) but then put Nichol back into the fourth (1996) and included some of Nichol's concrete poems.

35 See for instance Ubu Web Visual, Concrete, and Sound Poetry website, which includes some Canadian poets <www.ubu.com> and Coach House Books on-line publications <www.chbooks.com>. For more information on recent concrete poetry, see Jars Balan's "Cantextualities." See also the special issue on *Visual Poetics* (*Open Letter* 11.2 [Summer 2001]).

■

Nicole Brossard in English

Susan Rudy

> If the writer has a job to do it is to … make sure our language remembers us, and remembers the joy of free women and the disquietude of free men, the humid heat of July nights in Montréal, the softness of skin caressed, Dada, somersaults and Oulipo, and El Niño stroking our thoughts against our scalps and skulls as this twentieth century ends, while we cling desperately to our all-powerful present.
>
> Nicole Brossard, "The Giant Nature of Words and Silence around Identity"[1]

● Nicole Brossard's connections to radical poetics and feminist communities in English Canada can be traced to Barbara Godard, the bilingual feminist critic of Canadian and Quebec literatures who bought the first issue of Brossard's innovative literary magazine *la Barre du Jour* in 1965.[2] Between 1965 and 1970 Brossard published five books of poetry. In the 1970s she was a founding member of the Quebecoise feminist journal *Tête de Pioche* collective (1976–79). Realizing that Brossard was "one of the most influential writers of her generation" (Godard, "Nicole Brossard" 121), Godard suggested to Coach House Press that Brossard be featured in its "Quebec Translations Series." Edited by Godard and Frank Davey, the series published seven Brossard texts between 1976 and 1990, beginning with *Un livre* translated by Larry Shouldice as *A Book* (see fig. 8).[3] Although several authors were translated, Brossard alone "attracted a committed audience, particularly among other writers" (Davey, "A History of the Coach House Press Translation Series" n.p.).[4]

Since 1965 Nicole Brossard has published six collections of poems and three novels. She is a founding co-director of the important Quebec quarterly *La Barre du Jour*. Her most recent collection of poems, *Mécanique jongleuse*, received the 1975 Governor-General's Award. A translation of her second novel, *Sold-out*, will be published by The Coach House Press later in 1976.

Figure 8. Inside front cover of Nicole Brossard's *A Book* (Coach House Press translation).

For example, Fred Wah's fascination with *A Book* and *Turn of a Pang* led him to organize Brossard's "first-ever reading to an entirely anglophone audience, in Castlegar in 1979" (Davey, "A History").[5] Her work also caught the interest of feminist writers and readers in Toronto, Vancouver, and across North America. In 1981 she appeared with Adrienne Rich in the well-attended 1981 "Writers in Dialogue" series of Toronto readings featuring American and Canadian feminist poets and organized by a collective working through the Women's Bookstore.[6] In 1983 Brossard presented a paper in the session on "Writing in the Feminine: Language and Form" at Women and Words/Les femmes et les mots in Vancouver. With Luce Guilbeault she co-directed the National Film Board production *Some American Feminists* based on interviews during the mid-1970s with Kate Millett, Betty Friedan, Ti-Grace Atkinson, Rita Mae Brown, and Simone de Beauvoir. She participated in the first international feminist book fair in London (1984), the second in Oslo (1986), and organized the third international feminist book fair in Montreal (1988).

Brossard's impact on radical poetics has extended beyond Canada to readers and writers across North America.[7] Nonetheless, she continues to addresses the question "why write?" by insisting that literary form itself should accommodate the reality of the lives of women and other marginalized groups. To return to a key statement cited by Pauline Butling in the first chapter, "those who have never been able to speak the reality of their perceptions, those for whom the conquest of personal emotional territory has been precluded politically and patriarchally, will grasp that identity is simultaneously a quest for and conquest of meaning" (Brossard, *Aerial Letter* 67). What has not yet been said can still be grasped. Consider the following excerpts from "Matter Harmonious Still Maneuvering," Lise Weil's translation of "La matière harmonieuse manoeuvre encore," for example,

> at this late hour when naming is still a function of dreaming
> and of hope, when poetry separates dawn and the great rays
> of day and when many times over women will walk away—
> invisible and carnal—in the stories, I know that all has not
> been said because between urbane conversation and
> tradition it is cold in vertigo and sometimes in the volatile
> matter of tears a strange sweat of truth settles in as if life
> could touch its metaphors. (94)[8]

For bilingual readers, the line "I know that all has not been said" resonates with the French, "je sais que tout n'est pas dit," and produces additional meaning, since "tout" meaning "all" sounds like "tu" meaning the intimate "you."

Reading across languages, we can hear both "I know that *all* has not been said" and "I know that *you*"—which in Brossard's lexicon is always another woman—"have not been said" (italics mine). Through such linguistic manoeuverings, Brossard empowers women: you have not been spoken for, you are still possible, you have not been included in "the story so far" but now you are.[9] In so doing, she mingles and makes "harmonious" the feminist and the radically innovative, the corporeal and the abstract, the quotidian and the spiritual, a represented moment and a moment made present by the passage itself. By the last stanza, the poem moves, and moves us, from a known reality—which as Louise Forsyth has recently noted, "far from being real" is "fictitious and constructed by those who enjoy privilege and wish to keep it" (101 n3)—to a possible one, from old and tired metaphors to ones that are brave, broad and rich enough to "touch" reality's "unnameable poses" (Brossard, *Matter Harmonious* 94).

Brossard is perhaps best known in English Canada for her feminist critical writing—what she calls her "theoretical fiction" (*She would be* 38). Her first (and only) essay collection was published as *la lettre aérienne* in 1985 and in English translation as *The Aerial Letter* (1988). Since then, many of her more than two-dozen talks, articles, and papers have been published in English in North American radical and/or feminist contexts.[10] A key feminist essay, "Poetic Politics" (1990), for example, appears in Charles Bernstein's *The Politics of Poetic Form*. From this position within a radical, mostly male, North American context she articulates her politics by taking us to the year 1974 when she "became a mother and about the same time fell in love with another woman" (77). "Suddenly," she writes, she "was living the most common experience in a woman's life which is motherhood and at the same time [she] was living the most marginal experience in a woman's life which is lesbianism" (77). She explains the effect of these experiences on her understanding of the body and of reality this way: "Motherhood made life absolutely concrete (two bodies to wash, to clean, to move, to think of) and lesbianism made [her] life absolute fiction in a patriarchal heterosexual world. Motherhood shaped [her] solidarity with women and gave [her] a feminist consciousness as lesbianism opened new mental space to explore" ("Poetic Politics" 78).

Until that point, Brossard explains, "my private life would never have any relation to my texts." Rather, her "reserve" about writing her life is her "reserve of images, of hope, and of energy," a way to "reserve herself for the essential, the intuited matter" ("State of Mind" 39). "What is written in my texts," she says, "would always be overstepping who I am as an individual in the socio-cultural sense. That it would always be what is not said that I would look for in my texts" (Bayard and David, *Avant-poste/Outpost* 126). For her, the "essential—life, pain, extreme pleasure"—could not be told in her poetry: "Never. That has no words." Rather, "when one writes, one sends words that resurrect the forms, the images that circulate in the unconscious" and as such there is "no end to possibilities of combinations" (Bayard and David 126).

These possible combinations that Brossard refers to have begun to include writing in both English and in French. Brossard's portion of "Only a Body to Measure Reality By," a lecture jointly delivered in English with Daphne Marlatt at the University of Leeds in 1996, was her translation of a text that first appeared in the bilingual feminist journal *Tessera* (1995) under the title "Le corps du personage" and, in the accompanying abstract, given the English title "The Body/Core of the Character."[11] The title "Only a Body to Measure Reality by" is Marlatt's translation of another line in Brossard's French text, "un seul corps pour comparer," a line that appears not only in "Le corps du personage"/"The Body/Core of the Character," but repeatedly in Brossard's recent work. In the last diary section of her novel *Baroque d'aube*, for example, Patricia Claxton translates the phrase as "One Single Body for Comparison" (*Baroque at Dawn*).

In "Fluid Arguments," an essay Brossard wrote in French and English for Peter Baker's edited collection *Onward: Contemporary Poetry and Poetics*, the phrase appears in French (315) and is translated by Baker as "I will only have a single body" (335). The movement of meanings across these contexts, phrases, and translations gives another example of how Brossard understands the potentiality of transforming reality, poetics, and human connection. A literal translation of the early title "Le corps du personnage" would be "The body of the person." But the *Tessera* translation drew freely on the cross-lingual and other puns always encouraged in Brossard's work for the spaces they open up. The French word for body, *corps*, sounds like the English word "core," meaning the central part, like the core of an apple. But rather than translate *personnage* as "person," in the *Tessera* version it has been translated as "character." Moreover, the French word *personne* means nobody, no *one* body, at least.

These slips between someone and no one, persons and characters, are like the slip between person and persona in English, between fiction and reality, a slip that Brossard is always giving the slip to. But Marlatt foregrounds as the title of the piece a new translation of the phrase *Un seul corps pour comparer*: "Only a Body to Measure Reality By." This translation presents even more subtle complexities, since *un seul corps*, can mean both "only a body," and "a single body." The verb *comparer*—to compare—means, in the Brossard lexicon, not to catalogue differences but as Karen McPherson argued in a recent essay, to make connections ("Writing the Present" 10). Already in the title and its translations, we have Brossard's key terms of engagement, all of which encourage movement across, and indeed beyond boundaries: French and English, fiction and reality, characters and people, texts and translations, writers and readers, a woman and another woman, a single body and many bodies. Here is the first paragraph of the Leeds talk "Only a Body to Measure Reality By":

> Between *Mauve Desert* (1987) and *Baroque d'aube* (1995) my body will have aged seven years. Am I the same woman, the same novelist? How many characters does it take to transform a body and alter our features, our expression? How many pregnancies to change a woman? How many orgasms to transform the first person singular? How many funerals to introduce life once more as a vital principle in the narrative? How many trips to the sea to imagine what life is all about? (n.p.)

In this passage she invokes her aging, physical body. But she speaks later in the essay of the many bodies we all inhabit: "Between Plato's body-tomb, the theatrical-body, the feminine body of difference, the lesbian body of utopia, the queer body of performance, the body invents its surviving, its narrative which is its displacement in the middle of knowledge and beliefs. We need to place the body," she says "at the right place in the dreaming part inhabiting us" (2).

While Brossard's focus is always on women and women's lives, she is steadfastly not interested in being a "witness" to her own or others' experiences. Rather, as she writes in "Matter Harmonious," she bears witness to "the mobility of time and languages" (92). "Somehow," she writes, "we women have to invent our own idea of woman in order to enjoy being a woman and to proceed as a creative subject in language" (Huffer interview 117). In an essay on memory, Brossard reminds us that the verb "to refer" means "to be sent back to" ("Memory: Hologram of Desire" 45). As a formally innovative poet and lesbian, she has no interest in referentiality or conventional "sense," which she sees as sending readers back to the already known, the reality that her body has measured and found to be inadequate. In "A State of Mind in the Garden" (2000) she explains: "one is first lesbian because of the pleasure shaping the intelligence and the recognition that the other woman, *she* makes sense" (39).

Brossard insists that lesbian desire remain free, open, and "nomadic;" she does not consider a text "lesbian" simply because it was written by a lesbian, but "only if it alters the reader's sense of imagination" ("State of Mind" 40).[12] In an unpublished talk on ideology and the imagination, also written in English, she explained her thinking on the relation between the writer, reality, and change: "ideology works because it gets into the heart of our imagination by providing images of happiness." But "to whom are these promises being made" (n.p.)? Arguing against the familiar opposition between a functional ideology that connotes law, order, and the censorship of the individual and an experimental imagination that connotes freedom and creativity, she insists that in contemporary culture, the imagination has become functional: "we don't need it to write books," she said, "just to sell them."

Perhaps her greatest insight is that the ideology we live in is not, in fact, against the imagination, creativity, or pleasure. Rather, it is against the "first materials writers use for imagining that the world can mean something else"; that is, patriarchal ideology is against "memory, emotions, feelings and thoughts" as they are perceived by and through the body. As she writes in "Poetic Politics," "the body provides through our senses a network of associations out of which we create our mental environment, out of which we imagine far beyond what we in fact see, feel, smell, hear, or taste" (74). Our imagination, Brossard claims, is "proportional to the silence [w]e allow [ourselves]"; it is a "celebration of our capacity to reach beyond what we already know" ("Ideology and Imagination" n.p.). In "Writing as a Trajectory of Desire and Consciousness" (1988) she explains her theory of language:

> The life of a language is infinitely greater in what it connotes than in what it denotes. The life of a language is made of semantic and metaphoric circuits that are deployed around words and that give them either a negative or positive meaning. In fact, each word produces an odor, a perfume, a tempo. Each word has an aura. Further, we can say that all work of representation develops around this aura, that an imaginative and cognitive approach is worked out in the area of the aura. (182)

Her practice as a poet is to "conduct sense well beyond the signified. Then all the words can become the never-ending theatre of a series of apparitions where she who writes displaces imperceptibly but *radically* the order of the world" (182).

For Nicole Brossard, writing is a "trajectory," a transformative process that not only involves but returns to the body its desire and consciousness: "writing is a wager of presence in the semantic, imaginary and symbolic space" ("Writing as a Trajectory" 179). She speaks of "rituals" of "trembling," "shock," "sliding," and "breath" that "transform our relationship to writing and to reality" (180). In the ritual with trembling "the whole body concentrates intensely in order to re-member childhood and to untie the knots that have formed in its throat"; this ritual "permits us at once to exorcise fear, to make the first stories burst forth, and to make the body and thought available for new emotions" (181). "Words," she writes, "are made of a complex texture, of a succession of semantic layers under which we sleep, suffocate or cry" (181) and the ritual with shock has "the effect of making the word burst: certain words lose a letter, others see their letters reform in a different order. Thus image becomes magic; white, light; gain, pain; reason, season; ease, sea; mild, wild; require is transformed into desire" (181). The ritual with sliding displaces "slightly but sufficiently the semantic aura of words in such a way that they produce an unforeseeable resonance without alteration of the signifier" (182). The ritual with breath multiplies "energy by modulating it to the rhythm most appropriate to thought in the body" (183). She writes: "there is music that we carry in us, music made of silences and harmony, privileged moments that only come upon us when our availability is total. [...] It is a ritual in which our humility is at its greatest, and, paradoxically, our passion ultimate" (183).

Since the 1960s, Brossard has written on the side of possibility, of hope, of dream, of utopia, even though she knows the world has not yet changed. In "The Killer Was No Young Man," published in *La Presse* on 21 December 1989, for example, she wrote that the murderer of the young women at the Polytechnique on 6 December 1989 "was as old as all the sexist, misogynist proverbs, as old as all the Church fathers who ever doubted women had a soul. He was as old as all the legislators who ever forbade women the university, the right to vote, access to the public sphere. M.L. was as old as Man and his contempt for women" while the women who died were "as young as the gains of feminism ... as fresh as new life, which springs from the hope of each generation of women" (33). As the end of the twentieth century approached, Brossard became increasingly concerned about understanding "what it means to be a contemporary subject in a civilization about to shift into another dimension" (Huffer, interview 115). How can we, she asks repeatedly in recent years, move "from a culture of writings to one of digitalization and electronic image" while "more than three quarters of humanity are illiterate" ("Giant Nature" 2)? Acutely aware that she is living in a kind of "double-time"—both "historical linear time" and a "polysemic, polymorphic, polymoral time where the speed and volume of information erase depth of meaning," she has the courage to assert, "while scientific information and images of violence multiply to the point that ethics becomes a polymorphic version of virtual behaviour, I am still Nicole Brossard, born in Montreal, with a sense of the history of Quebec and of belonging to that part of the French North American continent" (Huffer, Interview 115).

The passage I cited at the beginning of this chapter comes from a talk Nicole Brossard gave on International Women's Day in March 2001. Speaking in English to a room full of women's studies students at the University of Ottawa, Brossard spoke of the writer's job: to "make sure our language remembers us." "International Women's Day comes around every year to remind us," she said, "that being born a woman, and above all, becoming a complete person in a patriarchal world, is no small task of life and courage" ("Giant Nature" 1).

For the past forty years Brossard's life and courage, as manifest in her poetry and prose, her editing and organizing, and the sheer fact of her presence at conferences or poetry readings in French and English contexts, have given two generations of women (and "free men" who are "disquiet[ed]") hope and the embodiment of alternatives. To hear Nicole Brossard read or speak is to witness the tenacity, creativity, and vigour of a woman who is a complete person, who presents her body for comparison in the fullest sense. She claims as her sites of investigation language and meaning, history and humanity, the present and the future. Reading her work we become, like her, explorers seeking "new territories" ("State of Mind" 37). And her work continues to remind us that even in our post-structuralist, post-industrialist, post-modernist, post-humanist, digitalized context, all women should be loved, taken seriously, and encouraged to become "complete persons," whatever that means to each of us.

Notes

1 Brossard's talk, "The Giant Nature of Words and Silence around Identity," was an extended version of Patricia Claxton's translation of Brossard's "Vingt pages entrecoupées de silence." A shorter version of the same paper was translated by Pierre

Joris and appeared in "99 Poets/1999: An international Poetics Symposium," a special issue (26.1) of *Boundary 2: An International Journal of Literature and Culture*, edited by Charles Bernstein.

2   See Godard's "The Avant-garde in Canada: *Open Letter* and *La Barre du Jour*" where she writes: "Back in 1965, I bought the first issue of *La Barre du Jour*, my curiosity piqued to see how the student editors, Nicole Brossard and Jan Stafford, proposed to challenge the dominancy of Parti Pris with its sociological poetics" (99).

3   The other Brossard texts in the series were *Sold-Out*, translated by Patricia Claxton as *Turn of a Pang* (1976), *Mécanique jongleuse* translated by Larry Shouldice as *Daydream Mechanics* (1980), *L'amèr on le chapire effrité* translated by Barbara Godard as *These Our Mothers or: The Disintegrating Chapter* (1983), and *French Kiss* translated by Patricia Claxton as *French Kiss* (1986). In the mid-1980s Davey and Godard left Coach House Press (for details see Davey, "A History"). But it went on to publish *Le Sens apparent*, translated by Fiona Strachan as *Surfaces of Sense* (1988) and *Le Désert mauve*, translated by Susanne de Lotbinière-Harwood as *Mauve Desert* (1990).

4   Victor-Lévy Beaulieu, Jacques Ferron, Claude Gauvreau.

5   Wah's fascination with Brossard's work continues. See "If Yes Seismal," Wah's "transcreation" of Brossard's poem "Si sismal" (38), for example. This was the first of numerous invitations she would receive to read in BC, including at the Kootenay School of Writing's "New Poetics Colloquium" in Vancouver, for example.

6   "The 500 seat auditorium at OISE [Ontario Institute for Studies in Education] was sold out several days before the event" (Lockey 9). My thanks to Frank Davey and Barbara Godard for their assistance in tracking down the details of this Toronto event. For details see Ottie Lockey's "Writers in Dialogue": the series "was a vision shared over dinner in 1978 by Marie Prins of the Toronto Women's Bookstore and Betsy Warland of the Women's Writing Collective. They wanted to present a dialogue between American and Canadian women writers to a Toronto audience" (9). In an email message, Barbara Godard tells me that she translated the poems for what became *Lovhers* for this occasion. In Godard's profile of Brossard ("Nicole Brossard") she suggests that *Lovhers* should be read in conjunction with Adrienne Rich's *Twenty-One Love Poems* (125).

7   She has delivered more than 180 talks, lectures, and inaugural addresses at Yale, Berkeley, the New School for Social Research, Princeton, and Bucknell Universities in the United States as well as at institutions and international conferences in Hungary, France, Belgium, Italy, Mexico, Amsterdam, Norway, Australia, the former Yugoslavia, Argentina, Portugal, Spain, England, Germany, and Croatia. She has been a visiting scholar at Queen's University, Bucknell, and Princeton. Since 1980 her poems have appeared in more than eighty anthologies. Over fifty articles and two books have appeared on her writing and more than thirty theses and dissertations. Her theoretical essays have appeared in academic and other journals and books in North America and internationally.

8   This poem has just appeared as part of Brossard's *Au présent des veines* (Les Écrits des Forges, 1999). See Louise Forsyth's essay "Bursting Boundaries in the Vast Complication of Beauty: Transported by Nicole Brossard's *Au présent des veines*."

Here is the same passage in its original "La matière harmonieuse manoeuvre encore":

> à cette heure tardive ou nommer est encore fonction de rêve et d'espoir, ou
> la poésie sépare l'aube et les grands jets du jour et que plusieurs fois des
> femmes s'en iront invisibles et charnelles dans les récits, je sais que tout n'est
> pas dit parce que, entre la conversation urbaine et la tradition, il fait froid dans
> le vertige et que parfois dans la matière volatile des larmes une étrange sueur
> de vrai s'installe comme si la vie pouvait toucher ses métaphores

9 Brossard edited *Les Strategies du Réel / The Story So Far* (1979), a bilingual anthology of new Quebec writing, for Coach House Press.

10 With Nicole Brossard's generous assistance, I am editing a new volume of her collected essays in English since *The Aerial Letter* to be entitled *Fluid Arguments* (Mercury Press, forthcoming).

11 The Arthur Ravenscroft Memorial Lecture.

12 See for example her comments in "The Idea of Your Lips": "lesbian desire has no rest. It is a subtle, floating desire which binds lesbians to lesbians but also lesbians to other women, it is a key element inspiring projects and activating creativity" (127).

■

Roy Kiyooka, Frank Davey, Daphne Marlatt, and George Bowering

Pauline Butling

> The word that we used all the time was "locus," which we
> liked partly because it came out of [Charles] Olson, partly
> because it didn't say setting, it didn't say place, it didn't say
> landscape, it didn't say all those things that are literary
> devices. Every time you use one of those terms you posit a
> person who is saying, OK, now how can I organize all this
> into a literary work. But if you said locus, it implies trying
> to find out where you are. It implies, I'm trying to locate
> myself.   George Bowering, interview
>   with Caroline Bayard and Jack David

● In 1960s Vancouver, several young poets began writing about place, landscape, the local, the city, the region, and the nation in an attempt to locate the I/eye of the poet within its social, discursive, and historical constructions. George Bowering puts it simply as "trying to find out where you are," echoing Northrop Frye's famous question some twenty years earlier, "where is here?" (Frye 68). However, for 1960s poets, "here" extends beyond geographic location; it includes the "linguistic landscape" of the place and of the poem.[1] As Bowering suggests in the epigraph above, language becomes not simply a source of literary devices that enhance the aesthetics of a poem. It is a "locus" that plays a crucial role in organizing identity and defining place.

The importance of this shift to language-centred poetics has often been noted as part of the radical shift to open-form and locally based poetics in English Canadian poetry in the 1960s.[2] Some forty years later, the notion of language as locus seems equally important as a shift away from the colonizing tropes of landscape poetry, or what Mary Louise Pratt aptly names an "imperial stylistics" (Pratt 199). In reaction to the domination of the Canadian cultural scene by a British/central Canada aesthetics, the young poets of the West refused the writing strategies of both the colonized—who view their world through the imported lenses of the imperial masters—or the colonizer—whose "imperial eyes" enact mastery and domination of the local (Pratt). Instead these poets explored the constitutive nature of language. In the process, they scuttled the dominant poetic I/eye in favour of a dispersed and interactive subjectivity. Viewed in its social/historical context, a poetics of the local is also an anti-imperialist poetics.

Mary Louise Pratt's analysis of the "imperial stylistics" (199) together with her critique of the colonizing mechanisms of travel writing provide some useful tools for my analysis of an anti-imperialist poetics. Pratt links modes of seeing to acts of domination in her title (*Imperial Eyes*). She then explicates an "imperial stylistics" in detail. First, she defines a "monarch-of-all-I-survey genre" (201), a genre in which the I/eye of the viewer occupies the centre of the scene (and the centre of the text). The writer's domination, however, is effectively concealed by the supposedly objective, painterly descriptions. Referring to Richard Burton's account of his "discovery" of Lake Tanganyika, published in 1860, for instance, Pratt shows how domination is enacted via descriptive techniques: "First, and most obvious, the landscape is *estheticized*. The sight is seen as a painting and the description is ordered in terms of background, foreground, symmetries between foam-flecked water and mist-flecked hills and so forth" (204).

But such aesthetic depictions of the landscape, Pratt argues, are by no means neutral. First, they establish the viewer's cultural superiority over the indigenous peoples in the sense that the foreign viewer alone has the ability to transform the landscape into an aesthetic experience. The link between aesthetic and imperial practices is that "the esthetic qualities of the landscape constitute the social and material value of the discovery to the explorers' home culture, at the same time as its aesthetic deficiencies suggest a need for social and material intervention by the home culture" (205). Pratt further notes that this strategy of "depicting the civilizing mission as an esthetic project is a strategy the west has often used for defining others as available for and in need of its benign and beautifying intervention" (205). Second, Pratt notes how the descriptive adjectives subtly privilege the imperial centre.

Of particular interest in this respect are a series of nominal color expressions: "*emerald* green," "*snowy* foam," "*steel*-coloured mountain," "*pearly* mist," "*plum*-colour." Unlike plain color adjectives, these terms add material referents into the landscape, referents which all, from steel to snow, tie the landscape explicitly to the explorer's home culture, sprinkling it with some little bits of England. (204)

Such writing practices, Pratt argues, constitute an "imperial stylistics": they privilege the I/eye of a single (and foreign) viewer, the descriptive terms colour the landscape with a European palette, and the local is devalued in the face of the viewer's ability to aestheticize (read "civilize") the scene. (204)

When the poets in 1960s Vancouver started to write about place, an imperial stylistics of civilizing via aestheticizing was still operative. In mid-twentieth-century Canada, the poet was valued for his/her ability to create an aesthetic landscape and/or to demonstrate the mastery of the seer over the seen. The imperialism in this paradigm derives both from the poet's position as a "monarch-of-all-I-survey" (disguised as aesthetics, not domination) and from the devaluing of the local that is the effect of that position. It is *against* this aesthetics that an anti-lyric poetics of the "local" began to emerge in 1960s Canada.[3]

A handful of poetry books written in response to place published in the 1960s and early 1970s demonstrate this emerging poetics: *Kyoto Airs* by Roy Kiyooka (1964), *City of the Gulls and Sea* (1964) by Frank Davey, *Lardeau* (1965) by Fred Wah, *Vancouver Poems* (1972) by Daphne Marlatt, and *Rocky Mountain Foot* (1968) by George Bowering. While their travel experiences and writing practices vary substantially, these poets share a resistance to the "monarch-of-all-I-survey" position implicit in the personalism of the lyric. They all work toward an articulation of place within a polysemic linguistic field.

For example, Roy Kiyooka's *Kyoto Airs*, a collection of poems written during his first trip to Japan in 1963, articulates a complex insider/outsider position in relation to both place and language, a relationship complicated by Kiyooka's Japanese/Canadian cultural hybridity.[4] Kiyooka was born in Japan and Japanese was his mother tongue, but he found himself to be a "tongue-twisted alien" when he travelled to Japan in 1963. His foreignness renders him silent; the speaking "I" all but disappears from the poems, except to note its alien location:

> I am among
> them a tongue-
> twisted alien.
> ("The Street" *Pacific Windows* 12)

Yet the perceiving eye of these poems is intensely aware, intensely engaged. While the pronoun "I" remains silent, the perceiving "eye" activates a semiotic field of colour, shapes, lines, and movements:

> green
>   green
>   green
>   green

> on the road
> to Yase
>
>   everything
>   is green   multitudinously
>   green
>
>   green trees on
>   green mountains
>   green fields &
>   a green stream
>
>   all things green
>
> including
> the shadows
> between boulders
> along the edge of the stream.
>   ("Road to Yase," *Pacific Windows* 11)

The absence of the pronoun "I" loosens the words from their grammatical moorings. By the fourth repetition of "green," the semantic context has all but evaporated; green becomes a sound, a shape, a word on the page. De-referencing is also partly achieved by the absence of any adjectives except for green. There is none of Burton's "nominal colour expressions," no "emerald" green, or any other kind of green that would remind the reader of "home." The word itself becomes a thing; *the eye* [is] *in the landscape*, to take a title from a later Kiyooka publication.

Frank Davey's *City of the Gulls and Sea*, also published in 1964, likewise attempts to shift away from the "monarch-of-all-I-survey" genre in part by de-emphasizing the "I." The book is written from the point of view of a newcomer to the city of Victoria, BC (Davey had recently moved there to teach at Royal Roads College). While the "I" dominates in Davey's poem more so than in Kiyooka's, Davey does question that dominance. In "Victoria IV," for instance, he questions the notion of "discovery":

> Much of this place
> has come to me.
> I might have said "I"
> actively (a lie)
> and "discovered"
> or "uncovered"
> but coverings are the way of people

> not land
> or cities. (16)

A decade later, in *The Clallam*, Davey more fully articulates and enacts this decentring:

> This is not a documentary of the *Clallam's*
> sinking. There are documents
> but no objective witnesses
> of the *Clallam's* sinking. The survivors
> were not objective. I
> am not objective. Only
> the objects we survive in.
>> (rpt. in *Selected Poems* 77)

Davey also offers a decidedly anti-romantic view of the city of Victoria in a poem published just one year after *City of the Gulls and Sea*:

> city of the dull
> and seedy, she would call it,
> where, if you pay attention,
> the hot rod
> outnumbers the sea-gull
> and beer
> outsells tea.
>> (*The Scarred Hull*, n.p.)

Fred Wah's *Lardeau* and Daphne Marlatt's *Vancouver Poems*, as their titles suggest, were also written in response to place, but their books trace their *rediscovery* of familiar places. Fred Wah rediscovered the West Kootenay region of BC where he had grown up, while working as a timber cruiser in the Lardeau area in the summer of 1964. Like Davey and Kiyooka, Wah resists the impulse to aestheticize the landscape:

> About the Lardeau?
> There is little to say.
> It is green, it rains
> often, the mountains
> are very beautiful,
> [...]
> the rivers and creeks
> flow south to the lake,

there are mosquitoes, the name
is Marblehead.
("Lardeau/Summer 1964," rpt. in *Loki is Buried* 36)

He names, but refuses to describe, the place; adjectives are conspicuously absent; and there is certainly no dominating I/eye.

Daphne Marlatt also resists the "monarch of all I survey" position, but she does so by diminishing the cognitive function of the "I" through immersion in an expanded field of sensory awareness. Based partially on the phenomenology of Merleau-Ponty, which Marlatt had studied in the 1960s, Marlatt's poems are shaped by "those aspects of the world that 'call our attention'" as much as by her own consciousness.[5] In preparation for writing the book, for instance, she read dozens of old newspapers and books about Vancouver and the poems themselves are filled with details from these sources.[6] At the same time, the poet actively works in and with the material. Merleau-Ponty's notions of a "to-and-fro relationship" between consciousness and the world could well be applied to Marlatt's compositional method in *Vancouver Poems*: "On the one hand, the speaking subject is rooted in the natural expressivity of the body situated in its perceptual field. On the other hand, the lived experience of the body as motor subject transcends itself through language and enters a linguistic field beyond its immediate perceptual one." There is thus a "two way relationship mediating language and perceptual life"; "through the body, consciousness is free to reach out to and intermingle with our environment, giving it meaning and form" (Chamberlain, "Merleau-Ponty" 424). Marlatt by no means simply or naively records this interaction. Even as she recognizes how received linguistic and semantic structures mediate experience, giving it meaning and form, she also deconstructs the received structures of self and place.

One of her main deconstructive strategies is to shake up the "I/you" structure, as in the following excerpt:

mute. mute. You ask me what news.
How far do 'I' go & where do 'you' begin.   To haul it
all in—the moon we knew, know. radioactive dust & dusty
voices calling, into the wilds of air waves the boats
ride, their message to be home at, someone's relative's
birthday, or someone's broken neck.

An ear.   an eye.

> The moon. A tree by a room no one knows, & only horizon
> to tell it by.
> (*Vancouver Poems* [32])

As a syntactic relationship, I/you establishes a one-to-one exchange in which the "I" dominates and/or controls the exchange. But Marlatt questions the potential for domination in that construct ("how far do 'I' go and where do 'you' begin") and then deflects to a broader linguistic field. In response to the question "what news?" the "I" does not answer directly but instead weaves together a mélange of unidentified voices overheard on the short-wave radio networks. "I" and "you" become elements among the list of *things* in the poem, not the dominating construction. The poet's I/eye is receptive ("An ear, an eye") and active (the one who "haul[s] it all in") but not controlling or dominating.

Another poem begins with "I" immediately disclaiming control—"But I don't drive." At the end of the poem, the "I" is aligned with the Hamats'a from Kwakwaka'wakw legend, a figure signified by an open mouth that sometimes suggests a flesh-eating monster but also simply a receptive figure. Like the Hamats'a, the poet can also be receptive rather than dominating or devouring. In this poem, they both open their mouths to the light; they wait for things to "walk in":

> Ideas, eye, I, deus .... let go & let the
> tide take.   A stream of perpetual grassgreen.   Light.
> Hamats'as open their gullets to, & walk in.
> ("But I don't drive" *Vancouver Poems* [42], Marlatt's ellipses)

Refusing to drive, going with the tide, opening the mouth to a "stream of perpetual grassgreen" are metaphors for an interactive rather than devouring relationship of person to place. Indeed throughout *Vancouver Poems*, the self becomes almost transparent: "I'm much more transparent in this book," Marlatt comments. "I had the sense of my self being used as a voice, as a channel for the city. I'm literally voicing the city" ("Given this Body" 71). The poet does not disappear altogether. Here, as in all her writing, one senses Marlatt's characteristically attentive consciousness. The poet is alert, embodied, responsive, precise, processual, but not controlling or dominating.

Rocky Mountain Foot

I have chosen George Bowering's *Rocky Mountain Foot* (1968) for detailed analysis, partially because it is a benchmark book in the sense that Bowering won the Governor General's award for it.[7] Also, in taking as his subject the famous Banff/Lake Louise tourist area, Bowering writes more overtly against the tradition of the travel poem. In Bowering's case, the shift from the imperial I/eye to a historicized and contextualized subjectivity, from language as literary device to language as part of "where you are," is achieved partly by developing a coalitional subjectivity via extensive use of collage. The book is made up of multiple texts, multiple discursive sites, and multiple viewpoints that include but are not limited to the poet's lyric I/eye. In an adaptation of William Carlos Williams's collage form in *Paterson*, Bowering combines fragments from newspapers, books, stories, oral histories, native legends, settler's diaries, radio broadcasts, and other poets with personal lyrics, often in ways that make it difficult to determine who is speaking.[8] He provides a list of sources at the end of the book, which includes:

The Imperial Oil Review,
Our Alberta ...,
The Badlands of the Red Deer River ...,
The Frank Slide Story by Frank Anderson,
The Calgary Albertan,
The Calgary Herald,
Program Notes of the Calgary Film Society
(127)

Bowering explains to Jack David and Carolyn Bayard that the collage enables him to get away from the "personalism" of the lyric:

That's when I'm dissatisfied with the lyric poem as a mode. Now there's got to be some way of getting away from the danger of the lyric which is the personalism that's involved, the seeing things from that personal point of view. I don't know what the model might have been but I had a sense that the way to do that was to inject or meet what you were writing with the other, so you can somehow move it out of the lyric mode so it no longer is my opinion on that or my response to that or my feeling on that, that there will be something like a collaboration perhaps. (Interview with Bayard and David 98)

The lyric poems become not the central consciousness of the book, but simply part of the textual collage, part of a polyvocal "linguistic landscape."

Bowering foregrounds this polyvocality at the very beginning of the book by including a First Nations' legend about the creation of Lake Louise on the same page as his lyric poem. The co-presence of two very different texts (signalled by differences in typography as well as the differences in discourses) immediately relativizes the authority of the poet as a so-called creator of the place. Here is the first page:

still in the sky

Clasp hands with the sun
at end of summer
driving thru purple Rockies
looking for the sky to end

(this time of year
the ice shifts in arctic weight.
A man's chest feels the finger,
his hand reaches for the sun)

The great hunter became dissatisfied with the
size of his bow & arrow. Looking up he saw a
rainbow over Lake Louise. It was a bow to match
his power. He climbed the tallest tree to grasp
it, but it melted thru his hand, spilling its
colours into the lake.

We might now question Bowering's use of a translated Native story as itself an imperialist act, but here the juxtaposition of personal lyric and local legend usefully foregrounds two contrasting constructions of place, two different discursive sites.

Bowering further undercuts the "personalism of the lyric" and its colonizing tropes by subtly mocking his own impulse to aestheticize the landscape, even as he proceeds to do so. In the first poem of the book ("still in the sky," above) we find the familiar lyric themes of transient beauty, the consolation offered by love in the face of approaching winter and death, and the solace found in nature. But to my ear, those themes—and the self-expressive ego along with them—are subtly parodied in the clichéd epithet of "purple Rockies." Purple, the only descriptive adjective in the poem, links the landscape to a cultural context (as do the colour adjectives in Burton's travel journal) but here the link is to a local, popular culture (such as cowboy songs about "the purple range" or the "the blue Canadian Rockies," etc.) not the "home" (and supposedly superior) culture, as in the explorers' journals. Purple also perhaps mocks poetic excess, as in the expression "purple prose." Rather than affirming the superiority of the speaker, the single descriptive adjective in Bowering's poem undermines his position as master perceiver by its links to "low" culture. In another poem in this opening sequence, the single descriptive adjective seems determinedly neutral (unlike the culturally laden adjectives that Pratt describes in Burton's travel writing):

> Walking thru Banff woods,
> our arms held out in front
> to hold off branches
> from our faces
>
> we came upon
> the old mossy cabin
> built by some man
> now dead.
>   ("the cabin," 47)

The self-protective gesture of arms out in front, together with the reference to the death of the cabin builder, suggests a vaguely threatening landscape. But the only descriptive modifier—"mossy"—is, as far as I know, culturally neutral. Bowering's insistently laconic lyric voice refuses to aestheticize or romanticize (read colonize) the scene.

    It's true that Bowering's lyric poems form a kind of classic travel narrative in that they trace a journey into new places. In typical tourist fashion, the "I" observes and comments on the weather, politics, history, dinosaurs, the stampede, "the grass," "the blue," "the frost," "the snow," "the dust" (used as poem titles) and so forth. He complains about the cold in winter, the dust in summer; and he longs for his "community of poets" that he left behind in Vancouver. Finally, at the end of the book, he ends up "back in vancouver/for a vancouver visit" where he realizes he belongs:

> We go
> to bed at six in the morning,
> full of joy weed & music,
> [...]

> Lets
>
> stay in Vancouver. Sam Perry's green truck
> has no dust, the sun of Vancouver
> warms my skin, Captain Vancouver
> is one of the boys...
>
> Here Angela says lets
> Stay in Vancouver we belong here.
> (122–23)

However, the "I" narrative is continually undermined throughout the book, as it was on the first page, by the co-presence of other narratives, other voices, other texts, other poets. One Moira O'Neill, in an 1898 diary entry, for instance, writes of her delight in the place, in contrast to the poet's endless complaining.

> Moira O'Neill said (1898): "A log or lumber
> house is built, then simply furnished.
> There are no elaborate meals or superfluous
> furniture. I like the endless riding
> over the prairie, the wind sweeping the grass,
> the herds moving from water to water,
> the fun of coyote hunting. I like the monotony
> and the change, the flannel shirts, the liberty."
> (41)

On the facing page Bowering's lyric laments "the dust." In another section, the thundering, Bible-belt rhetoric of Premier Earnest Manning ("'But men cant go on in depravity without bringing ultimate disaster and destruction of themselves'") co-exists with Bowering's laconic poems about the Calgary landscape (22–24). On another, he juxtaposes the voices of Christian fundamentalists (in a series of quotes from one William Tomyn) with a cluster of meditative lyrics. The poet asks himself "What are you doing, / a poet in cow country?" (32) and responds with poems about the subtle beauty of "the plain," "the grass," "the blue," "the frost," "the snow" (32–38). In contrast, the voice of fundamentalism thunders away at a separate textual site at the bottom of the page:

> William Tomyn, MLA, said: "In the classroom any teacher
> who deliberately conspires to destroy faith in God,
> our creator, is an intellectual leper."
> [...]

"... books and magazines are stenched
with the smell of filth"
[...]
"... pollute the minds of youth ... "
    (35–37)

Again, the personalism of the lyric is undermined by this polysemic linguistic landscape. Any claim to a "monarch-of-all-I-survey" position for the poet dissolves in the intertextual collage. The variety of perspectives and voices in the book points to the positionality of all discourse, including the poet's.

The polysemic linguistic landscape is also reinforced visually with most pages of the book having at least two different type styles and/or more than one margin. Double tracked, they offer a visual reminder of multiple discursive sites. Each text in some way questions or challenges other texts: the Native stories conflict with the settlers' views, the settlers' views conflict with the poet's lyric voice, and so on. Each version of place becomes culturally and/or geo-politically specific. Bowering's *Rocky Mountain Foot* reconfigures Alberta as a site of diverse discourses. The personal lyric becomes one discursive construction among many discourses of place.

While Bowering and Davey are writing about new places, Marlatt, Kiyooka, and Wah are rediscovering somewhat familiar ones. But they all actively work to develop alternatives to the "monarch-of-all-I-survey" genre of travel writing by exploring how place is as much mediated as represented by language. They do this by focusing on how both poet and place are constituted by and within language and by opening the poem to discourses other than the poet's. By re-locating the self within a "linguistic landscape" these writers decentre the poetic I/eye, re-value the "local," and disrupt imperial hierarchies of value that define the local as culturally deficient.[9]

In titling this chapter "more than meets the eye," I am underlining the duplicitous acts of cultural inscription enacted in the supposedly "objective" descriptions or "poetic" representations of place by poets and travel writers alike. My title implies the hidden, political agenda in such writing—definitely more than meets the eye. My title also suggests that a poetry of place can present more than what the eye sees insofar as it foregrounds a discursive landscape, which includes historical, mythic, and ideological discourses of place. By drawing attention to language as "part of where you are,"" poets such as Bowering, Marlatt, Kiyooka, Davey, and Wah not only show that place is as much mediated as represented by language (definitely more than meets the eye), but they also find a way out of the "monarch-of-all-I-survey genre" and the imperial baggage that goes with it. To the extent that they achieved this, theirs is a radical intervention indeed.

Notes

1 Carolyn Bayard introduces this term in an interview with Bowering. She notes: "While Souster and Purdy both have a very rooted sense of place, young Canadian poets, such as bpNichol or bill bissett, seem more concerned with the linguistic landscape." Bowering replies: "To me ... in the early sixties, those things seemed ... to be co-determinant, that if you're a poet the only way you can find out about the place, the configurations of the place in which you live, is with language" (Bayard and David 89).

2 See, for instance, Douglas Barbour's excellent essay, "Lyric, Anti-lyric." The anti-lyric poet, Barbour explains, foregrounds "the poet's speaking self" (55) rather than the poet's "fixed and transcendental ego" (46). Also, "in their retrieval of the poet's self as poetic speaker, such poems attack the idea of a modernist lyric" (55).

3 Note that the localism of these writers should not be equated with regionalism. George Bowering for instance, argues that "regionalism" reproduces the imperialist paradigm: "The word 'region' implies rulers, as regents, regimes, even rajahs, all those regal authorities who reign over Reich" (38). "It is significant," he continues, "that we had to find a new (for us) term. We could have said 'place,' I suppose, or more likely 'here.' But we at TISH did want to sound like theorists. Locus gives us lieu, a place to start, gives us the verb-clinging noun, location" ("Reaney's Region" 39).

4 Kiyooka was born in Japan and had returned once with his father as a very young boy, but he was too young to remember much (see note 5, to Roy Miki's afterword to *Pacific Windows* 318).

5 Chamberlain, "Merleau-Ponty," 424. Marlatt studied phenomenology in relation to poetics as part of her Master's program at Indiana University. Her master's thesis "consisted of translations of Francis Ponge's *Le Part pris des choses* and a critical essay comparing his work with that of William Carlos Williams" (Barbour, *Daphne Marlatt and Her Works* 1).

6 Marlatt explains that she looked through "hundreds of newspaper clippings" and a "whole shelf of books on Vancouver" (Bowering interview 70).

7 Since *Rocky Mountain Foot* is out of print and none of the poems have been reprinted in subsequent collections, I have quoted extensively from the book. Thanks to George Bowering for kindly granting permission.

8 For further discussion of the connections between *Rocky Mountain Foot* and Williams's *Paterson*, see Eva-Marie Kröller, *George Bowering* 42–43.

9 Not all the poets of the 1960s took this approach to place. Al Purdy's *Caribou Horses* (1965) or Margaret Atwood's *The Journals of Susanna Moodie* (1970), for instance, have a more unified lyric self, and use language to reflect or aestheticize rather than focus on how language constructs and/or mediates the experience of place.

Susan Rudy

> this is the plan
> // *and* the body
> Fred Wah, "household"

● Poet, critic, editor, and teacher, Fred Wah has lived on the edge or in the west of Canada for much of his life and in his more than twenty books he repeatedly writes out of liminal spaces. Like Nicole Brossard, he sees "writing as a way of using the body" (Brossard, *Aerial Letter* 91) that in his case is "half Swede, quarter Chinese, and quarter Ontario Wasp" (*Diamond Grill* 36). As early as 1972, inside the cover of *Among*, he locates himself in the assemblage of history, family, writing, and place that he now calls a "biotext": "living at South Slocan (editor of *Scree*) still on the Kootenay, with Pauline, Jenefer, Erika, Loki, Bonnie, Cedar, Birch and Mountains" (n.p.).[1] Twenty-four years later, *Diamond Grill* appeared, his prose biotext, a mixed genre about racial anger, that includes prose poems, anecdotes, and theoretical reflections on what it was like to be a young boy of mixed race growing up in a small BC town. Through *Diamond Grill* and the essays he wrote in the 1980s and '90s, collected in *Faking It, Poetics and Hybridity* in 2000, Wah has emerged as a central figure in the articulation of a hybrid, racialized poetics in North America.[2]

But as early as *Among* (1972), his poetry was tracking the experience of what he calls "living in the hyphen" (*Diamond Grill* 53). Consider the movement at the threshold of the inside/outside binary in this passage from the first poem in *Among:*

> The delight of making inner
> an outer world for me
> is when I tree myself
> and my slight voice screams glee
> [...]
> out of the trees
> among, among
> ("Among," *Among* 7)

"When I tree myself / and my slight voice screams glee" the pleasure of "making" takes the speaker "out of the trees / among, among." In "treeing"

himself to "scream" with a "slight voice," Wah suspends conventional gram-
mar and signification. Indeed Wah's practice is to take us repeatedly to
the "door" of suspended signification. In "Hermes in the Trees" (1), for
example:

> World word alive
> in the heart circle of the moon
> round and square
> the trees hum and whistle
> the trees bend slightly
> the wind is warm and it moves
> up the valley it moves
> as May 1st has today
> the warm spring advances
> the tops of them crown in the air that moves
> (can their own roots know any of it?)
> O word of the world
> round and square
> give me such graces (10)[3]

the juxtaposed words "World word alive" suggest that poets make the world
alive with words. But the supposedly inanimate world is also conscious:
"(can their [the trees'] own roots know any of it?)."

From his earliest work, Wah figures the speaker as a "tree" in poems that
ask questions about origins and roots, about ethnicity and mixed race even
though, as he said in a November 1999 interview with me that except "in
a very silenced and unproblematic way," a "dialogue about Asianicity in
Canada" was not possible until the late 1970s: "That whole process of the
bio, if you like, for me in my poetry, starts with a poem I wrote in *Picto-
grams*[4] in which I mention my [Chinese] cousins.[4] That poem became
provocative for me because I kept wondering how did that get in there?
Why all of a sudden 'cousins'?" Beginning in the mid-1970s, the Chinese
patronym "Wah" began to appear in the poetry itself in the material that
would appear as *Breathin' My Name with a Sigh*. In an essay entitled "Half-
Bred Poetics," Wah explains: "Through writing my book *Breathin' My Name
with a Sigh*, I realized the leverage the fractured and dissonant non-white
name can offer" (*Faking It* 60). Listen to this excerpt from *Music at the
Heart of Thinking*:

> Fred Was. Fred War. Fred Wan. Fred Way.
> Fred Wash. Fred Wag. Fred Roy. Fred What.
> (*Music* 55)

But that racialized, hybrid subject speaks also in a poem from *Among* entitled, tellingly, "For the Western Gate":

> Its hard to believe
> Enough of this to...
> trust my eyes to speak
> ...
> Now to know I go as I look
>
> Not otherwise   only
> Through the mouth of eyes
> I speak for myself I
> Want to go out there   out
> over the view to look for. (8)

Even the title is loaded with racialized significance. When considered in the context of race, the word "for" fully assumes its layered meaning, simultaneously signifying used by, representing, and speaking for. "Western" too takes on particular meaning when considered in relation to the East. "Gate," like "among," is a symbol of hybridization, a "moveable barrier, usually hinged," in an otherwise unmoving wall or fence.

The phrase "Now to know I go as I look" is opaque and suggestive, hinging on the meaning of the word "look." The phrase might mean, simply, I look where I'm going in order to know. It can also be read as suggesting that to know *now*, in the present, I need to go with consciousness of *how* I look, both how I see and how I seem—that is, whether racialized or not—to others. The word "now" initially situates the reader in a perpetual present. But the next line—"not otherwise only"—suggests both a resistance to being made other and a resistance to seeing himself as "other." In "through the mouth of eyes" the word "eye" puns on the "I" who says "I speak for myself" in the next line. That "I / eye" says "I / Want to go out there out / Over the view to look for" ("For the Western Gate" 8). But where is there? For Wah "there" is poetry, a place both here and there, in process, "over the view to look for" but not limited by an overview, a place over and above the present view where one "looks" for some end as yet unspoken: "I / want to go ... / Over the view to look for".... The meaning of what— or should I say w a h t —might be found is thus productively deferred.

The most powerful moment of this articulation of an identity at odds with itself appears in *Diamond Grill*: "Standing across the street from King's Family Restaurant" the narrator reflects on his strained relationship with a Chinese-Canadian childhood friend, Lawrence. Although they always say hello, he rarely goes into Lawrence's family's cafe.[5] On the street, Wah's mixed genetic inheritance allows him to pass as white, to say hello and realize he expects to be addressed in reply. But inside the cafe he is aware of how he would be seen differently: "he would know me, he would have me clear in his sights, not Chinese but stained enough by genealogy to make a difference" (137). Although he hesitates before such knowledge, he decides finally to "cross" into the space where his whiteness is a "stain" rather than a privilege:

> When Lawrence and I work together, him just over from China, he's a boss's son and I'm a boss's son. His pure Chineseness and my impure Chineseness don't make any difference to us in the cafe. But I've assumed a dull and ambiguous edge of difference in myself; the hyphen always seems to demand negotiation.
>   I decide, finally, to cross the street. (137)

The epigraph to *Diamond Grill* is from *Waiting for Saskatchewan*. Addressing his father, Wah writes, "You were part Chinese I tell them. / They look at me. I'm pulling their leg. / So I'm Chinese too and that's why my name is Wah. / They don't really believe me. That's o.k. / When you're not 'pure' you just make it up." Wah's self-deprecating humour speaks directly to his dilemma. Although "being there, in Lawrence's kitchen, seems one of the surest places [he] know[s]" (138), "back outside, on the street, all [his] ambivalence gets covered over, camouflaged by a safety net of class and colourlessness—the racism within [him] that makes and consumes that neutral (white) version of [himself], that allows [him] the sad privilege of being, in this white white world, not the target but the gun" (138).

Wah names his ambivalence about not being able to fulfill others' desires that he be either white or Chinese when he writes "I want to be there but don't want to be seen being there" (136). In crossing the street and entering the cafe, he has seen the face of the white "other," the face of racism, as his own. In Lawrence's kitchen he is sure only of what he has lost: an easy relation to a Chinese-Canadian community. But back outside on the street he is also sure that his privilege, his ability to pass as white, has produced that loss. For Wah, then, "crossing" means more than simply moving from one side of the street to the other; it means betraying himself. If "the hyphen is the door" (*Diamond Grill* 16), identity is liminal, not spatial; it's about doors not streets:

> In the Diamond [...] are two large swinging wooden doors, each with a round hatch of face-sized window. [...] looking through doors and

languages, skin recalling its own reconnaissance [...] mouth saying can't forget, mouth saying what I want to know can feed me, what I don't can bleed me. (1)

Like the swinging doors that look both ways, Wah figures his hyphenated subjectivity as an ambiguous yet substantial middle—a space *among* others. Language is the opening, the "door," the "mouth." The "face-sized window" looks both ways through doors and languages.

What is a "diamond grill"? To be "grilled" is to be subject to questioning, even torture. A diamond is a "colourless or tinted brilliant precious stone" (*Concise Oxford*). To be "in" the Diamond Grill is to be in this precious and yet contradictory space of interrogation, to be either "colourless or tinted." At the end of Wah's text, he returns to this place, his father's parking space, at the back of the restaurant:

Fred Wah

Diamond Grill

Private

(*Diamond Grill* 176)

The speaker goes through "the gates to the kitchen," which "are the same"

They swing and they turn, gate of to and gate of from, entrance and exit, the flow, the discharge, the access, the egress, the Mountains of the Blest, the winds of ch'i, mouth of Yin and eye of Yang, the Liver, the Stomach, the core and the surface, the rock and the lake. These are the gates and you can either kick them open or walk through in silence. Same dif. (164)

The fact of a gate is the "middle outside," the "same dif[ference]" provided by that disjunctive conjunction "and."

For Fred Wah, *and* is a word that is never neutral. Consider his renaming of the then-defunct literary magazine *Dandelion* as *dANDelion* when Wah and The Dandelion Magazine Society resuscitated it for the Creative Writing program at the University of Calgary.[6] This was achieved, he explains in an editorial postscript to the first issue, by "meld[ing] creative writing at the University of Calgary with the larger literary community in Calgary, beyond, and after."[7] With *dANDelion* Wah's editorial practice was to literally blow the "AND" out of the dandelion and generate connectivity "in Calgary, beyond, and after" (n.p.).[8] Wah's editorial practice has long involved finding life support in the sum total—in the hybridity if you will—of intense locality and productive multiplicity—international, cross-gender, cross-racial, and cross-genre. The front and back covers of that first issue of *dANDelion* (edited by Wah and Emily Cargan) exemplify this interweaving of the local and the international. The front cover photograph of "Nordic Constellations" is from an exhibition by local Calgary artist Tomas Johnsson who describes his work as "address[ing] the fluidity of national and cultural identities." Both inside and outside back cover images are from *Picture House*, an installation by John Havelda, a British-Hungarian poet and image-text artist who teaches at the University of Coimbra, Portugal. The inside back cover poem, entitled "Really Useful Knowledge," cites hypertext markup language as poem. The "readable" words "PAPER," "ORIENT," "PAW," "SAP," "NORMAL," "COLOURF DEFAULT," "COLORB DEFAULT," "EXPAND," "NORMAL" meld into a few readable phrases, "There is knowledge, and there is useful knowledge, and there is really useful knowledge, and really useful knowledge is knowing precisely when to stop."

Nine of the forty-eight writers whose poetry and image-texts appear in the issue are former or current members of Calgary's writing communities (all of them Wah's former students)—Louis Cabri, Susan Holbrook, Suzette Mayr, Jeff Derksen, Ashok Mathur, tom muir, r rickey, Ian Samuels, Jonathan C. Wilke. That the remaining writers are from Ireland, Austria, the United States, elsewhere in Canada, and that some have been publishing for forty years, some for a decade, some for a few years, becomes less important than the fact that they share an interest in a politicized, socially relevant, process-based poetics. The work of Ron Silliman, Richard Kostelanetz, Daphne Marlatt, George Bowering, Roy Miki, Fernando Aguiar, Erin Mouré, Lisa Robertson, Steven Ross Smith, Jan Zwicky, Darren Wershler-Henry, and Brian Kim Stefans appears alongside the work of younger writers Jean Bleakney, Philip Blair, Paula Meehan, Patricia-Anne Moore, Frank Sewell, Jo Slade, and Mairtin Crawford—all from Ireland—as well as Alanna F. Bondar, Jannie Edwards, Katherine Lawrence, and Margo Wheaton from St. John's, Edmonton, Saskatoon, and Halifax.

Wah has facilitated writing communities across North America, from Nelson to New Mexico, Vancouver to Buffalo, and Winnipeg to Edmonton. The titles of all the magazines he has been involved with—*Sum, Magazine of Further Studies, Scree, Open Letter, dANDelion*—foreground openness and contingency. For example, as "a magazine of current workings," *Sum* exists at this juncture between partiality ("some") and a total ("sum"), between gathering and inquiry, between the "current" and what works.[9] The May 1964 issue of *Sum* published work by writers from across North America: David Bromige, Robert Duncan, John Wieners, Frank Davey,

George Bowering, Carol Bergé, Gael Turnbull, and Denise Levertov.[10] The
Magazine of Further Studies presented itself as an invitation, a place to
begin working. It contained essays, bibliographies, and notices of readings
as well as poems. The back page was reserved for notices like the follow-
ing:

> COME!
>
> HEAR CHARLES DORIA'S MOUTH MUSIC
> in Wah's cellar / 3 pm / Sunday / 3 Oct
> and
> : There will be NO MORE DEADLINES for this magazine. submit
> continuously to
> anyone

"Notes on the Possibility of a Phenomenological Poetics—The Body's
World," by Charles Sherry, appears alongside George F. Butterick's "Notes
from Class." The transcript of a lecture on "Drugs and the Unconscious"
by John Wieners given on 5 March 1967 at the Institute of Further Studies
appears alongside Robert Duncan on poetics—on the "kinds of form and
their associations with ideas of the universe." Three substantial bibliogra-
phies on mythology and poetry were also published.[11]

Poetry too was published there. Consider John Wieners's poem "The
Jafferson Aweplane": "I want to be successful in other terms than lives. /
Loveliness among these people is no occurrence to me." Or Fred Wah,
22 May 1969:

> I point to my own absolute (?) experience of
> myself as a step towards which all
> my being flows (into) and fills and from that there
> a physical place out of which the possible

Or Charles Olson's poem/letter to Jack Clarke:

> My dearest Jack,
> I don't think one acquires
> knowledge (either of the future or
> of the past)
> What the Kahuna
> or I wld say [and there is no
> Secret. Or this is it] is that
> _____ & what makes time simply
> (as against all the still current

humanism) the "life" of space is
this fact that it is
                    Knowing is simply
purifying oneself to be tuned in
_____ to
play _____ (the music

The first issue of Wah's 8½ × 11 inch stapled-together magazine *Scree*, pub-
lished in March 1971, situates itself in terms of geography—"South Slocan,
BC"—and in the following epigraph on the front cover: "raise your sights."
The epigraph that appears on the reverse of *Scree*'s front cover indicates
its relation to the poetics of *Sum* and *Magazine of Further Studies*. Here is
an excerpt from that epigraph:

> In such a World man does not feel shut up in his own mode of exis-
> tence. He too is "open." He achieves communication with the World
> because he uses the same language—symbol.

The community of writers published in *Scree*—George Butterick, Robert
Duncan, Fred Wah—is contiguous with the earlier magazines. Ruth Fox
and Duncan McNaughton were from Buffalo, Brian Fawcett from Vancou-
ver. But new names from the local community—Derryll White, Gladys
MacLeod, Craig McInnes—also appear. Recipes and kitchen sketches also
appear for the first time in *Scree*.[12] The recipe for "Uga-Buga, or Polly's
Folly" appears in the February 1972 issue alongside increasingly politicized
poems, like Wah's "Havoc Nation" which would also appear in *Tree*:

How the earth
dangles
eyeing over the geographical heap
now the nation smothers
lays onto the private magic nation
its own fake imagination.
                    Backoff
[...]   I also know a man who is a tree
and he received a letter
from a friend back east which ends
"It must be a very real world where you are.
                    Love, George."
That man is me
as well a revelation.

> Well dangle then
> the revelation
> revolution nation
> (*Loki* 61–62)[13]

The immediacy and particularity of the community is conjured not only in the recipes, poems, and essays, but in lines like: "So Pauline says—'You'd better get some apples then.'"[14]

Like the titles of *Sum* and *Magazine of Further Studies*, the less common word "scree" signifies movement and process, not solid ground. Scree is "like snow that's made of rock, it gives and slides," Wah told me when I asked him "what's scree?" (personal interview). For Wah, writing gives and slides. A letter from poet Ron Loewinsohn to Wah dated 27 October 1963, published in the first issue of *Sum* (December 1963), explicitly recalls this sense that, like writing, magazines are also more like scree than mountains. Loewinsohn's reason for writing is to send Wah an excerpt from a 1936 letter William Carlos Williams sent to Marianne Moore. Why send it? Because it "touches so closely & importantly on *Sum*": "If only—I keep saying it year in & year out—it were possible for 'us' to have a place, a location, to which we could resort, singly or otherwise, & to which others would follow us as dogs follow each other—without formality but surely—where we could be known as poets & our work be seen—& we could see the work of others & buy it & have it!" Loewinsohn writes, "The idea of USING SUM as a working ground is one I'd hope for. As Duncan says in that letter to Wieners, 'this shd be the workshop, rather than the show-window.'" Writing and editing in this workshop, Fred Wah continues to push "for a place where we can thrash things out, reactions to what's being done now" (25). He pushes for conjunction and community, for being and beings who are similarly interested in the spaces between, in hybridity, in being among.

Notes

1 Here is the full text: "Born in 1939 in Swift Current, Saskatchewan. After the war we moved to Trail, BC and then finally to Nelson, BC in 1948 so I really sense I grew up on the shores of the Kootenay. Vancouver for university (co-editor of *Tish* magazine), Albuquerque (editor of *Sum* magazine) and Buffalo (co-editor of *Magazine of Further Studies* and *Niagara Frontier Review*) for graduate school; started teaching at Selkirk College in 1967, living at South Slocan (editor of *Scree*) still on the Kootenay, with Pauline, Jenefer, Erika, Loki, Bonnie, Cedar, Birch and Mountains."

2 *Faking It: Poetics and Hybridity* (2000) appears in NeWest Press's "Writer as Critic" series edited by Smaro Kamboureli. It won the Association of Canadian and Que-

bec Literature's Gabrielle Roy Prize for Literary Criticism in English. In 1994, Wah and Roy Miki co-edited *Colour. An Issue*, a special double issue of *West Coast Line* on racialized writing.

3 This and other poems from *Among* are reprinted in *Loki is Buried at Smoky Creek*, Wah's *Selected Poems*. See "Hermes in the Trees" (*Loki* 45).

4 He acknowledged that "George Bowering, for example, would know that [Wah was part Chinese] and would kid around a little bit about it maybe—but it was never an ingredient in any of our discourse around poetry and poetics. Race and ethnicity were not part of language, period." From the interview "On Asianicity in Canada: An Interview with Fred Wah," November 1999, Calgary, Alberta.

5 I follow the practice of Fred Wah and his father by not including an accent in the word usually spelled "café."

6 In 1999, the Dandelion Magazine Society had commemorated its twenty-fifth anniversary by publishing the final issue (25:2) of *Dandelion*. Wah's influence on the writing community in Calgary cannot be underestimated and includes support not only for *dANDelion* but for the origin of several magazines produced by his students, including *Absinthe* and *filling Station* magazines as well as the small presses DisOrientation Chapbooks and housepress (see chronology, 1991 and 1994.)

7 His unsigned comments appear on the last page of the first issue of the revived magazine.

8 His note on the last page of the magazine explains: "each issue will document a very distinctive and contemporary taste in prose, poetry, image, and text" (128); this first issue "represents both local and international threads of association and community" (128).

9 Three of the seven issues of *Sum* were guest edited and published in 1965. John Keys edited "Writing out of New York," featuring twenty-four poets, including Ted Berrigan, Diane Wakoski, Ted Enslin, Jackson Mac Low, Fielding Dawson, LeRoi Jones (Amiri Baraka), Frank O'Hara, and Barbara Overmyer. "Thirteen English Poets" was edited by Andrew Crozier, Gael Turnbull, Tom Raworth, and Basil Bunting, among others. Ron Loewinsohn edited "Writing from San Francisco," including work by David Bromige and George Stanley. Wah edited the last issue publishing work by Gerry Gilbert, Victor Coleman, Charles Olson, and Larry Eigner.

10 Levertov's widely anthologized poem "The Mutes" was published here.

11 The list of seventy-five texts in the first bibliography gives us a sense of what these young writers were reading: Whitehead on *Process and Reality*, Jung on *Psychology and Alchemy*, Whorf on *Language, Thought and Reality*, Sapir on *Language*, Neumann on *The Great Mother* and *The Origins and History of Consciousness*, L. Waddell on *The Aryan Origin of the Alphabet*, Olson, Duncan, Creeley, Hesiod, Homer, Plutarch, Ovid, Chaucer, Keats, Shelley, Stendhal, Melville, Hawthorne, Stein, Yeats, Lawrence, Williams, Pound, Heraclitus, *Webster's International Dictionary*, Scott's *Greek Lexicon*, Skeat's *Etymological Dictionary*, and Allen's *The New American Poetry*. The bibliography concludes with this phrase, in parentheses: "If this doesn't work, try the Tarot"! These bibliographies were sent to Jack Clarke by Charles Olson and then published in the magazine for the community to use. Lists of magazines to read include *Origin, Black Mt Review, Kulchur, Fuck You, A*

Magazine of the Arts, SᴜM, *Combustion, C, Niagara Frontier Review, Matter, The Nation, Paris Review, New Directions, Poetry Chicago, Contact, Foot, Tɪsʜ,* and *Snapping Pussy.*

12 In *Diamond Grill* Wah will return to this practice of valuing recipes and kitchen sketches.

13 Here is the "Uga-Buga" recipe:
"For each person:
1 or 2 eggs as desired
1 banana
½ to 1 onion
1 or 2 cups steamed brown rice
Put rice on to cook. Slice onions and fry in butter or margarine, keep warm. Slice banana once lengthwise and fry in butter or margarine until they are darker in colour and soft. Then fry eggs, sunny side up. Arrange in a pile with the brown rice at the base, then the fried onions, then fried bananas, and top with eggs. Believe it or not, it's good" (inside front cover says "Food by Polly Wilson out of *Argenta Cook Book*, p. 50," Kitchen by Debeck).

14 On the back cover of an issue that has a sketch of a bowl with the words "yogurt, applesauce" on the front cover.

■

Robert Kroetsch's *The Hornbooks of Rita K*

Susan Rudy

● Like bpNichol, Robert Kroetsch was a key figure in the 1970s poetry scene in English-speaking Canada. With Kroetsch's *The Ledger* (1975) and *Seed Catalogue* (1977), for example, he radically redefined the long poem, the work of the poet, and the function of poetry. His book *The Hornbooks of Rita K* (2001) continues this work.[1] In *The Hornbooks*, the "poet" is Rita K, a famous western Canadian woman writer who was last seen in the Frankfurt Museum of Modern Art. The "author" of the book is named Raymond. He is not only her editor, and one of her most devoted readers—he also loves her. Continually positing and then displacing author and reader, lover and the beloved, *The Hornbooks of Rita Kleinhart* reconfigures what Kroetsch calls "the desperate love story that poetry is" (letter to Susan Rudy). For example, "When I tell you that I love you" is a poem attributed to Rita K by Raymond, the fictional editor of *The Hornbooks of Rita K*:

> When I tell you
> that I love you
> I am trying to tell you
> that I love you.
> > Rita Kleinhart [hornbook #73][2]
> > (*The Hornbooks of Rita K* 97)

In that their initials are like his, both Raymond and Rita appear as doubles of Robert Kroetsch the poet/scholar. But while Raymond parodies the scholar, Rita is both the object of desire and a subject in her own right. Rita is both like and unlike Robert Kroetsch. Like Kroetsch, Rita Kleinhart lectures internationally and is "attempting to write an autobiography in which I do not appear" (29). But unlike Kroetsch, she lives on the site of Kroetsch's childhood home, a ranch overlooking the Battle River in central Alberta. At the Calgary launch of the *Hornbooks,* Kroetsch acknowledged that, among other things, this book is an attempt to imagine himself otherwise— as a poet who had stayed in Battle River County rather than leaving, as a poet who was not just a man.

> Why is a hornbook like a hand-held
> mirror?
> Take a look for yourself.
> > Rita Kleinhart [hornbook #69]
> > (*The Hornbooks* 100)

Let's begin by asking, not "why is a hornbook," but what is a hornbook? Several explanations are offered in *The Hornbooks of Rita K*, beginning with three of the four epigraphs: a "HORNBOOK ... [is] a leaf of paper containing the alphabet, the Lord's Prayer, etc., mounted on a wooden tablet with a handle, and protected by a thin plate of horn." And a "HORNBOOK ... [is] a treatise on the rudiments of a subject: a primer." Another explanation appears in the form of a nursery rhyme from 1717: "To Master John the English Maid / A horn-book gives of gingerbread, / And that the child may learn the better, / As he can name, he eats the letter (Mathew Prior)." Like Master John, to "learn the better" we are taught to take language into our bodies, as though we might digest meaning itself. Yet the purpose of the hornbook for the poet Rita K is rather different. As she advises in "[hornbook #__?]": "The body is. The body does. / The rest is all a vague because" (75).

Rita writes hornbooks that are "primers" for this "vague because," as Raymond notes to his disparagement:

> The hornbook is itself a book, but a book one page in
> length. Framed and wearing a handle, covered in
> transparent horn, it sets out to fool no one. It says its say.
> Rita Kleinhart seems not to have got a handle on this
> realization. What she claimed for her poems was exactly
> that which they did not provide: the clarity of the exact and
> solitary and visible page. The framed truth, present and
> unadorned. Not a page for the turning, no, but rather the
> poem as relentless as a mirror held in the hand.

Our work in making sense of this text begins even before we open the book, with the title certainly, but also with the front cover image. Three, perhaps four, abstracted but full-bodied women walk back and forth across the page on the front cover, a detail from Michael Snow's "Venus Simultaneous" (1962) that anticipates the absent but present poet Rita who "is always returning, even when she is here" (103). The image of the back door on the back cover and repeated throughout the text, invites us, in casual prairie fashion, to come on in. But if you enter this book expecting to know a poem when you see one, or hear the voice of an author, you will be disappointed. Beginning with the title, it is as much about what is not here as what is. Rita's last allegedly unpublished hornbook (#99) appears as the first hornbook in this book (8). But since Raymond finds that Hornbook #99 "exists in a number of versions, with no particular version indicated as her final choice," he gives us both: "The question is always a question of trace. / What remains of what does not remain?" (8) and "I am watching the weather channel. / It is that kind of day" (9). The poem becomes what we do with this juxtaposition.

This juxtaposition of different versions includes, as I have suggested, different versions of the author. Like Rita, Raymond is also "a voice without so much as a last name" (7). As Rita's reader/archivist/lover, he triangulates the relation between poet and poem, lover and beloved, self and other:

> We have made a small trade, you and I. I occupy your
> abandoned house. Therefore, by your crystal logic, it is I
> who am missing from the world, not you. But surely it is,
> always, the poet who is absent from the terrors of
> existence, not the reader. (54)

In addressing the absent writer Rita, Raymond speaks of making "a small trade." But like "you and I," he is also addressing her as a reader of *his* text. As readers, we always occupy the "abandoned house" of the text, left behind by the poet to face the terrors of existence.

Another epigraph to *The Hornbooks of Rita K* is an excerpt from the art critic Axel Muller's interpretation of *Twilight Arch*, 1991, an installation by the American artist James Turrell. *Twilight Arch* just happened to have been mounted at the Frankfurt Museum of Modern Art in the early 1990s, the site of the disappearance of Rita K and of her archivist Raymond. Muller's response to Turrell's work very accurately describes my response to reading the *Hornbooks*:

> No object can be seen, no shadow. The picture's optical framework, made by light, has no foreground, middle and background. Everything is light—even the room. Here a process of perception begins that is hardly describable or nameable. The gaze is now at rest. The constant and fruitless attempts to fix one's eye on something have been given up at last. (n.p.)

The fruitlessness of attempting to fix one's eye on something is foregrounded by what is at the centre of this book: disappearance.

Yet *The Hornbooks of Rita K* is a book about presence. According to Raymond, Rita Kleinhart disappeared in the Frankfurt Museum of Modern Art (on Kroetsch's sixty-fifth birthday!). But this is also the date on which Rita imagines that Raymond disappeared, while they were standing side by side, in the dark, looking at "Twilight Arch." He thought of himself as a poet until she chose to disappear there in Frankfurt (35). Here is Raymond's version, from "[hornbook #53]":

> There in Frankfurt, on the occasion of Rita's disappearance
> (and I was standing beside her in that darkened room
> where one believes one is looking at a framed painting only
> to discover, as one's eyes adjust to the dark, that one is
> staring into a faintly lit recession set blankly into a blank
> wall), I turned to remark that I found James Turrell's
> "Twilight Arch" compelling nevertheless, for all the
> absence of an image. I turned and she was not there. (37)

Here is Rita's version, in "[hornbook #20]," an early hornbook that appears mid-way through the book:

> Raymond, let me continue what I was about to say—when
> I turned to you there in a darkened room in the Frankfurt
> Museum of Modern Art and found that you had vanished.
> Yours is the pathos of the aging male. You think that now
> that your life is spent you have lived a full life—and arrived
> at wisdom. [...]
> And by the way, Raymond, life tonight is a sushi bar
> and a bottle of beer and a glass of sake and the touch of a
> knee against a thigh. (57)

Both seem to recognize in Turrell's work their own shedding of the requirements of an "image," the certainty of an objective gaze, unambiguous meaning. But in the figure of Rita in the *Hornbooks* (like Anna Dawe in *Badlands*), Kroetsch is also exploring the image of the woman writer in Canada.

In "Sitting Down to Write: Margaret Laurence and the Discourse of Morning," Kroetsch drew our attention to a woman writer, Morag Gunn in *The Diviners*, as a spokesperson "for a Canadian poetics" (155). In early morning "the time of the mind's revisioning" (148) Morag sits down to write and "finds she has already begun. Uncannily, the sheet of paper in her typewriter is written upon [by her daughter Pique who has 'up and cleared out']" (149). Not only has she already begun, "She has been begun" (149). Or in Rita Kleinhart's words (or perhaps in Raymond's), "We turn to speak and confront an absence. Thus we become, all of us, poets" (53). Kroetsch's reading of *The Diviners* suggests that all of us might begin in such moments of contradiction, in moments of loss that invite silence, that create "both the site for a speaking and a speaking out" (153). Frank Davey recognizes this contradictory positioning as an aspect of Kroetsch's "partisan postmodernism" ("American Alibis" 250). Distinguishing it from Lyotard's notion of the postmodern condition as one of ahistorical play, Davey identifies Kroetsch's focus on Canadian specificities and differences as a sign of an interested postmodernism. In Davey's reading through Foucault and Bakhtin, Kroetsch's postmodernism draws attention to materiality and historicity. As such, Kroetsch repeatedly mixes "similitudes with conflict and divergence" (Davey 250).

Like *The Hornbooks of Rita K*, "D-Day and After: Remembering a Scrapbook I Cannot Find" wrestles with the fragmentary nature of memory and text, as well as their interdependence. Both speak, in different registers, about "that essential recognizing, that compiling, that imagining, [that] enabled me then to survive—and even to hope" (147). Kroetsch is speaking of his survival through a World War II childhood on the prairies of western Canada. In "D-Day and After," Kroetsch traces his theory of writing, even his epistemology, back to a 1939 homework assignment. Given a blank scrapbook by his teacher, he was asked to keep a record of the war:

> A scrapbook is almost pathetically made up of scraps. Yet the idea of scrap implies a larger whole, an organized universe, an explanatory mythology, from which the scrap was taken or has fallen away. [...] What if the scraps are the story? Our lives on the prairies often went unrecorded; they survived as a collection of photographs in a shoe box, a scattering of stories told around a kitchen table. They survived as a scrapbook. But was there something else that was more unified, more complete? (136)

Reading Rita's poems and papers, Raymond writes, "one cannot help but detect a message even in scraps so / random as these doodled lines" (47).

In *A Likely Story* Kroetsch describes himself as having "reverted to hunting and gathering, trying to pick up a story after failing to grow my own (and I was a dismal failure at farming)" (28). On the farm, Kroetsch spent more time in the garden, with the women, rather than in the field, with the men. As the poet does in so much of Kroetsch's work, Raymond tells of the loss of the mother. In the garden after she has disappeared, he "burst[s] into words":

> The day they brought my mother's body home to our
> house for the wake, I went up the low hill behind our
> house. Rita, I wanted to tell you this. I went to a hollow

beside a large round rock, and I curled up in that hollow
and I cried until I had cried out my life. After that I was
empty enough to be a poet. I returned to the house and
went to my room and made a list of the names of the
neighbours who came with food and flowers.
"[hornbook #19]" (36)

Like this section of the *Hornbooks*, several poems in *Advice to My Friends*
are a son's elegies for his mother. The long poem "Sounding the Name"
speaks for the desperate child who imagines that "In this poem my mother
is not dead" (*Advice*).

The poet in "birthday: June 26, 1983" (a section of "Sounding the
Name") enters the fiction of his mother's presence, available in a snapshot
of her, age seventeen:

In the snapshot my mother is seventeen.
She is standing beside an empty chair.
Today is my birthday, I am fifty-six.
I seat myself in the empty chair

in the snapshot [...]

I am in the house, out of sight, hiding,
so that she won't remember I am not yet
born. Her waiting eyes contain my eyes. [...]

In this poem I rehearse my mother.
I hold the snapshot in my hands.
I become her approaching lover.
(*Advice* 132)

As he does in the *Hornbooks*, having seated himself in the chair, in the snap-
shot, in the fiction, the "I" hides, not only in the house, but also in the pro-
noun "she" and in the figure of the lover. "Her name," in Kroetsch's work,
usually signifies the absent mother: "I think some of the female presence
in my book is almost a parody of the absence which is really what the
book is about" (Kroetsch speaking to Shirley Neuman in *Labyrinths of
Voice* 22).

The Hornbooks of Rita K, with its curiously antiquated, scholarly, and
yet intimate title, inhabits and ultimately reconfigures the love poem as well
as the love poet: the poetry is written at the expense of the lover's presence;
it cannot bring her home. There is no single love poet in this book.

Although Robert Kroetsch's name is on the front cover, you won't find any poems in *The Hornbooks of Rita K* that are simply "by" Robert Kroetsch. You might even be uncertain about which of them are "by" Rita K since Raymond has added much more than a simple "footnote, a scrap of data, the slightest anecdote, at most a word, to Rita's dense poems." He has added his own poetry, his own narrative, his own story.

Kroetsch's obsessive relationship with the other or double that is the poet—and that is notation—is longstanding. In the *Hornbooks*, when Rita K reminds Raymond: "You must practice, she told me, and this in no uncertain terms, to confound the possibility of your encountering your own double" (47), one double speaks to another. Value in the world of Rita K lies in such uncertainties, juxtapositions, and possibilities, especially in "what remains unvisited" surrounding "each line of poetry" (76), "the hole in the middle of things" (101), the apparently expendable, the refused.

But *The Hornbooks of Rita K* is simultaneously intellectually challenging, moving, and hilarious. The first of five sections, for example, subtitled "The Marginalia Hornbooks" consists of six of Rita's hornbooks (6, 10, 31, 54, 75, and 89). Here are the first three:

[hornbook #6]

To see is not
to see ahead.
We cannot see
beyond the bed.

[hornbook #10]
Each line of a poem is a provisional exactness.
We write by waiting for the mind to dispossess.

[hornbook #31]
To you, dear reader, frequenter of airport lounges—
even a stand-by poem should tell you where you are. (3)

These lines can certainly be met with serious philosophical attention. How can a line of a poem be "a provisional exactness"? How is "to see" not "to see ahead"? But the last line undermines a too serious reading: "we cannot see beyond the bed"!! Every line, every section, every word is a puzzle. The contexts are both exotic and banal: from the dining-room table at Rita's ranch to a James Turrell exhibit at the Frankfurt Museum of Modern Art. The intimate moments of domestic life—eating breakfast, watching TV, making love, hiking, crying in the afternoon—all are listed with loving detail (like the "list of the names of neighbours who came with food and flow-ers" "[hornbook #19]" 36). Yet the poem is entranced by the abstract and philosophical. Raymond and Rita discuss the concept of "zero" and its origins in Western thought and ask repeatedly what is a poet, a poem, a per-son? Why write?

Two poets—Raymond and Rita—are asking "why write" in *The Horn-books of Rita K*. Raymond is waiting in Rita's ranch house, sitting at her dining-room table, reading her poems, writing about them, watching hockey, drinking scotch, believing she will return—which she does (I think!). According to Raymond, before she disappeared, Rita was working on "a huge—and I would say, bizarre—work" (16) in which she aestheticizes "the pathetic beauty that we create by way of discard" (173) by inscribing, in a series of ninety-nine poems, "the ninety-nine back doors that were nearest her own" (172–74). Raymond elaborates: "Her fascination with back doors—of houses, of apartments, even of garages and barns and public buildings—announces her interest in collective biography" (173).

For Raymond as for Rita, "poetry is excrement" (209); "writing is not about delivering messages" (25). "What rapacious need," he asks "makes the poet claim the multitude by the small ordering of a signature? / Does it not take a bundle of texts, a blather of loves, to bumble one poem out of one acquisitive poet?" (44). "Think of me," the archivist/narrator/poet/lover Raymond writes, "as a voice without so much as a last name" (7). (Having no last name we can't help but wonder, will he take hers?) As he sees it, "the presumption of the poet [that "we attribute to ourselves the poems we record on paper"] is one of technology's petty triumphs" (43). The poet is much more ordinary, more connected to and dependent upon the world, more temporary. Take "[hornbook for a young poet]" (92) in "The Red Shale Hornbooks" section for example. The advice to the young poet in this hornbook is to have a hearty (if high-cholesterol) breakfast, and then to reflect on the implications of having done so:

> Have bacon (four strips,
> preferably) and eggs (two, sunnyside up),
>
> hash browns with ketchup,
> toast (white) with real strawberry jam,
>
> a glass of orange juice (small will do),
> and three cups of black coffee;
>
> then mark one of the following
> (please, not with an X):

a) Tune-up and body-tone clinics are available
   at reasonable prices.
b) We do have to believe in something
   (don't we?).
c) We proceed by heresies, yet intend
   to get to where we are going.
d) Appetite will be the end of us. (92)

Unlike Rita, Raymond is a courier, not a poet, by trade. Until recently, he had spent his life delivering other people's documents, writing poems only in airplanes and flushing his words down the toilet before landing.

Paradoxically, by delivering Rita's poems into the hands of her readers, he becomes an acquisitive poet. *The Hornbooks of Rita K* is Raymond's text, what he would have called "The Poetics of Rita Kleinhart," and Rita's *Hornbooks*, his love poems and hers. Through this strategy she does not disappear, rather she remains in what "remains":

> To take poetry into one's hands is to take one's own life
> into one's hands. Surely Rita understood this when she
> asked me, late one evening, if I would, should the occasion
> arise, organize her papers and have them deposited in the
> vaults of the University of Calgary Special Collections
> Library. When I told her next morning that, yes, I would be
> happy to make her remains secure, she asked me what
> I was talking about. (45)

Her "remains" are the "neat stacks of scrawled notes, manuscripts, partially filled notebooks and, yes, unfinished (or unfinishable?) poems" (8) he finds on her ranch at the edge of the Battle River coulees in central Alberta after "the provincial authorities named [him] as the archivist who would put together her literary papers. The law recognized that our love relationship continued, even if that recognition was beyond Rita herself" (29).

Other "characters" include Rita's old friend "Robert," "sound poet" Doug Barbour, and writer George Bowering. In a deliberately playful way—and in a way that more conventional lyric poetry actually discourages—all correspondences between the fictional and the real become possible. Raymond introduces the book by saying he has "examined each hornbook as it comes to hand, here at the dining room table in the house that was Rita's study and her home," proposing to "add a footnote, a scrap of data, the slightest anecdotes, at most a word, to Rita's dense poems"(7).

In some respects, Raymond in the *Hornbooks* inhabits a very familiar fiction of femininity, one in which the woman is both desirable and inaccessible:

> I'm not convinced she ever heard a word I spoke to her. I
> offered her praise and love. She did not know how to
> accept either. We deceive ourselves into words when all
> that cries out is the body, wanting touch and taste and
> smell and sight. Do you hear me? (34)

Yet she is accessible. Rita is "present" throughout the text in the form of her poems. In the narrative frame, she comes home at the end:

> When I heard her key in the lock of the back door of her
> ranch house, I covered my face with a volume of her
> poems. I was lying on the couch in front of the TV, now
> and then sipping a very small scotch. The Edmonton Oilers
> were playing Ottawa. I am always waiting. She is always
> returning, even when she is here. (103)

Kroetsch, not the woman poet, is the absent one. She opens the door and comes home. Raymond thinks he can hide on the couch by covering his face with her book. I am reminded of [hornbook #13], which appears halfway through the book:

> We come, Rita, we come to apostrophe. We turn away to
> make address to whom or what we would address. But is
> that not always the predicament of both poet and poem? (56)

To come to apostrophe is to come, from the Greek word *apostrepho*, to the moment of turning away. This is the moment of loss for the conventional love poet who, in seeking connection, inevitably turns to words, not the beloved: "We turn to speak and confront an absence. Thus we / become, all of us, poets" (53). The next lines in [hornbook #13] play with this convention:

> I intended to compose a WANTED poster and circulate it
> on [the] Internet, only to find that what I had to say owed much
> to your own cryptic hornbooks. [...]
> I entered your abandoned house as I entered your abandoned
> poems, lovingly, I had proposed to write a description and
> put it into circulation in the expectation of bringing you

> back. Why then did your precious policeman come to find,
> not us, but me? (56)

What he has to say is what she has been saying. The dilemma of the love poet is that readers who are like policemen, speaking in the "single voice" (53) of "the law," may find only the archivist, not the beloved, not even the poem. But an apostrophe is also "an exclamatory passage in a speech or poem, addressed to a person (often dead or absent) or thing (often personified)" (*Concise Oxford*). As such, the *Hornbooks* are the poem as apostrophe, a turning that is a return, an address to and from the absent but ever-so-present poet as lover, as he, as she.

Notes

1. Earlier versions in their present or slightly different form appeared under the title "The Poetics of Rita Kleinhart" in little magazines during the 1990s, including *West Coast Line, Open Letter, Prairie Fire, Mattoid* (Australia), *The New Quarterly, Alberta Views, Canadian Literature*, and *Border Crossings* as well as in *A Likely Story: The Writing Life, The Oviedo Hornbooks*, and *The Red Shale Hornbooks*. See the bibliography for details.

2. Since Kroetsch repeatedly manipulates and undermines the convention of "author" and "editor" throughout *The Hornbooks of Rita K*, it is very difficult to use scholarly conventions to refer to passages from this book! For example, the "hornbooks" supposedly written by Rita K and now published by her editor Raymond do not appear in chronological order. Moreover, square brackets—for example "[hornbook #73]"—are used throughout to suggest that this numbering system is that of the fictional editor Raymond. My references throughout this essay play along. I cite the fictional author (Rita Kleinhart) and use the fictional editor's practice (I retain the square brackets). But these fictional references are followed by page references to Kroetsch's actual book called *The Hornbooks of Rita K*.

■

1980 **Theytus Books** (Penticton). Founded by Randy Fred. Current managing editor Greg Young-Ing. Publishes only Aboriginal authors. Owned and operated by First Nations people. "'Theytus' is a Salishan word meaning 'preserving for the sake of handing down'.... Theytus strives to play an active and important role in the development of Aboriginal literature through the promotion of Aboriginal authors" (Young-Ing, "Traditional" 186). Theytus Books also founded the magazine *Gatherings* (see 1990). Poetry titles include books by Jeannette Armstrong and Lee Maracle. Eventually housed at the En'owkin Centre (see 1981).

Williams-Wallace International (Toronto). Focuses on writers of colour in Canada. Published early books by Dionne Brand, M. Nourbese Philip, Betsy Warland, and Claire Harris. In 1990, published the anthology *Daughters of the Sun, Women of the Moon: Poetry by Black Canadian Women*. Edited by Ann Wallace.

Writing Magazine (David Thompson University Centre, Nelson and Vancouver; last issue 1993). Editors include David McFadden (1–5), John Newlove (6), Colin Browne (7–22), and Jeff Derksen (23–28). Moved to Vancouver in 1984 (issue no. 9) when the Vancouver section of the Kootenay School of Writing was established (see entry under 1984). Focused on Language writers in Canada and the USA.

1981 *The Coast Is Only a Line, Contemporary Poetry and Prose in BC* (Simon Fraser University, Burnaby). A six-week summer course that consisted of two full courses, one instructed by Warren Tallman and the other by Eli Mandel. There was also a weekend festival/conference by the same title halfway through the course. *Line* magazine (see 1983) grew out of this event.

Dialogue Conference/Colloque Dialogue (16–17 October 1981, York University, Toronto). Organized by Barbara Godard, participants included Himani Bannerji, Nicole Brossard, Louise Cotnoir, Daphne Marlatt, Kathy Mezei, Donna Smyth, Miriam Waddington, and Betsy Warland. Conference proceedings: *Gynocritics / La Gynocritique*. Ed. Barbara Godard (Toronto: ECW, 1987).

The En'owkin Centre (Penticton). Founded by the Okanagan Tribal Council. In 1986, Jeannette Armstrong became director. The name of the centre means "a group challenge to get the best possible answer" (Armstrong). The centre houses Theytus Books (see 1980), the En'owkin International School of Writing (see 1989), and *Gatherings: The En'owkin Journal of First North American Peoples* (see 1990).

Toronto South Asian Review (TSAR). Founded to provide a publishing venue for writers of South Asian descent. Eventually developed TSAR publications to publish new Canadian and American writers (regardless of ethnic origin) as well as world writing. Magazine contributors include Rajinderpal S. Pal, Lakshmi Gill, Ian Iqbal Rashid, Rienzi Crusz, Cyril Dabydeen, and Sadhu Binning. TSAR press published *Shakti's Words: An Anthology of South Asian Canadian Women's Poetry*, plus individual poetry books by Ian Iqbal Rashid, Rienzi Crusz, Lakshmi Gill, Ranjinderpal S. Pal, and others.

1982 ***Mondo Hunkamooga*** (Toronto 1982–98). Twenty issues. Founded by Stuart Ross "to reflect the world of small-press publishing, especially in Canada, but also with contributions from the USA and the UK" (Ross). Filled with reviews (by Stuart Ross, bpNichol, Nicholas Power, Kevin Connolly, Crad Kilodney, and others); interviews with writers and publishers (including David McFadden, Joe Brainard, Gil Adamson, Jim Smith, Kenward Elmslie); rants; cartoons; and "Mondo Editorialus," Ross's regular editorial.

Rampike (Ontario College of Art, Toronto). Ed. Karl E. Jirgens. Focuses on experimental writing and art. Contributors include bill bissett, Nicole Brossard, Christian Bök, Steve McCaffery, Laurie Anderson, France Theoret, bpNichol, Robert Zend, Robert Kroetsch, Fred Wah, Karen Mac Cormack, as well as Aboriginal writers including Tomson Highway, Roland Nadjiwon, and Norval Morrisseau.

1983 ***Line: A Journal of the Contemporary Literary Collection*** (Burnaby, Simon Fraser University, last issue 1989). Founded and edited by Roy Miki. "The materials it plans to publish—archival items, interviews, essays, review/commentaries, and bibliographies—will be related to the line of post-1945 Canadian, American, and British writers whose work issues from or extends, the work of Ezra Pound, William Carlos Williams, H.D., Gertrude Stein, and Charles Olson." Subtitle changed to *A Journal of Contemporary Writing and Its Modernist Sources* with issue no. 3. Merged with *West Coast Review* (see 1967) in 1990 to become *West Coast Line* (see 1990).

Nightwood Editions (Toronto). Started when Howard and Mary White and Alan Twigg bought Blew Ointment Press. David Lee and Maureen Cochrane became the press editors. In 1985, Lee and Cochrane took over the press, renaming it Nightwood Editions. (Howard and Mary White gave them their shares in the press as a wedding present.) Nightwood Editions published books by Steve McCaffery, Karen Mac Cormack, Chris Dewdney, bill bissett, and many others as well as the *Blewointment Anthology: 1963–1988* (2 volumes. Toronto: Nightwood Editions: 1985, 1986). In 1990, the press was re-established in Madeira Park, BC, under new owners.

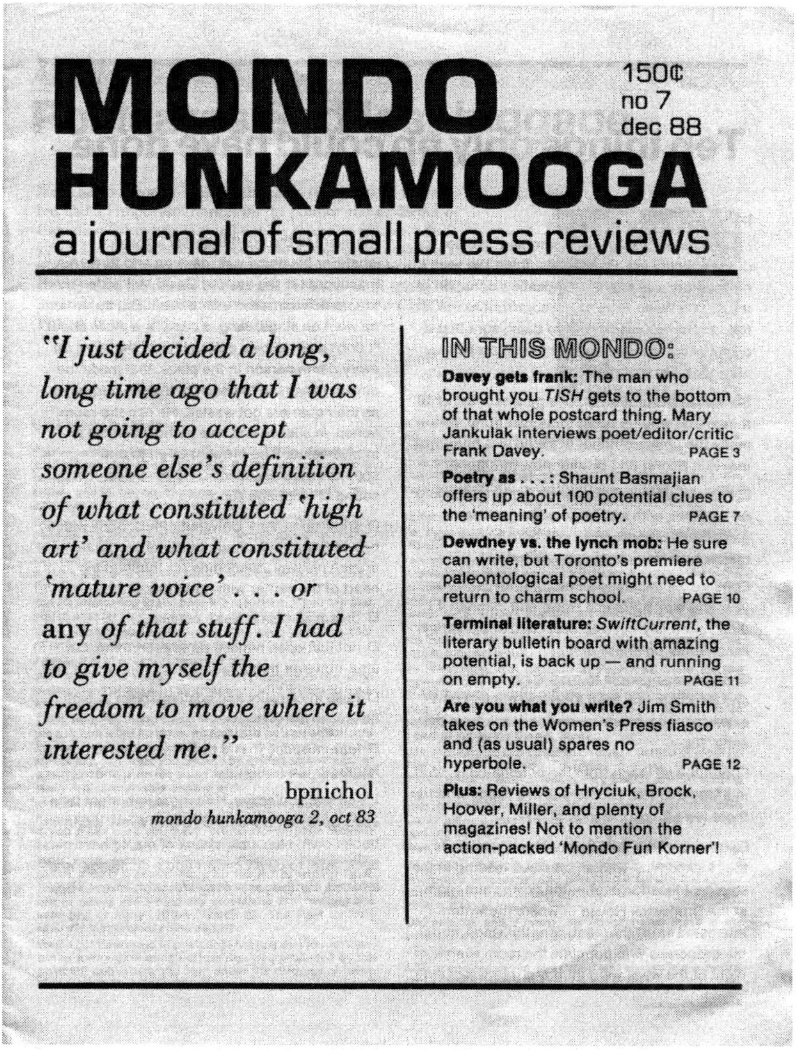

MONDO
**150¢
no 7
dec 88**

HUNKAMOOGA
a journal of small press reviews

"*I just decided a long, long time ago that I was not going to accept someone else's definition of what constituted 'high art' and what constituted 'mature voice' . . . or any of that stuff. I had to give myself the freedom to move where it interested me.*"

bpnichol
mondo hunkamooga 2, oct 83

IN THIS MONDO:

Davey gets frank: The man who brought you *TISH* gets to the bottom of that whole postcard thing. Mary Jankulak interviews poet/editor/critic Frank Davey. PAGE 3

Poetry as . . . : Shaunt Basmajian offers up about 100 potential clues to the 'meaning' of poetry. PAGE 7

Dewdney vs. the lynch mob: He sure can write, but Toronto's premiere paleontological poet might need to return to charm school. PAGE 10

Terminal literature: *SwiftCurrent*, the literary bulletin board with amazing potential, is back up — and running on empty. PAGE 11

Are you what you write? Jim Smith takes on the Women's Press fiasco and (as usual) spares no hyperbole. PAGE 12

Plus: Reviews of Hryciuk, Brock, Hoover, Miller, and plenty of magazines! Not to mention the action-packed 'Mondo Fun Korner'!

Figure 9. Front cover of *Mondo Hunkamooga*.

Prairie Fire (Winnipeg). Founded and edited by Andris Taskans. Grew out of *Writers' News Manitoba*. Began as "A Manitoba Literary Review" and would eventually become "A Canadian Magazine of New Writing." Contributors include a mix of prairie writers and writers from elsewhere, such as Di Brandt, Robert Kroetsch, Dennis Cooley, Adeena Karasick, David Arnason, Betsy Warland, and Fred Wah.

Raddle Moon (formerly *from an island*, Department of Creative Writing, University of Victoria, Victoria). Ed. Susan Clark (Yarrow), last issue 2002. Beginning with no. 13, published by Kootenay School of Writing Society, Vancouver. Emphasized international connections: "Internationalism seems to have come upon a number of us (Canadian Little Magazines), all at once. Each of us, perhaps, feeling suffocated: something had to be done" (Clark, *Raddle Moon* 3 [1985] 6). Had editors-at-large in Italy, France, Japan, China for several issues, then various contributing editors, including Nicole Brossard, Norma Cole, Lisa Robertson, Kathryn McLeod, Jeff Derksen, and Erin Mouré. Also published poems in translation and image-text works. Contributors include Jeff Derksen, Dan Farrell, Deanna Ferguson, Dorothy Trujillo Lusk, Catriona Strang, Kevin Davies, Peter Culley, Phyllis Webb, Susan Clark, Nancy Shaw, Maggie O'Sullivan, Joan Retallack, Christopher Dewdney, Lisa Robertson, Abigail Child, and Charles Bernstein.

Wolsak and Wynn (Toronto). Publishes only poetry: "We believe in the importance of widening the audience for poetry in Canada, and keeping it vital." < http://www.poets.ca/wolsakwynn/index.htm >. Has produced close to a hundred titles in its twenty-year existence, including recent books by Ashok Mathur, Douglas Barbour, Jeanette Lynes, and Nicole Markotić.

Women and Words / Les Femmes et les mots (30 June–3 July Vancouver). Over one thousand anglophone and francophone women attended, to "explore the tradition and context of our work with words, discuss existing power structures and the creation of alternative ones, and look at new directions evident in women's writing, criticism and cultural organizing" (Dybikowski et al., 9). Presenters included Beth Brant, Nicole Brossard, Louise Cotnoir, Jeannette Armstrong, Lillian Allen, Sharon Thesen, Daphne Marlatt, Makeda Silvera, and Phyllis Webb. (Conference proceedings: Dybikowski et al., *In the Feminine: Women and Words/Les Femmes et les Mots*. Edmonton: Longspoon, 1985).

1984 **The Kootenay School of Writing** (Vancouver and Nelson). Established as an independent, non-profit society by former faculty and students from David Thompson University Centre in Nelson, after the centre was closed in the spring of 1984. Founders of the Nelson section include Fred Wah, Irene Mock, Paulette Jiles, Rita Moir, Caroline Woodward, Pauline Butling, and Blake Parker. Founders of the Vancouver section include Tom Wayman, Colin Browne, Jeff Derksen, Calvin Wharton, Athena George, and Gary Whitehead. The Vancouver branch offers courses, lectures, workshops, and readings devoted to current theory and practice in all aspects of writing, publishing, and performance. The Nelson section organizes readings and workshops.

Long-liners Conference on the Canadian Long Poem (29 May–1 June, York University, Toronto). Organized by Frank Davey, Eli Mandel, and Ann Munton. Presenters included George Bowering, Louis Dudek, Roy Miki, Stephen Scobie, Charles Bernstein, Dorothy Livesay, bpNichol, and Fred Wah. Conference publication: *Long-liners Conference Issue. Open Letter* 6.2–3 (Summer–Fall 1985).

Tessera (Vancouver, Toronto, and Montreal). Founding editorial collective: Barbara Godard, Daphne Marlatt, Kathy Mezei, and Gail Scott. The idea for the magazine began at the Dialogue conference at York in 1981 when Marlatt approached Mezei, Godard, and Scott about starting a francophone/anglophone feminist journal (Marlatt, *Readings* 9). First four issues published as special issues in other magazines: no. 1 *Room of One's Own* 8.4 (1984); no. 2 *La Nouvelle barre du jour* 157 (1985); no. 3 *Canadian Fiction Magazine* 57 (1986); and no. 4 *cv2*, 11.2/3 (1988). Members of later editorial collectives include Louise Cotnoir, Susan Knutson, Katherine Binhammer, Lianne Moyes, Jennifer Henderson, and Nicole Markotić. "*Tessera* emerged from the discussions of a number of feminist critics and writers concerned about the absence in the Canadian critical institution of an appropriate frame for analyzing the exciting writing being produced by women in Canada working on language to develop new syntax, new narrative structures, new modes of subjectivity" (Godard, "Women of Letters" 258).

1985   *Contemporary Verse II* (Winnipeg). Beginning with vol. 8, no. 4 (February 1985) restructured with a feminist editorial collective of Pamela Banting, Di Brandt, Jan Horner, and Jane Casey "reinterpreting Dorothy Livesay's original vision for a national poetry magazine." Beginning with issue 9.1, the format and title changed to *Contemporary Verse II: A Literary Journal for Women and Men.* (It's short name was *cv2*.) Later members of the editorial collective include Keith Louise Fulton, Uma Parameswaran, Naomi Gilbert, and Patricia Rawson. Contributors include Kristjana Gunnars, Angela Hryniuk, Lydia Kwa, Marie Annharte Baker, Karen Mac Cormack, Janice Williamson, and Uma Parameswaran.

New Poetics Colloquium: A Celebration of New Writing (21–25 August, Emily Carr College of Art, Vancouver). Organized by the Kootenay School of Writing collective in Vancouver. Participants included Bruce Andrews, Charles Bernstein, Jeff Derksen, Sharon Thesen, Ron Silliman, Michel Gay, Steve McCaffery, Nicole Brossard, Lyn Hejinian, Susan Howe, and Daphne Marlatt.

Sister Vision Press (Toronto). Founded by Makeda Silvera and Stephanie Martin. Publishes women of colour in Canada, "especially those with a focus on lesbian writing." Poetry titles include books by Makeda Silvera,

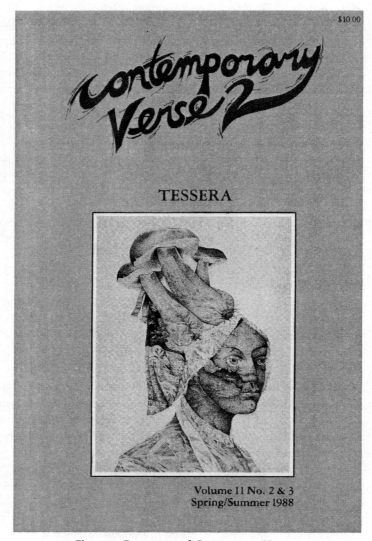

$10.00

TESSERA

Volume II No. 2 & 3
Spring/Summer 1988

Figure 10. Front cover of *Contemporary Verse II*.

Himani Bannerji, Lenore Keeshig-Tobias, Connie Fife, Afua Cooper, and Ramabai Espinet.

West Word Summer School/Writing Retreat for Women (University of British Columbia, Vancouver). The first of several summer workshops, with the last retreat held in 1993. Instructors included Daphne Marlatt, Gail Scott, Dionne Brand, Claire Harris, Smaro Kamboureli, and Nicole Brossard.

1986 **Split Shift: A Colloquium on the New Work Writing** (21–24 August, Trout Lake Community Centre, Vancouver). Sponsored by the Kootenay School of Writing and the Vancouver Industrial Writers' Union. Participants included Tom Wayman, Erin Mouré, Robert Carson, and Susan Eisenberg.

Tsunami Editions (Gibson's Landing and Vancouver). Founded by Larry Bremner (Timewell). Published chapbooks and perfect-bound books, including books by Jeff Derksen, Deanna Ferguson, Kathryn MacLeod, Lisa Robertson, Dorothy Trujillo Lusk, Kevin Davies, Dan Farrell, and Colin Smith.

1987 **(f.)Lip: A Newsletter of Feminist Innovative Writing** (Vancouver, last issue 1990). Eds. Sandy (Frances) Duncan, Angela Hryniuk, and Betsy Warland. "To state it simply, we are interested in new work which explores and alters content, form and language in ways that disturb our normal reading patterns, ways that delight, startle, subvert and liberate." Contributors include Di Brandt, Erin Mouré, and M. Nourbese Philip.

Toronto Small Press Book Fair (Annual event, 1987–current). Started by Nick Power and Stuart Ross. Coordinators include Clint Burnham, Katy Chan, Daniel Jones.

1988 **gynergy books** (Charlottetown). Founded as the feminist imprint of Ragweed Press (see 1980). Poetry books include titles by Nancy Chater, Gillian Chase, Liliane Welch, Diane Driedger, and Daphne Marlatt's and Betsy Warland's collaboration, *Double Negative*.

Pink Dog Press (Toronto, last publication 1997). Founded by Kevin Connolly. Published about sixteen chapbooks, including works by Greg Evason, Victor Coleman, Lynn Crosbie, David Demchuck, Brian Dedora, Stuart Ross, Daniel Jones, Kevin Connolly, Connie Deanovich, Randall Schroth, Gary Barwin, and Gil Adamson.

Telling It: Women and Language across Cultures (Vancouver). Conference organized by Daphne Marlatt during her appointment to the Ruth Wynn Woodward chair of Women's Studies at Simon Fraser University. Its purpose was "to showcase the writing of women who are marginalized in different ways ... it featured women writers and performers from the Native Indian, Asian-Canadian and lesbian communities in BC" (Marlatt, "Introduction" 12). Presenters included Jeannette Armstrong, Sky Lee, Lee Maracle, and Betsy Warland. Conference publication: *Telling It: Women and Language across Cultures*. Ed. Sky Lee, Lee Maracle, Daphne Marlatt, Betsy Warland (Vancouver: Press Gang, 1990).

The Third International Feminist Book Fair (Montreal, 14–22 July 1988). More than 6,000 women came to the fair, which consisted of two trade days and four days of panels and workshops "organized around the themes of memory, power, and strategies of feminist thought." It was "an event of historic importance" because it "established a space where crucial questions about women's relationship to language could be raised" (Nelson and Weil 3). Presenters included Montreal feminists Erin Mouré, Nicole Brossard, Gail Scott, Louise Cotnoir, and Mary Meigs as well as women from across Canada and around the world.

1989 **Desh Pardesh** conference/festival of diasporic South Asian art and culture (Toronto, annual event). Organized by Desh Pardesh, a Toronto-based organization of artists, cultural producers, and activists from the South Asian diaspora. Desh Pardesh grew out of "Salaam Toronto" (1988), a one-day arts event aimed at increasing the visibility of the South Asian lesbian and gay community, organized by Khush, an organization for South Asian gay men.

The En'owkin International School of Writing (Penticton). Founder and director, Jeannette C. Armstrong. The EISW offers creative writing courses that focus on Aboriginal creative processes and practices. Poetry, fiction, and publishing workshops also receive credit through the University of Victoria; other courses are accredited through Okanagan College.

Motel (Vancouver, last publication 1991: six issues). Edited by Kathryn MacLeod (with Lisa Marr, Julia Steele, and Douglas Stetar). "For your comfort and convenience." Published writers from Canada and the USA including Lyn Hejinian, Jeff Derksen, Nancy Shaw, Louis Cabri, and Erin Mouré.

Streetcar Editions (Toronto, last publication, 1993). Founded by Stuart Ross. Published poetry, and critical chapbooks by Kevin Connolly, Lynn Crosbie, Clint Burnham, Beverley Daurio, and others.

1990 **Fingerprinting Inkoperated** (1990–98: Victoria 1991, Vancouver 1992, Toronto 1993–1998). Founded and co-edited by Jon Adorno and damian lopes; edited solely by lopes after the second release. Purpose: to publish "intriguing & innovative 'writing' in any form, format or medium." Published leaflets, pamphlets, postcards, and small chapbooks. Published approximately one hundred titles, including works by damian lopes, Alana Wilcox, Christian Bök, Nelson Ball, David UU, jwcurry, Peter Jaeger, and Darren Wershler-Henry.

Gatherings: The En'owkin Journal of First North American Peoples (Published annually by the EISW, Penticton.) Editors and topics change each year. Editors include David Gregoire (1), Greg Young-Ing (2, 9, 10), Beth Cuthand (5), Kateri Akiwenzie-Damm and Jeannette Armstrong (7), and Florence Belmoe (11). Issue topics include *Metamorphosis* (6), *Shaking the Belly: Releasing the Sacred Clown* (8), and *Beyond Victimization* (9). Contributors include former students from the En'owkin Centre together with First Nations writers from Canada and the USA Canadian contributors include Lee Maracle, Drew Hayden Taylor, Marie Annharte Baker, Marilyn Dumont, Jeannette Armstrong, Daniel David Moses, and Louise Halfe.

hole (Ottawa, last issue, 1996). Founded and edited by Louis Cabri and Rob Manery as one offshoot of the ewg ("experimental writing group") that started in 1986 and "met regularly to read poetry alongside critical theory and poetics, and produce poetry seminars, talks and readings, in Ottawa, from 1986 to 1995" (Cabri, 6). The EWG also ran the "Transparency Machine" reading series from 1989–1991, featuring a number of writers from Canada, the USA, and UK, Canadian writers included Erin Mouré, Jeff Derksen, and Christopher Dewdney. *hole* published visual art, essays, reviews, and poetry (by Frank Davey, Karen Mac Cormack, Jeff Derksen, Deanna Ferguson, Lisa Robertson, and others). When *hole* magazine ended, *hole* became a chapbook series, which included books by Clint Burnham (*Pandemonium*), Deanna Ferguson (*ddilemma*), and Jeff Derksen *(But Could I Make a Living from It)*.

Nightwood Editions (Madeira Park, BC). In 1990, Kim and Carol La Fave, Alan Twigg, and Mary and Howard White purchased the company and moved it from Ontario to BC, with Kim La Fave as president. Marisa Alps becme the company director in the early 1990s and unofficial literary editor. In 2000 Alps also became the publisher. Silas White joined the company in 2002 (email from Silas White). Recent poetry publications include books by Pindar Dulai, Goh Poh Seng, Kuldip Gil, and Philip Kevin Paul.

West Coast Line (English Department, Simon Fraser University, Burnaby). Eds. Roy Miki (1990–99), Miriam Nichols et al. (1999–2001); Glen Lowry and Jerry Zaslove (2002–current). "The desire is to be in the midst somewhere in the doubts that plague us enough to keep us moving forward. Here, in this country, writers will have to continue the effort to resist the homogenization of imagination that everywhere threatens to dematerialize our language" (Miki, "Editor's Note). A product of the merger between *West Coast Review* (see 1967) and *Line* (see 1983), WCL includes poetry, fiction, critical essays, and visual art. The magazine took a proactive role in seeking out writers of colour and First Nations writers, who were published regularly in various issues, as well as in *Colour. An Issue,* a special double issue of *West Coast Line* (13/14, Spring–Fall 1994). Has had several guest-edited issues. Contributors include Marie Annharte Baker, Christian Bök, Clint Burnham, Jeff Derksen, Peter Hudson, damian lopes, Gerry Shikatani, Ashok Mathur, Steve McCaffery, Erin Mouré, Lola Lemire Tostevin, and Jacqueline Turner.

1991   *Absinthe* (Calgary, 1991–98). Began as an offshoot of *Secrets from the Orange Couch* (Red Deer, 1988–92). First issue of *Absinthe* is *Secrets* vol. 4.

no. 3 (Winter 1991). *Absinthe's* founding editorial collective was Ashok Mathur, Roberta Rees, Barbara Scott, Sonia Smee, and Jane Warren. Subsequent members of the collective included Suzette Mayr, Hiromi Goto, Aruna Srivastiva, and Rita Wong. The magazine began with the statement that "absinthe was said to evoke new views, different experiences and unique feelings." In 1993, it shifted its focus to race writing with the special issue, *This Skin on Our Tongues.* Published several other special guest-edited issues, including *HypheNation: a mixed race issue* (9.2, 1996); *sistaspeak: a collection of poetry and prose written and compiled by aboriginal women and women of colour* (8.1-2, 1995); *queering absinthe* (9.2, 1996); and *Women Writing Lives, Absinthe* (10.2, 1998). *Absinthe* also sponsored the Crow's Nest Pass Writing Workshops in the summer of 1993 and 1994.

DisOrientation Chapbooks (Calgary. Last publication 1997). Edited and produced by Nicole Markotić and Ashok Mathur). Titles included books by Suzette Mayr, Hiromi Goto, Greg Young-Ing, Robert Kroetsch, Méira Cook, and Roy Miki.

Interventing the Text (2-4 May, University of Calgary). "A symposium on the production and critical reception of language as text." Organized by Fred Wah, with assistance from Ashok Mathur, Brian Rusted, and Susan Rudy Dorscht. Conference proceedings: *Open Letter* 8.5-6 (Winter–Spring 1993).

1992 **above/ground press** (Ottawa). Founded by rob mclennan. Has published hundreds of inexpensive chapbooks and POEM leaflets (150 in the series to 2002) sold and handed out across Canada during mclennan's touring. Concentrates mostly on lyric poetry, with titles by George Bowering, Jay MillAr, Stephen Cain, Lisa Samuels, David McFadden, Ken Norris, Joe Blades, Stephanie Bolster, and mclennan himself.

The Appropriate Voice (Geneva Park, Orillia, ON). A three-day retreat organized by the Racial Minorities Committee of The Writers' Union of Canada to discuss common concerns and develop recommendations for proactive policies. The main recommendation was for a national conference for writers of colour and First Nations writers (see Writing thru Race entry, 1994).

Boondoggle Books/BookThug (London, ON, and Toronto. 1996–current). Founded by Jay MillAr. Name changed to BookThug in 1996. Publishes poetry and poetry criticism. Titles by Tim Conley, Stephen Cain, Christopher Dewdney, Alice Burdick, Gerry Gilbert, nathalie stephens, John Barlow, and MillAr himself.

Inglish: Writing with an Accent (20-21 November, Western Front, Vancouver). Sponsored by *West Coast Line*: "*Inglish* ... brought together some 70 writers, readers, artists and cultural workers participate to encourage a more open-ended way to circle the personal and theoretical implications of 'English' for contemporary issues such as writing, ethnicity, gender, racism, and subjectivity" (*WCL* 10, 27.1, 1993 [6]). Presenters included Ayanna Black, Robert Kroetsch, Aruna Srivastiva, Marie Annharte Baker, Fred Wah, and Betsy Warland. Proceedings published in *West Coast Line* 10, 27.1 (1993): 25–74.

Rungh (Toronto). "An interdisciplinary magazine committed to the exploration of traditional and contemporary south-Asian cultural production." Produced by the Rungh Cultural Society. Editor, Zool Suleman. First two issues included excerpts from the 1991 Desh Pardesh conference. Includes visual art, poetry and essays. Contributors include Ian Iqbal Rashid, Larissa Lai, Sujata Bhatt, Anita Rau Badami, and Ven Begamudré.

1993 **It's a Cultural Thing** (Calgary). A conference for First Nations artists and artists of colour, which featured the work of some forty First Nations and artists of colour. It preceded the AGM of ANNPAC (Association of National Non-Profit Artists Centres) and was organized by the Minquon Panchayat, a group that had formed at the previous AGM to develop anti-racism strategies for ANNPAC. At the 1993 ANNPAC AGM, the Minquon Panchayat's recommendations for policy changes were voted down. The result was the disintegration of ANNPAC into local organizations. Writers who participated included Lillian Allen, Jordan Wheeler, Hiromi Goto, Claire Harris, Lai-wan, and Ashok Mathur.

Scream in High Park: A Carnival of the Spoken Word (Toronto). Organized by Matthew Remski, Scream is an annual event featuring new writing and work in progress. Presenters have included Nicole Brossard, Jeff Derksen, Claire Harris, Dennis Lee, Fred Wah, Clifton Joseph, Robert Kroetsch, Makeda Silvera, and Darren Wershler-Henry.

1994 **filling Station** (Calgary). Editors include Doug Steedman, r rickey, derek beaulieu, Courtney Thompson, Jacqueline Turner, Paulo da Costa, Lindsay Tipping, Jill Hartman, and Natalie Simpson. A "stop between ... 'fixed' points on the map to get an injection of something new, something fresh that's gonna get you from point to point." "We'll publish any poem or story that offers a challenge; to the mind, to the page, to writers and readers." Publishes a mixture of writers from Calgary, other parts of Canada, the USA, and the UK.

Rice Paper (Vancouver). Published by the Asian Canadian Writers' Workshop. Facilitates "networking and information exchange among writers and artists from a common Pacific Rim heritage, and aims to inform, educate and promote a greater awareness of Asian Canadian literature and arts.... Through news, in-depth interviews, profiles, commentary, reviews and creative non-fiction, Rice Paper covers the people, events and issues shaping Asian Canadian contemporary culture" (Editorial statement 5.1 [1995], 2).

STANZAS (Ottawa). Photocopied, sporadically published magazine produced by rob mclennan. Concentrates on the long poem. Includes individual issues by Gerry Gilbert, Meredith Quartermain, nathalie stephens, Douglas Barbour, Sheila E. Murphy, and many more. Published by above/ground press. The press titles include books by Helen Zisimators, Victor Coleman, George Bowering, rob maclennan, Jay MillAr, jwcurry, and derek beaulieu.

Writing Thru Race (30 June–3 July, Vancouver). A conference for First Nations writers and writers of colour, organized by the Racial Minority Writers Committee of The Writers Union of Canada to explore the issues identified at The Appropriate Voice writers' retreat (see 1992). Coordinated by Roy Miki. Presenters include Lillian Allen, Dionne Brand, Ashok Mathur, Makeda Silvera, Lenore Keeshig-Tobias, and Daniel David Moses.

1995 **The Recovery of the Public World: A Conference and Poetry Festival in Honour of Robin Blaser's Poetry and Poetics** (Emily Carr Institute of Art and Design, Vancouver). Organized by Charles Watts, Jerry Zaslove, and others at Simon Fraser University. Participants included Steve McCaffery, Rachael Blau Duplessis, Daphne Marlatt, Charles Bernstein, Phyllis Webb, Michelle Leggat, Peter Middleton, Michael Davidson, Jed Rasula, and Michael Ondaatje. Conference publication: *The Recovery of the Public World: Essays on Poetics in Honour of Robin Blaser.* Edited by Charles Watts and Edward Byrne (Vancouver: Talonbooks, 1999).

1996 **Coach House Books** (Toronto). A literary publishing house and print shop established by one of the original Coach House Press founders, Stan Bevington, and others, following the demise of Coach House Press. First publication: *Nicholodeon: a book of lowerglyphs,* by Darren Wershler-Henry. Wershler-Henry was managing editor from 1998–2002, followed by Jason McBride (2002–current). Current poetry editor is Jay MillAr. damian lopes has been the web editor since the fall of 1998. Poetry titles include Steve McCaffery, Margaret Christakos, Suzanne Zelazo, derek beaulieu, Louis Cabri, Di Brandt, and Louise Bak.

Queen Street Quarterly (Toronto). Founded by Suzanne Zelazo, when she was an undergraduate at University of Toronto, as a "forum for the contemporary Canadian arts." Stephen Cain is the literary editor. Contributors include George Bowering, Jeff Derksen, bill bissett, Patrick Friesen, Victor Coleman, Sarah Dearing, and Keith Oatley.

TADS (Vancouver, last issue 2001; produced SIX issues in all). Founded by a group of "tads" (Chris Turnbull, Reg Johanson, Ryan Knighton, and later on Jason LeHeup and Karina Vernon) and the "dads" (George Stanley, George Bowering, and Jamie Reid). Its goal was to bring together poets from both generations. Contributors included work by the editors along with Thea Bowering, Renee Rodin, Mark Nakada, and others (email from Jamie Reid).

1997   **housepress** *(Calgary 1997–2003)*. Founded by derek beaulieu. A "micropress dedicated to experimental and unusual forms of poetry and prose" including concrete, visual, and language centred. Published as many as 10–12 chapbooks a year as well as numerous ephemera (postcards, broadsides, pamphlets, etc). Published *Courier: an international anthology of concrete and visual poetry* (2000) as well as titles by Christian Bök, tjsnow, Ian Samuels, Steve McCaffery, tom muir, Karen Mac Cormack, and Kenneth Goldsmith.

1999   *dANDelion* (Calgary). *Dandelion* (see 1975) ended with its twenty-fifth anniversary issue (25.2, 1999) but it was resuscitated and renamed almost immediately when the Dandelion Magazine Society "regrouped into an organization ... to meld creative writing at the University of Calgary with the larger literary community in Calgary, beyond, and after" (*dANDelion* 26.1). Edited by graduate students in Creative Writing/English at the University of Calgary, including derek beaulieu, Emily Cargan, and Jill Hartman.

     endNote (Calgary; last issue 2003). "Created with *Tish*, *Philly Talks* and the first series of *Open Letter* in mind, *endNote* promotes open communication between poets." Founding editors: derek beaulieu, r rickey, and tom muir. Six issues. Published reviews, poems, and letters. Contributors included jwcurry, Clint Burnham, Linda Russo, and others, along with Calgary-based poets Jill Hartman and Ian Samuels.

     Slought Networks: art and theory online < www.slought.net >. Founding curator/director: Aaron Levy. Co-curators: Louis Cabri, Jean-Michel Rabaté, Andrew Zitcer. Links include a sound archive; Fred Wah's audio recordings, 1963; Vancouver Poetry Conference, digitized; and PhillyTalks, since 1997, dialogue with contemporary poets < www.slought.net >. Poets from Canada include: Karen Mac Cormack, Roy Miki, George Elliott Clarke, Barry McKinnon, Lisa Robertson, Jeff Derksen, Fred Wah, Kevin Davies, Dan Farrell, Steve McCaffery, Clint Burnham, and Peter Jaeger.

     W (Vancouver). Edited by the Kootenay School of Writing Collective (Andrew Klobucar, Michael Barnholden, Ted Byrne, Margot Butler, Aaron Vidaver, and others). Contributors include Stephen Collis, Nicole Markotić, David Bromige, Clint Burnham, and Ian Samuels. Electronic version available at < http://kswnet.org/w>.

2000   **North American Centre for Interdisciplinary Poetics** (NACIP) <www. poetics.yorku.ca>. Founded July 2001, York University, Toronto. Interactive discussion of poetics. Articles received in English, French. Director: Steve McCaffery. Mandate: "to be nodal, catalytic, and non-censorial." Initial topics: poetics generally, ethnopoetics, cyberpoetics, parapoetics, cognitive poetics, architectural poetics, visual poetics; as interest arises, to include feminist, marxist, postcolonial, queer. Writers from Canada include Steve McCaffery, Karen Mac Cormack, and Meredith Quartermain. Linked to Toronto writer and editor Darren Wershler-Henry's "Poetechnology" site <alienated.net>.

2001 *Vallum* (Montreal). Published by the Vallum Society for Arts and Letters Education. "Provides a forum for emerging artists to interact with more established figures" and "encourages dialogue between Quebec and the rest of Canada" <http://206.191.48.25/vallummag/homepage.html>. Ed. Joshua Auerbach and Eleni Zisimatos Auerbach, the magazine includes poetry, reviews, and visual art. Contributors include George Elliott Clarke, Heather Spears, Karen Solie, John Kinsella, Elizabeth Harvor, Stephanie Bolster, Nicole Brossard, Virgil Suarez, and Norm Sibum.

2002 **Nomados** (Vancouver). Founded and produced by Meredith and Peter Quartermain. Publishes broadsides, chapbooks, and perfect-bound books up to 100 pages. Poetry titles include Robin Blaser, Charles Bernstein, and Susan Holbrook.

■

Inside/Outside Literary Communities

Pauline Butling

● For most of my life I assumed that belonging to a community was unquestionably a good thing. Whether I was thinking of the 1960s ideal that communal living could produce social change, or the modernist notion that avant-garde literary communities were crucial in supporting radical aesthetics, or the feminist practice of establishing collaborative structures to nourish women's activities, I did not question the basic value of community. I have spent thousands of hours doing volunteer work in various literary communities: I have organized poetry readings, hosted visiting writers, helped plan workshops and conferences, cooked party meals and cleaned up party wine spills, made posters, written press releases, helped with magazine production—all the while taking part in the ongoing dialogue, gossip, debate, and argument that is the life-blood of any community. Community was an expanded home, even a safe haven, a place to meet like-minded people, a context wherein my life and work had value.

Recently, however, I have come to see that this sense of comfort and belonging is not the whole story. Community *bonhomie* often camouflages sexist and other oppressive or subordinating structures. Membership in a community does not guarantee empowerment for all its members. Viewed from the inside, my communities seemed expansive, open, and welcoming to everyone. I had not noticed the internal hierarchies. Of course I have realized for some time, with the 1960s being increasingly analyzed and scrutinized, that even supposed counterculture communities have unequal power relations.[1] But I had not seen them at work in *my* communities.

Hierarchies in radical literary communities are often especially invisible to their members because of an assumption that aesthetic innovation goes hand in hand with progressive social relations; also because the inequities may be embedded in aesthetic positions. Michael Davidson points out the concealed gender bias in Charles Olson and Jack Spicer's poetics, for instance, a bias that is embedded in the "phallic ideals of power, energy, and virtuosity" which informs their poetics ("Compulsory" 190). Thus the absence of women from "from the centers of artistic and intellectual life in general in the 1950s," he continues, was not only an effect of 1950s social formations (which excluded women from the category of the artist) but also "a structural necessity for the liberation of a new, male subject" in the new poetics ("Compulsory" 198). As I argued in my analysis of the *Tish* community (chap. 3), radical literary communities are not immune from enacting the "symbolic violence" (Bourdieu 137) of oppression, exclusion, and subordination that is more often associated with mainstream groups.

I first questioned my assumptions about community-the-good when I began working on this book. Because we are a generation apart, Susan Rudy and I felt we should understand each other's history regarding why and how we became interested in experimental poetics, and so we wrote our respective stories in the form of letters to each other. It was a useful exercise in which I first articulated the importance of my life-long involvement in literary communities to my sense of self. The jolt came when I also saw that my position within those communities was often peripheral, that my memory of myself as a person with power and agency within those communities was somewhat illusory. I was left with several perplexing questions: How and why do I construct a memory narrative with an empowered "I" when, in the historical record, "she" was often invisible? Why do my memories of my actions as cultural worker/reader/critic tend to skip over my feminist work and emphasize my connections to male-dominated groups? What are the mechanisms of self-subversion? What is included, what is excluded in the historical record, in communal memory, in individual memory? Why and how are women's literary productions often forgotten? What is the role of memory narratives in identity formation? To answer these questions, I examine my insider/outsider status in my individual memory narrative and note that "I" acquire power and agency in this narrative by association with hegemonic narratives rather than by my individual actions. As a corrective, I reformulate a memory narrative in which the "I" is located within (and empowered by) a feminist community narrative.

Michael Lambek's essay on "The Past Imperfect" identifies some key issues for my analysis of memory processes. First he questions the tendency among memory theorists to dismiss individual memory as "direct, literal, and subjective" and to privilege communal memory (or what we call "history") as supposedly more reliable and objective. "It seems more interesting," he continues, "to take these ... as poles and to focus on the movement between them, on how one goes from the one to the other and back, how private experience and public narrative mutually inform each other" (241). He also introduces the term "situated distance" to emphasize that "memory is perspectival" (242) and that "neither personal memory nor scholarly history [is] ... literal." Both are "narrativized constructions" and thus open, to varying degrees, "to continuous reformulation" or "reinterpretation." Such fluidity, in turn, shifts the focus to "how such changes are legitimated" (243). These terms provide an apparatus for my own reformulation and legitimation of an alternative narrative.

Who Am I? Memory Narrative #1

Figure 11. Pauline Butling. University of British Columbia dormitory (1959).
Photograph courtesy of the author.

My story begins in Vancouver in 1960–61 when I was in my final year of a bachelor of arts degree (majoring in English and history) at the University of British Columbia. That year I took professor Warren Tallman's now-famous Studies in Poetry class where I was astonished and delighted to discover that English classes could include contemporary poetry and that poetry could be a place for addressing contemporary issues.[2] Tallman's course syllabus included Robert Duncan, Robert Creeley, Charles Olson, Allen Ginsberg, and other radical young American poets from the just-released *New American Poetry* anthology. I was also delighted to discover a community of poets on campus, some of whom were in Tallman's class that year. Through the class, I (and my boyfriend, Fred Wah, who also took Tallman's class that year) became part of the group of students/professors/poets/poetry aficionados that formed at UBC in the late 1950s and early '60s.

    Thus began a process in which community became central to my educational, emotional, and social life. We sat around for hours—in bars, in coffee shops, at parties—and talked about poetry and life. We formed a study group in the spring of 1961 that met every Sunday evening through-out the summer where we argued about how form changed the poem, why and how poetry could make a difference in Vancouver, what Charles Olson meant by "sprawl," how we hated the fraternity and sorority elite at UBC, why Vancouver was a great place to be, why start a poetry magazine, what was wrong with this or that line break, how to shake up the central Canada stranglehold on literary culture, and so on. We even donated money from our meagre resources to bring Robert Duncan to Vancouver to give three talks (three to five hours per evening for three consecutive nights).[3] His was a lived knowledge, delivered with such enthusiasm and passion that to this day I can still hear his voice and remember details from the talks. Duncan gave us an instant education in the modernist precursors of the new American poetry (Gertrude Stein, H.D., William Carlos Williams, Ezra Pound, Djuna Barnes)—as well as insights into the work of his contem-poraries (Charles Olson, Robert Creeley, Jack Spicer, Robin Blaser, and many more).

These were heady times. I remember explosive arguments, lots of laugh-ter, many parties, a steep learning curve, and a general excitement about challenging the status quo. I was hooked. When Warren Tallman suggested I apply to graduate school, I quickly shelved my plans to travel in Europe for a year, went to see Roy Daniells, the English department head, about getting a graduate teaching assistantship, and found myself embarked on an MA program the following September. My involvement in the commu-nity continued via friendships with fellow graduate students (George Bow-ering, Lionel Kearns, Gladys [Maria] Hindmarch), via marriage to Fred Wah in 1962, and through sharing in the excitement around the editing and production of *Tish*, which began in 1961. *Tish* was discussed, typed, and mimeographed in George Bowering and Frank Davey's graduate stu-dent office located in a cluster of temporary trailers where I also had an office.[4]

The high point of my UBC experience of community-the-good was the summer poetry workshop held at UBC in 1963.[5] This was one of those serendipitous historical moments when the marginal momentarily occu-pied the centre, thanks to the combined efforts of several, strategically located organizers, most notably Warren Tallman and Robert Creeley in the English department at UBC, a sympathetic ear in the UBC Extension Department, which officially sponsored the course, and another sympa-thetic ear in the person of Naim Kattan at the Canada Council, who provided some of the funding. To see Charles Olson, Allen Ginsberg, Robert Creeley, and others, with their long hair and hippie clothes inhabit the staid UBC classrooms, or the even more sedate faculty club with all the irreverence for established institutions that characterized the 1960s counterculture was itself a life-defining experience for me, not to mention the impact of all the lectures, discussions, and readings. Some fifty young poets signed up for the course; many more attended the evening readings and parties.[6] I had a part-time job assisting Warren Tallman with the pre-conference paper work, which also gave me free admission to the course. I went to all the morning lectures and evening readings (though not to the writing workshops). I was excited, exhilarated, and empowered (or so I thought) by these events. I even became part of a legendary narrative about a party that Fred and I had at our campus apartment. With some eighty people in our two-bedroom apartment, the only place to seat six-foot-six Charles Olson when he arrived was on the double bed in the bedroom. Others joined him (myself included), leading to Olson's boast, in his Berkeley lecture in 1965, of having five women in his arms.[7] Another legend developed around Allen Ginsberg, who spent most of the evening sitting on the landing at the apartment entrance chanting mantras with a group of his followers. When two police officers showed up later in the evening, ostensibly in response to a complaint about noise, but more likely to check for drugs and/or under-age drinking, the officers had to step through Ginsberg's magic circle to enter the apartment. I like to think that they were somewhat softened by this experience, since they only asked me to prove that I was twenty-one years old (the legal drinking age) and then left (though they later arrested several people as they were leaving the party for possession of marijuana).

These are some of the founding moments in the memory narrative of my life as a reader/writer/critic of contemporary writing. In a process typical of memory formation around life-defining experiences, "the conceptualization of experience ... took place fairly quickly after ... and provided the form in which the event would be remembered and could be recalled later" (Paul Thompson 4). Although I was not a poet, nor was I directly involved in either editing or producing *Tish* magazine, I saw myself as an active and indeed essential member of that community. And the community in turn was crucial to my individual formation. I always describe my master's thesis, for instance ("Robert Duncan: The Poem as Process") as informed by what I learned from the community events as much as by my UBC courses.

The same themes of community-the-good and myself as an integral member persist as my story continues on to Albuquerque, New Mexico (1963–64), and Buffalo, New York (1964–67), where Fred and I did graduate work, and then to the West Kootenay region of BC where we lived for twenty-two years (1967–89) in the village of South Slocan, taught at Selkirk College in Castlegar and David Thompson University Centre in Nelson, built a home, raised two daughters, grew vegetables, chopped wood, etc., and participated in a writing community that extended from our local node in the West Kootenay region out to Vancouver, Winnipeg, Toronto, Buffalo, San Francisco, and beyond.

In Albuquerque, Fred started *Sum* magazine (with John Keys and Ron Loewinsohn) and I typed, collated, licked stamps, and did other production work. In Buffalo, I was peripherally involved with the writing community that developed out of Charles Olson's graduate seminars at SUNY, Buffalo. I did typing and other production work for the *Magazine of Further Studies*, took one of Charles Olson's graduate seminars, and occasionally went to the bar with the boys, who gathered every week, following Olson's graduate seminar, at Onetto's Bar and Grill. I also completed all but the dissertation for a PhD, in between caring for our first child (who was just six weeks old when we arrived in Buffalo), and teaching part-time in the university Extension Department. To the extent that I took myself seriously as a PhD student (which is debatable since I characterized my graduate work in Buffalo as incidental and/or accidental) I would emphasize that it was made possible by my participation in the range of community activities described here.[8] Again, individual self-worth derived from community identity.

The same motif recurs in my story of life in South Slocan where we lived for some twenty years. At first my role was mainly social, hosting a continuing stream of visiting writers (including carloads of writer friends who often came from Vancouver to visit), putting on parties, and occasionally joining in the ongoing dialogue. Later I taught Canadian literature courses, organized readings, and began to write the occasional review or article. Fred again produced a magazine (*Scree*) and set up numerous workshops, conferences, readings, and informal writers' groups. When David Thompson University Centre (DTUC) opened in Nelson in 1978, I taught there until it shut down in 1984, and then helped set up the Kootenay School of Writing.[9] Our links to a cross-country writing community were sustained by the stream of new books and magazines that arrived at our house, often by the boxful (courtesy of Coach House Press) whenever

Figure 12. bpNichol and Pauline Butling. South Slocan, BC (1987).
Photograph by Fred Wah.

Fred went to Toronto, or hand delivered by the many poets who came to town to do workshops and readings. Talk spilled over from the readings and workshops to feed an ongoing dialogue about poetic forms and processes, about love affairs, and about literary cultural politics. Robert Kroetsch posited a grammar of narrative in a summer writing workshop based on Todorov's *Poetics of Prose*. Daphne Marlatt did a workshop on journal writing as a literary form, which raised intriguing questions about gender bias in literary forms. Myrna Kostash argued for the new, hybrid form of creative non-fiction. The Four Horsemen enacted Derridean deconstruction in sound poems that challenged all genres, definitions, and divisions. Nicole Brossard, as keynote speaker at the Language in Revolution conference at DTUC in 1982, argued for a link between language revolution and social revolution. Margaret Randall, the other featured speaker (the American poet who has just come back from several years in Nicaragua), argued just as strongly for the need for direct social action.

During DTUC's five-year existence, there was an intense continuum of talk, readings, parties, arguments, workshops, visiting writers, and a publication (*Writing* magazine started in 1981). I was not involved in the production of the magazine, but I continued to teach, organize, talk, write, and generally participate in the community. Again, my narrative reiterates the theme that the community did as much for me as I did for it. All of these activities, for instance, were crucial to my completing my long-abandoned PhD dissertation in the 1980s. My story again links the individual to the communal narrative by emphasizing a meaningful inter-relationship between the two. It constructs an "I" who is involved, important, productive, connected. It would seem, as Lambek explains, that we "create imagined communities ... and imagined selves and then attempt to live accordingly" (243). And also that "to remember is never solely to report on the past so much as to establish one's relationship toward it" (240). My memory narrative establishes a mutually beneficial relationship between self and community.

"Who Is She?"

> The question of who am I? has already generated a small industry as theorists turn to themselves, their own difference, trying to explicate the world metonymically from their own.... In arguing for the positivity of experience and the possibilities of using the self in theory ... we must articulate the question "who am I?" *and* the question "who is she?" Probyn, "Technologizing the Self" 503

When I shift from the individual and subjective "I" to the historical and public "she," I discover a very different relation between the individual and community. In the literary publications and historical accounts of the communities that I have briefly described above, Pauline Butling rarely appears. "She" makes a few brief comments in two interviews published in *Open Letter* in 1978 but her questions and comments are so sporadic as to seem almost intrusive.[10] I imagine readers might stumble when "she" speaks, they might mumble to themselves "who *is* she?" Even her name is uncertain: in the first, she is identified as Pauline Wah (her married name), in the second as Pauline Butling (her professional name). This was three years after "she" had started using Butling for all professional activities.

In terms of publications, Pauline Butling appears only as object (as the topic of a poem, for instance) not as speaking subject.[11] In the following poem by Fred Wah, "she" is a complex, active figure, but nevertheless still an object.

Pauline's House

Her mind and life-
time, yearning

for her life's
mind on it, heart
dance, literal
with her mouth

shoulders too
today years ago

I married her
Outside, the distant glaciers

crack and groan
with the same desire
    (n.p.)

In a poem by George Bowering, "she" provokes curiosity, even affection,
but Bowering does the talking.

Pauline Butling in Campbell Lake

The water of Campbell Lake is very cold,
& Pauline Butling is in it.

Her limbs are long & white, the glacier
is white, her one-piece bathing suit

is pale. She is still here
thirty years after our adult lives began,

doing breast stroke in Campbell Lake.

I have never been in love with her
but I would kill anyone

who tried to drown her. I would like
the sun to take the time to tan her,

to warm the water a little.
    (Bowering, "Pauline Butling in Campbell Lake"
    broadside)

Again, she is present only through the lens of the male viewer. In the pub-
lished accounts of the *Tish* group formation, only Gladys [Maria] Hind-
march mentions her name.[12] She herself published only one review (of

Margaret Lawrence's *The Diviners*) and one article ("Notes from Charles Olson's Classes") before the 1980s. In contrast to her perception of an empowered "I" in the individual narrative, "she" barely exists before the mid-1980s. Probyn's question ("Who is she?") reveals that she occupies the familiar, subordinate position of women, on the periphery of male-dominated public space.[13] She is reader, listener, friend, muse, supporter, lover, wife, hostess, and behind-the-scenes organizer. It seems that the "private experience" and "public narrative" do *not* "mutually inform each other" (Lambek 241). The I narrator does not see her subordination, nor her self-delusion.

Re-membering

However, this need not end as simply a victim story. I/she can reformulate the story by re-selecting the data and re-remembering an alternative story. Yes, "she" occupies a peripheral position in the historical records; yes, individual and communal memories construct different identities; yes, her power and agency in the autobiographical narrative proves to be mostly illusory. The "I" does not see that her self-narrative unwittingly reproduces the prevailing power structures, does not recognize her self-subversion. But an alternative story can also be constructed, beginning with Wendy Brown's very useful question, "what does politicized identity want?" Brown explains:

> if we are interested in developing the contestatory, subversive, potentially transformative elements of identity-based political claims, we need to know the implications of the particular genealogy and production conditions of identity's desire for recognition. *We need to be able to ask: Given what produced it, given what shapes and suffuses it, what does politicized identity want?* (my emphasis 209)

In my case, "politicized identity" wants/needs both to understand its "particular genealogy and production conditions" and to "imagine a different future," to steal a line from Phyllis Webb ("The Making of Japanese Print," *Hanging Fire* 77). This means resituating the "I" within a feminist genealogy. It means foregrounding the alternative "production conditions" that supported (rather than subordinated) my activities, and realigning the private and public. Then "I," "she," and "we" occupy parallel subject positions. Taking memory, "not as a neutral representation, more or less accurate, of the past, but as a claim or set of claims, more or less justified, more or less appropriate, about it" (Lambek 239), I reselect and reinterpret past events according to a revised "set of claims." My revised self-narrative still claims that community activities are crucial to the formation of the self, but the self is formed within a feminist context.

Memory Narrative #2

This story begins about a decade later than my first story, in the early 1970s, when, for the first time in almost ten years of married life, I found myself in the conventional role of stay-at-home wife and mother. Feeling isolated, disconnected, and devalued, I sought out women's groups such as the newly formed West Kootenay Status of Women's Council.[14] As a member of that group, I helped organize a lecture series on abortion, birth control, women's sexuality, and women's legal rights. These were big events for us. We felt bold and brash (and a little scared) to be speaking about supposedly private matters in a public forum. Yet we were exhilarated by a new feeling of power, power to put women's issues on a public agenda, power to speak and have an impact in a public space.

I also taught evening classes on women's literature, where the discussions often branched out into how to improve relationships, why some women accept the doormat role, how to get out of bad marriages, or how to find new pleasures. I read *Sisterhood Is Powerful: An Anthology of Writing from the Women's Liberation Movement* (Morgan) and loved every word; I pounced on the poems and stories by women that were beginning to appear in increasing numbers in little magazines and small presses. Yes, I thought as I read Margaret Laurence's *The Fire Dwellers* and *The Diviners*, there are others out there like me. Wow, I thought, as I dipped into *The New French Feminisms*, there's a huge, feminist discourse that I want/need to explore.

Although I had felt a few consciousness-raising jolts in the 1960s— such as hearing Denise Levertov read her poem about cunts and other unmentionable female body parts, or hearing Phyllis Webb's *Naked Poems* (1965) and their painful articulation of women's desire—my liberation did not begin until I formed intellectual, emotional, and political connections with women's communities.[15] Prior to my stay-at-home housewife/mother phase, I did not see a need for what Adrienne Rich calls "women-identified" activities ("Compulsory" 51). I was the "exceptional" woman, the one who stands apart from the group. Not only did that exceptional status prove illusionary, it also camouflaged a disempowering isolation and disconnection from other women. By contrast, forming connections and coalitions with women brought a genuinely empowering alignment.

This alternative memory narrative (of emergence and empowerment), however, is not one of moving quickly onward and upward. I did not feel immediately empowered when I became involved with women's communities, as I had when I connected to the *Tish* writing community where I acquired value immediately (albeit illusory) by association with a predominately male group. The women's community was itself struggling to establish its own social, material, and discursive spaces. Individuals and groups had to learn a new language, as Nicole Brossard would later explain so well.[16] They had to learn to inhabit public space, to risk exposure, failure, and censure. Only gradually did I find the collective identity necessary to sustain my individual momentum. The process was often painful. When Daphne Marlatt asked me to review Audrey Thomas's wonderfully nuanced novel of a woman's intense emotions and desires as she negotiates a complicated love affair (*Latakia* 1979), I was excited, but also terrified. The novel seemed so revealing of a woman's intimate thoughts, as was my own act of putting words on paper for all to read. When I saw my first reviews in print, I felt exposed and vulnerable.

At the Women and Words conference in Vancouver in 1983, while I was energized and exhilarated by the collective presence of so many women, I still hesitated to speak out in this very public space. But the sheer numbers, as well as the diversity of women, buoyed me up. Seeing the collective energy and the commitment to change, not only from women like me (middle-class, academic, heterosexual, white women) but also from women of colour, lesbian women, working-class women—many of whom had far more oppressive structures to deal with than I would ever encounter—was both humbling and inspiring. Also, by the early 1980s, there were more and more women working as editors, publishers, critics, poets, novelists, visual artists, and musicians. Their presence encouraged me. I felt empowered, too, by my shift in economic position that came with starting a full-time job in the mid-1970s, especially as I had to fight to get it.[17] The material and ideological shifts that I experienced at an individual level, combined with the material and ideological support of the emerging feminist communities, provided the springboards that launched me into the public domain.

In this revised memory narrative, I emphasize that my publications were mostly on women's texts, were published in magazines edited by women (*Periodics, Room of One's Own, A Mazing Space* [Newman]), and that finishing my PhD dissertation was linked as much to my emerging *feminist* trajectory as to the informal education that I got from the DTUC community.[18] I had abandoned the dissertation in the 1960s because I couldn't imagine myself fitting into that august category (also because I was too busy with babies, etc.) and then rationalized that I didn't want or need the degree, that there were other pathways to a professional life. (These I only vaguely imagined, and they usually turned out to be simply accidental opportunities.) With my new feminist awareness, I saw that my previous claim to successful back-door or ad hoc approaches had in fact camouflaged an anxiety about entitlement. But most important, in this reformulated story, the disjunctions and contradictions between the "I" narrative and the historical record disappear. The historical record corroborates her individual story. "She" *does* appear in the public record.

Yet even now, armed with a determination to recuperate a feminist history, I find this story difficult to remember. It keeps disappearing into the historical mists as my memory veers toward the hegemonic. I have to concentrate on deliberately constructing a genealogy of women, on reselecting past events to foreground a narrative of women's collective activities.[19] I do this not only for personal reasons but also because such stories of women's collective struggles for a share in the discursive field are essential for the continuation of a collective narrative. They provide historical continuity and momentum and prevent each generation from having to start over. These are the spurs that keep me on the track of a revised story with a "revised set of claims" (Lambek).

Reformulating

> For we think back through our mothers if we are women.
> It is useless to go to the great men writers for help, however
> much one may go to them for pleasure.
> Woolf, *A Room of One's Own* 72–73

A longer version of this reformulated memory narrative would include an account of literary magazines edited and published by women, such as *Room of One's Own, Fireweed, Atlantis, Tiger Lily, Periodics, (f.)Lip, Tessera,* and CV2; it would include a history of women's presses (such as Press Gang, Women's Press, and Sister Vision Press); it would note the publication of anthologies of writing by women, such as *Writing Right* in 1982; *A Mazing Space: Writing Canadian Women Writing* in 1986 (ed. Shirley Neuman and Smaro Kamboureli); *Poetry by Canadian Women* in 1989 (ed. Rosemary Sullivan); *Shakti's Words: An Anthology of South Asian Canadian Women's*

Poetry (ed. Diane McGifford and Judith Kearns); *Writing the Circle* (ed. Jeanne Perreault and Sylvia Vance); *Inversions: Writing by Dykes, Queers and Lesbians* in 1991 (ed. Betsy Warland); and *Gynocritics/Gynocritiques* in 1994 (ed. Barbara Godard). It would also include an account of women's literary conferences and festival such as the Dialogue Conference at York University in 1981 organized by Barbara Godard (where the idea for *Tessera* magazine began); Women and Words in Vancouver in 1983; Telling It: Women and Language across Cultures, held at Simon Fraser University in 1988 (organized by Daphne Marlatt); and The Third International Feminist Book Fair in Montreal (organized by Nicole Brossard), also in 1988.[20]

For this necessarily shorter version, I have selected one conference (Women and Words/Les femmes et les mots in Vancouver in 1983), one anthology (*Collaboration in the Feminine: Writings on Women and Culture from Tessera*), and one celebratory issue of a magazine, *Fireweed. Issue 56: Going on Twenty—A Celebration* (late winter 1996). The importance of the *Fireweed* and *Tessera* publications lies in the fact that they are commemorative events and as such perform the important "feminist memory-work" (Godard, "Women of Letters" 281) of reiterating and celebrating a collective history. Repetition is a well-known mnemonic device and celebration an effective mythologizing tool. Overall, both collections celebrate a "community of women of letters" (Godard, "Women of Letters" 258). The importance of Women and Words lies more in its groundbreaking status. Both types of events—founding moments and commemorative activities—are crucial ingredients in narratives of empowerment.

As a groundbreaking event, Women and Words/Les femmes et les mots "brought together over one thousand anglophone and francophone women involved in traditional and alternative forms of literary activity" (Dybikowski et al., Introduction 9). The sheer size of the conference, together with the publicity it received as the first all-women conference, helped to increase the visibility, credibility, and legitimacy of women's writing. Its long-term impact shows up in follow-up activities, including the start of *Tessera* (Mezei 16), the West Word Summer Writing Workshop for Women (1985–1993) and a feminist takeover of cv2. In the editorial statement for the first issue by the feminist collective of cv2, the editors explain that "*Women and Words* focused our frustrations and our energies and we began to think seriously about forming an editorial collective" (Banting et al., editorial 4).

The *Fireweed* publication commemorates eighteen years of existence for the magazine, certainly a history worth celebrating, as it was one of the first feminist literary magazines (founded five years before Women and Words). For this celebratory issue, the editors situate the publication emphatically within a genealogy of women: "This issue is a gift from a generation of women to the one that follows. A coming together of women in celebration and in support, women who value our cultural institutions" (4).

The editorial is both celebratory and polemical:

> And here is *Fireweed*, pulsing with women's creativity, already 18, verging on 19, preparing for 20. *Fireweed*, still edgy, still fresh, still eclectic, still independent. Celebrating the years that have passed and the work that has been done. Ready for new risks, new writers, new artists, new issues. (4)

Indeed, from its inception in 1978, *Fireweed* has consistently supported experiment and adventure. Its subtitle, "A Feminist Quarterly," together with its epigraph of "fireweed" as the "first growth to reappear in fire-scarred areas" and as "a troublesome weed which spreads like wild-fire invading clearings, bombsites, waste land and other disturbed areas," establish discursive and material sites for feminist innovation. The negative connotation of women's "troublesomeness" is redefined as a pioneering characteristic: like fireweed, "troublesome" women have the tenacity and resourcefulness to put down roots in the most barren ground. The actions of women writers and editors invading and reclaiming "fire-scarred areas" are legitimated as creative interventions rather than annoying intrusions. A sampling of subtitles for issues of *Fireweed* shows some of the diverse areas of reclamation: "Blood Relations" (no. 12, 1982); "Fear and Violence" (no. 14, 1982); "Feminist Aesthetics" (no. 15, 1982); "Women of Colour" (no. 16, 1983); "Atlantic Women" (no. 18, 1984); "Class is the Issue: The Issue is Class" (no. 25, 1987); "Lesbiantics" (no. 28, 1989); "Asian Canadian Women" (no. 30, 1990); "Sex and Sexuality" (no. 38, 1993); and "Revolution/Evolution Girl Style" (no. 59/60, 1997).

What I particularly like about the *Fireweed* birthday issue is the way it foregrounds individual excellence while celebrating a collective history. It presents a generation of Canadian women writers who have become well-known as individuals—Nicole Brossard, Daphne Marlatt, Susan Swan, Makeda Silvera, Claire Harris, Lillian Allen, Cécile Cloutier, Kate Braid, Libby Scheier, Erin Mouré, and Margaret Atwood among others—while also emphasizing a shared history. Its publication is an act of community building.

Collaboration in the Feminine (1994), which selected texts from previous issues of *Tessera* magazine (another commemorative publication that emphasizes a shared history and generational continuity), is also a community-building event. It does so first by its title—*Collaboration in the Feminine*—and second by Barbara Godard's reiteration of the original "project of *Tessera*":

> to constitute a space for women to exchange images and ideas in writing … [to] create the conditions of possibility for the constitution of women as speaking subjects … [and to] constitute the horizon of a discursive order in which "she" is determined as "subject" or author-function. Autherity. ("Women of Letters [Reprise]" 258)

Indeed *Tessera* has been instrumental in expanding the discursive space for women writers. Collecting some of its essays in book form gives wider circulation to some of the most useful discussions of feminist issues in Canada of the past decade.[21] Beginning with Lorraine Weir's article from *Tessera* no. 1, "'Wholeness, Harmony, Radiance' and Women's Writing," which Godard aptly describes as "a cautionary tale of the embattled state of feminist language-centred writing and theory in the patriarchal English Canadian critical institution" (Godard, "Women" 290–91), essay topics include "Theorizing Fiction Theory" (Godard et al., "Theorizing"); "the resistance to theory in the Anglophone Canadian literary institution … and how this works to marginalize feminist attempts to theorize gender in that institution" (Godard, "Women" 285); the connections between "feminist activists and theorists" (Godard, "Women" 286); "the feminist 'we,' as a political and ethical issue" (Godard, "Women" 287); the debate over essentialism, the issue of "Translating Women" (Godard, "Women" 291); and other ongoing debates about language, representation, and legitimation. These and other debates establish a discursive community where women are subjects rather than objects, where women work coalitionally to become producers of knowledge, producers of representations, and agents of change.

This brief narrative of emerging feminist communities, like my individual narrative of empowerment, is a much-abbreviated story, but long enough, I hope, to show how subjectivity can be differently constituted by reselecting, reformulating, and thereby legitimating, alternative histories and subjects. As Louise Cotnoir so eloquently puts it, feminist subjectivity is given life and substance by women's collective activities:

> I am, we are, *women of memory*. By its presence, *Tessera* has and will contribute, I hope, to leaving traces of women's History, Thought and Imaginary. Because we have dreamed, we still dream, of a world where we will be visible and vital, I am, we are *women of words*, and it is undoubtedly on this territory that *Tessera* has and will be for me most

necessary. I have discovered in its pages, along with other women, intelligence, imagination, the literary wealth of women, and I have had many amorous encounters with their texts, their hopes and their ideas which each, in her own way, has nourished my reflections, my fictions and my desires. (10)

Yes indeed! Remembering my feminist self has likewise been nourished by many "amorous encounters" with other women's texts, encounters that link the individual to the collective. Only then does "the constitution of the collective subject work analogously to the constitution of the individual one" (Lambek 245). Only then can I override the subordinating, exclusionary, and self-deluding mechanisms that came into play in my first story to keep me subordinated to the hegemonic track. To repeat Lambek's comment cited earlier, "to remember is never solely to report on the past so much as to establish one's relationship to it" (240). As here my discursive acts of speaking and writing an alternative memory narrative locate "I," "she," and "we" on mutually enhancing, parallel tracks.[22]

Notes

1   The gender bias in revolutionary groups as diverse as the Solidarity movement in Poland, the hippies and Beat protest groups of the 1960s in the USA and Canada, or the Black power movement of the 1960s are other well-known examples.

2   It was famous because of Tallman's unusual curriculum choices and because so many *TISH* and *blewointment* poets took Tallman's course. They include Frank Davey, Gladys [Maria] Hindmarch, Daphne Marlatt, bill bissett, Jamie Reid, Maxine Gadd, David Dawson, Judith Copithorne, and Lionel Kearns. The class I took included student/writers Fred Wah, Judith Copithorne, David Bromige, and Mike Mathews.

3   Duncan's talks were given 23–25 July 1961 in the Tallmans' living room. Audio tapes of these lectures are available at Simon Fraser University, Contemporary Literature Collection.

4   Three graduate students shared the *TISH* office. The third was Canadian literature scholar and editor W.H. New.

5   See Issue no. 30 of the *Minutes of the Charles Olson Society*, guest edited by Aaron Vidaver, for documents relating to the conference. It includes letters planning the conference between Warren Tallman and Robert Creeley, the list of course participants, and a transcript of the 31 July morning session with Robert Creeley, Robert Duncan, Allen Ginsberg, and Charles Olson. Audio tape recordings of the lectures and readings are available in the Contemporary Literature Collection at Simon Fraser University, Burnaby, BC, and on-line at Slought Networks < www.slought.net >. See also the entry in the chronology (1963).

6   See Aaron Vidaver's essay "Vancouver, 1963" and the accompanying archival material for names of students and other course details. *Minutes of the Charles Olson Society* 30 (April 1999).

7   Charles Olson tells the story in his *Reading at Berkeley*: "there was a party of 75 of us—And right next to the Royal Mounted Canadian Police. No kidding. I mean it was a narrow little walk to get to the Wah apartment.... Fred and Pauline Wah. And we had to bring our whiskey because the Wahs haven't yet got any money ... I was on the bed—I don't mean in—... in copulation, but I had five women in my arms, and that's the best I've ever done.... And Robert Duncan was behind me, like a Sabine or a Catullan feast. It was wonderful"(18–19).

8   My story describes a self whose actions are based on practical considerations and haphazard academic adventures: as a married couple, Fred and I had to enter the USA with the same visas. We chose student visas rather than work visas as the latter would make Fred draftable. Thus I had to be a student too, so I took one or two classes each semester to keep my student status and to be eligible for part-time teaching. It was only when we had decided to leave that I counted up my course credits, discovered that I had completed the required number of course credits for a PhD, and decided to write the PhD comprehensive exams.

9   For information on the formation of the Kootenay School of Writing in both Nelson and Vancouver, see the 1984 entry in the chronology.

10 Both were published in the same issue of *Open Letter* magazine, mischievously subtitled by bpNichol as the "All-Incest Issue." One was a discussion led by bpNichol with Fred and me titled "Transcreation: A Conversation with Fred Wah"; the second was a discussion initiated by Fred with Steve McCaffery and me (Wah, "Mrs. Richard's Grey Cat: A Discussion with Steve McCaffery and Pauline Wah"). Both took place at our dining-room table in South Slocan.

11 See Robert Kroetsch's "To the Wahs, on the Kootenay River" (*Completed Field Notes* 107); Fred Wah's "five ones for p." (*Border Crossings* 10.1: 24 and *So Far* 86); and Daphne Marlatt's "arriving," for Fred & Pauline (*here & there* [5–6]).

12 See Irene Niechoda and Tim Hunter, "A *Tish* story." The participants were Warren Tallman, Roy Miki, Gerry Gilbert, Gladys [Maria] Hindmarch, George Bowering, Frank Davey, David Dawson, Lionel Kearns, Fred Wah, Ellen Tallman, and Dan McLeod. Hindmarch remembers:

> I guess a thing that really pulled it [the *Tish* group] together was the New American poetry book, which came out in 1960, but which people didn't really read in Vancouver until 1961. I remember getting that in the spring of '61. And through talking about that, Warren told me that Pauline Butling had written a very interesting essay on one of Robert Duncan's poems, and I read this essay; and then I read an essay by Fred Wah, which I think was on William Carlos Williams. Suddenly I wanted to meet these two people. (Niechoda and Hunter 86)

13 I don't mean to position myself here as simply a victim of male oppression or as having been silenced by others. I am more interested in my self-silencing. To the extent that I can analyze why I was happy with this vague role, I would say that it was a combination of my own hesitation to take myself seriously as a professional person, reinforced by the prevailing uncertainty about women's role in the workforce. While my mother offered a non-traditional role model—she founded and developed the physiotherapy department at the Nelson hospital in a thirty-year career as well as achieving local and national fame as a mountaineer and conser-

vationist, she characterized her work as a fall-back position. For me, going to university did not necessarily mean taking up a career. But nor did I see marriage and family as my main goal. I played out that ambivalence by a combination of doing and not doing. I concealed my intelligence (I remember the astonishment of a male student/friend at a party when he found out that I was on scholarship) yet I continued my education. I did not take myself seriously as a scholar, yet bristled if others did not and was surprised if they did. I did not plan a career, yet resented the fact that, for a few years, I didn't have one.

14 Numerous such organizations were established across Canada, following the recommendations of the Royal Commission Report on the Status of Women (1970). The report was the most comprehensive and radical report of its kind to that time.

15 I heard Levertov read "Hypocrite Women," at the summer poetry workshop in Vancouver in 1963. The poem begins: "Hypocrite women, how seldom we speak / of our own doubts / while dubiously / we mother man in his doubt! // And if at Mill Valley perched in the trees / the sweet rain drifting through western air / a white sweating bull of a poet told us // our cunts are ugly—why didn't we / admit we have thought so too" (*O Taste and See* 70).

16 This notion of having to learn a new language recurs throughout the essays collected in *The Aerial Letter*. In a subsection titled "Having an Accent," Brossard complains that the term "women" is "rooted in foreign semantic earth" and asks "how does one succeed in getting ahead of one's thinking with foreign words?" (*Aerial Letter* 105–106).

17 I had been recommended by the hiring committee for a full-time, permanent teaching position in the English Department at Selkirk College in Castlegar, BC in 1974, but the college principal overruled the committee, saying that he was opposed to nepotism (an argument that often served, among other things, to keep wives in part-time, temporary positions). Only when I threatened to appeal to the BC Human Rights Commission did the appointment go through. I also changed my name from Wah (my husband's name) to Butling at that time. The change was prompted by my fury at finding my job contract in my husband's mailbox (he taught at the same college). I saw this not as a simple mistake of confusing the names, but as an act that relegated me to the subordinate position of wife, not an employee in my own right.

18 Frank Davey's *Open Letter* was also an important publication outlet for me. He published my first review, of Margaret Lawrence's *The Diviners,* and a number of other essays.

19 This is not to essentialize the category of woman. As Teresa de Lauretis explains, to construct a genealogy of women "is not a biological or metaphysical essentialism but a consciously political formulation of the specific difference of women in a particular sociohistorical location" (qtd. in Knutson, "Imagine Her Surprise" 229).

20 As explained by Marlatt, "*Tessera* began with conversations, both formal and informal around the Dialogue conference Barbara [Godard] organized in 1981" (Marlatt "Introduction: Women of Letters" 13). The *Tessera* founding editorial collective of Gail Scott, Barbara Godard, Kathy Mezei, and Daphne Marlatt met as a group for the first time at the Women in Words Conference in Vancouver (Mezei 16) and formulated more specific plans and goals for the magazine.

21 In this connection Godard reminds us of "the lesson Gwen Davies has drawn from the past" which is that magazine publication is often ignored in "charting the periods and genres of literary production in Canada" (qtd. in Godard, "Women" 265). Book publication, on the other hand, has more visibility, credibility, and legitimacy.

22 My first presentation on this topic was in oral form, at Women and Texts, Les Femmes et Les Textes: Languages, Technologies, Communities / Langages, Technologies, Communautés, University of Leeds, 26 June–4 July 1997.

■

Claire Harris's Liminal Autobiography

Susan Rudy

● Here is how Ian Sowton describes Claire Harris after her 1993 York University reading from *Drawing Down a Daughter*: she "gracefully and patiently answered the apparently unavoidable question about how much of [her] own life/experience went into" the book. "A good deal," she said, and went "on patiently to explain how mediated and overdetermined and edited is that life/experience into text."[1] Like Claire Harris, Patricia Whittaker-Williams, the narrator of *Drawing Down a Daughter,* is a teacher and a Black woman from Trinidad who has lived in Canada for quite some time. Like Harris, she has a complex analysis of racism in Canadian culture. But in other ways, what Ian Sowton calls the "autonarrating self" (4) in *Drawing* is not at all "like" Claire Harris. She is in her mid-thirties, pregnant, married. Harris, born in 1937, was fifty-six the year *Drawing* was published (1993). Harris has never married, and has no children. And *Drawing* narrates, not the life of Claire Harris, but a single day in the life of another Black woman writer in Canada. In so doing, it reconfigures the relation of "presence" to autobiography by positing a liminal space in which autobiography does not represent but corresponds with—in the sense of writing back and forth to—the writer's "life."

Many subjectivities speak in *Drawing Down a Daughter.* The first-person narrative configures the consciousness of "Patricia Whittaker-Williams, author of her own story." This "I" is active; she speaks aloud, makes jokes, sings, showers, complains. Reading *Drawing Down a Daughter* we sense that, as John Sturrock claims, "in autobiography, if anywhere in literature" the text is "inhabited by a living person," "that an author who was peculiarly present to himself [*sic*] while he [*sic*] was writing is now present to us as we read" (3). But the autobiographical first person, in being twice removed from Harris herself, offers a space of "liminality," what Harris herself calls "the space between two worlds," a "place of paradox. A potent space of creativity and fullness" ("Poets in Limbo" 125).[2] Harris teases the reader beyond the edges of our singular selves, histories, ideologies.

In an essay on the ontology of autobiography, James Olney admits that "a legitimate definition of life—real life—can be 'consciousness' with its now and now and now immediacy" (243). But for Olney consciousness is a synonym for bios "only insofar as it is untouched by either time or history"

(243). Harris's "Authobiography. Of sorts" is just the opposite: it fore-grounds both a situated consciousness and a particular history. After mov-ing to Canada in 1966, Harris encountered both subtle and overt forms of racism: "Everything I had observed about the Western World, most specif-ically the vast gulf between its moral and social philosophies, and its unre-strained violence in the 'south' slotted quietly into place. I had been taught that I was a writer. I had my subject": "everything I had observed" ("Why Do I Write?"). Dialoguing in the first person plural out of a complex pronominality, Harris's embedded narrator can use what Harris speaks of as "words that are *real*" (122).

In "Ole Talk," Harris's "view on writing and gender" that appeared in an essay collection called *Language in Her Eye*, she explains that "the text is a fabric of quotations … the writer can only imitate an ever anterior, never original gesture: her sole power is to mingle writings, to counter some by others" (130). Her ability to counter dominant narratives assumes that the writer is larger than the patterns of the culture, what Bakhtin calls the "perceiving consciousness."[3] *Drawing Down a Daughter* demonstrates that "what there is teasing beyond the edges" (96) of a text is the embodied con-sciousness of its writer, a consciousness the reader is invited to inhabit. If "the fiction persists," as the narrator in *Drawing Down a Daughter* says, "that autobiography is non-fiction. A matter of fact. The question, of course, is what is fact: what is reality" (62). The text proceeds from a life and an embodied knowledge of politics.

The narrator/mother/writer in *Drawing Down a Daughter* addresses the unborn child as an/other within herself who is like herself in that she is black and female. But that other within is also radically other in that she has not been subjected to racism or sexism. The narrator's dialogue with the other within herself is with that which she inhabits—black femaleness—and yet which also inhabits her—some "body" not raced, not sexed. The mother's text, in addressing the other as daughter, celebrates the self as (m)other.

The first page of *Drawing Down a Daughter* begins, as no other sec-tion of the book does, with a title—the words "THE GATHERING"—in bold type, capitalized, and centred at the top of the page. Functioning as a sub-title to the book, the meanings of the word "gathering" include "drawing," the image evoked in the title: to gather is to "draw (material, or one's brow) together in folds or wrinkles" (*Concise Oxford*). To gather is also to "stitch along the seam line and ¼ inch inside the seam line, using a long machine stitch" (*Simplicity Pattern* no. 8671). To gather is to participate in the weave at the edge of what seams. So *Drawing Down a Daughter* "gathers" but comes to no conclusions about the narrator's present life.

Formerly a teacher, still a writer, the self-naming narrator in *Drawing* is alone, in her apartment, very pregnant, awaiting her husband's return from Trinidad where he has gone to seek employment and to plan a life in which she is not eager to participate. Her account includes, at various intervals, entries in the journal she is writing as a "birthgift" for her unborn daughter. This "birthgift" includes poetic accounts of nightmares and dreams, poems, stories, and memories. These accounts are written, not only from the narrator's perspective, but also from that of her Great Aunt, whom she refers to as "The Storyteller." Great Aunt speaks several times, in dialect, in the first person. Gathered in this way, the text is what Daphne Marlatt calls the "cloth of our life as we want it to be" (*Labyrinths* 17). It constructs the narrator's—and her daughter's—possible subjectivities. To continue the sewing metaphor, the book functions as a kind of "seaming" (and seeming).

The narrator acts as a "seam"—she contains within her physical self another subject in process (she is pregnant); she stitches the narratives from the past together for that daughter and thereby "draws" her daughter and/as her self down. *Drawing Down a Daughter* begins with an account of a dream; significantly, only after the mother is found in the dream does "she" speak as "I":

> she flees before a red sun that slips across raw earth road /
> that draws its cloth of colour away from/ dust rising red to
> greet it   now she scurries before dark pan   this is a dream
> (7)

In this dream narrative, the pregnant narrator is the past daughter, asking her mother to come with her; the mother refuses to leave the house "your father bought ... for me" (7). The daughter says "'you can't ... it's rotting'... I hear my voice   a knife bright with knowledge" (8). At this point, the nightmare becomes even more confused, since the woman in the dream seems to be writing or reading: "the book leaps from my hands pages rattle in reluctant / flight   I am screaming   'you are not... you are not...' she vanishes."

The "book" which leaps from her hands is, like the book "she" is writing, that we are reading, both there and not there; full of consciousness and yet represented, an attempt to make sense of the dream and a fiction. To "wake" from the dream is to stop the writing. The "book" draws down "a" daughter—her self, her daughter, her mother—by "dreaming the mother/ dreaming myself dreaming / the mother." The dream is "potent as love / or hate / helpless as a daughter" (8). In Harris's interview with Janice Williamson, she says that the woman writing in the poem "needs to make the world safe for her child; the poem prepares a safe space" (123). But the poem also creates a safe space for the mother who writes "helpless as a daughter":

> still and all for this your birthgift   Child who
> opens me
> I prefer the third
> person ...
>   (8–9, ellipsis in original)

The "Child"—a daughter—"opens" the mother in that her "birthgift" is a living "present": the liminal space of third-person narration that is much like the "selvage / selvedge" on a piece of cloth.

Following Harris, I find the sewing metaphors useful. The "selvage / selvedge" is both the "edge of cloth so woven that it cannot unravel" and a "border of different material or finish along the edge of cloth intended to be removed or hidden" (*Concise Oxford*). If the self's edge is kept from unravelling by the selvage of consciousness, then our borders are much greater than our texts. But what if the self's edges are limited by much narrower seams—the limiting discourses of sexism and racism, for example—created by the "pattern" itself? Filmmaker Trinh T. Minh-ha, whose work involves production in another kind of cutting room, insists on including in her films the repetition, bad cuts, and mistakes that usually get edited out: "Despite our desperate, eternal attempt to separate, contain, and mend, categories always leak" (vi). But in whose interests is it that we separate and contain ourselves? Notice Trinh's "mending" metaphor which, unlike the semantic fields produced by the words "separate" and "contain," suggests a deliberate repairing.

If clothes are the designed, patterned, cut, sewed, hemmed, and occasionally mended product of someone's—usually not our own—labour with "material," they are, like many aspects of our daily lives, evidence of the patterns of ideology. As such, the "selvage" can be considered as either discardable excess or as potential. To explore the self's edge as a liminal space of potentiality is to reach "what there is teasing beyond the edges," to acknowledge the experiences of self beyond the seams, beyond what seems to be one's experiences. In *Drawing Down a Daughter*, these "selves" are figured as

1. The "i" at the very edge of self, the salvaged self, the self constructed in early childhood;
2. The "I" as a self that both is and is not self because it is limited and made possible by the language within which it speaks;
3. The "she" who watches, records, analyzes, writes, lives, showers, eats, breathes;
4. The doubly embedded "I" of the Great Aunt who speaks, in dialect, and so is drawn out of the past and into the present.

Harris's "Poets in Limbo" cites many other Black women poets for whom their grandmothers' and great aunts' stories offered an image of self as potentiality. For example, Dionne Brand spoke, in an unpublished interview with Harris, of the effect of her grandmother's and great aunts' stories: "they made me an image of me … I'm still working towards" ("Poets in Limbo" 117). Because the moment the child is born the "space of potentiality" or "selvage" is threatened—it can be cut, wasted, hidden by any number of patterns imposed by the dominant ideology (by hunger, sexual abuse, racism, poverty, for example)—Harris takes up the Black woman poet's challenge "to restore the sense, the ability to perceive, of the real self" (118). *Drawing Down a Daughter* interpellates the daughter as "Black! And radiant" even while acknowledging that "there is no language / i can offer you no corner that is / yours unsullied / you inherit the intransitive/ case Anglo-Saxon noun" (24).

In the following poems, the words become, like the skin of a pregnant belly, both the centre and the limit. They seam and yet open:

> for
>   her
>   self
>   for
>   the
>   child
>   roped
>   in
>   her
>   womb
>   she
>   refuses
>   (16)

This passage is preceded by the words "she hears her name again calling" (15), which make intriguing sense of the words "as she were lost" (16), which I first misread as "as if she were lost." The meanings of "she hears her name again calling / as she were lost" are unusual. "She" hears her name calling her as if "she," in the plural (as signified by the verb "were") were "lost." She is and is not lost for she can call herself, and hear herself calling.

The poem across the page looks like this:

She rises
        going
               out to
                       day that existed
              in/   and
          before
    her body
    her body
        day's
             memory
                of it   illusive
            imprint
        waiting for
    her nakedness

    inside her the child thrashing
    daughter she needs
    dreads
    for who would bring a child
        (17)

Note the clear, black words, which suggest breasts and engorged or aroused nipples. The words "her body / her body" are repeated at the place where the breasts meet. And yet the repeated words mean that the breasts don't touch one another. The words function to represent, intimately and particularly, the body that is "going / out to / day that existed / in / and / before / her body." A number of unusual semantic oppositions are set up by the formal arrangement on the page. "Going" is set against "before"; "day's" set against "waiting for"; "She rises" against "her nakedness"; "out to" against "in / and"; "memory" against "imprint"; "day that existed" against "of it illusive." This poem offers both a powerful representation of pleasure in a full, pregnant body and an empowering language for a complex, and clearly not binary, experience in the world in such a body. The cover of the book resonates with this poem. A side-view image (after a photograph by Craig Schneider) of a seated, pregnant, brown- or black-skinned woman's belly and upper thighs occupies two thirds of what might be called the "bitter orange glow" of the brown-shaded cover.

Drawing Down a Daughter makes its argument in many contexts, utilizing many strategies. Consider the following passage, which consciously destabilizes, through its place in the embedded writing of a fictional author, its status as "truth":

> Take, for instance, the laughable, the incontrovertible
> idea that I am writing this. True, these are my hands that strike the
> keys. But I have so little control over what is being written that I
> know the story is writing me. I have been brooding over these
> events since I rediscovered them in 1983. Once I was determined to
> write a straightforward narrative. A soupçon of horror. A fiction.
> Yet this has become an autobiography. Of sorts. (58)

As this narrator seems to know, poststructuralist theories of subjectivity have convincingly argued that stories write us. She acknowledges that we speak from within a much larger fabric of discourses, that we are shaped by the languages and worlds that precede us and into which we are born, that "we," and the worlds we inhabit, are the products of material conditions. But rather than add fuel to the poststructuralist fire, Harris's text counters with an alternative reading of the constitution of her subjectivity.

This alternate reading or alternate subjectivity can be understood as a critique of poststructuralism. It's a critique that is also described by Jane Flax in her book called *Fragments: Psychoanalysis, Feminism, and Postmodernism in the Contemporary West*. Here is how Flax describes the dilemma that poststructuralist and postmodernist theories of the subject present for women: "the postmodernist narratives about subjectivity are inadequate. As postmodernists construct subjectivity, only two alternatives appear: a 'false' unitary and essentialist self or an equally nondifferentiated totally historically or textually constituted 'true' one" (210). Flax's alternative to the dichotomy is what she calls the "core self"—an image I find useful but not entirely accurate for my understanding of Claire Harris's text, since it suggests something recessed within the individual rather than something equally materially constructed and often sacrificed by the dominant ideology.

Flax argues that "those who celebrate or call for a 'decentered' self seem self-deceptively naive and unaware of the basic cohesion within themselves that makes the fragmentation of experiences something other than a terrifying slide into psychosis" (218). If Flax were the analyst of Harris's narrator, she might argue that Harris can write in liminal spaces, in multiple voices, precisely because she takes for granted a "core self": "only when a core self begins to cohere can one enter into or use the transitional space in which the differences and boundaries between self and other, inner and outer, and reality and illusion are bracketed or elided" (219). But as my reading will demonstrate, these boundaries are not bracketed in Harris's text but made functional in her articulation of her "autobiography. Of sorts."

The representation of alternative subjectivities works in other ways in *Drawing Down a Daughter*. In the following section, Patricia Whittaker-Williams writes of a dream she's had of herself at the selvage "where a poem begins" (96):

> in such a space the night is wet   dank
> streetlights are blue/orange/red in pavement a   wind
> a plastic bag that lifts and skids and blows
> gleams *ghostly as flimsy as i in the schoolyard*
> twirling   twirling to music that not even the dream
> reveals   what is a dream *without revelation*
> i watch as from a great distance above how *she*
> *comes face to face with her self   that other*

In this dream-poem, embedded in the narrator's story, the child is "i in the schoolyard" (96), "she" who comes face to face with "her self that other that/ in the dream *is glimmering* trailing not always/ there not all there" (96). The small "i" "watches." The body is present as "her self," "her forehead," "her eyes," "her face." Only the mouth—that powerful place where one's words are in one's body—is claimed with the possessive adjective "my":

> my mouth open straining to fit in to   reach what
> is there   on that street corner in Calgary below
> the bluffs and dry poplars   *to fit into*
> infiltrated by the bitter orange glow of midnight streets
> *to reach what there is teasing beyond the edges.*
>   (96; Harris's italics)

In *Drawing Down a Daughter* Claire Harris produces an autobiographical self ("Of sorts") within what Shirley Neuman calls "a poetics of differences" (225). She accesses "some vital truth of herself, some proof susceptible to the hand, the eye, [that] lingered on the surface of things. So could bear witness" (97). Harris's notion of self as self/edge offers "a complex, multiple, layered subject with agency in the discourses and the worlds that constitute the referential space of [...] her autobiography" (Neuman 225). In her view, "self-clothing," affirms the "real self" against the perilous cutting away (self-loathing) of racism and misogyny. Harris's representation of a Black feminist consciousness requires a complex, constructed, and yet particular and unequivocal subjectivity that is "not always / there." She writes, not just her life, but *for* her life by speaking out against the inhumanity of racism and sexism in contemporary Canada. In the process, she refashions poetry, narrative, autobiography, and the English language itself.

Notes

1 As part of her "long, generous reply" she apparently held up *Drawing Down a Daughter* and "matter of factly, in passing," said "This is my life" ("An Autobiography: Of Sorts [Reading Claire Harris, *Drawing Down a Daughter*]" 25–34).

2 According to Linda Woodbridge and Roland Anderson, in an *Encyclopaedia of Contemporary Literary Theory*, the concept of liminality comes from Arnold Van Gennep's work on ritual (578). The second of three phases, the liminal, or threshold phase is usually marked by signs of "inertness and indeterminacy." According to Victor Turner, "liminality is no thin line but an expanded zone ... [which] involves namelessness, absence of property, nakedness or uniform clothing, transvestism, sexual continence, minimized distinctions of sex, rank and wealth" (*Ritual Process* 106–107). Harris's notion of the liminal as a potent space of creativity—figured in this book by the overarching presence of a pregnant writer/ narrator—both participates in and extends the possibilities of the threshold space. Harris's text consciously inhabits and reconfigures the potential of the liminal space by imagining it as a space, not of indeterminacy or meaninglessness, but of pregnancy.

3 For Harris as for Bakhtin, language, like consciousness, is "a living, socio-ideological concrete thing": "for the individual consciousness lies on the borderline between oneself and the other" ("Discourse in the Novel" 294).

■

Pauline Butling

● Robin Blaser began formulating his poetics with Robert Duncan, Jack Spicer, and other young writers in Berkeley and San Francisco in the late 1940s. In the 1950s this group became famous (at least in poetry circles) for an avant-garde, open form, innovative poetics, and for their equally radical actions as gay men who were out at a time when homosexuality was still officially illegal.[1] Robert Duncan's 1944 essay "The Homosexual in Society" was one of the first public discussions of the subject.[2] *Gino and Carlos* bar in San Francisco, where Jack Spicer presided for many years, was a well-known gathering place for homosexual and other writers in the Bay area in the 1950s and early '60s. While Blaser's poetry does not often directly address issues of homosexuality, his work celebrates a multiple and diverse world which allows for unfixed and variable erotics. He celebrates the *"anal and oral poetics"* of Hieronymus Bosch's *Garden of Earthly Delights*, a world that includes a homosexual erotic:

> de Certeau tells us, *a reality made up of*
> *peaks, beaks, arrows and sharp points: an anal and oral poetics,*
> *a marvelous animality of asses and mouths, a greedy flowering*
> *of amorous play—*
> ("Image-Nation 25," *Holy Forest* 369)

Following Hannah Arendt, whose work Blaser first encountered in the 1950s, Blaser has always affirmed a heterogeneous public realm.[3] Like Scheherazade, whose ongoing narrative of "A Thousand and One Nights" is echoed in my title, Blaser sustains an open-ended discourse, affirms an open universe with a poetry that offers a "thousand and one celebrations" ("Image-Nation 25," *Holy Forest* 371).

Curiously, however, in Blaser's 1975 essay "The Practice of Outside" on the poetics of Jack Spicer (a poetics that he largely shared), Blaser makes no mention of a homosexual outside. "The Practice of Outside," he explains, refers to Spicer's notion of a poetic process based on dictation, on the poet as "a conveyor of messages" (276), on "Jack's discipline of emptying himself in order to allow his language to receive an other than himself" (279). Blaser's main concern in the essay is to define Spicer's processual poetics and the resulting serial form that both Blaser and Spicer used extensively. The outside is defined very broadly as the realm of the unknown: as "god, world, spirit, angel, ghost" (295); the outsider is simply the stranger.[4] However, the effects of this "emptying... to receive an other than himself" certainly include destabilizing the boundaries that define otherness. And in a major essay on his own poetics published in 1974, Blaser emphasizes the potentially disturbing and transformative effects of open-form poetics: "The Other is not an object," he explains, " but acts chiasmatically.... Not a stillness. Not a rest" (*Stadium* 55).[5] In Blaser's poems, a chiasmic relation to otherness breaks the inside/outside binaries. His emphasis on a poetics of receptivity and openness, on paying attention to the unseen or unspoken, produces an expansive and heterogeneous social as well as poetic realm.

I have chosen some of Blaser's most recent poems, the last section of *The Holy Forest: The Collected Poems* (1995), where Blaser directly addresses issues of outsiderdom and exile, to explore the links between his social concerns and his poetic practice. Appropriately titled "Exody," these poems take on the discourses of exclusion and homogenization that, in Blaser's view, so impoverish the public realm. In "Even on Sunday," a poem "written for Gay Games III, Vancouver, August, 1990" (351), Blaser describes his life work as one of "breaking... boundaries," partially because he is one of those whose *"existence itself becomes a breaking of boundaries"* (349). On behalf of the homosexual who is *"shut out of the social order"* in the sense that he is prevented from *"being alive / in the full sense of body and soul"* (347–48, Blaser's italics), the poem rages against "the manipulated incompetences of public thought // where I had hoped to find myself ordinary among others in the / streets" (346). Blaser condemns hierarchies of value in which

> Woman is not equal to man. Man is manly man, whatever is to be
> understood
> by that: the feminine man stands out from the race and thereby becomes
> worthless
> life. Shylock must be exterminated: the only final solutions are fire and
> gas
> ("Even on Sunday," *Holy Forest* 350)

More generally, he critiques any discursive boundaries that deny multiplicity and exclude or devalue minorities. The enlightenment promise of *"equality to / men and / women, including homosexuals!"* (350–51), he suggests, disappears in the face of a reductive push for the normative.

His work in poetry has been to resist that "normative," to resist discursive closure, to work against homogenization:

the work of a lifetime—in this breaking of boundaries—

against,

as Mayer says, *a global disposition of thought toward annihilation,*
which
thinks to admit only majorities in the future and is determined to
equate
minorities with 'worthless life'   Worthless are the Jews, there the
blacks [and
aboriginals], somewhere else (and everywhere) the homosexuals, women
of the type of Judith and Delilah, not least the intellectuals keen on
individuation . . .
("Even on Sunday" 349; Blaser's ellipses, parentheses, and square
brackets)

The poem critiques social, political, and religious systems for their exclu-
sion of "outsiders" in the name of a *"unified mankind"* or *"homogenized
humanity"* (350). Blaser's critique of Christianity, one of the most repres-
sive systems in Western history, begins with the poem's title—"Even on Sun-
day"—a title that plays against the movie title *Never on Sunday*, a film in
which the prostitute / heroine shuts down her sexual service business every
Sunday. In the movie, the no-sex-on-Sunday rule is established to enable
her to see her beloved Sunday drama performances, not because of a puni-
tive Christianity. But a punitive system is nevertheless implied in the title
because it recalls the prescriptive nature of Christian doctrine. Blaser's
poem argues against a Christianity that not only forbids or limits pleasur-
able activities, but also more seriously excludes those who are labelled
outsiders *"by virtue of our existence"* (351)—such as the homosexuals,
blacks, Jews, aboriginals, and prostitutes in the passage cited above (349).

On a positive note, Blaser and the other speakers cited in the poem
work to recuperate *"all / forms of outsiderdom"* as part of the *"existential
given"* (348), work to counter the *"metaphysical / washout"* (351) caused by
homogenizing discourses. Despite the indictment of those who speak of
AIDS as God's revenge and of other punitive thought systems, the position
of the writing subject in this poem is, as always in Blaser's poetry, one of
entanglement. The poet remains "a shadowy participant in a folding with
something outside himself" ("Practice of Outside" 281). The poem ends by
embracing the "quantified multitudes who / wander *the computations and
rationalities that belong to no one*" (351). Blaser's discussion of the "Practice
of Outside" in Spicer's work in his 1975 essay becomes a clearly articulated
ethical position in these recent poems.

Before discussing the poetics and ethics of the "Exody" poems in more detail, I want to briefly turn to Blaser's response to another outsider experience—that of the immigrant. Blaser was almost forty years old when he moved to Canada in 1965—not an easy age to change countries and citizenship—and he initially described himself as "in exile."[6] However, unlike many American intellectuals who moved to Canada to teach at Canadian universities in the 1950s and '60s, Blaser chose to join his adopted country. In 1972, at the age of 47, he became a Canadian citizen. He also started a magazine two years after he arrived for the express purpose of building a "Pacific Nation": "I wish to put together an imaginary nation," he explains in his preface to the first issue of *Pacific Nation.* He envisions a heterogeneous nation, that brings together politics and poetry: "Images of our cities and of our politics must join our poetry" (preface n.p.)[7]

Blaser's "citizenship" in the public realm is also demonstrated by his two major critical essays on Canadian writers—introductory essays to the *Selected Poems* of George Bowering (1980) and of Louis Dudek (1988). The essays are acts of citizenship in the sense that they help to define a wide-ranging modernist/postmodernist tradition within a Canadian context. Blaser emphasizes the relation between the individual poets and their social and political contexts—which reflects Blaser's own priorities of bringing politics and poetry together. Blaser says:

> On the one hand I want to place Bowering's work within the modernist condition—that is, to see its significance within "the enormity of present experience." On the other, I am concerned with his contemporaneity. The term, "post-modern," so conscientiously inserted into Canadian criticism by Frank Davey—and supported by Bowering's own literary essays—signals a strong movement among important Canadian writers to separate themselves from certain characteristics of modernism. Their emphasis is upon the democratic and against the authoritarian, upon naturalness of language, and upon fragment-structures of thought and feeling without undue anxiety about the absence of reconciliatory and conservative structures of meaning. ("George Bowering's Plainsong" 24)[8]

I find Blaser's emphasis on Bowering's Canadian context especially interesting, given the fact that Bowering, like Blaser, is more often aligned with the transnational literary tradition of Ezra Pound, William Carlos Williams, and other modernist writers. Blaser emphasizes Bowering's debt to Louis Dudek, Irving Layton, and Raymond Souster, for instance, and also Bowering's early critical work on Al Purdy and Margaret Avison: "when Bow-

ering comes to measure his place in Canadian poetry, he does so with ...
a book on Al Purdy (1970), and a fine essay on Margaret Avison, 1971"
(21). Bowering's anti-lyric stance and subsequent work in the "large imag-
inative structures" of the serial poem (11), Blaser continues, show Bower-
ing's commitment to the "democratic and against the authoritarian."
Blaser's "careful tracing of Bowering's Canadian connections in order to say
that Bowering is not foreign here" (21) is, perhaps, also a way of saying that
Blaser, too, is "not foreign here." Certainly, Blaser defines a Canadian tra-
dition that is broad enough to include both himself and Bowering. Again,
we see Blaser's concern to establish an inclusive public realm.

In his own poetry, Blaser generates openness and heterogeneity by a
variety of writing strategies, all informed by a projectivist practice that
locates the self as object among other objects, by his and Spicer's notions
of "the practice of outside," and by his life-long critique of oppression in
twentieth-century discourses.[9] Blaser's serial forms, coalitional subjectiv-
ity, and dense intertextuality destabilize the self/other, inside/outside bina-
ries that exclude or devalue difference. In responding to a letter from a
student who finds his poetry difficult, Blaser explains: "I suppose syntax is
one difficulty—how is so much going on without the 'I' of the poem tak-
ing imperial power over the flow? ... The arrangement of my sentences is
meant to deny the simplicity and danger of such a relationship as owner-
ship—why, the language isn't yours alone—it's older than you are, and
largely other than you are, and it's never transparent to any reality you can
think of" ("Letter from a Student" 6). The disjunction and fragmentation
maintain a flux of semantic, phonic, and morphemic particles where self
and world, self and other, are intermingled rather than reduced to oppo-
sitional and/or transparent positions. Blaser works within an iterative and
coalitional economy to activate "*the man of the multiple*" (*Holy Forest* 367).
As with Bosch's "anal and oral poetics," Blaser's poetics opens the poem to
unfixed erotics, to unfixed identities, and to multiple discourses.

What does this look like in practice? In terms of the movement from
word to word, line to line, Blaser pays attention to the silences "between
words and at the beginning and end of sentences,"—pays attention to the
unspoken. He explains:

> If we take the order of language to be the arrangement of words with-
> out noting the silence between words and at the beginning and end of
> sentences, we have lost the protagonist language is.... All language is
> musical, even idle talk, but the rhythm of poetry brings forward the
> silence and tension of words—rhymes and older metered patterns did

not originally close lines, but open their silence, as if the words burst
into flame out of an absence of words. ("Stadium," 53)

Blaser listens at the edges of words, at the ends of lines, to hear the unspo-
ken. The edges expand to become liminal spaces where absence can become
presence, where silence can generate noise. Giorgio Agamben's discussion
of the "outside" in *The Coming Community* is helpful here: he describes the
outside as a "bordering . . . that knows no exteriority, but a threshold . . . , that
is, a point of contact with an external space that must remain empty"
(67). If the external space is emptied of meaning (by dissolving insider/out-
sider binaries) the border becomes not a dividing line but an inhabited
space, as indicated in Agamben's shift to the active, verbal noun *bordering*
from the static noun, *borders*. Borders thus become potential sites of plen-
itude, of excess, which in turn disturb or change the settled meanings on
the inside. Similarly Blaser opens his poems to what he calls commotion,
noise, and turbulence, which continually unsettle the poem's semantic
fields.[10] In a "Letter to a Student" having difficulty reading Blaser's *Pell
Mell*, he explains: "a poem is a commotion among things—a search for
form—because form is alive—and the poet is, thereby, a *commotor* not a
commuter of meaning" (6). For Blaser, borders are liminal spaces in the
sense defined by cultural anthropologists such as Victor Turner where
"liminality is no thin line but an expanded zone, in which liminars may
spend much time" (qtd. in Woodbridge and Anderson 578–79). The exter-
nal space remains empty, as Agamben says, because no inside/outside
binary locates difference beyond the borders of normalcy or sense. Blaser's
description of "tourbillions" in "Image-Nation 25 (Exody" both enacts and
describes such an expanded zone:

> tourbillions, that is, whirlwinds, whirlpools, vortexes, fireworks,
> the writer writing twists there—his or her *chance-possessed
> breath*—blew out the sentinal sentences, ancestral and beauti-
> ful—they are now of changed substance—perhaps, of joyous tour-
> maline, often black, sometimes blue, red, green, brown, or
> colourless—polished pieces—of jewellers' tourmaline tongs that
> would distinguish glass from crystal.
> (*Holy Forest* 367)

In the turbulence and asymmetry of Blaser's poems, it becomes difficult to
differentiate positive/negative, inside/outside binaries: "and I asked
St. Clare," Blaser writes in the first poem of the "Exody" series, "to help this

kaleidoscope be asymmetrical, as / the / world is in mind and heart" ("Muses, Dionysus, Eros," *Holy Forest* 345).

Another way Blaser generates commotion and plenitude in the poem is through a coalitional subjectivity. The speakers in his poems are folded or layered together in a structure resembling a chorus, though they don't necessarily speak in unison, or as independent voices in an intertextual dialogue. Rather, the subject(s) in Blaser's poems are variously entangled: they collaborate, or angle away from each other, or become fragmentary and segmented. In the absence of any single voice or position, subjectivity remains coalitional. Take "Image-Nation 25," for instance: to say that the poem begins with a quotation from Michel Serres does not adequately describe the complex intermingling of Serres's text with other trajectories that take shape within the field of the poem as Blaser explores what constitutes creative turbulence. Blaser first introduces Serres as "a town crier" who raises crucial questions (Blaser's italics indicate quotations from Serres):

> trying to imagine *the intermediary states,* trying to imagine *the*
> *man of the multiple, trying to imagine the margin that separates*
> *the multiple from the ordered, the moment when the solid is at*
> *the point of setting, in agitated crystals, when turbulence spins*
> *in its whirlwind, when life is connected, liberated, awakened,*
> *organized ...*
> this admirable, charmed mind of Hermes
> (*Holy Forest* 367; Blaser's ellipses)

Further on, Blaser joins Michel de Certeau in applauding another kind of turbulence—the curved, circular, elliptical movements in Hieronymus Bosch's painting, *Garden of Earthly Delights*. De Certeau's voice is spliced into Blaser's text without introduction or comment: the "I" of the poem simply "join[s] him now with / my magnifying glass" to observe Bosch's "*interpretive delirium,*" described by de Certeau as a process of

> *coming into meaning and going out—this space is curved inward*
> *upon itself, like the circles and ellipses Bosch endlessly gen-*
> *erates, there is no entrance, only interpretative delirium, frag-*
> *ments of a language, a lacunary system, a cosmos unsure of its*
> *postulates—*
> ("Image-Nation 25," *Holy Forest* 368)

De Certeau's text continues to intermingle with Blaser's comments for another page-and-a-half discussion of Bosch's aesthetics. "[My] eyes strain, even with a guide" (369), Blaser says at one point, indicating his dependent relationship. Blaser and de Certeau work together in a coalitional subjectivity to develop an explanation of Bosch's unfixed erotics:

> an aesthetic exercise (in the sense in which one speaks of
> spiritual exercise), de Certeau tells us, a reality made up of
> peaks, beaks, arrows and sharp points: an anal and oral poetics,
> a marvelous animality of asses and mouths, a greedy flowering
> of amorous play—
>   ("Image-Nation 25" Holy Forest 369)

The poem not only celebrates "the circles and ellipses Bosch endlessly gen- / erates" (368) but is itself in a circular form that turns and returns "inward / upon itself" as Blaser folds together his words with other voices/texts. From Michel Serres's discussion of how to resist the forms of closure that exclude "the / man of the multiple" (367), to Blaser's description of the "writer writing" (367) within a multiplicity of vectors, to Mark C. Taylor's comments on how "God, self, history, and book ... each mirrors the other" (367), to a parallel image of a "fun-house" (368) of distorting mirrors, to a two-stanza poem on the mirroring relationship of "space/time time/space" (368), the poem circles around themes of multiplicity and Bosch's "anal and oral poetics." The poem reminds me of the movements of a three-dimensional kaleidoscope where, as in Deleuze's description of a labyrinth cited toward the end of the poem: "The multiple is not / only what has many parts but what is folded in many / ways" (370). Like the self, the poem is multilayered. As Blaser so clearly explains to his puzzled student reader: "we're not wandering around looking for a SELF that preceded experience, but, rather, we are looking for a world in which to find ourselves—alive and celebrating" ("Letter" 6).

Also crucial to Blaser's coalitional poetics is a nomadic, unfixed subjectivity, defined by Rosi Braidotti as a state of "becoming" as a result of "emphatic proximity, intensive interconnectedness" (5). Although I am uneasy about using a term which, as Braidotti admits, is "inspired by the experience of peoples or cultures that are literally nomadic" (5) especially as Braidotti sometimes equates nomads with tourists, which is hardly the same as Blaser's exiled "wandering Jew and nomad" who appears in the final poem (371), I do find her discussion helpful in describing the nomadic subjects in Blaser's poems. "Nomadism," Braidotti claims, "refers to the kind of critical consciousness that resists settling into socially coded modes of thought and behaviour"; it produces "the subversion of set conventions"(5). The process of "coming into meaning and going out" that Blaser speaks of requires such a subversive and mobile subject who refuses to settle down into meanings. This is not to say that the subject becomes the perpetual tourist, detached and/or voyeuristic. Nomads live in homes, albeit moveable ones. By nomadic subjectivity I mean a mobile but always engaged subject, a subject who resists staying in one place ("resists settling into socially coded modes of thought and behaviour" to repeat Braidotti's definition) but who recognizes that subjectivity is always "among things," as Blaser puts it:

> the "I" of my poems is among things, people, etc. (images)—say, "Drive I Car"—there's a fancy word for this—parataxis—a placing alongside—or, to put it my way, the "I" of my poems is discovered among things, not in charge of them, not owning them, not drowning them in my sentiments—the "I" then, found among things, is also in great part created by them—whether they be loved, hated, or simply met—   ("Letter" 6)

Such a locally constellated subject avoids the reductive self/other boundaries produced by an egocentric "I." It enacts *"a breaking of boundaries"* (349) and opens the border to the *"man of the multiple"* (367). More specifically, in the "Exody" sequence, a coalitional subjectivity opens the poem to an expansive, unfixed erotics that can include homosexual subjectivity. As in the last poem of the series, where Blaser (again speaking to and with de Certeau) "proposes this, that Bosch's garden says to me or 'you'—*You / there, what do you say about what you are, while you are say- / ing what I am?"* His answer is that "one might celebrate this *unintelligibility that extinguishes / itself"* (370).

Other methods of generating discursive openness and heterogeneity—even a welcome "unintelligibility"—in Blaser's poetic practice include repetition, which provides linkages, combined with segmentation, which sustains openness.[11] The third poem of the "Exody" sequence works mainly via this process ("Image-Nation 24 ('oh, pshaw,'"). Fast-paced and full of the "commotion" and "noise" of personal memories, family stories, and societal dictates, the poem traces the recurring tropes of exile and outsiderdom. Prose clusters, punctuated mostly by dashes, have the rapid-fire rhythm of the telegraph messages described at one point in the poem as "dot— / dash—spaces—sounds … quick as the platinum / points come together, quick as the mind can" (358). The poem's turns, folds, shifts, and returns prevent discursive or imagistic closure and make its conceptual and formal margins fluid "borderings." Meanwhile, the nomadic "I" of the poem wan-

ders within the folds of personal and social history, unravelling (and some-
times rewinding) the many narrative threads that entangle "Robin."

The poem begins, for instance, with a story of the young boy playing
"with the / lacy iron treadle" of his great-grandmother Ina's sewing machine,
an action that causes the bobbin thread to become tangled (353). The
grandmother then untangles and rewinds the bobbin as she also rewinds
narratives of gender for the young boy. She, who "had been secretary to
Brigham Young," scolds him for hanging around in the women's world of
the kitchen reading *Redbook* or *Ladies' Home Journal* and throws him out-
side to play in the masculine world, among the chickens and jackrabbits
(353). The poem then shifts abruptly to a different kind of unravelling. In
the next segment, the letters of the word g-o-d are scrambled and reformed
in multiple combinations, in effect scattering the *idea* of a unified God along
with the letters. There is to be no unified God hovering over this poem:

> g & d retained become *gad, gawd, gud*
> or only the g becoming *gog, golly, gosh, gum*
> or disguise g as c and *cock, cor, cod* appear
> or drop g for untold suffixes, *od, ud,* etc.
> or add relationship, *begad, begar, bedad, egad*
> or take up possession, *swounds, zounds*
> or reduce the whole busyness to 'drat'.
> (*Holy Forest* 353)

Again, Blaser shakes up the poem's semantic field. "Drat" indeed says the
poem to the whole notion of an authoritarian, punishing, and controlling
God "at / whose fiat the world came into being, and whose im- / posed will it
obeys" (362). "Drat" to the racism and homophobia that are some of the
effects of such a punitive "*christianism*" (362). As Blaser writes toward the
end the 'I' of this poem "cannot exist there" (362), cannot exist in those nar-
ratives of exclusion and repression, such as the recent right-wing "*god-lore
spattering*" everything with its messages of rejection: "Pat Robertson at the
Republican / Convention proposing a social future excluding homosexu-
als and / women's choice" (361):

> here, plagues galore weave among us—aids, racism, homophobia,
> displacement and poverty, *christianism* with its political plans,
> the Vatican sending out 'advisory letters' to the Bishops that
> it's okay to discriminate against gays in jobs, housing, and
> professions—wacky—
> (*Holy Forest* 362)

The poem continues to segment, entangle, and sometimes untangle the constitutive narratives of the boy Robin, whose name itself creates confusion because he is named after the girl Robin in Frances Hodgson Burnett's novel *Robin* (354). Both Robins were misfits: s/he is "an intruder and a calamity" (354, 357).

The boy's stories in this poem include stories of family hardship and survival during the Depression, "bunched there on an embankment by the railroads" in a boxcar home where they clung desperately to their whistle-stop town of Blaser, Idaho (354). Within the family, the boy's "cultural kitchen" (361), "Robin" is entangled in many narrative threads. His grandmother Sophia Nichol tells him "stories of Odysseus" (358) which then provide a narrative frame for his own "'circuitously Odyssean'" journey when she sends him on his first major adventure, across a flooding river and back to get supplies (359). She also unwittingly introduces him to the discourse of Christian fundamentalism by sending him to the nearby town of Boise ("my first city") where he heard about the "stench and corruption of the body" (360) from a street-corner preacher. This experience, in turn, becomes entangled with (and changed by) several literary narratives that celebrate rather than condemn diverse sexual experience that the boy encounters when he reads Joyce, *Ecclesiasticus*, *The Homeric Hymn to Aphrodite*, and Calvino (361). As well as his excursions into the vocabulary and narratives of the outside world, there are the experiences inside the house where his mother sang with him as he sat under the ironing board—everything from *The Star Spangled Banner* in Latin to *Hallelujah, I'm a Bum* (359). There were also silences, most notably from his grandfather, "a Mormon Bishop" and "roadmaster on The Union Pacific" (355), who hinted at the hidden knowledge and visions of a forbidden, mystical Christianity in a secret *Golden Bible* (356).

Even in the privacy of his favourite reading spot under the library table, the boy does not escape the constitutive power of narrative. The "piercing eye" of "the wandering Jew / or nomad," a figure painted on the leather back of the rocking chair that sat in the centre of the family home, follows him everywhere.

> the rocking chair from their lost house in Salt Lake City, often
> talked about, had a painted leather back—the wandering Jew or
> nomad—whose marvellous, piercing eye followed everyone up and
> down the boxcar parlour—into corners—even under the library
> table, also from the lost house—*eros* of wandering—*eros* of

being sought in every nook and cranny—that, so far as I'm con-
cerned is where vocabulary begins—fierce eyed—dot—dash—
space—and syntax is later and difficult
("Image-Nation 24," *Holy Forest* 359)

However, the poem ends on a positive note, with the "ashen boy" Robin
becoming "exodic" (363)—which I take to mean that he is revived by enter-
ing the poem's heterogeneous discursive space. Similarly, in the boy's "'cir-
cuitously Odyssean'" journey within the multiple folds of poem, he becomes
more than an "intruder and calamity" (357). At the end of the poem, he has
a chance at love; he inhabits a discourse that is expansive enough to include
him:

I tell 'you,' my love, these tales—*fold according to fold*—
my chances—it may be

a crap game—hoping for a nick—7—or a natural—11—

on a startled day—the ashen boy—becomes—exodic
("Image-Nation 24," *Holy Forest* 363)

Similarly, at the end of the last poem in the "Exody" series, when the tropes
of exile and outsiderdom return along with the images of multiple folds,
the boxcar parlour, the "wandering Jew or nomad" on the back of the
rocking chair, and the boy reading under the library table, the "I" reappears
sitting comfortably in the family rocking chair. In this position, a position
that entangles the comfort of the rocking-chair home with the condition
of exile pictured in the "wandering Jew and nomad" carved into the back
of the chair, the "I" can "imagine *evolutionary* love" (Blaser's emphasis, 371).
Like Scheherazade, who daily wins a reprieve from her death sentence
with her stories that go on for a thousand and one nights, "Robin" wins a
reprieve from the life-denying discourses that produced "the ashen boy" by
means of his multiple narratives, his "thousand and one celebrations":

nevertheless, I rock there,
wandering Jew and nomad

I imagine mortality,
its unrest and process

I imagine *evolutionary love,*

my thousand and one celebrations
(*Holy Forest* 371)

Notes

1 Blaser has often commented on how crucial this connection was for him, referring to it as "the fateful meeting of Jack, Robert Duncan and myself" in "The Practice of Outside" (323). See also Michael Davidson, *The San Francisco Renaissance*, for a discussion and analysis of the literary and social impact of this group.

2 The essay was first published in a left-wing magazine called *Politics* and reprinted in Ekbert Faas, *Young Robert Duncan: Portrait of the Poet as Homosexual in Society*.

3 Blaser has often acknowledged his debt to Hannah Arendt. In his preface to *The Early Poems of Robert Duncan*, he explains: "We discovered *The Origins of Totalitarianism* when she taught at Berkeley in 1955" (4). Or in "Particles," an essay "prepared for the Arts council Symposium on Art and Politics, University of British Columbia, 1967," he begins by noting his "dependence on two scholars who act as masters in my life and thought: Ernst Kantorowicz, who taught me to read history in terms of events, actions, and men in relation to ideas, rather than as a process and generality; and Hannah Arendt, whose work has clarified the partnership of politics and society for me" (27).

4 It is important to note that Blaser is not referring to the supernatural: "To understand the 'outside,'... it will not do to take off on those supernaturalisms which precondition and explain the experience. The dictation remains persistently of the world and as it is unknown, it moves into the language as the imageless moves into image" (279).

5 See Blaser's essay "The Stadium of the Mirror" which accompanies the publication of his *Image-Nations 1–12*.

6 See, for instance, Blaser's autobiographical note in *Pacific Nation* [1967]: "Robin Blaser, the editor of *The Pacific Nation* is ... currently in exile" (114).

7 See Chronology (1967) for details.

8 In his reference to Frank Davey, Blaser is referring to Davey's introduction to *From There to Here* (1974) where Davey announces "the demise of the modernist period and the beginning of a decentralized, 'post-electric', post-modern, non-authoritarian age" (19).

9 See Charles Olson's essay "Projective Verse": "Objectism is the getting rid of the lyrical interference of the individual as ego, of the 'subject' and his soul, that peculiar presumption by which western man has interposed himself between what he is as a creature of nature (with certain instructions to carry out) and those other creations of nature which we may, with no derogation, call objects. For a man is himself an object, whatever he may take to be his advantages, the more likely to recognize himself as such the greater his advantages, particularly at that moment that he achieves an humilitas sufficient to make him of use" (395).

10 In a similar vein, Daphne Marlatt describes her poems in *Salvage* as releasing a "flood" of different meanings: they are "littoral poems, shoreline poems ... the whole book—written on that edge where a feminist consciousness floods the structures of patriarchal thought" ("Foreword" 9).

11 For a very interesting and useful analysis of repetition as a structuring device, see Joseph Conte's discussion of lexical and semantic repetition and the effects of constant and variant in *Unending Design: The Forms of Postmodern Poetry*.

■

Daphne Marlatt's "Booking Passage"

Pauline Butling

● Even a cursory look at Daphne Marlatt's publications shows a life-long attention to gendered subjects in terms of both the poetry's speaking subject and its subject matter. Before Marlatt consciously articulated a feminist politics, her writing questioned the received definitions of female subjectivity and female experience.[1] *Frames of a Story* (1968) reworks the heroine of Hans Christian Anderson's "The Snow Queen"; *leaf leaf/s* (1969) explores a leafing out of language through a restive but still fairly tentative consciousness, a process which led to personal changes.[2] In *Rings* (1971) the speaking subject is decidedly active and female, writing of marital breakdown, pregnancy, and birth. In the 1980s, Marlatt became one of the leading figures in the formation of feminist communities and in the articulation of feminist practices. She was a founding member of the feminist journal *Tessera* and one of the organizers of two important conferences—Women and Words (1983) and Telling It: Women and Language across Cultures (1988). Her publications included two groundbreaking collections of lesbian love poems, *Touch to My Tongue* (1984) and *Double Negative* with Betsy Warland (1988), as well as the novel *Ana Historic* (1988), which explores the erasure of women from history.

The distinguishing feature of Marlatt's writing is not only her critique of oppressive gendered systems and ideologies; she also focuses on how gendered subjects are constructed by and embedded within received structures of language and form. I have always enjoyed this latter focus in Daphne Marlatt's writing. Her multidirectional meanings, participatory processes, and feminist sensibility engage the reader's ear, eye, mind, and body simultaneously. Entering a Marlatt text is like entering a playground where many different activities take place at the same time: there are words at play, subjects in motion, images forming, dissolving, reforming, and frames shifting in kaleidoscopic motion. Sometimes I feel a little disoriented. But invariably a second or third reading brings participatory pleasures along with an appreciation of the critical edge made possible by this interactive process. Her mode of communication has never been the direct I/you exchange in which the sender encodes a message and the receiver decodes the exact same message. Hers is a field model. She treats the poem as a linguistic, semantic, semiotic field within which she (and the reader) finds points of intersection, conjunction, and disjunction. In this field-based communication process, meanings are inflected by multiple trajectories, including discursive modes, social/geopolitical formations (place, community, gender, class, and sexuality), as well as by individual life experiences. My discussion of the closing section of Marlatt's *Salvage* (1991) explores how this field model of communication facilitates Marlatt's project of "salvaging" a lesbian language and history, together with how I as a reader develop an affective reading process.

I have chosen the last section of the book because the title,"Booking Passage," intrigues me: The parallels between booking a ticket for travel across physical spaces and the writer writing a book (*book*ing) that will take her across discursive territory also apply to the reader: how to find (book) my passage/pathway into this book? I do not just pick up my ticket at the nearest travel agent (i.e., pick a critical apparatus) and get on board. I pick up words. I play with meanings. I construct scenes and stories.

> gazing at trees, rocks, boats, we feel the boats rock waves
> in our arms, these arms of land go out of focus up the pass,
> ça gaze? things go okay? like us, "like ones," who come and
> go in the watery sound a sailboat makes, no wind, engine
> drone, and the wake rolls to us, eyes closed to avoid our
> gazing (gauze of a certain hue—nothing distinct beyond
> blue) we find how things are in each other's skin, undone
> up close, we rock our ends in each other's surge, wake on
> wake of desire's passing, shudders, shifts ...
>
> ("To Write," *Salvage* 113, Marlatt's ellipses)

I picture a West Coast scene of tree-lined shores with rocky cliffs and outcroppings, a geography of trees, rocks, and water. I also see the landscape as a metaphor for the lover's body, as the poet links the physical sensation of being in a boat to the sensation of making love: the body rocking to the inner surge of desire ("we rock our ends in each other's surge, wake on / wake of desire's passing, shudder, shifts ..."). As well, the rhythms and textures of words foreground the physical presence of language and the erotic connections between words: "gauze of a certain hue—nothing distinct beyond / blue."

Words "call each other up" Marlatt writes in "musing with mother-tongue," and in so doing generate "a form of thought that is not rational but erotic because it works by attraction" (224). The sound pattern in "trees, rocks, boats" reverses into "boats rock waves" (113) producing a rocking motion of words, of a boat, of two bodies making love. But some words and phrases seem detached, disconnected from the rest. For exam-

ple, questions interrupt the narrative and rhythmic flow—"ça gaze? things
go okay?" (113). Other phrases seem built more on rhyme than reason, as
with the lines cited above "gauze of a certain hue—nothing distinct beyond/
blue" (113). Desire comes into language in Marlatt's texts at the pre-sym-
bolic level, in the tissue, texture, and rhythms of language more than in the
meanings because, as Julia Kristeva claims, that is where the libidinal
energy finds expression (79–83). For Marlatt, coming out of the closet
means *coming* into language—both sexually and discursively:

> nothing in the book says where we might head. my tongue
> in you, your body cresting now around, around this tip's
> lip-suck   surge   rush of your coming in other words.
>   (116)

Having recognized the lesbian erotic in the poem, my reading becomes
more purposeful. I see that the poems enact as well as thematize the strug-
gle to articulate lesbian sexuality:

> we haven't even begun to write ... what keeps us going,
> this rush of wingspread, this under (nosing in), this wine-
> dark blood flower, this rubbing between the word and our
> skin.
>   (116, Marlatt's ellipses).

"To write in lesbian" (118), as the speaker says further on in this poem,
becomes one of the poem's directives: to articulate the unspoken, to find
words for the eroticized female body, to articulate the gap "between the word
and our / skin" (116).

Identity Politics, Feminist Politics

But how do I, a heterosexual reader, read these poems? I am not the "i" of
these poems, yet I share the feeling of dislocation, as in "(Dis)spelling":

> the alphabet of fear, a current running just offshore, off
> the edge of some clan pier which wasn't mine, the sinking
> feel of footings underwater, ankle-deep on what remains,
> afraid i'll drown, swept out (there was a broom) to sea.
>   (*Salvage* 114)

Not walking on water, but walking in water. Not an easy thing to do, walk-
ing against the resistance of the water. Will I/she drown? be swept out by

the tide? by that pull of the symbolic order that takes you where you hadn't intended, didn't want to go? No, the footings hold, feet on the ground. But the ground keeps shifting. If I conflate lesbian desire with all female desire (and thereby identify with the "i" of the poem) do I then appropriate the lesbian experience? If I resist the identification, do I erase that experience? How can women share in the processes of empowerment without erasing differences?

These questions lead me to feminist theory, in particular to Nicole Brossard's essay "From Radical to Integral" where Brossard posits ways of creating the "integral" woman through radical action. While the forms of radical feminism may differ, Brossard suggests, depending on one's particular experience of marginalization, the process of creating a female culture has a common purpose, to redefine woman as sign. Creating a female culture involves literally *making* sense (103), that is to say, making up new meanings for the term "woman" within the semiotic system:

> For as soon as we speak of culture, we necessarily speak of codes, signs, exchanges, communication, and recognition. Likewise, we must speak of a system of values which, on the one hand, determines what makes sense or non-sense and which, on the other, normalizes sense so that eccentricity, marginality, and transgression can be readily identified as such, in order to control them if need be.
> (Brossard, "From Radical to Integral" 103)

The radical feminist literally *makes* sense out of the supposed "eccentricity, marginality, and transgression" attributed to women. She invests the term "woman" with meanings other than the "patriarchal one-way sense" (109) by "unfurling of polyvalent and multi-directional words" (111). Such a process shatters the "one-way sense" of patriarchal meaning. It produces a void, a mental space that, little by little, will become invested with feminist subjectivities, thus constituting an imaginary territory where women's energies will begin to be able to take form (111). Integration takes place when the closed circle of sense is disrupted by a spiral that loops out into the unspoken and incorporates women's subjectivities into an expanded circle of meaning: "we quit the circle in order to enter into the spiral" (111). The radical becomes integral when the "integral woman" enters the sentence:

> When I saw you right in the middle of a sentence, it occurred to me I was naturally inclined toward you, as real as the idea I have of us, as real as the energy which speaks me emerging from our life stories.
> (Brossard, "From Radical to Integral" 115)

Brossard's delight here in recognizing the emergent woman "right in the middle of a sentence" parallels my own experience of reading Marlatt's section "Booking Passage." It is not a matter of identification but of recognition, even celebration, of new meanings of "woman." In such a context, the term *woman* "speaks me," as Nicole Brossard would put it; that is, it gathers my own experience of female subjectivities into its circle of sense. It spirals out to "speak" many female subjectivities.

From Radical to Integral: I to We

In Marlatt's poem, the movement from radical to integral involves, among other things, moving from a singular subject ("i") to a plural and communal subjectivity ("we"). The speaker discovers "the energy which speaks me emerging from our life stories" (as Brossard says) through writing her particular lesbian experience into the poem. From there, she finds a ground for identification with, and recognition of, other lesbian writers. The expanded circle of sense extends back to Sappho and forward to writing this poem:

> *She shouts aloud, Come! we know it; / thousand-eared night*
> *repeats that cry / across the sea shining between us.*
> (*Salvage* 117, Marlatt's italics and backslashes)

Earlier in the sequence, however, in "(Dis)spelling" for instance, the speaker is singular and isolated, on the edge of the circle of sense, engaged in dispelling "the alphabet of fear, a current running just offshore" (*Salvage* 114). The pronoun configuration is the lyric I/you that separates "I" from "you" and demands negotiation of the distances between. In a (male) culture, which valorizes individuality, such a structure works well. The form is ideally suited to the expression of individual male desire for the female object. It enacts the patriarchal structures of desire, what Brossard calls the patriarchal "one-way sense" ("Radical to Integral" 104): the "I" seeks to possess and/or gain mastery over "you." "To write in lesbian," however, requires other relational networks. In Marlatt's "(Dis)spelling," the "i" explores her fear of erasure, of drowning, of being silenced. She returns to childhood to find footings, to "this once bombed island" (the island of Penang where Marlatt spent her childhood) and re-enters her "singular, [/] body alive in the halflight morning." The speaker is a shadowy, solitary, half-formed figure—unable to speak to "you": "you call me and i am speechless. you call me and i am [/] still" (114).

Increasingly, in the next (and final) poem of the sequence (also titled "Booking passage"), the grammatical subject becomes "we," as the speaker dis-spells, dismantles the spells that oppress and silence this lesbian woman. She recognizes "the wall that isolates, that i so late to this" ("Booking passage" 117) and discovers connections to others, dis-covers hidden lesbian texts within the patriarchal structures of language and "his-toricity":

> one layer under the other, memory a ghost, a guide, his-
> tolytic where the pain is stored, murmur, *mer-mére*, his-
> toricity stored in the tissue, text … a small boat, fraught.
> trying to cross distance, trying to find that passage (se-
> cret). in libraries where whole texts, whole persons have
> been secreted away.
> (117, Marlatt's ellipses)

This is not a search for a female essence, as some have argued, but for female presence.[3] In this poem, the search is for a specifically lesbian presence in language. Marlatt expands the circle of sense so that the "radical" woman (the ex-centric and transgressive) becomes integral. She seeks a shared ground in language so that the "i" can say "we":

> the dark swell of a sea that separates and beats against our
> joined feet, islands me in the night, fear and rage the iso-
> late talking in my head   to combat this slipping away, of
> me, of you, the steps … what was it we held in trust, tiny
> as a Venetian bead, fragile as words encrusted with pearl,
> *mathetriai*, not-mother, hidden mentor, lost link?
> (118, Marlatt's ellipses)

Moving "into awake"

Moving "into awake," the closing metaphor of the first poem of the sequence, offers another way of moving from radical to integral, of "book-ing passage" for lesbian desire. "Awake" suggests both a mental state (being awake) and a physical phenomenon (the wide swath behind a moving boat). Metaphorically, "moving into awake" implies both coming to con-sciousness (an awakening) and moving into a specific space, the space in language behind the patriarchal boat. Like the wide swath that a boat leaves in its wake, language too offers a wide space behind the straight and narrow path of patriarchal meaning. Marlatt's creates this "wake" in her poems by interrupting the linear flow of meaning. Parentheses and dashes,

repetition, or incomplete syntactic units create lateral and spiralling seman-
tic trajectories:

> this is not the distinction of looking (long and fixed the
> gaze) as in backward ("summer is over") or back at you ("i
> want to memorize your face forever ...")—thoughts up
> the pass.
>
> it's us who move into awake, finding our calling.
>   (*Salvage* 113, Marlatt's ellipses)

Also, the ambiguous grammatical function of "awake" and "calling" in the
last line makes the reader stop and reread. How can one move into awake?
"Awake" is an adjective, or a verb, not a noun; it's a state of mind, not a des-
tination (one is awake or asleep or one awakens). Likewise "calling" is an
action, not an object to be found. But the syntax demands/produces a
nominative function for "awake"; I make sense of the non-sense by dwelling
in the word until it separates into article and noun (a wake). The wake gen-
erated behind the patriarchal boat becomes a metaphor for lesbian writ-
ing. "Calling" also doubles as both noun and verb. As a noun, it signifies a
"strong inner impulse toward a particular course of action" (*Webster's*). In
Marlatt's poem, that "strong inner impulse" is the "lesbian in us," to use
Adrienne Rich's phrase. Reading further in the dictionary entry, I discover
that calling also means "the characteristic cry of a female cat in heat." The
combined noun/verb potential of the two words deepens and widens their
meanings. As I explore these trajectories, I join the writer in producing the
polyvalent context necessary for writing/reading the lesbian experience.

Changing the Sentence: The Prose Poem

Marlatt resists and subverts the sentence, both the patriarchal sentencing
of women to secondary status in the social order and the grammatical
sentence that demands linearity, order, and closure in writing. In Marlatt's
writing, the period marks a break in the movement of thought, but not the
completion of a thought. Notice the unstable sentence units in the first seven
stanzagraphs of the poem "Booking passage":

> this coming and going in the dark of early morning, snow
> scribbling its thawline round the house. we are under-
> cover, under a cover of white you unlock your door on this
> slipperiness.

to throw it off, this cover, this blank that halts a kiss on the open road. i kiss you anyway, and feel you veer toward me, red tail lights aflare at certain patches, certain turns my tongue takes, provocative.

we haven't even begun to write ... sliding the in-between as the ferry slips its shoreline, barely noticeable at first, a gathering beat of engines in reverse, the shudder of the turn to make that long passage out—

the price for this.

we stood on the road in the dark. you closed the door so carlight wouldn't shine on us. our kiss reflected in snow, the name for this.

under the covers, morning, you take my scent, writing me into your cells' history. deep in our sentencing, i smell you home.

there is the passage, there is the *booking*—and our fear of this.

(*Salvage* 115–16, Marlatt's ellipses)

The first sentence contains actions without agency (verbs but no sub-jects). The second seems conventional at first, but the adverbial phrase "under a cover of white" shifts into a clause in which the subject changes from "we" to "you." The second stanzagraph begins with an infinitive phrase (again action without agency) followed by a sentence that starts out on the straight and narrow, but then veers off with a string of qualifiers that are connected paratactically (by association) rather than syntactically (by grammatical links). The third and fourth stanzagraphs together form one sentence unit, consisting of a series of phrases and clauses linked by com-mas and dashes. Again the structure is paratactic rather than syntactic, with words, phrases, or clauses linked by association rather than by grammat-ical structures. In contrast to the conventional sentence, which provides con-nection and integration, Marlatt's sentences refuse integration.[4] She decontextualizes and disintegrates meanings; she works with rhythmic units which bring words together in metonymic relationships, rather than with syntactic structures which integrate all the parts. The dislocated syn-tax works against a narrative line of discovery and exploration that propels the text toward closure and creates instead a countermotion—Gertrude Stein's "continuous present." Like the cubist painters (from whom Stein derived her concept) who refused the integrative structures of perspective and three-dimensionality, and instead placed all the visual elements on the same plane, Marlatt resists the linear relations of conventional grammar.

The subject/verb differentiation is blurred, for example, in the many "ing" forms that appear throughout the above passage: "booking," "gazing," "looking," "finding," "calling," "(Dis)spelling," "sentencing." These words combine verb and noun functions and so loosen the lock-step progression from subject to verb to object. They redirect attention to the *thingness* of the word. Roland Barthes describes this focus on the specificity of the word as the hallmark of contemporary poetry: "The poetic word," he suggest, is "an act without immediate past, without environment, and which holds forth only the dense shadow of reflexes from all sources which are associated with it" (*Writing Degree Zero* 47–48). And further that "each poetic word is … a Pandora's box from which fly out all the potentialities of language" (48).

Indeed the propulsion toward sentence and paragraph integration is constantly interrupted, suspended, or slowed in Marlatt's poems, but Marlatt does not, as Barthes suggests, reduce the word to a "zero degree" (48). Instead, there is a to-and-fro relationship: even as the thingness and presence of each word pushes against the narrative line, the narrative and metaphoric connections constantly pull the individual words into their integrative structures. This seesaw motion is partially an effect of the prose poem, a form that combines narrative and poetic elements in a constructive tension. The horizontal movements of prose (enacted in sentence and paragraph forms) intersect the verticality of the poetic word, creating multidirectional vectors. As well, in Marlatt's texts, there is an integrative movement at the phonic, or rhythmic level. The flow of the stanzagraph often enacts sexual rhythms. The pace quickens, climaxes, subsides. Marlatt describes the rhythmic units in physical terms, as "multiple orgasms" ("On Salvaging" 34).

To take an example: the final stanzagraph of the poem "Booking passage" in part follows a story line that moves toward closure. It tells the story of her struggle "to write in lesbian" and her discovery of a community of lesbian writers. When Sappho's words flow into the blood/language/desire of the text, the poem comes to a satisfying emotional conclusion. The stanzagraph also moves toward a rhythmic climax at the word "rush," and then levels out with a closing cadence. However, Marlatt's fragmented language works against these integrative structures. Phrases such as "this page," and "this mark" interrupt the narrative line and foreground the presence of the word on the page:

like her, precisely on this page, this mark: *a thin flame
runs under / my skin.* twenty-five hundred years ago, this
trembling then. actual as that which wets our skin her
words come down to us, a rush, poured through the blood,
this coming and going among islands is.

(*Salvage* 119, Marlatt's emphasis)

Throughout all three poems that make up the section "Booking Passage,"
Marlatt continuously enacts "this coming and going" of words, sentences,
lines, and stanzagraphs to produce vertical/horizontal, semantic and syn-
tactic tensions. The resulting polymorphous form generates multidirec-
tional meanings, mobile subjects, and kaleidoscopic slippages that loosen
the boundaries of meaning. This loosening in turn makes new meanings
possible. In this particular section of poems, Marlatt recuperates lesbian his-
tory and extends the meaning of "woman" to include lesbian subjectivity.

Notes

1 She reiterates this position in a recent interview: "It has always been important for
  me to write out of my experience as a woman because I felt that was the unspeak-
  able, the ignored, the elided. I wanted to make it present in the same way as the TISH
  group of writers wanted to make Vancouver present. There was this sense that this
  place is unwritten and should be on the map and I had that same sense about female
  experience. That's why I was writing about giving birth and nursing and adolescent
  sexual conditioning" ("On Salvaging" 30).

2 Marlatt explains to George Bowering that writing *leaf leaf/s* led to her change her
  life: "I started living my own life. My phrase for it was 'taking on more ground.' I
  wanted to feel that I had a right to live in the world" ("Given this Body" 55–56).

3 See, for instance, Frank Davey, "Words and Stones in *How Hug a Stone*" and Den-
  nis Cooley, "Recursions Excursions Incursions: Daphne Marlatt Wrestles with the
  Angel Language." See also Stan Dragland's response to Davey and Cooley in his *Bees
  of the Invisible* (186) and Julie Beddoes's critique of Davey in "Mastering the Mother
  Tongue: Reading Frank Davey Reading Daphne Marlatt's *How Hug a Stone*."

4 For further discussion of the "new" sentence see Ron Silliman, *The New Sentence*
  and Lyn Hejinian, "Language and 'Paradise.'"

■

Jeff Derksen's "Rearticulatory Poetics"

Susan Rudy

> I want to see
> the real relations
> but you've got Nikes on and I like you
> so I have to try and understand. And if
> that shirt's from The Gap, then one arm was sewn
> in Malaysia, the other in Sri Lanka. Why then
> is it hard to "see" ideology when you're
> wearing it? Is it "out there"? Or deeper inside
> than even desire could get?
>
> Derksen, *Transnational Muscle Cars* 10

● A poet and cultural critic who moved back to Vancouver in 2003 to teach at Simon Fraser University, Jeff Derksen has had what he calls a "transnational" existence over the past decade.[1] Most recently he lived in New York City where he was conducting post-doctoral research on globalization and national cultural formations at CUNY's Graduate Center for Place, Culture and Politics, and Vienna where he lived with his partner, the conceptual artist Sabine Bitter.[2] But he was born in Murrayville, BC, in 1958, grew up in New Westminster, BC, and was educated in British Columbia and Alberta.[3] During the 1980s Derksen was a founding member of Vancouver's influential Kootenay School of Writing (KSW), a writer-run centre that continues to offer workshops, talks, readings and colloquia.[4] Derksen's publication history as poet and critic is international in scope, linked to the Language poets in the United States as well as to various poetry communities in Canada, most obviously KSW.

Derksen's substantial contribution to both cultural studies and poetics involves his investigations, in several media, of what he calls "the burden of history carried by language" ("Sites Taken as Signs" 148) by focusing on the "local" as "an intersection of ideology, signification, and subjectivity" (151). In "Central [Canada] Party Haus," for example, first published on *The East Village Poetry Website*, Derksen writes,

> Localism robs us
> of our history.
> [...]   Your shirt
> is a living example

of the alienation of labour.
[…]   The Gap
just across the tracks
shows how the forces
of NATO and NAFTA have made
it easy to look good casually.
[…]   I'm specific, I'm
particular platinum at
a pronounced pace: one
can only negotiate
these contradictions textually
or risk a president's choice.
(*Transnational* 66–67)

In Canada, "president's choice" is a brand of grocery product available at the "Real Canadian Superstore," and in other large chain stores. The poem advises us to negotiate the contradictory relation between lived experience and mass production or else risk being commodified.

"Jerk" puts it this way: "My idealistic belief/ is that historical consciousness may come. / My sad cognitive mapping / is that overdetermined contradictions/ don't lead to new social relations" (*Transnational* 10). Or consider a line from *Dwell*, "Jeanine is a living example of Noranda's attitude to employees" (8, from a Noranda TV ad), which also opens Derksen's essay "Sites Taken as Signs: Place, the Open Text, and Enigma in New Vancouver Writing" where he argues: "In the face of corporate constructions of our subjectivity that reduce a person to a 'living example,'" how "can we assert a space for the subject that goes beyond the limited official versions" ("Sites" 144)? In several talks in the 1990s, Derksen begins to call this investigative practice a "rearticulatory poetics."[5]

Long before developing this critical vocabulary, Derksen's work was rearticulating, or making politically overt through startling juxtaposition, the meanings of apparently ideologically neutral terms. Consider even the titles of his books. His first chapbook, *Memory Is the Only Thing Holding Me Back* (1984), juxtaposes the philosophical category of "memory" with the clichéd, corporate phrase "the only thing holding me back [from success?]." As a result, both concepts are rearticulated. "Memory" is linked to economic reality, and the desire produced by late capitalism to not be held back is linked to the unconscious. Another chapbook has a title almost as long as the text itself: *Selfish: Something Deep Inside Liberal Cultural Relativism Says "Yes I Can"* (1993). Here, the imprint of cultural discourse on the self is demonstrated in the juxtaposition of the usually derogatory and colloquial category "selfish" with the discourse of cultural theory—"Liberal Cultural Relativism"—which here is also assigned conventional personhood, as having "Something Deep Inside." Derksen's *But Could I Make a Living from It* (2000) takes its title from a line in his full-length poetry book *Dwell* (1994): "I could learn how to do that, but could I make a living / from it?" (64).[6] Again the line juxtaposes the reality it demonstrates—the speaker has learned how to do "that"—question "liberal cultural relativism"—but can "he" (the poet, the speaker) survive? Could he make a living from it?

In "Poetry and Social Relations: Recent Rearticulatory Practices," Derksen argues that "cultural production lies at a particularly bound yet contingent and potential crossroads" (n.p.) since political art, once it sees ideology as "a constructing and constructed effect," can make "ideology tangible, [make] ideology ideological." In a kind of "Marxist critique in reverse," Derksen engages "the complications of social relations by showing the links between the subjective, the everyday, and the most widely circulated ideological sites and nets" ("Poetry and Social Relations" n.p.).

With his website project "MyNewIdea," Derksen moves from print to new media. To enter Derksen's website—what he calls "the reading space"—you click on an image of Russian Constructivist Elena Semenova's design of a Workers' Club Lounge (1926). You may not know what you are looking at until you click on "WHO" in the menu:

The information on the "WHO" link tells us that other images on the site are from another workers' club lounge—from Aleksandr Rodchenko's

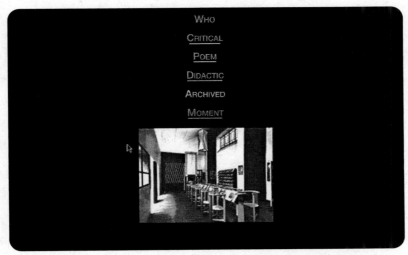

Figure 13. Jeff Derksen's website menu. "Reproduction of Russian Constructivist Elena Semenova's design of a workers' club lounge (1926)."

contribution to the 1925 *Exposition Internationale des Arts Decoratif et Industriels* held in Paris, which "did not progress past the 1:1 model stage: it was never built and put into use. This reading room represents a conceptual reading space where reading was also ideologically imagined as work (and workers as readers)."

"MyNewIdea" appears near "But is it Politics?"—a website Derksen worked on in collaboration with Sabine Bitter and Helmut Weber:

> "But is it politics?" flips the still-circulating question of "But is it art?" from the 70s in order to pose a new set of questions regarding cultural production's potential or effect. Art can no longer be imagined as an autonomous field, but is mediated and negotiated as any other social field. Today's politicized art practice that is engaged in the rearticulation of social, political and economical formations is confronted with a multilayered determining system of legitimation and identification. This system forecloses and appropriates the space and strategies that politicized art once claimed as its own site of opposition and legitimation. (Derksen, Bitter, Weber n.p.)[7]

Moving horizontally one line at a time, the text above runs across the bottom of the screen under a view, from a highway, of the backyards of a suburban streetscape, also moving across the screen, situating the reader overtly in a space "mediated and negotiated as any other social field."

On his website, Derksen uses the resources of web-based technology to bring into collision and intersection more ideological contradictions and elisions. He invites readers to enter the site, to engage with him in the work of unmasking ideology while remaining fully aware of the difficulties we encounter in trying to do so. If you click on "DIDACTIC," for example, you will find "JERK," the poem with which I began this chapter: "I want to see / the real relations / but you've got Nikes on and I like you / so I have to try and understand" (*Transnational* 10). Here is another section from that poem:

> The sun glints off the chrome bodies
> of the gondolas of late capitalism
> as they labour up the mountain.
> The mountain is named
> after a commodity. Art has made this
> a nonalienated view. Is that what
> we asked it to do? If "each day seems
> like a natural fact" and if "what we think
> changes how we act" should art not

reveal ideology
rather than naturalize it?

These old idealisms, they burn me up
These old idealisms, what do they cover up?
 (*Transnational* 9)

"JERK" was written in the fall of 1998 while Derksen was artist in residence at the Banff Centre for the Arts in Alberta. Clearly the "I" is positioned as the kind of "jerk" our culture can produce, one who grapples with the contradictory desire to have both an explicit and relentless politics and remain connected to the world as it has been given to him: "My idealistic belief / is that historical consciousness may come. / My sad cognitive mapping / is that overdetermined contradictions / don't lead to new social relations. / I want an art / more complicated than that" (*Transnational* 10).

 "MOMENT" links us to an image-text piece called "Perceived Accepted Suffered" where the following image-texts appear:

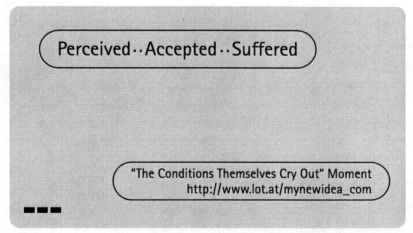

Figure 14. From Jeff Derksen's "'The Conditions Themselves Cry Out' Moment."

The images in / on / at these "moments" are either of a young white man on a motorcycle (see figs. 15 and 16) or of a high-tech sofa in bright green and orange. The images are repeated in various degrees of detail and the text is not linked to any one image. Both image and text repeat in several combinations. In fact, they become a moving image of what Derksen describes in *Dwell*: "My tropes peel off the / landscape, moving in an apparently opposite direction / to what I have to 'leave out.' Becomes body. Here is / the closest place of social and beauty. The sentence / that focuses attention" (38).

Figure 15. From Jeff Derksen's "'The Conditions Themselves Cry Out' Moment."

As this example demonstrates, Derksen's "here"—his primary unit of composition—is quite often what looks like an ordinary sentence. But these sentences are constructed to point out the contradictions inherent in the most common of discourses. Consider another example as illustrated in figure 15. If "I" think I can "question authority" and the question itself can win, what is my relation to authority? How did "the question" get so much power? What is the question? What does it mean if the question, rather than the questioner, can win? And what of this question?

By asking whether a system of power relations—capitalism—can experience a highly individualized human emotion—can it be embarrassed?—this question points out the gap between such a system and the actual human beings who suffer under it. In these ways, Derksen aggressively, ironically, mischievously inhabits the dehumanizing discourses of his—and our—moment in history in order to get us to see them. (See fig. 16.)

Web technology has facilitated Derksen's representation of what he calls, in the first section of *Dwell*, the "Interface": "Interface of self and place passes me through a/translation machine" (3). The effect of this poetics is to foreground the interface between the putative "inside," which he defines as "the reiterative act of a community," and a similarly putative "outside," a "powerful if mistakenly totalizing, value-defining discursive exterior":

Figure 16. From Jeff Derksen's "'The Conditions Themselves Cry Out' Moment."

> You had a lovely critique
> and you looked great, sexy
> really, the way your world-market
> pants might shock the bourgeoisie
> into consciousness. But these days
> I'm yearning not for a little outside
> to call homeland, although I like good
> design too and do feel that "workers"
> (morphed "multitude") also live
> outside of quotation marks
> in this "the highest stage"—
> but now I'm wanting transformation
> rather than "structural adjustment"
> to go with the primitive accumulation
> and worn contradictions. Not more
> of these natural facts ("globalization is").
>
> ("Jerk," *Transnational* 9–10)

These interfaces where Derksen's poems "dwell" reproduce the energetic, humourous, and acutely accurate recognition that one is complicit in the very ideology one wants to critique: "I still answer the phone as if I were 'employed': that / reminds me that the structure [I] hate, hates [me]" (*Dwell* 12).

Always attentive to the interests served by both multinational and disciplinary boundaries, Derksen's move to web culture has accompanied his widening interest in the discourses of architecture and geopolitics. *Transnational Muscle Cars* opens, for example, with a quotation from David Harvey: "But we cannot make either our history or our geography under historical-geographical conditions of our own choosing." Like his earlier poetry, Derksen's work on the web involves a desire to make an art complex enough to counter the dehumanizing effects of globalization: "an art more complicated than The Gap." His answer to the question"what happens to the poetics of place when your only / 'place' is your body and it's not moving?" (*Dwell* 63) is that you can be "Happy Locally, Sad Geopolitically" (*Transnational* 11). Derksen's website, like his poetry itself, disrupts the surface of the local with global effects and in so doing makes room for a geopolitics of poetic form.

Notes

1 He has published six books of poetry and his articles appear in scholarly books and journals across North America, including Mark Wallace and Steven Marks's *Telling It Slant: Avant-Garde Poetics of the 1990s*, Bruce Andrews's *Paradise and Method: Poetics and Praxis*, Paul Delaney's *Vancouver: Representing the Postmodern City*, and Douglas Barbour's *Beyond TISH*. Other articles appear in *Cross Cultural Poetics*, *C Magazine*, *Open Letter*, *West Coast Line*, and *Poetics Journal*. As well, he edited the "Disgust and Overdetermination: A Poetics Issue" of *Open Letter* (10.1 Winter 1998).

2 See Derksen's PhD dissertation, "Globalism and the Role of the Cultural."

3 He attended the David Thompson University Centre in Nelson, BC, where he earned a BA in Creative Writing and English (with distinction) conferred through the University of Victoria. In the early 1990s he moved to Calgary where he earned an MA (1995) and a PhD (2000) in English from the University of Calgary and held Killam Memorial Fellowships (1996–1999) and Social Sciences and Humanities Research Council of Canada Doctoral Fellowships (1995–1999). In 1999–2000 he held a Fulbright Scholarship through the Canada-US Fulbright Program, which he carried out at the City University of New York Graduate Center.

4 See their website at < http://www.KSW.net > and the chronology entry in 1984.

5 "Poetry and Social Relations" and "Poetry and Other Rearticulatory Practices," unpublished.

6 A selection from *Dwell*—"Host Nation, Host Society"—was included in Messerli's *The Gertrude Stein Awards in Innovative American Poetry 1993–94*. Derksen's poetry also appears in Sharon Thesen's *The New Long Poem Anthology*, Klobucar and Barnholden's *Writing Class: The Kootenay School of Writing Anthology* (New

Star 1999), Douglas Messerli's *The Poet's Calendar for the Millennium* (Sun and Moon 1999), and Jerome McGann's guest-edited issue of *Verse* on "Postmodern Poetries" (1990).

7 "MyNewIdea" is linked to "But Is it Politics?" a project initiated alongside the artists' residency "The Long March," 5 October–11 December 1998 at the Banff Centre for the Arts, by Sabine Bitter and Helmut Weber. The project is hosted on their site <www.lot.at>.

∎

Excessively Reading Erin Mouré

Susan Rudy

> The truest things, spoken here,
> would sound like nonsense.
> Erin Mouré, "Rain 10," *wsw*

● With each book since *Furious* won the Governor General's award for poetry in 1988,[1] Erin Mouré has posed increasingly complicated challenges to herself as a writer and to her readers. The titles of her recent books tell the story: *A Frame of the Book / The Frame of A Book* (1999); *Pillage Laud: Cauterizations, Vocabularies, Catigas, Topiary, Prose: Poems* (1999); *Sheep's Vigil by a Fervent Person: A Translelation of Alberto Caeiro / Fernando Pessoa's O Guardador de Rebanhos* (2001); and *O Cidadán* (2002). The first has two titles; the second uses an unfamiliar vocabulary; the third an unknown genre (a "translelation"), the fourth, well, what is a "Cidadán" and what language is she writing in anyway? In a long epigraph to *O Cidadán*, Mouré explains: "I, a woman: o cidadán. As if 'citizen' in our time can only be dislodged when spoken from a 'minor' tongue, one historically persistent despite external and internal pressures, and by a woman who bears—as lesbian in a civic frame—a *policed sexuality*" (n.p.).[2] As she speaks "the truest things" about living in her body, with her desires, at her—and our—moment in history, Mouré agrees with Gilles Deleuze, whom she cites in an epigraph to *Pillage Laud*: "experimentation on ourself, is our only identity, our single chance for all the combinations that inhabit us" (n.p.).

As early as "The Acts" (*Furious* 83–99), Mouré recognizes that changing "the weight and force of English" will not necessarily "make women's speaking possible" (98). Rather, she wants to "move the force in any language, create a slippage, even for a moment ... to decentre the 'thing,' unmask the relation" (98). To this end, she writes in excess of signification; refuses conventional word order and usage; redeploys grammar, punctuation, syntax, and spelling; juxtaposes as many as ten versions of a poem; and ignores the conventions of pronominal and prepositional reference. Mouré sees the "accessible" as "just a way of reading" (Williamson 210), and in asking that we read in excess of signification, generates different ways of reading and other points of access. Not that all readers will be willing or able to meet her high expectations. Book reviewers often describe Mouré's poems as "too obscure, too difficult—ultimately too dangerous" (Denisoff, "Merger, She Wrote" 114). If these poems are dangerous and difficult, however, it is not just because they are formally experimental but also because they not only expose and critique the realities of many women's lives; they affirm the ongoing possibility of alternatives.

In an interview with Pauline Butling and me, Mouré translated France Théoret's epigraph to *Sheepish Beauty, Civilian Love*:

> There's another world, I'm sure of it. My interior voice, especially that of my mother that I hear, affirms this. I am troubled by this experience because that voice of my mother in(to) myself seems charged with contradictions. I never heard my mother pronounce the word happiness. I imagine that it has to do with that—with an undefinable happiness the search for which is born in present unhappiness.[3]

The "voice" of the mother is "charged with contradictions." Although unable to "pronounce" the word happiness, she is still in search of it. Like an "undefinable happiness," the truest things in Mouré's texts may sound like nonsense because they celebrate what Foucault called "illegitimate sexualities" (*The History of Sexuality* 4). Stephen Scobie argues that Mouré uses a "'strategic incoherence' to keep the discourse open, to leave no settled position for the reader" (71). But on occasion a settled, if unsettling, position is offered to the reader—albeit a counterdominant one.

Mouré's poetry not only takes as its subject and form the ways language is not working in the interests of desiring women. It often speaks directly—and only—to women, a mode of address that is often unrecognizable, even incoherent, in the dominant discourse.[4] Note the speaker's articulation of this (dis)location as "I am not, have not, will not" in the passage below:

> The room hot full of women. The room hot full of
> women's whispers in the foreign place a few blocks
> from home. My t-shirt & beige shorts, their clothes
> & lifted knees, the floor full of women & I see her
> there. Stand away from her. The seam folded &
> sewn shut between us, she smiles over the border
> here I watch her arms listening she looks up. Her
> smile & curious distance. The seam I break with
> my eyes breaking the seam the space between the
> real & imagined meetings not to be broken I break it
> with my eyes. On the real floor in real windows
> in real room several sewn & buttressed borders.

I am not, have not, will not.
    ("Meeting," Seams, *Sheepish Beauty* 51)

Through the pronoun "her," the poem interpellates women readers, the rhetorical effect of which is to include them as lesbians: "The trouble is, the pronouns: *her, & her*. No one / knows who they belong to!" (What Is: Jeanne-Mance & Villeneuve, *Sheepish Beauty* 59).

Since *Furious*, Mouré has made use of formal innovation for the purposes of feminist critique. "Unfurled & Dressy" (*Furious* 51), for example, collapses the relations between women readers, writers, and lovers:

> Frontally speaking […]
> It is your voice which I am speaking over & over
> because I like to hear you
> inside my mouth
> where I can touch our futures with my tongue
> & throw down my names & embrace you
> & forget which one of us I am
> Frontally speaking
> Frontally speaking.
>   (51)

The phrase "Frontally speaking," the first and last lines of this excerpt, invites readers to imagine what "speaking" "frontally" might be like. Is the speaker, in "frontally speaking," giving an opening address? Or is she just speaking "in front" of me? Is she speaking forthrightly? Or is it aggressive (a full-frontal attack)? And if it "is your voice which I am speaking over & over," what am I doing while she is speaking frontally? Repeated six times, the phrase "Frontally speaking" names the impossible relationship lesbians have to the sign "woman," a relationship not available on the surface of sense, in reality, since "what seems is not what is" ("Seams," *Sheepish Beauty* 50). By the end of the poem, however, the phrase accumulates a specifically lesbian sexual connotation (to be more direct, two women—in the poem? reading the poem? after reading the poem?—are facing each other, making love), and suggests speaking frontally can be done only with another woman who also forgets "which one of us I am" ("Unfurled & Dressy," *Furious* 51).

Also in *Furious*, "Betty" speaks with a woman's name to liberate the unspoken, to name the difference between women speaking and women being heard, between women speaking as subjects and women being recognized by others, and by each other, as subjects: "women / speaking light words into the cups of each other's fingers."

> Our small hands frozen, without fingers, claws of ice holding stiff snouts of fur,
>
> strange sprung words leaking
>
> into our sentences.
> "*A-girls,*" the 2 year old girl called out at the supper table.
> Let's not say "Grace" again, she said, let's say "Betty." (78)

Not a naming but a "saying," the poem speaks women otherwise in its pun on "hey girls," in the hyphenated "A-girls." Mouré, like the filmmaker Yvonne Rainer, invents a new spelling of her name "in the direction of unwomanliness. Not a new woman, not non-woman or misanthropist or anti-woman, and not non-practicing lesbian. Maybe unwoman is also the wrong term. A-woman is closer. A-womanly. A-womanliness" (qtd. in de Lauretis, "Strategies of Coherence" 123).

"Speaking of Which" works on the ambiguity and yet specificity of the seemingly innocuous shifters "which," "this," and "something" (*Furious* 38–39). It requires readers able to attach signifieds to these signifiers, readers who "know us" by "women's / talk & whispers, by these signs" (39), readers who become "us." It figures a space where women walk away from certain words into "uncertain territory," toward a naming as yet unspecified:

> because this fury is our hardest core, because the bar is full of women's talk & whispers, by these signs you shall know us,
>
> the bright oxygen, the air inside us who stared
> then walked away, from the word *cock,* & *ravishment*
> To name what our own tongues will call *something.* (39)

The movement into the infinitive—"to name"—and the specificity and yet potentiality of the word "*something,*" these movements of desire out of possibility and in contradiction, are what most characterize Erin Mouré's work, making all of it "excessible" (*wsw* 107)—that which appears beyond what she calls the "visible spectrum."[5] Her writing moves toward "the word for this," "the green word."[6] Like the theatre's green room (a place that accommodates actors when they are offstage) her words "for this" are waiting to go on, to be visible, to be heard. But to "create a slippage, even for a moment" (*Furious* 98), she will need us to read as excessively as she does.

In *Pillage Laud*, a more recent text, Mouré draws on the uncanny potential in software-generated prose. At its Calgary launch she explained that, to write the book, she selected "from pages of computer-generated sentences" (what she calls "MacProse") to produce "lesbian sex poems":

> Where were we racing? To spread was laughter.
> Her knees I wantonly adored
>
> While sex was the structure's industry,
> both were appearing.
>
> The vested interest balanced. A master had slipped
> A riposte her contusion.
>
> Such a twelfth floor: pleasure.
> Vocabularies were those empires.
> Wit inside wounds.
>
> To cry out determined her. Because we won't trust fate,
> bereaved are balances.
>
> What can atmosphere with
> vocabularies delight?
>
> We have desired those knees.
> So arbitrary a vulva.
>   ("Oakland" 5)[7]

This passage from "Oakland" appears in one of thirteen sections named after particular cities or neighbourhoods. Other sections include "High Prairie," "Bowness," "Burnaby," "Rachel-Julien," and "Anaximenes." Readers from California, Alberta, Montreal, or British Columbia may attach signifieds to these signifiers. But real and imagined places are given equal attention. The last section—"Anaximenes"—is named after a place on the moon where Apollo 13 did *not* land.

One of the first pages of the book also looks like a table of contents but is not. Instead it is a "Vocabulary Grid" with sections listed according to their email suffixes. But rather than the suffixes conventionally used for countries—".ca" or ".uk" for example—the real and imagined local place names are linked to a list of nouns (see fig. 17). Each section consists of six to ten pages. Each page repeats its particular vocabulary grid in italics along the bottom. The grid functions as a kind of chorus. Because the nouns are linked to cities and neighbourhoods, the local and social context of the production of meaning is foregrounded. Most overtly, readers of this text

SECRET DE LA RENCONTRE

Intus haec ago, in aula ingenti memoriae meae.
St. Augustine, *Confessions,* Bk. 10, Sec. 14

Pillage Laud – Vocabulary Grid

.Oakland	*fate sex vocabulary library citizen presence thwack*	1
.High Prairie	*prairie pioneer cattle beds feeling field*	11
.Roselawn	*fist flow archive finger textile book ambition congregation*	19
.Bowness	*vandal tissue curl plaster smell body bent*	25
.Fairview	*childhood fist grace belt feeling mustard burst charm*	31
.Bloorcourt	*airport stroke maid toast envelope belt whoosh vagina*	37
.Burnaby	*doctrine girl bath library essay discipline extend hotels*	43
.tout cela se passe à l'intérieur de moi-même, dans l'ample palais de ma mémoire.		st.a.
.Rachel-Julien	*speech power exchange metabolism hospital lisp*	49
.Burnside	*livings vesicle split texts gallery burst swollen stroke*	55
.Glorieta de Bilbao	*harness size plug bottom top vibrate camp ambition*	63
.Fra Mauro Hills	*legs vestibule vagina marriage envelope grieve flow*	77
.Anaximenes	*history belief event burnt air beginning temperature law*	83

In Tenebris, or *The Gate*	87
"to exist is reading"	95
Pillage's Lauds	98

Figure 17. Vocabulary grid from *Pillage Laud*.

become aware of the unexpected surplus of meaning *we* can attach to words by confronting them in unusual and unexpected combinations and contexts. While none of the "vocabularies" in Mouré's text are unfamiliar—the words "*fate sex vocabulary library citizen presence thwack*" generated the "Oakland" section for example—their randomly generated syntactic combinations place them in strange contexts and make their combinations entirely unpredictable: "so arbitrary a vulva," for example. Thus while the basic unit of composition—the sentence—is familiar, the relations between words is endlessly shifting.

The sentences in *Pillage Laud* are gathered into what Mouré calls "couplets." Her invention of one-, two-, and three-line "couplets" draws our attention to the assumption that, in culture as in poetry, a meaningful "couplet," like a couple, consists of two. She shows us other possibilities. Unlike speech, the freeware program "MacProse" is "incapable of generating a cliché because it has no culture and it has never met anyone."[8] By generating sentences using "MacProse"—which is capable of working with a vocabularly of only 1500 words—she foregrounds the myriad effects language has the potential to have on us, the limitless connotations that can be generated. When used in such deliberately unconventional ways, we see both the possibilities and restrictions of language usage. It is easy to see Mouré's experiments as "nonsense"; it is more difficult to see them as generating an excess of meaning. For Mouré, textual experimentation is "our single chance" (Deleuze); it generates and draws us toward the risks we can take in language and reminds us that, by not pushing the limits of language, we risk being reduced to clichés defined by endlessly repeatable but inadequate—even inhuman—significations.

Mouré's work demonstrates how and why "The truest things, spoken here, / *would* sound like nonsense" (italics mine). For the "truest things"—in this case, the fact that women can and do speak and desire—to make sense, the relationship between what can be heard and what is said must shift. Consider an experiment from *wsw*: two very similar-looking poems with the same title are set across from one another. The first—"The Beauty of Furs"—documents the talk among women:

At lunch with the girls, the younger ones are talking about furs, & what looks good with certain hair colours. Red fox looks no good with my hair, says one. White fox looks snobbish, beautiful but snobbish, says another one. […] I remember, I say, I remember my mother had a muskrat coat, & when she wore it & you grabbed her too hard by the arm, fur came out. Eileen, fifteen years older than me, starts to laugh, & puts her hand on my shoulder, laughing. We both start laughing. I start to explain to her that it was old; my mother wore it to church on Sunday & got upset if we grabbed her arm. We're laughing so hard, now the young ones are looking at us, together we are laughing, in our house there was a beaver coat like that Eileen said, then suddenly we are crying, crying for those fur coats & the pride of our mothers, our mothers' pride, smell of the coat at church on Sunday, smell of the river, & us so small, our hair wet, kneeling in that smell of fur beside our mothers. (68)

THE BEAUTY OF FURS: A SITE GLOSSARY

Later you realize it is a poem about being born, the smell of the fur is your mother birthing you & your hair is wet not slicked back but from the wetness of womb, the fur coat the hugest fur of your mother the cunt of your mother from which you have emerged & you cower in this smell The fur coat the sex of women reduced to decoration, & the womb the place of birth becomes the church in which you are standing, the womb reduced to decoration, where women are decoration, where the failure of decoration is the humiliation of women, to wear these coats, these emblems of their own bodies, in church on Sunday, children beside them The church now the place of birth & rebirth, they say *redemption*, everyone knows what this signifies & the mother is trying to pay attention, all the mothers, my mother, & we are children, I am children, a child with wet hair cowlick slicked down perfect, no humiliation, the site still charged with the smell of the river, the coat smell of the river, smell of the birth canal, caught in the drown-set is to be stopped from being born, is to be clenched in the water unable to breathe or see the night sky, the *coyohts* calling me upward, as if in these circumstances, so small beside my mother, I could be born now, but cannot, can I, because we are inside this hugest womb which has already denied us, in which we are decoration, in which men wear dresses & do the cooking, & the slicked hair is not the wet hair of birth but the hair of decoration, as if I could be born now, I am born, my snout warm smelling the wet earth of my mother's fur

Figure 18. Erin Mouré's "The Beauty of Furs: A Site Glossary."

Across the page (see fig. 18) "The Beauty of Furs: A Site Glossary" (69) comments on what the women say about their mothers' fur coats. Both are prose poems; both occupy, as few of Mouré's poems do, the whole width of the line. But "A Site Glossary" overtly rereads and interprets "The Beauty of Furs." It inhabits a space similar to that of the first poem (both occupy one page in the same book) and yet is on site (in the collection) differently. "A Site Glossary" interprets "The Beauty of Furs" and gives meaning to the women's shared narrative, pleasure, and memory. In its invocation of "you" and "we" it also invites ongoing interpretation and analysis, seeks other readers, other poems: "Later you realize it is a poem about being born, the smell of the fur is / your mother birthing you & your hair is wet not slicked back but from the / wetness of womb, the fur coat the hugest fur of your mother the cunt of / your mother" (69).

The communal narrative—the girls eating lunch, telling stories, laughing—in the first poem makes the intimate, reflective, and yet shared feminist analysis in "The Beauty of Furs: A Site Glossary" possible. The poem demonstrates the ways "you" arrive at such a thought, how "you" might read when you are not alone. Since much of Mouré's work invites, indeed requires, a feminist reader, she shares Nicole Brossard's sense that "it is not in the writing that a poetic text is political, it is in the reading that it becomes political" (78).[9] Addressed by a feminist, women readers of Mouré's poems are addressed as subjects, and are able to experience what this address enables: subjectivity, agency, and desire.

Erin Mouré is not naive about how political change can be effected. When Janice Williamson asked, in an interview, about "the relationship between poetry and social change" Mouré replied: "I don't think it's possible to talk about poetry in those terms. [...] Poetry should bug people. Then *they* can change" (208). She "bugs" us because she insists that like reality itself, poems should acknowledge several versions. "Three Versions" in *Furious* begins with an epigraph from Gail Scott: "Why do you have to choose a definitive version?" (75).[10] Beginning with *Furious* Mouré's books have increasingly required her—and us—to be aware of how many versions we are reading.[11] The rereading, thinking, theorizing subject is, as Mouré said to Dennis Denisoff, "pulled into the poems themselves" (130). "Visible Spectrum" in *Sheepish Beauty*, illustrates:

> In such a territory we found ourselves. The visible
> spectrum. In which we saw for the first time
> the light of the other, the curious crown of light
> inhabiting the other, released by talk &
> hesitation, non-talk, released by
> silent looking. The cup of coffee held in the fingers,
> held & released by the tips of the fingers,
> their soft surge of capillary blood giving a shimmer
> of colour,
> of memory,
>
> the "speech" of motion, the sound of, continual. (33)

To "see" one needs light; to see otherwise, "the curious crown of light / inhabiting the other," what the poem later refers to as "the 'speech' of motion, the sound of, continual." Reading. Excessively.

Because they take women seriously and speak to women directly, Mouré's poems politicize their women readers by affirming that, as she asserts as early as *Domestic Fuel* (1985), "The Words Mean What We Say" (48). Mouré challenges readers to notice the ways that women are not included in a notion of humanity that takes as its signifier the word "man": "The word human being has stood for men / until now" Mouré writes in "Ocean Poem" (*Furious* 48). Her use of the past tense, "the word ... has stood for," rather than the more common "the word stands for," reminds us that the meanings of words do change. The possibility of being human "has stood for" men "until now [in this instance of reading; as we women read together]. / Until now" (48):

> & the sentence goes on & on excessive I don't want it to
> end the blank space beyond the period hurts I want
> everything to occur before it & you don't hear me & the
> snow is excess & the flowers are excess
> & as for me standing here
>
> *what am I writing*
>
> this too is excess
>   ("Excess" wsw 106)

Erin Mouré does not "perceive [herself] to be this transparent kind of writer that's speaking the poem to you, like 'I, the poet, will now speak.' [...] the centred speaking subject that is 'entire' apart from context" (Denisoff, "Acknowledging" 130). Rather, her poems insist that we question the "*I writing.*"

One continues to wonder, of course, about the relationship between the poet and the text. Again Brossard is useful. When writing, Brossard says, she is "the same person, but a more thoughtful person and therefore a person that is ahead of herself. Between the individual and the writer there is a free space, a mysterious landscape where one discovers and dares things that the individual cannot afford. It is in that space that I learn about myself and can transform myself" (interview in O'Brien 137). In "that space," what Mouré calls "the gaps we long for" ("It Remained Unheard" 83)—where "what seems is not what is" (*Sheepish Beauty* 50)—the "sewn & buttressed border" ("Meeting," *Sheepish* 51) breaks open. To cite a passage from *Pillage Laud*, "to exist is reading" (n.p.); writing exists to be read excessively—by the poet and others. Attending to what "seems" through words that both "seam" and undo reading, in the "free space" that she opens up, we too can transform ourselves.

Notes

1   Shortly after *Furious* won the Governor General's Award, Sonja Skarstedt asked "was Canada (finally) offering its stamp of approval to feminism, vis-à-vis one of its most visible proponents" (10)? While Skarstedt recognizes the inseparability of Mouré's poetry and her feminism, the reviewer participates in the reinscription of gender binaries [masculinity and femininity] insofar as she sees Mouré's interrogation of form—what Mouré calls "a theory of deregulation regarding (the English) language" (Skarstedt 10) as being for the purposes of legitimating "the *feminine* voice" (10, italics mine). Not "feminine" but feminist, Mouré's poems make visible, not the feminine voice, not even "her" voice, but feminists' voices, and lesbians' subjectivities: as Mouré once said in an interview, "I always consider my poems to be public events" (O'Brien 233).

2   Here is the full passage: "To intersect a word: citizen. To find out what could intend/distend it, today. *O cidadán.* A word we recognize though we know not its language. It can't be found in French, Spanish, Portuguese dictionaries. It seems inflected 'masculine.' And, as such, it has a feminine supplement. Yet if I said 'a cidadá' I would only be speaking of 52 percent of the world, and it's the remainder that inflects the generic, the *cidadán.* How can a woman then inhabit the general (visibly and semantically skewing it)? How can she speak from the generic at all, without vanishing behind its screen of transcendent value? In this book, I decided, I will step into it just by a move in discourse. I, a woman: o cidadán. As if 'citizen' in our time can only be dislodged when spoken from a 'minor' tongue, one historically persistent despite external and internal pressures, and by a woman who bears—as lesbian in a civic frame—*a policed sexuality.* Unha cidadán: a semantic pandemonium. If a name's force or power is 'a *historicity*... a sedimentation, a repetition that congeals,' (Butler) can the name be reinvested or infest, fenestrated ... set in motion again? Unmoored? Her semblance? Upsetting the structure/ stricture even momentarily. *To en(in)dure, perdure. / To move the force in any language, create a slippage, even for a moment ... to decentre the 'thing,' unmask the relation ....*"

3   France Thèoret, from "Ceci n'est pas un lac" in *L'Homme qui peignait Staline.* Significantly, Mouré translated the phrase "*je n'ai jamais entendu ma mère prononcer le mot bonheur,*" not as "I never heard my mother *speak* the word happiness," but as "I never heard my mother *pronounce* the word happiness" (italics mine). The difference between speaking and pronouncing in French is slight; in English it has more resonances. "Pronouncing" implies not only speaking, but a way of speaking, reminding us that the same letters can sound—and therefore signify—differently. Speakers of new languages quickly realize that unless their words are pronounced "correctly" they will not be understood; they will not have spoken because they will have not been heard. Women speaking in any language often have the opposite experience—of speaking meaningfully without having been heard to be saying anything. Women do not often make pronouncements. Especially for an anglophone living in Montreal the difference between speaking and pronouncing might be the difference between uttering meaningless sounds (speaking) and being heard to be making sense (pronouncing). In an email message to me dated

24 April 1995, Mouré explained that her translation had a great deal to do with the practice of Montreal English. She wrote: "in Montreal we often use French words directly in English, with the French 'weight' or meaning predominating, even though the word has another predominant meaning in English." While taking her point, I nonetheless cite this slippage as an instance of the ways that meaning's excesses do give readers opportunities to think about real relations of power, and power's relation to language.

4 In the Williamson interview Mouré responded to the question "Who am I addressing?" by saying "I'm talking to women, and if I'm talking to men that's I think when my furious, my terrible aliveness, becomes rage. Because I have this strong sense that there are lots of problems right now with heterosexual love. Men don't acknowledge their love for each other in the same way that women do. A lot of heterosexual love is men using women as an intermediary to get at their love for each other" (216).

5 See for example *Visible Spectrum* (1992) her chapbook in Roy Miki and Irene Niechoda's pomflit series.

6 I quote here from "THE GREEN WORD," part 5 of the long poem "The Trepanation: Cinq Morceaux en forme de Poire" (wsw 35). The title of her book of selected poems is also *The Green Word*.

7 The reading was at Pages Bookstore, Kensington Road, Calgary, Alberta, 30 September 1999.

8 Explained in her introductory remarks at the Calgary launch.

9 Brossard is talking about her experience of writing and commenting on her own process. She says: "While writing this essay [for a series of lectures on "The Politics of Poetic Form"], I found myself saying: 'It is not in the writing that a poetic text is political, it is in the reading that it becomes political'" (78). The form which Brossard chooses to say what she says—she quotes herself, she "reads" what she "found [her]self" saying—exemplifies her statement. It is in reading that "she," as reader, becomes politicized.

10 Many of Mouré's books are dedicated to the Montreal novelist and essayist Gail Scott. The dedication in *Furious* exemplifies the intensity of Mouré's affection: "(Immeasurable) thanks to Gail Scott, whose fiction, voice, and thinking helped seed the light that is in this book."

11 See, for example, "Executive Suite" and "Corrections: 'Executive Suite'" in *Sheepish Beauty* (14–19) or "The Acts" in *Furious*. "The Acts" are also the first example of the metacommentary and footnoting that is now regularly incorporated into Mouré's poems.

Lisa Robertson's Poetics of "Soft Architecture"

Susan Rudy

> Architecture, fashion—yes, even the weather [...] stand in
> the cycle of the eternally self-same, until the collective seizes
> upon them in politics and history emerges.
>
> Walter Benjamin, *The Arcades Project*[1]

> Repeat rather than narrate.
>
> Lisa Robertson, *The Apothecary*

> What is fact is not necessarily human.
>
> Lisa Robertson, *The Weather*

● Born in Toronto in 1961 with both Canadian and British citizenship, Lisa
Robertson currently lives in Paris. Since 1979 she has been a camp cook and
private cook on Saltspring Island, BC, and in Normandy, France (1979–83);
a student of English and fine and performing arts at Simon Fraser Univer-
sity in Vancouver (1984–88); the proprietor/bookseller of Proprioception
Books in Vancouver (1988–94); a member of Vancouver's Kootenay School
of Writing collective (1990–98); a visiting fellow at Cambridge (1999); and
a board member of Artspeak Gallery, Vancouver (1990–2002). Perhaps
most notoriously, she is among what Ann Vickery calls the "new genera-
tion of language-centred writers in Canada" whose "literary entrée" was
marked by the New Poetics Colloquium organized by the Kootenay School
of Writing in 1985 (129).[2] Since 1995 Lisa Robertson has been a freelance
writer, editor, and teacher. Her poetry appears in journals and magazines
across Canada, the USA, Great Britain, Australia, France, and New Zealand
and she has published seven chapbooks and four books: *Xeclogue* (1993; 2nd
ed. 2000), *Debbie: An Epic* (1997), *The Weather* (2001), and *Occasional
Works and Seven Walks from the Office for Soft Architecture* (2003).[3] *Debbie*
was nominated for the Governor General's Award in 1998; *The Weather* won
the Relit Award for Poetry in 2002. She has also published dozens of poet-
ics essays, talks and reviews, art and architectural criticism, and, under the
pseudonym Swann, a quarterly column for *Decorators' Horoscopes*.[4]

Not surprisingly, Robertson's methodology was influenced by art and
architecture even before she read poetics or theory. In a *PhillyTalks* conver-
sation with Steve McCaffery she writes: "I started to read architectural
theory before any exposure to contemporary avant-garde poetics. Then it

was Heidegger—*Poetry Dwelling Thinking* [*sic: Poetry Language Thought*]—
was important—and other phenomenological approaches. Bachelard was
a huge figure for me (*The Poetics of Space*)" (32). In her discussion with
McCaffery, Robertson cites not only the architect and architectural theo-
rist Rem Koolhaas, but also Judith Butler, Michel de Certeau, Gilles Deleuze,
Michel Foucault, Elizabeth Grosz, Raymond Williams, and Monique Wit-
tig, among many others. Her poetics is research-based, dissatisfied with "the
abjected notion of gendered otherness [she] came across in some feminist
and psychoanalytic work" (*PhillyTalks* 33). The "big question," she writes,
"was how could a subject construct temporary agencies, when the social-
sexual axis would always have already cast her outside of authority, power,
agency" (33)?

   The Weather begins to answer such questions. Created as a site-specific
work while she was a visiting "fellow" at Cambridge University in the late
1990s, Robertson follows Walter Benjamin's epigraph from *The Arcades Pro-
ject* and seizes upon the "huge open metaphor of the weather" (Robertson
and McCaffery, *PhillyTalks* #17) to create a long poem.[5] Based on "intense
yet eccentric research in the rhetorical structure of English meteorological
description" (*The Weather* 80) at Cambridge, Robertson read Wordsworth's
Prelude, Wells's *Essay on Dew*, Howard's *Essay on the Modification of Clouds*,
and Aikin's *Essay on the Application of Natural History to Poetry*. Other
research involved listening to the BBC shipping forecasts at 1:00 a.m., mak-
ing friends by talking about the weather, reading chaos theory and Hesiod,
and looking at John Constable's cloud sketches with their written annota-
tions: "all of these texts, broadcasts, conversations and their rhythms con-
tributed to the composition of this poem. It is weather, and it is for
friendship" (*The Weather* 80; *PhillyTalks* #17, "Newsletter" n.p.). As such,
it demonstrates, in Gertrude Stein's words, that "Nature is not natural and
that is natural enough."[6]

   Following a reading in Philadelphia in October 2000, Robertson talked
about the process of writing *The Weather*: she wanted to find a way to re-
present change itself, how it occurs across time. She found a vocabulary by
using terms for local conditions (those of the West measured in days,
weeks, months and in terms of the earth, globe, sky), the days of the week,
the weather in England (a phatic and for her non-representational dis-
course). Her intervention begins with a section called "SUNDAY" followed
by six additional sections corresponding to the days of the week. The
"days" begin with long (three- to five-page) prose poems and end with
two-page lyric poems.[7] As the opening lines of "Sunday" exemplify, Robert-

son's prose poem utilizes a "protracted sentence structure based on repetition:"[8]

> About here. All along here. All along here. All the soft coercions. Maybe black and shiny, wrinkled. A sky marbled with failures. A patterned revision. And got here about one o'clock. And got here wet to the skin. And here are houses too, here and there. And luck, too, whenever. And here experienced the benefits. And here again wisps. And here gained real knowledge. And here got into the wild. And here, too. Arrived here about two o'clock. Here alone the length. There is a bed of chalk under this. (2)

"SUNDAY" is not "about *here*" (italics mine). Rather, through the repetition of the word "here" an alternative structure emerges: the relentlessness of the long prose line is undercut by another pattern building within. Watch what happens when I change the line breaks to emphasize the repetition of the word "here":

> *Here* is a house.
> *Here* is a system. […]
> *Here* as everywhere else. […]
> In short, not *here*.
>   (italics mine, 3–4)

Like "here"—any house, any system, anywhere—reality is a human construction, a "fact that is not necessarily human" (20). Such facts and realities both establish the present and build on layers of fiction from the past: "upon a bed of chalk" (3–5).

Following the long-line prose sections named after the days of the week, the "lyric" sections are all entitled "RESIDENCE AT C_____." These sections consist of short lines, the punctuation varies, only the first-person singular pronoun is employed:[9]

> Give me hackneyed words because
> they are good. Brocade me the whole body
> of terrestrial air. Say spongy ground
> with its soft weeds. Say self because it can. (14)

This section ends with the word "Sincerity" (15). With its "hackneyed words," this self-reflexive poem reflects on the lyric genre, the "it" that can "say self," that "say[s] self because it can" (14).

At the end of *The Weather* we find a section called "porchverse." Lyric in tone, more minimal than the "ʀᴇsɪᴅᴇɴᴄᴇ ᴀᴛ ᴄ_____" sections, it functions as both an appendix and a textual "porch" on which to rest:

> The porch unclasps each word
> of what I say: are these words
> perhaps nothing in July?
> What makes pronouns, problems.
>   (75)

This "porch" that "unclasps each word / of what I say" provides another layer of defamiliarization, another questioning of the status of language that, "like 'pronouns, problems'" is made. But by what? For whom?

"Mᴏɴᴅᴀʏ" overtly investigates the attraction and malleability of ideology: "First all belief is paradise. So pliable a medium. A time / not very long. A transparency caused. A conveyance of / rupture. A subtle transport" (10). The energy generated by the repetition of two seemingly innocuous words (*a* and *and*) becomes evident when the long prose line is again broken to reveal the repetitious sentence structure and vocabulary:

> *A* time not very long.
> *A* transparency caused.
> *A* conveyance of rupture.
> *A* subtle transport.
>   Scant *and* rare.
> Deep in the opulent morning, blissful regions,
>   hard *and* slender.
>   Scarce *and* scant.
>   Quotidian *and* temperate.

Let's "begin afresh in the realms of the atmosphere" (10), the poem suggests; let's take on the weather as system since "The sky is complicated and flawed and we're up there in it" (10).

Interrupting the "meteorological surface" ("Webcast Reading" n.p.) of the poem is a radical feminist politics that challenges the "dream of obedience and authority" (19). In "ᴛᴜᴇsᴅᴀʏ" Robertson invokes the first names of a number of women, many of them recognizable as first-wave radical feminists (Ti-Grace Atkinson, Shulamith Firestone, Valerie Solanis):

> Days heap upon
> us. Where is Ti-Grace. But darker at the bottom than the
> top. Days heap upon us. Where is Christine. Broken on

the word culture. But darker at the bottom than the top. Days heap upon us. Where is Valerie. Pulling the hard air into her lung. The life crumbles open. But darker at the bottom than the top. Days heap upon us. Where is Patty. (18)

Again, the underlying structural repetition becomes apparent when the lines are broken. This passage continues:[10]

> Days heap upon us. Where is Shulamith.
>   Abolishing the word love.
> The radical wing crumbles / open.
> The scorn is not anticipated.
> We have given our / surface.
>   Darker at the top than the bottom.
> Except one / large opening with others smaller.
> Except one large / opening with others smaller.
>   Gradually.
> Days heap upon / us. Where is Patricia.
> In the dream of obedience and
> authority. The genitalia crumbles open.
>   (18–19)

The repetition of the question without the question mark—"Where is" Ti-Grace, Christine, Valerie, Patty, and Shulamith—the names of radical feminists interspersed with the names of women Lisa Robertson knows—makes it an elegy for all the women missing from history. But it also "returns the content of an earlier generation of radical feminists to a moment in the present" ("Webcast Reading").

At fourteen pages, "WEDNESDAY" is by far the longest section of *The Weather*. It begins: "A beautiful morning; we go down to the arena" (28). The poem's movement occurs through the repetition of two little words, *we* and *a*, where *we* signifies "the nightreading girls" "thinking by their lamps" (37):

> we make use of their work. We cannot contain our plea
> sure. The rain has loosened; we engage our imagination.
> The sentence opens inexpensively; we imagine its silence.
>   (37–38)

The working girls in this poem are intellectuals whose thought is made use of by other girls. Seeing the word "pleasure" break at the end of the line, their "plea" can "sure" not be contained: "The sentence opens inexpensively."

In a 2001 "How Poems Work" column for the *Globe and Mail*, Robertson deliberately recuperates the word "girl" to read Denise Riley's "In 1970":

> the eyes of the girls are awash with violets
> pansies are flowering under their tongues
> they are grouped by the edge of the waves
> and are anxious to swim;
> each one is on fire with passion to achieve herself.

Contrasting the "muteness" of "the feminine image" in "men's verse" (D14) with "the girls" who are "on fire with passion" to achieve themselves, Robertson recuperates the meaning of the word "girl." In Riley's poem "the girls" are to be admired, valued, claimed: "The girls are the girls who walk with suppleness and wit through Sappho's fragments, through Ovid's changes [...] in old holiday photo albums, and they are today's fine girls out sale-shopping." Insisting that "when a girl steps forward, she does not leave herself behind," Robertson claims that "she becomes several, and with a fidelity both passionate and discriminate" (D14). In her "Essay on Heaven" Robertson also reclaims the word girl: "when winter closes in on a girl she needs the richest possible decoration. She needs rest. She needs enormous eschatological bouquets"(*Office of Soft Architecture* n.p.). As early as her 1993 text *Xeclogue*, Robertson expressed her need to rewrite and reclaim conventional genres, histories, and language itself for women's purposes. She makes what we have been given into what "she needs"— "eschatological bouquets" for example, and a new meaning for the word "girl."

With *Xeclogue* Robertson even invented "a genre for the times that I go phantom" ("How Pastoral: A Prologue" n.p.). She welcomed as her "house-guest," the eighteenth-century poet, traveller, and political critic Lady Mary Wortley Montague, whose "City Eclogues" introduced Robertson to the "eclogue." *The Weather* continues this work: "We flood upwards into the referent" (31). Words accumulate new meanings: she gives us "Shadow for Hour," "For for Five," "Curious for Lucid," "Door for Bridge," "Rustic for Cunt" (41). She would have us experience "the extraordinary foreignness of the concept" when it is "returned" to us in different form and asks "For whom are *we* that form?" (italics mine). In the lyric section following "THURSDAY" the "I think[s] of this stricture"—

                              —rain
language, building—as a corset: an
outer ideal mould, I feel
the ideal moulding me the ideal
is now my surface just so very
perfect I know where to buy it and I
take it off. I take it off.
          ("RESIDENCE AT C_____" 52)

"Rain, language, building" are all, like "corsets," restrictive, "an outer ideal
mould." The word "mould" itself both signifies decay and construction or
shaping. As form and content, words are like both meanings of mould. And
so is the first person pronoun. In correspondence with McCaffery, Robert-
son wrote: "I don't know whether what 'I' experience is 'myself' but to some
extent, in order to be useful, I have to suspend disbelief" (*PhillyTalks* 37).

The "we" who speak in "THURSDAY" remind us that "when threat-
ened, we study everything, / no shape is for later, inside the cliché" (49).
Urgency of meaning accumulates around the words *now, come,* and *when,*
emphasized in the following by breaking the lines into shorter units:

All around is the mould of distance.
          Come we now prefer / ring.
Nothing else is happening.
          Come we now walking.
                    Now also be here.
                    Now bending,
          come we crawling.
                    Now / crisp,
          come we falling.
Now sparkle, eating.
Now swagger, / drinking.
Now transmit, smelling.
Now yellow, sucking.
When a mass,
          come we avoiding.
When by the margin,
          come we now ignoring.
When clouds go,
          come we now / tripping.
When conditions of freedom come.
     (46)

The incessant "Come we now" is followed by a series of paradigmatically-linked verbs: *preferring, walking, crawling, falling, avoiding, ignoring, tripping*, and *describing* how "we" will come "when conditions of freedom come." But the repetition of the present tense in the phrase "Come we now" overrides the possible future of "When conditions of freedom come" making the phrase "When women./When women. When world no longer determines, this / artificial obscurity" (50) a declarative statement rather than a question.

Rest finally comes on "FRIDAY": "We rest on the city or water or forms assumed in a fine / evening after showers" (56). Since "the real is not / enough to pleasure us," the equally real and fabricated "city or water or forms" on which "we rest" are contrasted with "the uninhabitable streets of our life" (57),

> We rest on the fringe of a vigorous archi-
> tecture fighting and sliding as the orange lights of descrip-
> tion therefore we're inflected by the site. Construct the
> real games and emotions. Blocked soliloquy. Tacit.
> (57–58)

In this "city of hunger and patience" (60), "we / want to speak the beautiful language of our times. Lashed / by change. With no memory. Without admonishment" (*The Weather* 58). Against the "mass rhetorics of structural permanence" we find that the weather like "our city is persistently soft": "Under the pavement, pavement. Hoaxes, failures, porches, archaeological strata spread out on a continuous thin plane; softness and speed, echoes, spores, tropes, fonts; not identity but incident and the accumulation of air-miles" (n.p.).

In the discourse of what Robertson calls a "soft architecture," "Words are fleshy ducts. Description decorates" ("The Office of Soft Architecture Introduction," *The Weather* n.p.). As "fleshy ducts" words are both human and mechanical. "Because the present is not articulate" ("For Soft Architects" n.p.), the poet as soft architect makes new descriptions on "the warp of former events" ("Soft Architecture: A Manifesto" n.p.). In *The Weather*, words, like ducts, convey meaning at a layer both in and above the structural. The book's building materials include weather words: *sunny, cloudy, windy, showers, rain, wet, fresh, bright, fine*. And words from many other discourses—pastoral, architectural, philosophical, quotidian. But the words that move the poem are the usually overlooked words *here, where, and, it, we,* and *a*, they are its "fleshy ducts."

Figure 19. Nicole Brossard and Lisa Robertson at Assembling Alternatives Conference. Photograph by Susan Rudy.

The soft architect, opening the folds we move among, exposes the ductwork, the torn places in the texture of any structure, the "fretted gap in the sheet where our feet get caught" ("Soft Architecture: A Manifesto" n.p.).[11] *The Weather*'s "Introduction" is quite literally a fold, a "fretted gap" we move into when we read it. It consists of a twice-folded 8½ by 11 inch sheet of blue paper folded within the pages of the book. In its 4 by 5¼ inch folded form, the words "Published as a component of THE WEATHER by Lisa Robertson" are written. On the first fold are the words "Introduction to THE WEATHER." The second fold is an address from "THE OFFICE FOR SOFT ARCHITECTURE" dated April 2001, Vancouver. The text begins: "We think of the design and construction of these weather descriptions as important decorative work. What shall our new ornaments be? How should we adorn mortality now? This is a serious political question." And ends with the words "Dear Reader—a lady speaking to humans from the motion of her own mind is always multiple. Enough of the least. We want to be believed."

The Weather, too, wants "to be believed" in an unusual sense: through an interrogation of the discourse of the weather, Robertson's *The Weather* achieves "a stunningly imaginative recitation on feminist art and politics."[12] Urgency of meaning arises, not through didacticism or critique, but through repetition, a "fine and beautiful," relentlessly unconventional and repetitious syntax: "My purpose here is to advance into / the sense of the weather, the lesson of / the weather" ("RESIDENCE AT C_____" 24). It explores, not the interior of the self—*The Weather* is never autobiographical—but the interior of the collective. The "I" speaks but soliloquy is blocked: "We speak as if in you alone" (60). As a line from "porchverse" puts it, "It is too late to be simple" (76).

Robertson's *The Weather* is another superb example of how the radically feminist and the radically innovative can productively intersect. Her methodological proposition was that she read the weather as structure, to consider it a kind of architecture, a "soft architecture."[13] Well aware that "some bodies are indeed constrained to a subjectivity and a space" (*PhillyTalks* 38) there are, nonetheless, "unbuildable or unbuilt architectures folded into the texture of the city and our bodies are already moving among them" ("Newsletter Dialogue" n.p.). Reading the weather as such a space to move among, she not only imagines but produces "an architecture, a poetry, that is both delusional and critical, a ludic zone" ("Newsletter Dialogue" n.p.). That architectural poetry is *The Weather*. And it is especially for women's friendships.

Notes

1   In *The Weather*, Lisa Robertson's reference to Walter Benjamin's *The Arcades Project* includes more than I have here: "Architecture, fashion—yes, even the weather—are, in the interior of the collective, what the sensoria of organs, the feeling of sickness or health, are in the individual.... They stand in the cycle of the eternally selfsame, until the collective seizes upon them in politics and history emerges" (n.p.). Robertson had also abbreviated the passage, which is worth citing in full: "It is one of the tacit suppositions of psychoanalysis that the clear-cut antithesis of sleeping and waking has no value for determining the empirical form of consciousness of the human being, but instead yields before an unending variety of concrete states of consciousness conditioned by every conceivable level of wakefulness within all possible centers. The situation of consciousness as patterned and checkered by sleep and waking need only be transferred from the individual to the collective. Of course, much that is external to the former is internal to the latter: architecture, fashion—yes, even the weather—are, in the interior of the collective, what the sensoria of organs, the feeling of sickness or health, are inside the individual. And so long as they preserve this unconscious amorphous dream configuration, they are as much natural processes as digestion, breathing, and the like. They stand in the cycle of the eternally selfsame, until the collective seizes upon them in politics and history emerges" (389–90).

2   Although a number of feminist poets—Lisa Robertson among them—did emerge out of KSW, I disagree with Vickery's claims that poets from the Kootenay School of Writing generated "one of the most innovative and strongly feminist of poetic

communities existing in Canada today" (133). In fact, the school is fairly infamous for its complicated relationship to feminist politics.

3 In addition, her work appears in many exciting and innovative anthologies, including Krukowski, Yang, and Gizzi's *Exact Change Yearbook 1995*, Messerli's *The Gertrude Stein Awards in Innovative Poetry 1993–94*, *Out of Everywhere: Innovative Writing by Women in North America and the UK* (O'Sullivan), *Moving Borders: Three Decades of Innovative Writing by Women* (Sloan), *Writing Class: The Kootenay School of Writing Anthology* (Barnholden and Klobucar), *The New Long Poem Anthology*, 2nd Ed. (Thesen), *Love Poems for a Media Age* (Samis), and *An Exaltation of Forms: Contemporary Poets Celebrate the Diversity of Their Art* (Finch and Varnes).

   Robertson's chapbooks are *The Apothecary* (1991; reissued 2001), *The Badge* (1994), *The Glove: An Essay on Interpretation* (1993), *The Descent* (1996), *Soft Architecture: A Manifesto* (1999), *A Hotel* (2003), and *Face* (2003).

4 See especially "How Pastoral" in Wallace and Marks's *Telling It Slant: Avant Garde Poetics of the 1900s* and "My Eighteenth Century" in Huk's *Assembling Alternatives*.

5 Robertson held Cambridge's Judith E. Wilson Visiting Fellowship in Poetry in 1999.

6 From the back cover of Robertson's *Xeclogue*.

7 Except for "Wednesday," which I discuss later in the chapter.

8 Note that this "title" appears only in the footer on the page and that the historical authenticity of "Cambridge" is severed through its reduction at the level of the signifier to "C———."

9 Robertson and McCaffery, *PhillyTalks* 17.

10 Unless otherwise indicated, all citations from *The Weather* have been reconfigured to emphasize their structural repetition and complexity.

11 Paradigmatically, the soft architect produces a "fretted gap" through the motion of feet in a bed, as Robertson writes in "Soft Architecture: A Manifesto": "The worn cotton sheets of our little beds had the blurred texture of silk crêpe and when we lay against them in the evening we'd rub, rhythmically, one foot against the soothing folds of fabric, waiting for sleep. That way we wore through the thinning cloth. Our feet would get tangled in the fretted gap" (*Occasional Work* 13).

12 From the "Content" description of a tape of Robertson reading from *The Weather*, held in the American Poetry Archives at San Francisco State University.

13 Her playfully serious recuperation of that most ubiquitous of urban spaces—the "office"—and her positing of a "soft" architecture, can be traced to her "manifesto" on "Soft Architecture." Several of her recent publications have even been attributed to "THE OFFICE FOR SOFT ARCHITECTURE." On the San Francisco State University Web site for the journal of innovative prose, Robertson cites herself this way: "Lisa Robertson writes under the alias of Office for Soft Architecture (Vancouver). Presently the office is conducting research on tailoring. Previous projects include *Debbie: An Epic* and *Xeclogue*, both from New Star Books (Vancouver)." In her conversation with McCaffery she explains: "the ad hoc 'office' formed itself, obviously with a strong nod toward Koolhaas's influence, but also as an attempt to escape the author called 'Lisa Robertson'" (33).

■

1990s Editing and Publishing

Pauline Butling

● In chapter 1 I argued that the discourses of avant-gardism could not adequately define radical poetry and poetics in the late twentieth century. Especially in the 1990s, literary innovation has been signified as much by class, gender, sexuality, and race-based critiques of power relations as well as by formal experiments. Also, a striking feature of the 1990s literary/ cultural field has been the increased presence of writers of colour and First Nations writers in little magazines and small presses as well as in mainstream media. This upsurge of race-identified writers continues the feminist, gay and lesbian, and First Nations incursions that began in the 1970s and '80s when the alternative poetics networks were reconfigured to include these subjectivities. However new subjects do not birth themselves, fully formed by their individual talent and energy alone, as the restricted economy of capitalism would have us believe. They enter the social imaginary via the material spaces of little magazines and small presses and by virtue of the work of editors who change the discursive terms within those sites. Editorial activism, in turn, like poetic innovation, does not take place in isolation from its social/historical contexts. The literary struggles of the 1990s are informed by the broader social/political justice movements of the past few decades that sought self-government, territorial rights, redress, and legislated equality by and for historically disadvantaged groups. The difference is that *editorial* activism works toward a share of *discursive* territory, for ownership of *cultural* property, and for the right to self-representation (self-government) in the social imaginary. In this chapter I focus on some of those editing and publishing initiatives of the 1990s that created discursive contexts and material sites for "new" subject positions.

In order to locate editorial activism within its social/political contexts, however, I begin with a brief summary of legislative initiatives and social justice movements that changed the discursive terms and legal frameworks of the nation and its subjects after World War II. For starters, one needs to know that until the Canada Citizenship Act of 1947, race-identified groups were denied full participation in Canadian society by several discriminatory laws. The first of these and arguably the most injurious, was the Indian Act of 1880 and its subsequent additions/revisions, which created "special" status (read second-class status) for First Nations people and instituted a policy of forced assimilation.[1] Other well-known instances of legislated racism included the Chinese head tax (introduced in 1885), immigration laws that excluded or severely limited race-identified groups (Blacks, Asians, and Jews), and the application of the War Measures Act in 1942 to suspend the basic civil rights of Canadians of Japanese origin.

The Canada Citizenship Act of 1947—so named because it extended full citizenship (i.e., the right to vote) to Chinese and South Asian Canadians—marked the beginning of a series of legislative initiatives to end discrimination against race-identified groups. The right to vote was extended to Japanese Canadians in 1948, to the Inuit in 1950, and to status Indians in 1960.[2] Prior to 1947, all of the above groups were literally second-class citizens in that they were denied the most basic right of a citizen in a democratic society. Not being on the voters list, in turn, served as a basis for further discrimination: for instance, a person had to be on the voters list to get a licence to practise as a doctor or lawyer.[3] Enfranchising all Canadians was obviously an important first step toward social justice. Also in 1947, the ban against Chinese immigration was lifted. Many of the restrictions against Black immigrants ended in the 1960s. In 1988, The War Measures Act was repealed and the Japanese-Canadian redress movement achieved its goal of getting a public apology together with monetary compensation from the federal government for the government's illegal seizure of assets during the Second World War.[4] As of 2004, The Indian Act remains in place.[5]

In addition to removing some of its discriminatory laws, the federal government has also initiated rights legislation. The most important for minority groups, The Canadian Charter of Rights and Freedoms, passed by the Trudeau government in 1982, opened the door to legal challenges based on charter rights. Another equality initiative, The Multiculturalism Act of 1988, legislated a nation of different but equal races and ethnicities. Many have argued that official multiculturalism simply camouflages rather than eliminates inequality and that it was introduced more to facilitate global economic agendas than to eliminate discrimination, especially as the act was passed just weeks before the Canadian government signed the free trade agreement between Canada and the United States (1 January 1989). Smaro Kamboureli, for instance, argues that official multiculturalism enacts a "sedative politics" which "allows the state to become self-congratulatory, if not complacent, about its handling of ethnicity" (*Scandalous Bodies* 82). Clint Burnham and others are more damning, claiming that official multiculturalism ... functions as an attempt to cement over the cracks in a violently unequal society" ("Introduction: Toronto since Then," 5).[6] Certainly official multiculturalism facilitates free trade and multinationalism insofar as it encourages the easy circulation of capital and labour across national borders, an essential process for multinational corporations to thrive: a multicultural society implies the necessary welcoming environment for this process. Nevertheless, I include it in my list of social justice initiatives because it launched a redefinition of nationhood, together with more public debate about minority rights issues. On a practical level, it also provided financial support for ethnic and race-identified projects through the Secretary of State for Multiculturalism (now the Ministry of Canadian Heritage). Generally speaking, the various legislative initiatives listed here signal a national policy change to redefine the nation as inclusive of difference. Obviously such legal changes don't erase discriminatory practices immediately but they do provide a legal framework for the slower process of social/cultural change.[7]

Equally important in putting discrimination issues on the public agenda has been First Nations' political and social activism that began in the 1960s with Red Power movements in Canada and the USA. Also in the 1960s, books such as Cree writer Harold Cardinal's *The Unjust Society* jolted the conscience of the nation with its "unrelenting and articulate denunciation of Canadian Indian policy" (Young-Ing, "The Estrangement" 25). Since the 1960s, First Nations' protests in the form of blockades, standoffs, and sit-ins, together with land claims, abuse charges, and court appeals over treaty rights have become a regular feature of Canadian public life. First Nations' activism not only raised public awareness of indigenous rights; it also had some political successes in settling land claims, achieving self-government, and gaining recognition of Aboriginal rights. Some notable successes include the Nisga'a land claims treaty of 1973 (the first treaty to be signed in BC since 1899); the James Bay Agreement in Quebec in 1975 which granted self-government to the Inuit and Cree in the James Bay region in Quebec; the Nunavut land claims agreement in 1993, which paved the way for the creation of the Eastern Arctic self-governing jurisdiction of Nunavut in 1999; the Nisga'a Agreement on self government in BC in 1999; and the Supreme Court ruling recognizing Aboriginal fishing rights in 2000.[8]

The 1990s began with First Nations issues front and centre with several highly publicized events. First Elijah Harper, an Oji-Cree and member of the Manitoba legislative assembly, precipitated the very dramatic, eleventh-hour defeat of the Meech Lake Constitutional Accord.[9] Next came the standoff at the small Quebec town of Oka through the long, hot summer of 1990, when the Mohawk Warrior Society from the nearby Kanesatake reserve set up a blockade to prevent the development of a golf course on Indian land. The image from that event that has been emblazoned in cultural memory encapsulates the increasingly defiant stance adopted by race-identified groups throughout the 1990s. The image is of two heads in profile—a Mohawk warrior named Lasagne, and Canadian army sargeant Patrick Cloutier—just a few inches apart, in fact almost nose-to-nose, in a standoff that bespeaks intense confrontation and hostility (see < http:// www.vigile.net/00-7/oka-pc.html >).

The literary/cultural field was equally fraught at the start of the 1990s with explosive confrontations about theft of cultural property, cultural appropriation, and the persistence of racist stereotypes in cultural productions.[10] Major cultural institutions—the Canada Council and The Writers' Union of Canada (TWUC)—responded with proactive policies and structural changes. In 1990, for instance, TWUC established a Racial Minorities Committee in response to demands from some of its members to address access and appropriation issues. Chaired by Lenore Keeshig-Tobias, the committee's first action was to organize a retreat, called The Appropriate Voice, held at Geneva Park, Orillia, Ontario, in the spring of 1992. At the retreat, First Nations writers and writers of colour identified common issues and developed an action plan, including a recommendation that TWUC sponsor a national conference for First Nations writers and writers of colour.[11] In the same year (1992), the Canada Council adopted an official policy on cultural appropriation based on the recommendations of its Advisory Committee for Racial Equality in the Arts.

The heated debates that erupted in the national media over these cultural policy initiatives pitted the discursive terms of liberalism—freedom of expression and individual rights—against the emerging discourses of minority rights such as ownership of cultural property and the right to control its representations. In a flurry of articles, editorials, and letters to the editor following the Canada Council's announcement of its policy on cultural appropriation for instance, charges of censorship were met with countercharges of cultural theft.[12] Demands to preserve freedom of expression, terms that reflect the liberal, individual rights position (most often expressed by white writers), were countered by demands for policy initiatives in support of minority *group* rights. While the furor raged on without any apparent resolution, it did trouble some of the assumptions of liberalism—suggesting, for instance, that the individual rights argument camouflages white privilege.

Writing Thru Race

The discursive/power struggle between individual and group rights came to a head in 1994, in the public debates about Writing Thru Race, a three-day conference held in Vancouver for First Nations writers and writers of colour. The struggle began at the 1992 Writers' Union AGM with accusations of censorship and violation of individual rights because white writers would be excluded from the conference's daytime events. Two years later, just two months before the conference, another debate at the union's AGM was picked up by the national media. Critics of the conference again attempted to recast it as an act of censorship, political correctness, reverse racism, and violation of individual rights: "George Orwell, Call Your Office" is the headline of an article by Robert Fulford in which he accuses the Writers' Union of "reinventing apartheid," engaging in Orwellian double-speak, and asserting group over individual rights:

> The no-white rule symbolizes a startling change in the way Canada handles issues of this kind…. We have apparently moved from the era of pluralism to the era of multiculturalism. The old liberal pluralism holds that each of us has rights as an individual: this is the idea that has animated social progress for generations. The new multiculturalism, on the other hand, focuses on rights of groups, and sees each of us as the member of a racially designated cluster…. Now the Writers' Union of Canada want to tell us that closed is open, limited is free, exclusion is inclusion. (*Globe and Mail*, A1)

Roy Miki, chair of the conference planning committee, responded a week later with a careful explanation of both historical and current reasons for the conference. He accused Fulford of being "mean-spirited" and applauded the writers "for taking on the national task of constructing social and cultural justice" ("Why We're Holding the Vancouver Conference," A17). Bronwen Drainie also challenged Fulford with articles titled "Controversial Writers' Meeting Is both Meet and Right" (E3) and "Colour Me Politically Correct and Proud of It" (C3). Myrna Kostash, weighed in with the point that, "contrary to liberal desire, we do not check our skin colour at the civic door" (C5). Even members of parliament entered the fray, prompted by Reform Party member Jan Brown protesting the exclusion of white writers from the publicly funded conference. Brown's protest in turn led to the minister of Canadian Heritage, Michel Dupuy, in a "personal" decision (and surely a political one), to withdraw his ministry's funding for the conference.[13] Again, the discourse of liberalism and *individual* rights was pitted against an increasingly articulate counter-discourse about structural discrimination and minority *group* rights.[14]

Roy Miki's interview with Pamela Wallin, aired on CBC television's *Newsworld* following an explosive debate at the TWUC AGM, offers one example of a relatively successful voicing of that counter-discourse. As the interviewer, Wallin set the initial terms of the discussion. The program began with a full-screen text, "NO WHITES ALLOWED," followed by a clip of Canadian icon Pierre Berton protesting "reverse racism." However, Miki's reasoned and articulate responses to Wallin's inflammatory questions shifted the terms to issues of minority rights and needs. Against Wallin and Burton's "reverse racism" allegations, Miki offered the notion of "the retreat format" as a long-established practice that is used by all sorts of groups to examine problems and develop solutions. Racialized writers in particular need such a format, he explained, in order to be able to focus on common issues rather than be forced to spend their time explaining their concerns to a dominant group. He also stressed the conference's *inclusivity* (against accusations of exclusivity), this being the first time writers of colour and First Nations writers had come together as a group.

The conference was a success on many fronts. It was a community-building event that concluded with recommendations for follow-up actions, such as mentoring programs and publishing initiatives, that would continue to build group strength, empower individual writers, and expand the discourse around minoritization and racialization. As a social justice initiative, it emphatically inserted First Nations writers and writers of colour into the cultural and discursive spaces of the 1990s. It did so both by rearticulating the terms of engagement as well as by simply increasing the visibility of the group. There were important effects of the conference *within* the group as well; not least was a greater awareness the group's internal diversity. According to Monika Kin Gagnon, "the concluding sessions … profoundly revealed the radically different ideological positions that First Nations and writers of colour occupy in relation to dominant culture and cultural organizations: from assimilative to radically transformative" (71). Kin Gagnon goes on to argue for "the radical possibilities of cultural transformation" by insisting that the idea of a "shared politic" that the conference began with "must give way to different, if more dramatically effective, crises of representation" (71). Kin Gagnon's comments further expand the discursive field to include the notion of cultural transformation (as opposed to the one-way street of assimilation).

All of the above—legislative initiatives, social/political activism, discursive struggles, and institutional change—helped to create a receptive environment and provide the discursive terms for 1990s editorial activism. As examples of particular activist initiatives in the literary field, I look at the editorial strategies in four anthologies, one magazine, and one small press. Bennett Lee and Jim Wong-Chu, for instance, claim the right to self-representation and argue for a group identity (based a shared history of discrimination) to legitimate Chinese-Canadian subjects in *Many-Mouthed Birds: Contemporary Writing by Chinese Canadians* (1991). First Nations writers and activists Daniel David Moses and Jeannette Armstrong likewise use identity narratives and refer to a shared history of colonization to provide coherence and value to an "emerging" literature (Moses xiii) in two major anthologies of First Nations writing that bookend the decade: *An Anthology of Canadian Native Literature in English* (edited by Daniel David Moses and Terry Goldie in 1992) and *Native Poetry in Canada* (edited by Jeannette C. Armstrong and Lally Grauer in 2002). Both also use a coalitional strategy, of co-editing with white editors Terry Goldie and Lally Grauer respectively. Roy Miki, as editor of *West Coast Line* from 1990–1999 and especially in *Colour. An Issue*, a Special Issue of *West Coast Line* (1994), takes a slightly different tack, that of "cultural transformation" (Kin Gagnon 71). He sought out First Nations writers and writers of colour in order "to bring the minoritized or racialized writers into the mix," in order to create "a dialogue, even a tension between the dominant and the marginalized" (interview).

Editorial activism on behalf of First Nations writers and writers of colour was not the only story of the 1990s. Class politics also prompted at least one editorial initiative. Michael Barnholden and Andrew Klobucar provided a discursive reframing of the Kootenay School of Writing poets by linking its disjunctive poetics to a Marxist analysis of class politics in *Writing Class: The Kootenay School of Writing Anthology* (1999). I also include an example of the editorial activism usually associated with the traditional avant-garde, that of experimenting with new technologies to publish work that would be uneconomical in conventional forms and/or requires inventive formats to do justice to the work, with a brief outline of Coach House Books. When Stan Bevington, Victor Coleman, Hilary Clark, Darren Wershler-Henry, and others established Coach House Books in 1997, they did so in order to continue the original Coach House Press tradition of publishing experimental poetry that would not otherwise be available. All of the above editorial initiatives not only provided material sites for writing by various outsider groups; they also provided much-needed discursive terms and critical frameworks for articulating and/or legitimating that work. I conclude the chapter with an analysis of the links between poetry and politics in a book of poetry, *Monkey Puzzle* by Rita Wong.

●

Many-Mouthed Birds: Contemporary Writing by Chinese Canadians
edited by Bennett Lee and Jim Wong-Chu (Douglas and McIntyre, 1991).

The first major anthology of Chinese-Canadian writing to be published in Canada, edited by two members of that community, appeared in 1991. The process that preceded its publication demonstrates the effectiveness of one set of discursive terms—those associated with identity narratives—as an activist tool. The process began in the mid-1980s when a mainstream (white) editor received preliminary funding from the Secretary of State for Multiculturalism to edit and publish an anthology of Chinese-Canadian poetry and fiction. When the editor approached the Chinese-Canadian community, however, as poet/activist Jim Wong-Chu explains, he "met considerable resistance from a community that was distrustful and militant about having outsiders control the product which is so important to represent the community" (email to Pauline Butling). That community had already been politicized through forming the Chinese-Canadian Writers' Workshop more than a decade earlier (later renamed the Asian Canadian Writers' Workshop). So they already understood the importance of *self*-representation in asserting their identity as a legitimate group within the dominant literary culture. Now they took control of the production: Bennett Lee and Jim Wong-Chu took over as editors and also chose the publisher.

The discursive terms that came to the fore in the process of producing this anthology highlight the politics of representation. For the Chinese-Canadian community it was crucial that, instead of gaining visibility (both discursively and materially) by a dispensation from the dominant group (the hallmark of the imperialist model), they had to achieve it by their own agency and on their terms.[15] As many a colonized or excluded group has discovered, taking control of their representations is vital to community empowerment and identity formation. The anthology intervenes overtly in the social order as much as in the literary field in that it presents "new" subjects as well as new writing. Bennett Lee, in his introduction to *Many-Mouthed Birds*, emphasizes the anthology's social role. He begins by naming

Chinese-Canadian writers as a category deserving attention (and outlining some of the challenges of doing so). Lee then legitimates the outsider group by associating their work with a mainstream aesthetic: "the sole criterion" for inclusion in the anthology, he explains, apart from being Chinese Canadian, was "well-crafted and honest writing which could surprise, enlighten and entertain an ordinary reader (1)." Lee here surely echoes Ezra Pound's dictate earlier in the century that the purpose of poetry is to teach, to move, and to delight ("A Retrospect"). But then Lee quickly returns to the discourse of minoritization, with two pages devoted to the history of discriminatory legislation against the Chinese Canadians. He concludes the introduction by reiterating the opening discourses of liberation and transformation. The anthologized writers are indeed "many-mouthed birds," he suggests, "because they are breaking a long and often self-imposed silence" (8). Lee thus reaffirms the point that the anthology is a social intervention that contributes to cultural transformation.[16]

●

An Anthology of Canadian Native Literature in English
edited by Daniel David Moses and Terry Goldie (Oxford, 1992)

Native Poetry in Canada
edited by Jeannette C. Armstrong and Lally Grauer (Broadview 2002)

These two anthologies of Native literature that bookend the decade also intervene in the social order by inserting two substantial bodies of Native writing into the literary/cultural field together with a discursive framework that legitimates and values that work. As with *Many-Mouthed Birds*, a major goal of the anthologies is to establish group identity and legitimacy. While emphasizing diversity in writing styles and topics, both note common values, a shared history of colonialism, and a need for group visibility. At the same time, like Bennett Lee, they also note connections to "the literary avant-garde" (Armstrong xvii), although Goldie offers the qualification that Native writers are often more interested in reclaiming the past, "unlike innovative mainstream writers, who often seem to be tearing things down" (xiv). Moses adds: "If we become part of the mainstream we're going to be the deep currents" (xiv). They assert both their difference from and connections to the dominant culture.

In contrast to Wong-Chu and Lee, Moses and Armstrong chose to co-edit with white scholars. The primary purpose of the anthologies—to show the range and quality of Native writing—is well served by this strategy in that both Terry Goldie and Lally Grauer are respected scholars in the field of Native Studies.[17] At the same time, both emphasize that their role is to stay in the background. Goldie sees himself as a silent facilitator: "to create an anthology would not give my comments about a Native voice but rather do a little bit to get the Native voice heard" ("Preface: Two Voices" xii). Lally Grauer characterizes her role as a listener and learner and encourages the reader to do likewise. She thereby offers a role model for white readers of Native literature and simultaneously argues for transforming "the interpretive field" (xxvii) by including Native literature in university curricula.

Daniel David Moses and Jeannette Armstrong diverge, however, in their discursive strategies. Moses collaborates with Goldie in writing the introduction and they choose a dialogue form. They focus on the politics of anthologizing, the distinct features of Native literature, and some of the landmines associated with presentations of Native culture and history. Moses, who chose most of the historical material (Goldie did the contemporary), comments that he did not want "to place native people in the museum with all the other extinct species" (xiii), nor to feed "white guilt": "It seems to me you don't want to heal, you want to keep the wound ... You're dancing around a wound" (xvii). Goldie speaks of making political as well as aesthetic choices, for instance, in selecting Lenore Keeshig-Tobias's "After Oka—How Has Canada Changed" (235–36), which raises the question of whether purely aesthetic decisions are possible given the political role of the anthology (xxi). As Moses notes: "the decisions on what would go in something that you might call the canon can be easily disguised as aesthetic decisions, but if we are making a canon the decisions are definitely political, especially with a literature that is emerging even as we speak" (xii). The dialogue form, together with the editors' frankness about the politics of anthologizing, has the effect of legitimating the project. They take the value of Native literature as a given and proceed to a discussion of specific issues. Also the dialogue creates an atmosphere of open discussion that diffuses the emotional baggage of guilt, blame, or reformist zeal that surrounded Native issues, especially in the early 1990s when the anthology appeared. The dialogue form invites the reader to ponder the questions along with the editors, while also providing contexts and concepts to facilitate that discussion. It is an effective strategy that subtly expands the discursive field.

Armstrong and Grauer take a very different track. For starters, they write two separate and quite distinct introductions: Armstrong's is personal and Grauer's is scholarly. Armstrong offers a moving account of her life as

a writer. Her story follows the tropes of identity narratives, noting origi-
nary moments and subsequent benchmark events in a process that leads
to individual/group empowerment. She starts in the late 1960s with an
account of hearing Duke Redbird's poetry on late-night CBC radio, and con-
tinues through her gradual discovery of a group identity in "our own col-
lective colonized heritage of loss, pain, anger and resistance, and of our pride
and identity as Native" (xvi–xvii). She then notes a paradigm shift at the
start of the 1980s. Daniel David Moses's *Delicate Bodies* (1980) marked
the start of a "decade of Native literary experimentation" (xix) that contin-
ued in the work of "Beth Brant, Beth Cuthand, Lenore Keeshig-Tobias, and
Emma Laroque" (xix). In the 1990s, Native literature completed its com-
ing-of-age process with "an era of poetic celebration of being Native" (xx).
Beginning with Marie Annharte Baker's *Being on the Moon* in 1990, the
process continues, she explains, in the work of a new generation of writ-
ers such as Joanne Arnott, Louise Halfe, Gregory Scofield, and Randy
Lundy.

Interwoven with this coming-of-age narrative is a parallel narrative of
the development of Native publishing. Armstrong thus links the liberatory
discourse of empowerment with a historical materialist focus on the con-
ditions of cultural production. Group identity formation takes place only
when "Native alternative press broke the print barriers" (xvii). She also
emphasizes the importance of public gatherings, such as the coming
together of "over fifteen prominent Native women writers from Canada and
the United States" (xix) at the International Feminist Book Fair held in
Montreal in 1988. At such moments, shared concerns can be more fully real-
ized and articulated. In this instance, ad hoc groups and loosely organized
networks "suddenly solidified around concerns of marginalization, ghet-
toization, and misappropriation of cultural voice" (xix). One immediate
result of the formation of North America-wide networks, she notes, was the
En'owkin School of Writing in Penticton. Again she links individual and
group empowerment to publishing ventures, political and cultural activism,
and institutional changes. As an activist strategy, Armstrong's narrative skil-
fully combines liberatory and materialist methodologies; she legitimates and
celebrates the achievements of Native poets without losing sight of the his-
torical conditions and social formations that facilitated those achieve-
ments.

●

Colour. An Issue
A Special Issue of *West Coast Line* (13–14, Spring/Fall 1994)
edited by Roy Miki and Fred Wah

Many-Mouthed Birds and *Writing Class* both stake a claim to discursive space by articulating a group identity. *Colour. An Issue*, as the title suggests, takes on the "issue" of colour directly. Colour, period. No hyphen. No comma. Colour is a matrix to explore, not an identity marker. This is not, the editors declare, "a collection of texts that has been selected, arranged, and edited into a 'whole' that advances the coherence of collectivity" (Miki and Wah 5). Working against the "homogenization and the elision of racialization," they offer "the unpredictability of writing," that produces a kinetic and provisional discursive field. The word "issue," they suggest, not only refers to this particular publication but also to a "transitional zone" where "imagined possibilities in language and thought" can be "kindled" (5). They do not isolate the group as "special" (read peripheral); the words COLOUR. AN ISSUE declare themselves to the reader from the front cover.[18] The cover image also foregrounds race issues with a side view of two silouetted heads (one African, one Asian) face-to-face, almost nose-to-nose, profiled against a white background. The figures pulsate with blackness. The contrast is reversed on the back cover with the two white heads set against a black background. Also, their position has changed to a back view, which eliminates some of the physical race markers (such as nose, head, and lip shape). Shoulder to shoulder they seem joined in camaraderie. In the sequence of five images, which is reproduced within the issue (Yoon 297–301), the heads are all black but the combinations change from African/Caucasian, to Asian/Caucasian, to African/Asian. Created by Vancouver artist Jin-me Yoon, the image sequence enacts both the rigidity and instability of "colour" signifiers.

The nose-to-nose confrontation on the front cover resonates with the image of the Mohawk warrior staring down the sergeant that I referred to earlier in this chapter, but with a significant difference. Certainly the image emanates tension, but the changing combinations in the image sequence, together with the black-and-white reversal on the back cover, suggest fluid and provisional positions and relations, including the possibility of dialogue *between* people of colour. Also worth noting is the activist role of the artist. Jin-me Yoon does not simply present a parade of race-identified silhouettes. She disturbs the signs of race; she provokes the viewer to think

COLOUR.AN ISSUE

EDITED BY
Roy Miki and Fred Wah

Figure 20. Cover image, *Colour. An Issue.*
West Coast Line 13–14, 28/1.2 (Spring/
Fall 1994). Photography by Chick Rice;
concept by Jin-me Yoon.

about white/black subject positions
and relations. She offers the possibil-
ity of cultural transformation.

More than three hundred pages
in all, with some sixty contributors,
Colour. An Issue offers variable, pro-
visional, even conflicting responses
and "side by side tensions" (Miki and
Wah 6). In terms of literary forms,
there is fiction, poetry, memoir,
visual art, and theoretical essays.
Contributors vary in age, geographic
location, and individual histories.
They include First Nations writers Marilyn Dumont, Marie Annharte
Baker, George Morrissette, Victoria Walker; South Asian Canadians Ashok
Mathur, Kanwaljit Kaur, Ian Iqbal Rashid, Haruko Okano, and Yasmin
Ladha; Asian Canadians Henry Tsang, Gerry Shikatani, Kyo Maclear,
Hiromi Goto, and Larissa Lai; African Canadians Mercedes Baines, Peter
Hudson, Janisse Browning, and Nicole Holas. White writers also enter the
mix, with poetry by Erin Mouré, r rickey, Jacqueline Turner, and Susan Hol-
brook and essays by critic/theorists Jeanne Perreault and Dawn McCance.
Taken together, the texts articulate many pathways in the complex process
of imagining "possibilities in language and thought" (Miki and Wah 6). As
a material object, the issue claims public space for "colour" and provides
a textual grounding in race-identified writing that others can build on. As
a discursive intervention, it posits provisionality, heterogeneity, and con-
tingency. These terms circulate throughout the "issue" to both trouble and
expand the discourses and practices associated with "colour."

●

Writing Class: The Kootenay School of Writing Anthology
edited by Andrew Klobucar and Michael Barnholden (New Star, 1999)

Writing Class: The Kootenay School of Writing Anthology presents poems by
fourteen writers associated with the Vancouver-based Kootenay School of

Writing (KSW). In 1984 KSW was established in Nelson and Vancouver, BC, as a writer-run, volunteer organization. It was founded by a group of former students and faculty from the School of Writing at David Thompson University Centre (DTUC) in Nelson when the centre was shut down in 1984 as part of an economic and ideologically driven "restraint" program that had been introduced by the right-wing provincial government the previous year. Following the DTUC closure, former students and faculty banded together to establish their own "school," first in Nelson and shortly after in Vancouver, where many of the DTUC students and faculty relocated. The anthology title, *Writing Class*, encapsulates two central KSW activities—the provision of an alternative writing "classroom" together with a critique of class relations. Like the Asian/Canadian Writers' Workshop, KSW writers produced an anthology that articulates a shared identity and history. In the words of editors Klobucar and Barnholden, the anthology documents "a shared approach towards class position and politics" (4). In their lengthy introduction (close to twenty-five percent of the total book) they articulate a historical and ideological position that supports this claim.[19] A major goal of the anthology is thus to both assert and expand the discursive context within which KSW writers might be read. Curiously, however, this claim is made retroactively. The anthology was published in 1999, while the anthologized poems are taken from the 1980s (even though all the anthologized writers continued to publish throughout the 1990s). They legitimate the group in the present moment by articulating the terms of their formation, presumably because KSW writers became well known for their experimental poetics, but less so for their Marxist analysis of class oppression.

Editors Klobucar and Barnholden set out to claim both discursive and material space for the group, using the now-familiar strategies of outsider groups; that is, by claiming originary historical moments and constructing identity narratives. In terms of origins, they locate KSW within a network that includes the American Language poets and the Vancouver experimental poetics tradition (going back to the *TISH* poets and the summer poetry workshop at the University of British Columbia in 1963). The anthology defines a community of writers who shared "a critical sense of language itself as a prime constituent of community" (5). On the class front, the editors link the KSW writers' class-consciousness to their historical moment, their experience of oppression and exclusion during the decade of "restraint." Although only two of the fourteen writers in the anthology were DTUC students and/or founding members (Jeff Derksen and Dennis Denisoff were DTUC writing students and Derksen was one of

KSW's founders), as young poets trying to survive in the hostile arts environment and economic downturn of the 1980s, all the anthologized writers would have felt the effects of the provincial government's Reagan/ Thatcher copycat program. The editors argue that the restraint program provoked an articulate class politics, that KSW writers explored the links between the social/economic marginalization of the artist and class oppression, and that their disjunctive poetics reflects those concerns. Gone is the romantic notion that outsider status is a necessary prerequisite for creative activity. In its place came a barrage of questions about who wields the power to exclude, who is excluded, who benefits, and how such inequities can be addressed. The publication intervenes in the social/discursive order with a retroactive rearticulation and historicization of KSW's social critique and disjunctive poetics.[20]

●

Coach House Books (1996)

When the venerable Coach House Press folded in 1996, Stan Bevington and Hilary Clark began talking about starting a new press (Victor Coleman joined in shortly after) that would follow the original Coach House Press path of combining innovative book design with innovative writing.[21] Coach House Books was subsequently founded in 1996 to re-establish the "best of the small press tradition" while also venturing into the new technologies: "Preserving the best of the small press tradition, we produce finely designed and crafted books in limited editions with the author integrally involved in the process. Simultaneously, we are redefining the concept of publishing by offering all our texts online" < http://www.chbooks .com >. When Darren Wershler-Henry became editor in 1998 and damian lopes took on the specific job of web-editor, Coach House Books launched several innovative web publishing projects, such as the bpNichol project (an ongoing archive of information about Nichol's work) or the "Cybrarian book finder" (a reference tool), or the "Digital Ephemera" project in which works would appear for only a short time.[22] They also experimented with web-based publishing for texts that might not otherwise be available because of their formal challenges, such as Steve McCaffery's *Carnival*, originally published by CHP as a text that the reader literally cuts up as s/he reads it. Overall, they saw "electronic publishing not as a marketing gimmick but as a reality and a necessity. After all, publishing means to make public, and the Internet has become an important public 'space'" < http:// www.chbooks.com >.

Another Coach House Books initiative was to reprint former Coach House Press books (titles ranging from Nichol's *The Martyrology*, to Diana Hartog's *Matinée Light*, and David McFadden's *Great Canadian Sonnet*) that had disappeared with the demise of Coach House Press, thereby reinserting those poets into the current discursive field. Another neglected group of poets, in Wershler-Henry's view, were the writers associated with the Kootenay School of Writing in Vancouver in the 1980s, many of whom had languished in the publishing sidelines with only one or two chapbooks to their names. Wershler-Henry sought books by Dan Farrell (*The Inkblot Record*), Nancy Shaw and Catriona Strang (*Busted*), and Clint Burnham (*Buddyland*). CHB's list also increasingly includes books by formally innovative writers of colour, such as damian lopes (*Sensory Deprivation*) and Louise Bak (*Gingko Kitchen*). Other experimental poets—both young and old—have found a publishing home at Coach House Books. The CHB 2001 list includes Karen Mac Cormack (*At Issue*), Louis Cabri (*The Mood Embosser*), Christian Bök (*Eunoia*); in 2002, Margaret Christakos (*Excessive Love Prostheses*), David Young (*Clout*), and Beth Follett (*Tell It Slant*).

Coach House Books' various projects show the extent to which it supports a wide range of innovation. Wershler-Henry argues that CHB and other small presses such "Krupskaya, New Star, Anansi, and Arsenal Pulp," can and do "make a difference in the national literary culture.... Just getting the writers I've mentioned into print is an act with aesthetic and even political implications" (Bök and Wershler-Henry 113). These presses provide an alternative to what Wershler-Henry calls the "generic poetry press producing lyric verse" (Bök and Wershler-Henry 113). They are reinventing the social: "the most important radical gestures that an artist makes have to do with reinventing the social—perpetuating a free and vigorous exchange of ideas, information and access to the means of publication" (Bök and Wershler-Henry 112).

Rita Wong's "puzzles"

Finally, to conclude this chapter on literary activism, I return briefly to a question that recurs throughout this book: how are critiques of power-relations enacted within the poem? What is an activist poetics? So many of the cultural activists of the 1990s are also poets, but how are their politics and poetics linked? The poetry of Rita Wong, a young Chinese-Canadian poet who began writing in the 1990s, offers one example of a politicized poetics in her first book, *monkeypuzzle* (1998). In her words, "political consciousness and emotional grounding" are "inseparable" and her poetry offers that grounding ("The 'I' in Migrant" 108). Wong's activism began in the early 1990s with various anti-racism projects. She joined the editorial collective of *Absinthe* magazine, joined Minquon Panchayat (a national organization of artists and writers of colour), joined the Calgary Women of Colour Collective, and took part in educational initiatives such as a Writers for Change project (interview with Larissa Lai 80).[23] When she moved to Vancouver in 1998, she continued her activist work by joining DARE (Direct Action against Refugee Exploitation[24]). Wong joined the organization, she explains, not "out of altruism"; her motives had to do with her own survival: "as someone affected by this history of discrimination and racism, I feel the need to work against its continuance. It is a matter of my own survival" ("The 'I' in Migrant" 106).

In *monkeypuzzle*, Wong begins with a critique of that history. The first section of the book is a "memory palate" of her personal experiences of racism. Born in Calgary to a working-class, Chinese-Canadian family, Wong's childhood is marked by silence and invisibility. She discovers that "the price for a respectable daytime existence is / high. it is my own desire. creating a vacuum, / the hollow space which i become" (14). The child learns early of racial stereotyping, while working in the family business, the "sunset grocery":

> i learn the word "inscrutable" & practice being so
> behind the cash register. however, i soon realize that i
> am read as inscrutable by many customers with absolutely
> no effort on my part, so i don't bother trying any more.
> (11)

Within the family, there is little nourishment for a desiring self. She and her family work "nine to nine seven days a week" in the ubiquitous Chinese-Canadian corner store, putting in long hours for meager returns:

> the store is where i develop
> the expected math skills: $60 net one day divided by
> twelve hours is $5 an hour, divided by two people is
> $2.50 an hour, or divided by five
> people $1.00 an hour.
> (11)

Weighed down by the "penny nickel dime tedium" (13) of the working poor that so often accompanies racialization, she learns to hide both her fears and desires:

part fire, part water, part air & part earth, i try to distance myself from
the fire within, fear that i cannot control its random blasts. i learn
to cultivate that part of me which is earth, sowing gradual seeds of
pragmatism, small quiet sprouts in the spring, studious endeavours
reaping scholarly harvests, parental approval,
respectable tunnels for escape.

(13)

Adolescence brings further wounds when a boy that she has a crush on calls her a "chink." Or when, in the teenage search for role models, she finds herself "caught between wannabe bad girl & good chinese girl" (16).

Section one also includes a positive role model, in the story of China Annie of Idaho who acted on, rather than suppressed, her desires. She ran away from her owner and *"escaped to / Boise to marry her lover Ah Guan. her owner charged her with grand / larceny for stealing herself* (Judy Yung, qtd. in *monkeypuzzle* 23). Following China Annie's example, Wong's "i" narrator likewise takes ownership of her physical/symbolic body:

i want it back. my eyes, my lips, my
fingers, my breasts, my rumbling stomach. all mine. my blood
thundering to deafen an army. jab of my insistent elbow. my pulse
beats defiance: i am i am.

(23)

In a reversal of the poststructuralist decentering of the Cartesian I, the racialized subject reclaims the "i." For her it is a much-needed site of agency and self-determination.

As important as such self-affirmation is in combating the effects of racialization, Wong drops the first person narrative mode in the second section of the book. Her critique of power is not so much expressed via an individual narrative of identity formation as enacted in disjunctive writing strategies that break up "the steamroller of the english language, / its etymology of/ assimilation / [that] tramples budding/ memory into sawdusty/ stereotypes" (29). Certainly Wong also thematizes the complexities of hybridity, both in the section title ("monkeypuzzle") and in individual poems that explore the intersecting trajectories of foreignness and "home." Her description of the monkey puzzle tree in an essay on migrancy aptly describes the thematic concerns in this section:

this type of tree hails from the chilean andes and gets its common name
from the shape of its spiraling green spikes. monkeys can climb up its

branches but can't get down. because of how the spikes are now point-
ing up at them, there's no easy way out. no escape. on a bad day, i feel
like those monkeys caught in the monkeypuzzle. here i am in canada.
dealing with the chance racist, sexist, classist, homophobic encounters
of any given day, stuck in this tree i can't leave. and to top it off, some
jerk yells, "why don't you go back home?" not understanding that this
monkeypuzzle is my home.

("the 'I' in migrant" 105–106)

But Wong also critiques the prickly spaces of hybridity and migrancy via
formal interventions that break up restrictive if not oppressive semantic and
symbolic structures. Creative page layout, variable typography, right jus-
tified margins, intermingled Cantonese and English words, exaggerated

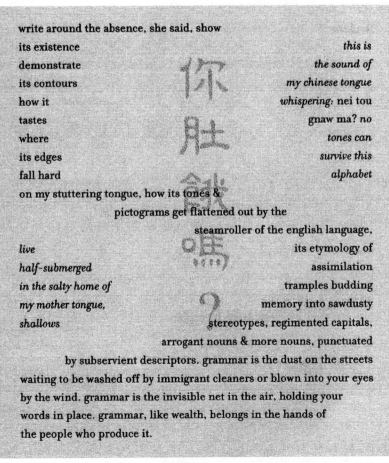

Figure 21. From *monkeypuzzle* by Rita Wong, page 29

white space, and other disjunctive practices literally create space on the page that enables her to "write around the absence" (29), to expand the semantic space, and to break up oppressive stereotypes.

Hybridity is enacted visually in the first poem of the section by double columns of text (see Fig. 21). The speaker starts off with a command to herself to "write around the absence," but in the middle of the page, her "stuttering tongue" collides with the "steamroller of the english language." At the point of collision, the watermark/ideograms that move vertically down the middle of the page and signify the linguistic and cultural ground of an ethnic Chinese-Canadian subject are overwritten by the colonizing force of English. That effect is enacted visually in the spread of its "arrogant nouns," "subservient descriptors," and "invisible net[s]" of grammar across the page, overriding the individual narrative. The *sound of / my chinese tongue*" fades to a whisper. Visually, the two margins—one flush right and the other flush left—set up two opposing points of departure and two colliding realities: the cultural/linguistic reality on the right-hand margin and the individual narrative on the left. The Cantonese words running down the middle, if understood, could bridge the gap: they express a very basic greeting—the equivalent of "how are you?" in English. But they, like the ethnic Chinese-Canadian subject, remain "inscrutable" to most Western readers. Also, Wong varies the phrase slightly. The Cantonese greeting translates as "have you eaten yet?" Wong's phrase says "are you hungry?" Wong explains: "there is a reference to the greeting but if you said 'are you hungry' to someone it would not quite come across as a hello. repetition with a difference" (email to Pauline Butling). Likewise the poem enacts various estrangements ("repetition with a difference") within familiar language/cultural structures.

Similarly, in "puzzlinen," double columns loosen the grip of imposed identities, in this instance, by continuously interrupting the narrative flow. Disjunction breaks up those "invisible nets":

everyone else	can
they don't see it	laugh
basket	chase
re	run
suzy wongs	pocohontas! run!
give them	hot food?
rotsa raffs	voice? what voice?
you must	make this up

(46)

The imperative voice in the last line speaks of liberation through the creative act ("you must make this up") even as it also critiques the interpellation of the racialized subject enacted in the command performances of the Suzy Wongs and Pocohontases of popular culture.

In section three, Wong introduces another barb in the monkeypuzzle of hybridity, that of the privileged position of the Chinese Canadian in China. When she goes "back" to China to travel and work, she recognizes she is inseparable from the patronizing, candy-throwing Westerner. Indeed "so much depends on the direction in which one is travelling," Wong notes sardonically, in a revision of the objectivism of William Carlos Williams ("'I' in Migrant" 107). Travelling from West to East, from North America to Asia, puts her on the literal and metaphoric "silk road," complicit with other westerners (despite her ethnic Chinese origins) and the imperialist/capitalist project:

> i touched the tip of the mythical silk
> road one afternoon as the bus
> sputtered to our impoverished
> destination.
> [...]
> a merchant's daughter raised on a
> practical diet counting change day in
> day out. i can smell how money snakes
> along the city road, only occasionally
> meandering to leak a few coins into the
> surrounding countryside.
>> ("I was dreaming my geography but
>> it's time to wake up," MP 67)

In the closing section, titled "passion rampant in small secret rooms," the subject becomes more active as she goes further inward, into "the secret rooms" of lesbian love. In "parchment" the "i" speaks an embodied, passionate lover/self into being. While racialization and cultural hybridity continue to inflect the self, the speaker "wrestle[s] new stories" with "each sweaty assertion." Note the active verbs: *write, wrestle, mark, inscribe*. Wong inscribes the lovers onto the "parchment" of the page (and into the cultural script):

> this globe my body so dry its surface flakes white, the only time this
> skin is white. upon contact, your eyes on my skin write an old tale,
> words we know too well. with time, we wrestle new stories from each

other, nets rip with each sweaty assertion. we are not all the same. the
trail of saliva leads here to your tribe & my tribe in this room private
as the histories in our stretched muscles. i mark you with my fingers,
my hair, my teeth. inscribe my body's anecdotes upon you so that you
cannot name me foreign. i speak myself against you, year after year,
replenish the oasis in this desert. you will learn my dialect as i have
learned yours, the pages of our exchange rustling anew. a pact,
you & i, a pact.

    (*monkeypuzzle* 89)

This is decidedly the most expansive and inclusive "you" of the book:
"you" includes the self, the lover, the page, and the reader as well as the face-
less "you" of previous poems. Writing a lesbian and racialized body, the poet
at once unravels imposed categories of class, race, and sexuality even as she
also *claims* and rewrites those identities. Hers is an emphatic act of "self-
writing"—in the sense defined by Jeanne Perreault—an act which "make[s]
the female body of she who says 'I' a site and source of written subjectiv-
ity, investing that individual body with the shifting ethics of a political,
racial, and sexual consciousness" (*Writing Selves* 2). As readers, we have the
pleasure of watching that "self-in-the-making" (Perreault 2) within the
"puzzles" of migrancy, identity, and hybridity. In relation to my opening
question of how poetry contributes to an activist agenda, Wong's poems
both critique and enact various exclusions in a creative/critical explo-
ration that moves both to the heart of language and form as much as to the
heart of the matter.

    In relation to the broader question of new directions in writing and
publishing in the 1990s, *monkeypuzzle* shows one writer's response to some
of the challenges of the decade, the challenges of producing self represen-
tations and of effecting the cultural transformations, for instance, that
Monika Kin Gagnon identified in her commentary on Writing Thru Race
(71). Rita Wong enacts class, gender, sexuality, and race-based critiques of
power in poems that are both formally innovative and politically engaged.
In so doing, she, along with many others, significantly expands the defini-
tion of radical poetics at the end of the twentieth century.

Notes

1 The first Indian Act, passed in 1880, assigned Indian "status" to First Nations peo-
ple (hence the term "status Indians"). The act established land reserves and allo-
cated funds for housing and farming on those reserves. The rationale for the act
reflects the racist premises of an imperialistic paternalism. Its purpose was to
oversee the transition of First Nations people from "primitive" peoples ("noble sav-

age," etc.) to civilized Canadians. To do so, Aboriginals were supposed to learn farming, learn English, convert to Christianity, and generally adopt the traditions and cultural practices of the European settler society. In the interim, the department of Indian Affairs would "manage" their lives and oversee their assimilation. Notwithstanding the "good" intentions (or perhaps because of those intentions), the Indian Act often had disastrous effects on First Nations people. Arguably the most injurious aspect of this policy was the forced attendance of thousands of Indian children at residential schools: the children were taken from their families, forbidden to speak their native languages, and forced to adopt white, Christian beliefs and practices. Many were also subjected to physical and sexual abuse. The effect was not only personal injury but also cultural genocide.

2   The provinces followed suit over the next twenty years, beginning with the province of British Columbia, which granted the vote to Chinese Canadians and status Indians in 1947, and to Japanese Canadians in 1949. Non-status Indians were also granted voting rights in the provinces, again beginning with BC in 1949 and ending with Quebec in 1969.

3   The restrictions extended into other areas as well: for instance Chinese Canadians were prohibited from working with white women, from getting a liquor license, a logger's license, or being hired on public works projects (Li 267).

4   The War Measures Act was replaced by the Emergencies Act, with more limited powers. Impetus to change the War Measures Act came both from Quebec (Front de Liberation de Québec) as a result of the outrage felt by civil libertarians and others over the Trudeau government's invocation of the act in 1970 for wholesale arrests of suspected FLQ terrorists, and from the Japanese-Canadian redress movement. Regarding the redress, surveys showed that two thirds of Canadians favoured a settlement, a further indication of the extent to which race issues had become a concern in the national consciousness.

5   Amendments to the act have been proposed on several occasions, but First Nations leaders, who insist that outstanding land claims and the issue of Aboriginal and treaty rights must be settled first, have rejected them. A significant amendment to the act was passed in 1985 (Bill 3-31) to address discrimination within the act against women and mixed-race Aboriginal people. The massive *Report of the Royal Commission of Aboriginal Peoples* released in 1990 contained many recommendations for changes to the act. In 2002, some amendments to the act were passed in parliament.

6   This statement comes from the editors' introduction to *Toronto Since Then (part 1)*. However in the introduction to *Toronto Since Then (part 2)*, written by Burnham alone, he argues for a more productive role: "Multiculturalism can subvent nationalism so long as the nation-state is willing to protect all of its citizenry .:. (there has to be some positive way to reclaim Pearsonian-Trudeau diplomacy as a counterargument to Kennedy-Kissinger-Reagan-Bush interventionism or Clinton isolationism)" (9). See also Roy Miki's "Sliding the Scale of Elision: 'Race' Constructs / Cultural Praxis" and Scott McFarlane's "The Haunt of Race: Canada's *Multiculturalism Act*, the Politics of Incorporation, and Writing Thru Race." For a comprehensive analysis of the problematics of multiculturalism, see Jeff Derksen's PhD dissertation, University of Calgary, 2000.

7 Historian Peter S. Li offers one example of a link between legislative and social change. He suggests that the rapid rise of a Chinese-Canadian middle class since mid-century and a parallel increase of "second-generation Chinese Canadians... in managerial and professional occupations" (273) was made possible by changes in immigration policy in the late 1940s, although he also notes continuing economic inequalities (272).

8 Unless otherwise indicated, historical dates and other facts in the preceding section have been taken from *The Canadian Encyclopedia Year 2000 Edition*.

9 The Accord needed unanimous approval in the federal parliament and in all provincial legislatures. On the final day for approval in the Manitoba legislature, Elijah Harper announced that he would not vote in favour of the accord because it failed to adequately address First Nations issues. Harper's act was the beginning of the end of the Accord.

10 They include a public outcry when the public policy group of the Women's Press turned down three stories (which had been previously accepted by the fiction editors) for a proposed anthology, *Imagining Women*; public demonstrations by Toronto's African-Canadian community against an exhibit at the Royal Ontario Museum ("Into the Heart of Africa") because of its "colonial perspective" (The Coalition for the Truth about Africa, Information Kit, qtd. in Tator et al. 41); and protests against two musicals (*Miss Saigon* and *Show Boat*) for their racist representations of black people. See Tator et al., *Challenging Racism in the Arts*, Nourbese Philip, *Frontiers*, and Brand, *Bread out of Stone* for accounts of some of these events.

11 For many of the seventy or so First Nations writers and writers of colour who attended, the retreat inspired them to immediate action. Suzette Mayr, for instance, came back from the retreat "full of energy and excitement" to "do something" (personal interview). Mayr, along with Hiromi Goto and Ashok Mathur who also attended the retreat, volunteered to do a 1993 special issue of *Absinthe, This Skin on Our Tongues*, on race issues. Roy Miki also credits the retreat with prompting him to be more proactive in seeking racialized writers for *West Coast Line* (personal interview).

12 See, for instance, "Canada Council Asks Whose Voice Is It Anyway?" by Stephen Godfrey (*Globe and Mail*, 21 March, 1992*)*; the reply by Joyce Zemans (director of the Canada Council),"Council's Policy 'Remains the Same'" (*Globe and Mail*, 4 April 1992); followed by Godfrey again with "The Problems Posed When Picking the Pickers Becomes Political" (*Globe and Mail*, 2 May 1992: C1); and "Artists Must Resist Political Pieties of Left and Right" by Ray Conlogue (*Globe and Mail*, Saturday, 6 June 1992: C3). Or check out the letters to the editor section on Saturday, 28 March 1992, where writers such as Timothy Findley express outrage at the new Canada Council policy on cultural appropriation.

13 The initial funding bodies included TWUC, the Heritage Ministry, and the Canada Council. Only the Heritage Ministry funding was withdrawn. The shortfall was covered through personal donations (including donations from some high-profile members of TWUC such as Margaret Atwood and Pierre Berton) and from organizations such as the Japanese Canadian Association.

14 See for instance, Dionne Brand's "Notes for Writing Thru Race" in her essay collection *Bread Out of Stone*.

15 Ten years earlier, Coach House Press had published an anthology of Japanese-Canadian poetry, *Paper Doors*, edited by Gerry Shikatani and David Aylward. It's interesting to note the similarities in editorial positions stated in the respective introductions. Both begin by noting the relatively recent appearance of Asian-Canadian writers because of the long history of exclusion and oppression. Shikatani and Aylward comment: "nothing hampered the development of a generic poetry more than that period of Japanese-Canadian history which has come to be called, 'the Evacuation'"(7).

16 Andy Quan makes a similar claim, some ten years later, in his introduction to *Swallowing Clouds, An Anthology of Chinese-Canadian Poetry* (edited by Andy Quan and Jim Wong-Chu, Arsenal Pulp Press, 1999). By anthologizing a self-identified "minority group" he argues, the group both enters and alters the mainstream: "We're walking through the door and bringing in the outcast, taking the outsider inside ... we are identifying ourselves as 'minority' writers at the same time as we are entering and altering and creating a 'mainstream'" ("Introduction" 8).

17 Terry Goldie published *Fear and Temptation: The Image of the Indigene in Canadian, Australian, and New Zealand Literatures* (1989) and Lally Grauer teaches Native and other literatures at Okanagan University College.

18 A recent glaring example of peripheral status for "colour" is the supplement to *Prairie Fire. Race Poetry Eh? A Poetic Supplement to Prairie Fire* produced to commemorate UNESCO's World Poetry Day and the United Nations International Day for the Elimination of Racial Discrimination. March 21, 2001." The collection is a supplement to the regular issue, volume 21, no. 4. It has the same number as the regular issue and is identified only as "Special Issue" even though it is a separate publication.

19 Unfortunately the introduction contains many inaccurate historical details. For instance, Warren Tallman and Robert Creeley organized the summer poetry workshop at UBC in 1963, not "Tallman, along with Duncan, Olson, and Ginsberg" (21); Charles Olson began teaching at the State University of Buffalo in 1963 and Robert Creeley in 1965; they did not both arrive "at the end of the 1960s" (24); John Newlove was not involved in founding the writing program at David Thompson University Centre in Nelson, nor did he teach in the Nelson area for any length of time (24). He taught at DTUC for one year. He was editor of *Writing* magazine for only one issue. *Writing* magazine continued in Vancouver under the editorship of Colin Browne. Not until much later was it edited by Nancy Shaw and Jeff Derksen (19). See *Writing* magazine entry in the chronology (1980).

20 For further discussion of the anthology, see my article "Writing as Social Practice: *Writing Class: The Kootenay School of Writing Anthology*," in *Xcp Cross-Cultural Poetics: Writing (working) Class 9* (2001): 85–92

21 Stan Bevington (along with Victor Coleman, Dennis Reid, and Wayne Clifford) had been one of the founders of the original Coach House Press and a member of its editorial board for many years, but he had resigned from the board because of their shift away from the original Coach House mandate. He set up a specialty print shop, named Coach House Printing, which did some contract printing for CHP.

22 Darren Wershler-Henry had been an active member of the small press movement in Toronto since 1989, editing and contributing to zines such as *n-1*, *SinOverTan*, *Virus 23*, and *TORQUE*.

23 Writers for Change was a secondary-school reading tour by a group of writers of colour to raise awareness of race-identified writers and writing. See *West Coast Line* 30 (Winter 2000) for a collection of some of the material presented during this tour.

24 DARE was formed to help the woman migrants from Fujian province who were placed in immigration jail after their illegal arrival in Canada in 1999.

■

Agamben, Georgio. *The Coming Community*. Trans. Michael Hardt. Minneapolis: U of Minnesota P, 1993.

Allen, Donald, ed. *The New American Poetry, 1945–1960*. New York: Grove, 1960. Rpt. 1999.

Allen, R.E.N. "Editor's Note." *Matrix* 55 (2001): 1.

Andrews, Bruce. *Paradise and Method: Poetics and Praxis*. Evanston, IL: Northwestern UP, 1996.

Armstrong, Jeannette C. "Four Decades of Canadian Native Poetry from 1960–2000." Armstrong and Grauer, eds., *Native Poetry*. xv–xxi.

———, ed. *Looking at the Words of Our People: First Nations Analysis of Literature*. Penticton: Theytus Books, 1993.

———. "'What I Intended Was to Connect...and It's Happened.'" Williamson, *Sounding Differences*. 7–26.

Armstrong, Jeannette, and Lally Grauer, eds. *Native Poetry in Canada: A Contemporary Anthology*. Peterborough: Broadview, 2001.

Atwood, Margaret. *The Journals of Susanna Moodie*. Toronto: Oxford UP, 1970.

Baker, Marie Annharte. *Being on the Moon*. Winlaw, BC: Polestar, 1990.

———. *Coyote Columbus Cafe*. Winnipeg: Moonprint, 1994. First section rpt. in Armstrong and Grauer, eds, *Native Poetry*. 71–76.

———. "I Make Sense of My World through Writing." Interview with Pauline Butling. Butling and Rudy, *Poets Talk*. 89–113.

Bakhtin, M.M. "Discourse in the Novel." Trans. Caryl Emerson and Michael Holquist. *The Dialogic Imagination: Four Essays by M.M. Bakhtin*. Ed. Michael Holquist. Austin: U of Texas P, 1981. 259–422.

Balan, Jars. "Cantextualities: Because one picture-poem can say more than a thousand words..." *Open Letter* 10.6 (Summer 1999): 7–17.

Banting, Pamela, Di Brandt, Jan Horner, and Jane Casey. Editorial. *Contemporary Verse 2* 8.4 (February 1985): 4.

Barbour, Douglas. *bpNichol and His Works*. Toronto: ECW, 1992.

———, ed. *Beyond TISH. New Writing, Interviews, Critical Essay*. Special issue of *West Coast Line* 25.1 (Spring 1991) and NeWest Press. Edmonton: NeWest, 1991.

———. *Daphne Marlatt and Her Works*. Toronto: ECW, 1994.

———. "Lyric/Anti-lyric: Some Notes about a Concept." *Line: A Journal of Contemporary Writing and Its Modernist Sources* 3 (1984): 45–63. Revised in Barbour, *Lyric/Anti-Lyric*. 7–32.

———. *Lyric/Anti-lyric: Essays on Contemporary Poetry*. The Writer as Critic VII. Gen. ed. Smaro Kamboureli. Edmonton: NeWest, 2001.

Barbour, Douglas, and Stephen Scobie, eds. *Carnivocal: A Celebration of Sound Poetry*. Calgary: Red Deer, 1999.

Barbour, Douglas, and Marni Stanley, eds. *Writing Right: Poetry by Canadian Women*. Edmonton: Longspoon, 1982.

Barnholden, Michael, and Andrew Klobucar, eds. *Writing Class: The Kootenay School of Writing Anthology*. Vancouver: New Star, 1999.

Barthes, Roland. *The Pleasure of the Text*. Trans. Richard Millar. New York: Hill and Wang, 1975.

———. *Writing Degree Zero*. Trans. Annette Lavers and Colin Smith. New York: Hill and Wang, 1968.

Bayard, Caroline. *The New Poetics in Canada and Quebec: From Concretism to Post-Modernism*. Toronto: U of Toronto P, 1989.

———, and Jack David, eds. *Out-Posts / Avant-Postes: Interviews, Poetry, Bibliographies and a Critical Introduction to 8 Major Modern Poets*. Erin, ON: Porcepic, 1978.

"BC poet faces critics." *Quill and Quire* 44.9 (July 1978): 27.

Beddoes, Julie. "Mastering the Mother Tongue: Reading Frank Davey Reading Daphne Marlatt's *How Hug a Stone*." *Canadian Literature* 155 (1997): 75–87.

Benjamin, Jessica. *The Bonds of Love: Psychoanalysis, Feminism, and the Problem of Domination*. New York: Pantheon, 1988.

Benjamin, Walter. *The Arcades Project*. Trans. Howard Eiland and Kevin McLaughlin. Cambridge: Belknap, Harvard UP, 1999.

Benson, Eugene, and William Toye, eds. *The Oxford Companion to Canadian Literature*. 2nd ed. Toronto: Oxford UP, 1997.

Berland, Jody. "Nationalism and the Modernist Legacy: Dialogues with Innes." Berland and Hornstein, *Capital Culture*. 14–37.

Berland, Jody, and Shelley Hornstein, eds. *Capital Culture: A Reader on Modernist Legacies, State Institutions, and the Value(s) of Art*. Montreal: McGill-Queen's UP. 2000.

Bernstein, Charles., ed. *Close Listening: Poetry and the Performed Word*. New York: Oxford UP, 1998.

———. "Optimism and Critical Excess (Process)." Bernstein, *A Poetics*. 150–78.

———. *A Poetics*. Cambridge: Harvard UP, 1992.

———, ed. *The Politics of Poetic Form: Poetry and Public Policy*. New York: Roof, 1990.

Billings, Robert. "Changes the Surface: A Conversation with Erin Mouré." *Waves* 14.4 (1986): 36–44.

bissett, bill. "untitled poem." *Catalogue*. Toronto: Nicky Drumbolis, 1986. n.p.

Black, Ayanna, ed. *Fiery Spirits: Canadian Writers of African Descent*. Toronto: HarperCollins, 1994.

Blaser, Robin, ed. *The Collected Books of Jack Spicer*. Los Angeles: Black Sparrow, 1975.

———. "George Bowering's Plainsong." Bowering, *Particular Accidents*. 9–28

———. *The Holy Forest*. Toronto: Coach House, 1993.

———. "Image-Nation 24 ("oh, pshaw,'." *The Holy Forest*: 353–63.

————. "Image-Nation 25 (Exody." *The Holy Forest*: 367–71.

————. "Letter from a Student—Letter to a Student." *Capilano Review* 2.13 (1994): 5–8.

————. "Particles." (Prepared for the Arts Council Symposium on Art and Politics, University of British Columbia 1967.) *The Pacific Nation* [2] (1969): 27–42.

————. *Pell Mell*. Toronto: Coach House, 1988.

————. "The Practice of Outside." Blaser, ed. *The Collected Books of Jack Spicer*. 271–329.

————. Preface. *The Pacific Nation* 1.1 (1967): 3.

————. Preface. *The Early Poems of Robert Duncan*. Buffalo: Shuffaloff, 1995.

————. "The Stadium of the Mirror." *Image-Nations 1–12 & The Stadium of the Mirror*. London: Ferry, 1974. 51–64.

Bloch, Maurice. "Internal and External Memory: Different Ways of Being in Memory." *Tense Past: Cultural Essays in Trauma and Memory*. Ed. Paul Antze and Michael Lambek. New York: Routledge, 1996. 215–34.

Bök, Christian, and Darren Wershler-Henry. "What Poets Are Doing: An Interview." *Brick* 69 (Spring 2002): 106–23.

Bordo, Susan. *Unbearable Weight: Feminism, Western Culture and the Body*. Berkeley: U of California P, 1993.

Bourdieu, Pierre. *The Field of Cultural Production: Essays on Art and Literature*. Ed. Randal Johnson. New York: Columbia UP, 1993.

Bowering, Angela, George Bowering, and David Bromige. *Piccolo Mondo: A Novel of Youth in 1961 as Seen Somewhat Later*. Toronto: Coach House, 1998.

Bowering, George. *Al Purdy*. Toronto: Copp Clark, 1970.

————. "the cabin." *Rocky Mountain Foot*. 47.

————. "The End of the Line." *Open Letter* 5.3 (Summer 1982): 5–10.

————. *Genève*. Toronto: Coach House, 1971.

————. *George: Vancouver*. Kitchener, ON: Weed/Flower, 1970.

————. Interview with Caroline Bayard and Jack David. Bayard and David, *Outposts*. 77–99.

————. Introduction. Nichol, *An H in the Heart*. xi–xiv.

————. *Particular Accidents: Selected Poems / George Bowering*. Edited with an Introduction by Robin Blaser. Vancouver: Talonbooks. 1979.

————. "Pauline Butling in Campbell Lake." 1987. Nine Poets Printed. Eleven broadsides in portfolio. Toronto: imprimerie dromadaire, 1986–1988.

————. "Reaney's Region." *A Way with Words*. Ottawa: Oberon, 1982. 37–53.

————. "still in the sky." *Rocky Mountain Foot*. 14.

————. *Rocky Mountain Foot, A Lyric A Memoir*. Toronto: McClelland & Stewart, 1968.

Braidotti, Rosi. *Nomadic Subjects: Embodiment and Sexual Difference in Contemporary Feminist Theory*. New York: Columbia UP, 1994.

————. *Patterns of Dissonance: A Study of Women in Contemporary Philosophy*. Trans. Elizabeth Guild. Cambridge: Polity, 1991.

Brand, Dionne. *Bread Out of Stone: Recollections Sex Recognitions Race Dreaming Politics.* Toronto: Coach House, 1994. 9–23.

———. "Canto III." Wallace, *Daughters.* 26–31.

———. *Land to Light On.* Toronto: McClelland & Stewart, 1997.

———. *No Language Is Neutral..*Toronto: Coach House, 1990.

———. "Notes for Writing Thru Race." Brand, *Bread out of Stone.* 173–83.

———. *Primitive Offensive.* Toronto: Williams Wallace, 1982.

Brandt, Di. *Mother, Not Mother.* Stratford, ON: Mercury, 1992.

Bronson, A.A., ed. *From Sea to Shining Sea: Artist-Initiated Activity in Canada, 1939–1987.* Toronto: Power Plant, 1987.

Brossard, Nicole. *The Aerial Letter.* Trans. Marlene Wildeman. Toronto: Women's P, 1988.

———. "The Aerial Letter." Brossard, *Aerial Letter.* 67–87.

———. *L'amèr ou le chapitre effrité (théorie/fiction).* Montreal: Quinze, 1977.

———. *Au présent des veines.* Trois-Rivières: Écrits des Forges, 1999.

———. *Baroque at Dawn.* Trans. Patricia Claxton. Toronto: McClelland & Stewart, 1997.

———. *Baroque d'aube.* Montreal: L'Hexagone, 1995.

———. *A Book.* Trans. Larry Shouldice. Toronto: Coach House, 1976.

———. "Le corps du personage." *Tessera* 19 (1995): 63–71.

———. *Daydream Mechanics.* Trans. Larry Shouldice. Toronto: Coach House, 1976.

———. "December 6, 1989 Among the Centuries." Ed. Louise Malette and Marie Chalouh. *The Montreal Massacre.* Charlottetown: Gynergy, 1991. 91–101.

———. *Le Désert Mauve.* Montreal: Hexagone, 1987.

———. "Écriture lesbienne: Stratégie de marque." Eribon, *Les études.* 51–56.

———. "Fluid Arguments." *Onward: Contemporary Poetry and Poetics.* Ed. Peter Baker. New York: Peter Lang, 1996. 315–46.

———. *Fluid Arguments.* Trans. Anne-Marie Wheeler. Ed. Susan Rudy. Stratford, ON: Mercury, forthcoming.

———. *French Kiss or, A Pang's Progress.* Montreal: Editions du Jour, 1974.

———. *French Kiss.* Trans. Patricia Claxton. Toronto: Coach House, 1986.

———. "From Radical to Integral." Trans. Marlene Wildeman. Brossard, *Aerial Letter.* 103–19.

———. "The Giant Nature of Words and Silence around Identity." Unpublished ts. Written in English by Brossard based on an extended version of Patricia Claxton's translation of Brossard's "Vingt pages entrecoupées de silence" and Pierre Joris's translation "I like to say we and look elsewhere."

———. "I like to say we and look elsewhere." Trans. Pierre Joris. Bernstein, *boundary* 2 (1999): 60–62.

———. "The Idea of Your Lips." *Tessera* 9 (1990): 126–29.

———. "Ideology and Imagination." Unpublished ts. 4 pps.

———. Interview with Carolyn Bayard and Jack David. Bayard and David, *Outposts.* 57–92.

————— . Interview with Clea Notar. O'Brien, ed. *So to Speak*. 122–43.

————— . "The Killer Was No Young Man." *The Montreal Massacre*. Ed. Louise Malette and Marie Chalouh. Charlottetown: Gynergy, 1991. 31–33.

————— . *la lettre arienne*. Montreal: Les Éditions du remue-ménage, 1985.

————— . *Lovhers*. Trans. Barbara Godard. Montreal: Guernica, 1986.

————— . "La Matière harmonieuse manoeuvre encore / Matter Harmonious Still Maneuvering." Trans. Lise Weil. *The Massachusetts Review: An/other Canada, another Canada? Other Canadas* 31.1–2 (1990): 86–95.

————— . *Mauve Desert*. Trans. Susanne de Lotbinière-Harwood. Toronto: Coach House, 1990.

————— . *Mécanique jongleuse*. Paris: Génération, 1973.

————— . "Memoire: hologramme du desir." *Quebec Studies* 31 (2001): 8–11.

————— . "Memory: Hologram of Desire." Trans. Lucille Nelson. *Trivia* 13 (1988): 42–47.

————— , and Daphne Marlatt. "Only a Body to Measure Reality By: Writing the In-Between." *The Journal of Commonwealth Literature* 31.2 (1996): 5–17.

————— . "Poetic Politics." Bernstein, ed., *The Politics*. 107–26.

————— . *Le Sens Apparent*. Paris: Flammarion, 1980.

————— . *She Would Be the First Sentence of My Next Novel / Elle serait la première phrase de mon prochain roman*. Trans. Susanne de Lotbinière-Harwood. Toronto: Mercury, 1998.

————— . *Sold-Out*. Montreal: Editions du Jour, 1973.

————— . "A State of Mind in the Garden." *Lesbian Selfwriting: The Embodiment of Experience*. Ed. Lynda Hall. New York: Haworth, 2000. 35–40.

————— , ed. *Les strategies du réel / the story so far*. Montreal and Toronto: La Nouvelle Barre du Jour / Coach House, 1979.

————— . *Surfaces of Sense*. Trans. Fiona Strachan. Toronto: Coach House, 1988.

————— . *These Our Mothers or: The Disintegrating Chapter*. Trans. Barbara Godard. Toronto: Coach House, 1983.

————— . *Turn of a Pang*. Trans. Patricia Claxton. Toronto: Coach House, 1976.

————— . "Writing as a Trajectory of Desire and Consciousness." Trans. Alice Parker. Parker and Meese. 179–85.

Brown, Wendy. "Wounded Attachments: Late Modern Oppositional Political Formations." *The Identity in Question*. Ed. John Rajchman. New York: Routledge, 1995. 199–228.

Burnham, Clint. *Allegories of Publishing: The Toronto Small Press Scene*. Toronto: Streetcar Editions, 1991.

————— . Introduction. *Open Letter* 8.9 (Summer 1994): 5–10.

————— , Lance La Rocque, and Lisa Narbeshuber. "Introduction: Toronto Since Then." *Open Letter* 8.8 (Winter 1994): 5–7.

————— . *Pandemonium*. Ottawa: hole chapbooks, 1996.

Butler, Judith, and Joan W. Scott, eds. *Feminists Theorize the Political*. New York: Routledge, 1992.

Butling, Pauline. "'Hall of Fame Blocks Women': Re/Righting Literary History: Women and BC Little Magazines." *Open Letter* 7.8 (Summer 1990): 60–76.

———. "Play and Carnival in the Formation of a Postmodern Aesthetic: A Study of Robert Duncan, Phyllis Webb and bpNichol." PhD Dissertation. State University of New York at Buffalo, 1987. UMI Dissertation Information Service, 1988.

———. "Robert Duncan: The Poem as Process." MA Thesis. University of British Columbia, 1966.

———. *Seeing in the Dark: The Poetry of Phyllis Webb.* Waterloo, ON: Wilfrid Laurier UP, 1997.

———. "Willow Wand Pen." Review of *The Diviners* by Margaret Laurence. *Open Letter* 3.2 (Fall 1975): 125–28.

———. "Writing as Social Practice: *Writing Class: The Kootenay School of Writing Anthology.*" *XCP Cross Cultural Poetics: Writing (working) Class* 9 (2001): 85–92.

Butling, Pauline and Susan Rudy. *Poets Talk: Conversations with Robert Kroetsch, Daphne Marlatt, Erin Mouré, Dionne Brand, Marie Annharte Baker, Jeff Derksen, and Fred Wah.* Edmonton: University of Alberta Press, 2005.

Cabri, Louis. "hole Magazine." *Capilano Review* 2.34 (Spring 2001): 5–22.

Canadian Encyclopoedia: Year 2000 Edition. Toronto: McClelland & Stewart, 2000.

Canadian Magazine Publishers' Association. July 2000. <http://www.cmpa.ca>.

Canadian Magazines for Everyone. Toronto: Canadian Magazine Publishers' Association, 1993.

Cardinal, Harold. *The Unjust Society.* 1969. 2nd ed. Vancouver: Douglas & McIntyre. 1999.

Chamberlain, Daniel. "Merleau-Ponty, Maurice." Woodbridge and Anderson, eds. 423–24.

Chronology of Canadian Poetry 1916–1989. National Library of Canada. <http://www.nlc-bnc.ca/services/quickref/echrpoe.htm>.

Clark, Susan. "Notes Towards." *Raddle Moon* 3 (1986): 2–4.

Claxton, Patricia, trans. "Vingt pages entrecoupées de silence." By Nicole Brossard. *Les écrits* (1999): 117–40.

Coach House Books. 9 March 2004: <http://www.chbooks.com>.

Coleman, Victor. "The Coach House Press: The First Decade: An Emotional Memoir." *Open Letter* 9.8 (Spring 1997): 26–35.

Collins, Jim. "Post-Modernism as Culmination: The Aesthetic Politics of Decentred Cultures." *The Post-Modern Reader.* Ed. Charles Jencks. New York: St. Martin's Press, 1992. 94–118.

Conlogue, Ray. "Artists Must Resist Political Pieties of Left and Right." *Globe and Mail* 6 June 1992: C3.

Conte, Joseph. *Unending Design: The Forms of Postmodern Poetry.* Ithaca: Cornell UP, 1991.

Cooley, Dennis. "Recursions Excursions and Incursions: Daphne Marlatt Wrestles with the Angel Language." *Line* 13 (1989): 66–79.

Cotnoir, Louise. "Introduction: Women of Letters." Godard, ed. *Collaboration.* 10.

Creeley, Robert. "Why Bother?" *Tish* 13 (14 September 1962): 2. Rpt. in Davey *Tish* 1–19. 251–52.

Culley, Peter. "Because I Am Always Talking." *Whispered Art History: Twenty Years at the Western Front.* Ed. Keith Wallace. Vancouver: Arsenal Pulp, 1993. 189–97.

Damon, Maria. "Was That 'Different,' 'Dissident' or 'Dissonant'? Poetry (n) the Public Spear: Slams, Open Readings, and Dissident Traditions." Bernstein, ed., *Close Listening.* 324–41.

Davey, Frank. "American Alibis: A Search for Kroetsch's Postmodernism." *Open Letter* 9.5–6 (Spring–Summer 1996): 241–51.

———. "The Beginnings of an End to Coach House Press." *Open Letter* 9.8 (Spring 1997): 40–77.

———. *Canadian Literary Power.* The Writer as Critic: Series IV. Gen. Ed. Smaro Kamboureli. Edmonton: NeWest, 1994.

———. *City of the Gulls and Sea.* Victoria: Morriss, 1964.

———. *The Clallam.* Vancouver: Talonbooks, 1973.

———. "Dear Fred, David, George, Others." *The Open Letter* 1.2 (March 1966): 3.

———. Editorial. *Open Letter* 9.8 (Spring 1997): 5–8.

———. Editorial. *Tish* 1 (September 1961): 1. Rpt. in *Tish 1–19.* 65.

———. "Editorial Changes." *Open Letter* 7.5 (Summer 1989): 5–6.

———. *From There to Here: A Guide to English-Canadian Literature since 1960.* Vol. 2. *Our Nature—Our Voices.* Erin, ON: Porcepic, 1974.

———. "A History of Coach House Quebec Translations." Forthcoming in Barbara Godard, ed., *Translation Studies in Canada.*

———. "The Problem of Margins." *Tish* 3 (14 November 1961): 11. Rpt. in *Tish 1–19.* 65.

———. *Selected Poems: The Arches.* Ed. bpNichol. Vancouver: Talonbooks, 1980.

———. *The Scarred Hull, A Long Poem.* Calgary: *Imago* 6, 1966.

———, ed. *Tish 1–19.* Vancouver: Talonbooks, 1975.

———. "Words and Stones in *How Hug a Stone." Line* 13 (1989): 40–46.

David, Jack. Introduction. *Selected Writing: As Elected bpNichol.* By bpNichol and Jack David. Vancouver: Talonbooks, 1980. 9–31.

———. "A Published Autopopography." *Essays on Canadian Writing* 1 (1974): 39–46.

Davidson, Michael. "Compulsory Homosociality: Charles Olson, Jack Spicer, and the Gender of Poetics." *Cruising the Performative: Interventions into the Representation of Ethnicity, Nationality, and Sexuality.* Eds. Philip Brett, Sue-Ellen Case, and Susan Leigh Foster. Bloomington: Indiana UP, 1995. 197–216.

———. *The San Francisco Renaissance: Poetics and Community at Mid-Century.* New York: Cambridge UP, 1989.

Davidson, Michael. "Language Poetry." Preminger and Brogan. 675–76.

de Lauretis, Teresa. "Strategies of Coherence: Narrative Cinema, Feminist Poetics, and Yvonne Rainer." *Technologies of Gender: Essays on Theory, Film, and Fiction*. Bloomington: Indiana UP, 1987. 107–26.

Delaney, Paul, ed. *Vancouver: Representing the Postmodern City*. Vancouver: Arsenal Pulp, 1994.

Deleuze, Gilles, and Félix Guattari. *A Thousand Plateaus: Capitalism and Schizophrenia*. Trans. Brian Massumi. Minneapolis: U of Minnesota P, 1987.

Denisoff, Dennis. "Acknowledging the Red Spades: An Interview with Erin Mouré." *West Coast Line* 11, 27.2 (1993): 124–35.

———. "Merger, She Wrote: Politicubism in Gertrude Stein and Erin Mouré." *Open Letter* 9.2 (Spring 1995): 114–22.

Derksen, Jeff. *But Could I Make a Living from It*. Philadelphia/Vancouver: hole chapbooks, 2000. Rpt. in Derksen, *Transnational*. 24–39.

———. *Down Time*. Vancouver: Talonbooks, 1990.

———. *Dwell*. Vancouver: Talonbooks, 1993.

———. "Globalism and the Role of the Cultural: Nation, 'Multiculturalism,' and Articulated Locals." PhD Dissertation. Department of English, University of Calgary, 2000.

———. "Making Race Opaque: Fred Wah's Poetics of Opposition and Differentiation." *West Coast Line* 8, 29.3 (1995): 63–76.

———. *Memory Is the Only Thing Holding Me Back*. Nelson: David Thompson UP, 1984.

———. *MyNewIdea*. 12 March 2004: <http://www.lot.at/mynewidea_com>.

———. "Poetry and Other Rearticulatory Practices." Unpublished ts.

———. "Poetry and Social Relations." Unpublished ts.

———. *Selfish: Something Deep Inside Liberal Cultural Relativism Says "Yes I Can."* Vancouver: Pomflit, 1993.

———. "Sites Taken as Signs: Place, the Open Text, and Enigma in New Vancouver Writing." Delany, ed., *Vancouver*. 144–61.

———. *Transnational Muscle Cars*. Vancouver: Talonbooks, 2003.

———. "Torquing Time [Fred Wah]." Barbour, ed., *Beyond TISH*. 161–65.

———. "Unrecognizable Texts: From Multicultural to Antisystemic Writing." Wallace and Marks, ed., *Telling It Slant*. 145–60.

———. *Until*. Vancouver: Tsunami, 1987. Rpt. 1989.

———, Sabine Bitter, and Helmut Weber. "But Is It Politics?" 12 March 2004: <http://www.lot.at/politics>.

Deckter, Ann. "Going on Twenty—A Celebration." *Fireweed* 56 (Winter 1996): 4.

Dorn, Edward. *Slinger*. Berkeley: Wingbow, 1975.

Douglas, Stan, ed. *Vancouver Anthology: The Institutional Politics of Art*. Vancouver: Talonbooks, 1991.

Dragland, Stan. "Coach House Poetry, 1965–96." *Open Letter* 9.8 (Spring 1997): 78–91.

———. *Bees of the Invisible: Essays in Contemporary English Canadian Writing*. Toronto: Coach House, 1991.

———. "Messages from Don McKay and Stan Dragland, founding partners of *Brick* on the 20th Anniversary of Brick Books in 1995." 12 March 2004: <http://www.brickmag.com>.

Drainie, Bronwen. "Controversial Writers' Meeting Is Both Meet and Right." *Globe and Mail* 16 April 1994: E3.

———. "Colour Me Politically Correct and Proud of It." *Globe and Mail* 25 June 1994: C3.

Duncan, Robert. "For the Novices of Vancouver, 25–28 August 1962." *TISH* 13 (1962): 3–5. Rpt. in Davey, ed., *TISH* No. 1–19. 251–56.

———. "The Homosexual in Society." Faas, *Young Robert Duncan*. 319–22.

———. "Ideas of the Meaning of Form." *KULCHUR* 4 (1961): 60–74. Rpt. in Duncan, *Fictive Certainties*. New York: New Directions, 1985. 89–105.

———. Lectures in Vancouver, 24–26 July 1961. Audio tape recordings. Contemporary Literature Collection, Simon Fraser University Library.

———. "Letter to John Wieners." *Measure* 3 (Winter 1958): n.p.

Dybikowski, Ann, Victoria Freeman, Daphne Marlatt, Barbara Pulling, Betsy Warland, eds. *In the Feminine: Women and Words / Les Femmes et les mots: Conference Proceedings*. Edmonton: Longspoon, 1985.

En'owkin Centre, Theytus Books. March 2004 <http://www.enowkincentre.ca/>

Eribon, Didier, ed. *Les études gay et lesbiennes*. Paris: Centre Georges Pompidou, 1998.

Faas, Ekbert. *Young Robert Duncan: Portrait of the Poet as Homosexual in Society*. Santa Barbara: Black Sparrow, 1983.

Fawcett, Brian. Interview with Barry McKinnon. McKinnon, ed., *BC Poets*. 29–39.

Ferguson, Deanna. *Ddilemma*. Vancouver: hole chapbooks, 1997.

Finch, Anne, and Kathrine Varnes, eds. *An Exaltation of Forms: Contemporary Poets Celebrate the Diversity of Their Art*. Ann Arbor: U of Michigan P, 2002.

Fireweed Collective. Fireweed: Going on Twenty—A Celebration. *Fireweed* 56 (1996).

Flax, Jane. *Thinking Fragments: Psychoanalysis, Feminism, and Postmodernism in the Contemporary West*. Berkeley: U of California P, 1990.

Forsyth, Louise. "Bursting Boundaries in the Vast Complication of Beauty: Transported by Nicole Brossard's *Au présent des veines*." *Verdure* 5–6 (February 2002): 100–108.

Foucault, Michel. *The History of Sexuality*. Trans. Robert Hurley. Vol. 1. New York: Vintage, 1980.

The Four Horsemen. *CaNADAda*. LP. Griffin, 1972.

———. *Live in the West*. LP. Starborne, 1977.

Fournier, Suzanne. "BC Poetry: Off the Page, onto the Stage." *MacLean's* 7 May 1979: 20d, 20f.

Frank, Thomas. "Why Johnny Can't Dissent." *Commodify Your Dissent: Salvos from the Baffler*. Ed. Thomas Frank and Matt Weiland. New York: Norton, 1977.

Friedman, Susan Stanford. "Creativity and the Childbirth Metaphor: Gender Difference in Literary Discourse." *Speaking of Gender*. Ed. Elaine Showalter. New York: Routledge, 1989. 73–100.

From the West: 'Writing in our Time': Seven Benefit Readings for West Coast Literary Presses. Vancouver: Vancouver Poetry Centre, 1980. Poster.

Frye, Northrop. *The Bush Garden: Essays on the Canadian Imagination.* Toronto: Anansi, 1971.

Fulford, Robert. "George Orwell, Call Your Office." *Globe and Mail* 30 March 1994: A1.

Gadd, Maxine. *Lost Language: Selected Poems by Maxine Gadd.* Ed. Daphne Marlatt and Ingrid Klassen. Toronto: Coach House, 1982.

——— . "Squabbling Through Eternity." Interview by Daphne Marlatt and Ingrid Klassen. Gadd, *Lost Language.* 165–80.

Gagnon, Monika Kin. "Building Blocks: Anti-Racist Initiatives in the Arts." Gagnon, *Other Conundrums: Race, Culture and Canadian Art.* Vancouver: Arsenal Pulp, 2000. 51–72.

Geddes, Gary, ed. *Twentieth Century Poetry and Poetics.* Toronto: Oxford UP, 1969.

——— . *20th Century Poetry & Poetics.* 2nd ed. Toronto: Oxford UP, 1973.

——— . *20th Century Poetry & Poetics.* 3rd ed. Toronto: Oxford UP, 1985.

——— . *20th Century Poetry & Poetics.* 4th ed. Toronto: Oxford UP, 1996.

Gilbert, Sandra M., and Susan Gubar, eds. *The Norton Anthology of Literature by Women.* New York: Norton, 1985.

Ginsberg, Allen. "Notes for *Howl* and Other Poems." *The New American Poetry.* Ed. Donald M. Allen. San Francisco: Grove, 1960. 414–18.

Godard, Barbara. "The Avant-garde in Canada: *Open Letter* and *La Barre du Jour.*" *ellipse* 23/24 (1979): 98–113.

——— , ed. *Collaboration in the Feminine: Writings on Women and Culture from Tessera.* Toronto: Second Story, 1994.

——— . "Epi(pro)logue: In Pursuit of the Long Poem." *Open Letter* 6.4 (Summer/Fall 1985): 301–35.

——— , ed. *Gynocritics/La Gynocritique: Feminist Approaches to Writing by Canadian and Quebecoise Women/Approaches féministe a l'écriture canadiennes et québécoise.* Toronto: ECW, 1987.

——— . "Nicole Brossard." *Profiles in Canadian Literature.* 87. Toronto: Dundurn, 1986. 121–28.

——— . "Structuralism/Poststructuralism: Language, Reality and Canadian Literature." Moss, *Future Indicative.* 25–51.

——— , Daphne Marlatt, Kathy Mezei, and Gail Scott. "Theorizing Fiction Theory." Godard, ed., *Collaboration.* 53–62.

——— . "Women of Letters (Reprise)." Godard, ed., *Collaboration.* 258–306.

Godfrey, Stephen. "Canada Council Asks Whose Voice Is it Anyway?" *Globe and Mail* 21 March 1992. C1, C5.

——— . "The Problems Posed When Picking the Pickers Becomes Political." *Globe and Mail* 2 May 1992: C1.

Goldie, Terry, and Daniel David Moses, eds. *An Anthology of Native Canadian Literature in English*. Toronto: Oxford UP, 1992.

Grauer, Lally. "Tuning Up, Tuning In." Armstrong and Grauer, eds. *Native Poetry*. xxi–xxviii.

Harris, Claire. *Drawing Down a Daughter*. Fredericton: Goose Lane, 1992.

——— . "'I dream of a new naming…'" Williamson, *Sounding Differences*. 115–30.

——— . "Ole Talk: A Sketch." Scheier et al. 13–41.

——— . "Poets in Limbo." Neuman and Kamboureli, *A Mazing Space*. 115–25.

——— . "Why Do I Write?" Morrell, ed., *Grammar of Dissent*. 26–33.

Harvey, David. *Spaces of Hope*. Berkeley: U of California P, 2000.

Hejinian, Lyn. "Language and 'Paradise.'" *Line* 6 (1985): 83–99.

Henderson, Mae Gwendolyn. "Speaking in Tongues: Dialogics, Dialectics, and the Black Woman Writer's Literary Tradition." Butler and Scott. 144–66.

Hindmarch, Gladys [Maria]. Interview with Brad Robinson. "Before *TISH*: from Oral History of Vancouver." *Open Letter* 2.1 (Winter 1971–1972): 30–36.

——— . *The Watery Part of the World*. Vancouver: Douglas & McIntyre, 1997.

Huffer, Lynne. An Interview with Nicole Brossard, Montreal, October 1993. Trans. David Dean. *Yale French Studies* 87 (1995): 115–21.

——— . "From Lesbos to Montreal: Nicole Brossard's Urban Fictions." *Yale French Studies* 90 (1996): 95–114.

Huk, Romana, ed. *Assembling Alternatives: Reading Postmodern Poetries Transnationally*. Middletown, CT: Wesleyan UP, 2003.

Hunt, Erica. "Notes for an Oppositional Poetics." Bernstein, ed., *The Politics*. 197–212.

Hutcheon, Linda. *The Canadian Postmodern: A Study of Contemporary English-Canadian Fiction*. Toronto: Oxford UP, 1988.

——— . "Present Tense: The Closing Panel." With Stephen Scobie, George Bowering, and Robert Kroetsch. Moss. 239–45.

Hyde, Lewis. *The Gift: Imagination and the Erotic Life of Property*. New York: Vintage, 1975.

Imagining Women. Second Story Collective. Toronto: Women's Press, 1988.

Jaeger, Peter. *ABC of Reading TRG*. Vancouver: Talonbooks, 1999.

Jencks, Charles. "The Post-Avant-Garde." *The Post-Modern Reader*. Ed. Charles Jencks. London: St. Martin's, 1992. 215–24.

Jones, Daniel. "Towards a Theory of Small Press." *Paragraph* 13.3 (1991): 21–24.

Kalaidjian, Walter. *Languages of Liberation: The Social Text in Contemporary American Poetry*. New York: Columbia UP, 1989.

Kamboureli, Smaro, ed. *Making a Difference: Canadian Multicultural Literature*. Toronto: Oxford UP, 1996.

——— . *On the Edge of Genre: The Contemporary Canadian Long Poem*. Toronto: U of Toronto P, 1991.

——— . *Scandalous Bodies: Diasporic Literature in English Canada*. Don Mills, ON: Oxford UP, 2000.

————— . "The Technology of Ethnicity: Law and Discourse." *Open Letter* 8.5–6 (Winter–Spring 1993): 202–17.

Kearns, Katherine. *Psychoanalysis, Historiography, and Feminist Theory: The Search for Critical Method.* Cambridge, UK: Cambridge UP, 1997.

Keeshig-Tobias, Lenore. "After Oka—How Has Canada Changed." Moses and Goldie, *An Anthology.* 235–36.

Kerouac, Jack. *The Dharma Bums.* New York: Viking, 1958.

Kertzer, Jon. *Worrying the Nation: Imagining a National Literature in English Canada.* Toronto: U of Toronto P, 1998.

Kiyooka, Roy. *The eye in the landscape: Retinal/Images of The Point, Hornby Island; THE EYE IN THE LANDSCAPE: photo/graphs, of The Point, Hornby Island. August 1st thru 31st 1970.* Vancouver: National Film Board. 1970.

————— . *Kyoto Airs.* Vancouver: Periwinkle, 1964. Rpt. in *Pacific Windows* 7–24.

————— . *Pacific Windows: Collected Poems of Roy K. Kiyooka.* Ed. Roy Miki. Vancouver: Talonbooks, 1997.

————— . "Road to Yase." *Kyoto Airs.* Rpt. in *Pacific Windows*: 11–12.

————— . "The Street." *Kyoto Airs.* Rpt. in *Pacific Windows*: 11–12.

Klobucar, Andrew, and Michael Barnholden, eds. *Writing Class: The Kootenay School of Writing Anthology.* Vancouver: New Star, 1999.

Knutson, Susan. "Imagine Her Surprise." Godard, *Collaboration.* 228–36.

————— . *Narrative in the Feminine.* Waterloo: Wilfrid Laurier UP, 1999.

Kostash, Myrna. "You Don't Check Your Colour at the Door." *Globe and Mail* 2 May 1994: C 5.

Kostelanetz, Richard. "The New Poetries in North America." *Open Letter* 2.7 (Spring 1974): 18–35.

————— , with assistance from H.R. Brittain et al., *Dictionary of the Avant-Gardes.* New York: Shirmir, 2000.

Kristeva, Julia. *Revolution in Poetic Language.* Trans. Margaret Waller. New York: Columbia UP, 1984.

Kroetsch, Robert, ed. *A Canadian Issue.* Special issue of *Boundary* 2. 3.1 (1974).

————— . *Completed Field Notes: The Long Poems of Robert Kroetsch.* Toronto: McClelland & Stewart, 1989.

————— . *Completed Field Notes: The Long Poems of Robert Kroetsch.* 2nd ed. Edmonton: U of Alberta P, 2001.

————— . "D-Day and After: Remembering a Scrapbook I Cannot Find." Kroetsch, *A Likely Story.* 127–47.

————— . *The Hornbooks of Rita K.* Edmonton: U of Alberta P, 2001.

————— . *The Ledger.* London, ON: Applegarth Follies, 1975.

————— . *A Likely Story: The Writing Life.* Red Deer, AB: Red Deer College P, 1995.

————— . "The Poetics of Rita Kleinhart." *Open Letter* 9.2 (Spring 1995): 61–74.

————— . "The Poetics of Rita Kleinhart." Kroetsch, *A Likely Story.* 171–216.

————— . "The Poetics of Rita Kleinhart." *West Coast Line* 10, 27.1 (1993): 34–39.

————— . *Seed Catalogue.* Winnipeg: Turnstone, 1977.

———. "Sitting Down to Write: Margaret Laurence and the Discourse of Morning." Kroetsch, *A Likely Story*. 148–56.

———. "To the Wahs, on the Kootenay River." Kroetsch, *Completed Field Notes* [1989]. 107.

Kröller, Eva-Marie. *George Bowering: Bright Circles of Colour*. Vancouver: Talonbooks, 1992.

Krukowski, Damon, Naomi Yang, and Peter Gizzi, eds. *Exact Change Yearbook 1995*. Boston and Manchester: Exact Change and Carcanet Presses, 1995.

LaCapra, Dominick. *History and Criticism*. Ithaca: Cornell UP, 1985.

Lambek, Michael. "The Past Imperfect: Remembering as Moral Practice." *Tense Past: Cultural Essays in Trauma and Memory*. Ed. Paul Antze and Michael Lambek. New York: Routledge, 1996. 235–54.

Laurence, Margaret. *The Diviners*. Toronto: McClelland & Stewart, 1974.

———. *The Fire Dwellers*. Toronto: McClelland & Stewart, 1973.

Lauterback, Ann. "Pragmatic Examples: The Nonce." Sloan, *Moving Borders*. 600–602.

Lazer, Hank. *Opposing Poetries*. 2 vols. Evanston, IL: Northwestern UP, 1996.

Lecker, Robert. "The Canada Council and the Construction of Canadian Literature." *English Studies in Canada* 25.3–4 (September and December 1999): 322–45.

Lee, Sky, Lee Maracle, Daphne Marlatt, and Betsy Warland (the *Telling It* book collective), eds. *Telling It: Women and Language across Cultures*. Vancouver: Press Gang, 1990.

Levertov, Denise. "Hypocrite Women." *O Taste and See*. Norfolk, CT: New Directions, 1962. Rpt. in Gilbert and Gubar, *Norton Anthology*. 1943–44.

———. "The Mutes." Rpt. in Gilbert and Gubar. *Norton Anthology*. 1951–53.

Li, Peter S. "The Chinese Minority in Canada, 1858–1992: A Quest for Equality." *Chinese Canadians: Voices from a Community*. Ed. Evelyn Huang with Lawrence Jeffery. Vancouver: Douglas and McIntyre, 1991. 264–75.

Literary Press Group. 2000. < http://www.lpg.ca >.

Lockey, Ottie. "Writers in Dialogue." *Broadside: A Feminist Review* 2.8 (June 1981): 9.

Long-liners Conference Issue. The Proceedings of the Long-liners Conference on the Canadian Long Poem, York University, Toronto, 29 May–1 June 1984. Ed. Frank Davey and Ann Munton. *Open Letter* 6.2–3 (Summer/Fall 1985).

Lyotard, J. *The Postmodern Condition*. Manchester: Manchester UP, 1986.

Maart, Rozena. "Pain and Glory." Review of *Drawing Down a Daughter* by Claire Harris. *Books in Canada* (May 1993): 48.

Mackey, Nathaniel. *Discrepant Engagement: Dissonance, Cross-Culturality, and Experimental Writing*. Cambridge Studies in American Literature and Culture. Vol. 71. Cambridge: Cambridge UP, 1993.

Magazine of Further Studies. Edited and produced by Jack Clarke, George and Collette Butterick, Mike [Albert] and Pat Glover, Fred and Pauline Wah, [Butling] and others. Six Issues (Fall 1965–Spring 1969). Buffalo, NY.

Mandel, Eli. "Talking West." Interview with Roy Miki. *Line* 1 (Spring 1983):26–43.

Mann, Ron. *Poetry in Motion.* 1982. VHS/DVD, 2002.

Marks, Elaine, and Isabelle de Courtivron, eds. *New French Feminisms: An Anthology.* New York: Shocken, 1981.

Marlatt, Daphne. "arriving, for Fred & Pauline." *here & there.* Lantzville, BC: Island Writing Series, 1981. 5–6.

——— . "Booking passage." *Salvage.* 115–19.

——— . "Editorial." *Periodics: A Magazine Devoted to Prose* 4 (1978): 78–80.

——— . *Frames of a Story.* Toronto: Ryerson, 1968.

——— . *Ghost Works.* Edmonton: NeWest, 1993.

——— . "Given This Body: An interview with Daphne Marlatt" by George Bowering. *Open Letter* 4.3 (Spring 1979): 32–88.

——— . *here & there.* Lantzville: *Island* Writing Series, 1981.

——— . *leaf leaf/s.* Los Angeles: Black Sparrow, 1969.

——— . "The Measure of the Sentence." *Open Letter* 5.3 (Summer 1982): 90–92.

——— . "In the Month of Hungry Ghosts." *Capilano Review* 16–17 (1979): 45–95.

——— . "Introduction: Meeting on Fractured Margins." Lee, *Telling It.* 9–18.

——— . "Introduction: Women of Letters." Godard, *Collaboration.* 13.

——— . "musing with mothertongue." *Touch to My Tongue.* Edmonton: Longspoon, 1987. 45–49. Rpt. in "Musing with Mothertongue." Marlatt, *Readings.* 9–13.

——— . *Net Work: Selected Writing/Daphne Marlatt.* Ed. Fred Wah. Vancouver: Talonbooks, 1980.

——— . "On Salvaging: A conversation with Daphne Marlatt." Pauline Butling and Susan Rudy. Butling and Rudy, *Poets Talk.* 29–41.

——— . *Readings from the Labyrinth.* The Writer as Critic VI. Gen. Ed. Smaro Kamboureli. Edmonton: NeWest, 1998.

——— . *Rings.* Vancouver: *Georgia Straight* Writing Supplement, 1971.

——— . *Salvage.* Red Deer, AB: Red Deer College, 1991.

——— . "Self-Representation and Fictionalysis." *Tessera* 8 (1990): 13–17. Rpt. in Godard, *Collaboration.* 202–206; Marlatt, *Readings.* 122–30.

——— . *Steveston.* Vancouver: Talonbooks, 1974.

——— . "The Story, She Said." Pacific Rim Express: Excerpts from a Group of Eight Writers. *The British Columbia Monthly* 3. 8 (December 1977): n.p.

——— . *Touch to My Tongue.* Edmonton: Longspoon, 1984.

——— . *Vancouver Poems.* Toronto: Coach House, 1972.

——— . *What Matters: Writing 1968–70.* Toronto: Coach House, 1972.

Marlatt, Daphne, and Nicole Brossard. *Mauve.* Vol. 40. Montreal: NBJ, 1985.

Marlatt, Daphne, and Betsy Warland. *Double Negative.* Charlottetown: Gynergy, 1988.

Mathur, Ashok. "Panel Discussion on Marginalized Voice." *Open Letter* 8. 5–6 (Winter–Spring 1993): 146–47.

———. "Race Poetry: An eh-ditorial." Mathur, *Race Poetry, Eh?* 5–10.

———, ed. *Race Poetry, Eh? A Poetic Supplement to Prairie Fire.* [Produced to commemorate UNESCO's world poetry day and the United Nations International Day for the Elimination of Racial Discrimination, March 21, 2001.] *Prairie Fire* 21.4 (Winter 2000–2001).

Mauss, Marcel. *The Gift: Forms and Functions of Exchange in Archaic Societies.* Translated by Ian Cunnison. Glencoe, IL: Free Press, 1954.

Mayr, Suzette, Hiromi Goto-Tongu, and Ashok Mathur. "Of Skins, Tongues, and Many Voices." *This Skin on Our Tongues.* Special Issue of *Absinthe.* Precedes 6.1 (Summer 1993): 4.

McCaffery, Steve. "The International Festival of Sound Poetry: A Brief History." McCaffery and Nichol, *Sound Poetry.* 19.

———. "Voice in Extremis." Bernstein, *Close Listening.* 162–78.

———. "Writing as a General Economy." *North of Intention: Critical Writings 1973–1986.* Toronto: Nightwood Editions, 1986. 201–21.

McCaffery, Steve, and bpNichol. "Intro: The Open Ladder Essay." McCaffery and Nichol, *Rational Geomancy.* 227–29.

———. Introduction. *Canadian "Pataphysics [sic].* Ed. The Toronto Research Group. *Open Letter* 4.6–7 (Winter 1980–1981): 7–8.

———. *Rational Geomancy: The Kids of the Book-Machine. The Collected Research Reports of the Toronto Research Group: 1973–1982.* Ed. with an Introduction by Steve McCaffery. Vancouver: Talonbooks, 1992.

———. "Research Report 3: The Language of the Performance of Language." McCaffery and Nichol, *Rational Geomancy.* 224–90.

———, eds. *Sound Poetry: A Catalogue for the Eleventh International Sound Poetry Festival. Toronto, Canada. October 14 to 21, 1978.* Toronto: Underwhich, 1978.

McCarthy, Cavan, et al., eds. *Tlaloc 10, New Canadian Poets, 1960–65.* (1966).

McClure, Michael. *Ghost Tantras.* San Francisco: Four Seasons, 1969.

McFarlane, Scott. "The Haunt of Race: Canada's *Multiculturalism Act,* the Politics of Incorporation and Writing Thru Race." *Fuse* 18.3 (Spring 1995): 25–31.

McGann, Jerome, ed. "Postmodern Poetries: Jerome J. McGann Guest-Edits an Anthology of Language Poets From North America and the United Kingdom." *Verse* 7:1 (Spring 1990): 6–73.

McKinnon, Barry. BC *Poets and Print: Barry McKinnon Talks with Ten British Columbia Poet/Publishers.* Special Issue of *Open Letter* 7.2–3 (Summer–Fall 1988).

———. "The Caledonian Writing Series: A Chronicle." *line* 2 (Fall 1983): 2–17.

McKnight, David. *New Wave Canada: The Coach House Press and the Small Press Movement in English Canada in the 1960s.* Ottawa: National Library of Canada, 1996.

McPherson, Karen S. "Writing the Present in Nicole Brossard's *Baroque d'aube.*" *American Review of Canadian Studies* 30.3 (2000): 361–82.

Melanson, Holly. *Literary Presses in Canada, 1975–1985. A Checklist and Bibliography*. Occasional Paper. Vol. 43. Halifax: School of Library and Information Studies, 1988.

Messerli, Douglas, ed. *The Gertrude Stein Awards in Innovative American Poetry 1993–94*. Los Angeles: Sun and Moon, 1995.

Messerli, Douglas, ed. *The Poet's Calendar for the Millennium*. Los Angeles: Sun and Moon, 1999.

Mezei, Kathy. "Introduction: Women of Letters." Godard, ed., *Collaboration*. 16.

Michelût, Dore, Anne-Marie Alonzo, Charles Douglas, Paul Savoie, Lee Maracle, Ayanna Black. *Linked Alive*. Toronto: Editions Trois, 1990.

Middleton, Peter. "The Contemporary Poetry Reading." Bernstein, ed., *Close Listening*. 262–99.

Miki, Roy. "Afterword: Coruscations, Plangencies, and the Syllibant: After Words to Roy Kiyooka's *Pacific Windows*." Kiyooka, *Pacific Windows*. 301–20.

———. *Broken Entries: Race, Subjectivity, Writing*. Toronto: Mercury, 1998.

———. Editor's Note. *West Coast Line* 1, 24.1 (Spring 1990): 7–8.

———. "From Exclusion to Inclusion." *The Canadian Forum* 73.832 (1994): 5–8.

———. Interview with Pamela Wallin. CBC Newsworld. [14 May] 1994.

———, ed. *Meanwhile: The Critical Writings of bpNichol*. Vancouver: Talonbooks, 2002.

———. Notes on Contributors. *West Coast Line* 10, 27.1 (1993): 5–8.

———. Notes on Contributors. *West Coast Line* 24, 31.3 (1997): 95–96.

———, ed. *Pacific Windows: Collected Poems of Roy K. Kiyooka*. Vancouver: Talonbooks, 1997.

———. Preface. *line* 1 (spring 1983): 1–2.

———. "Sliding the Scale of Elision: 'Race' Constructs / Cultural Praxis." Miki, *Broken Entries*. 125–59.

———, ed. *Tracing the Paths: Reading ≠ Writing The Martyrology*. Vancouver: Talonbooks, 1988.

———. "Why We're Holding the Vancouver Conference." *Globe and Mail* 7 April 1994: A17.

———. "Writing Thru Race: Chair's Report." *The Writers' Union of Canada Newsletter* 23.3 (September 1995).

Miki, Roy, and Fred Wah. Preface. *Colour. An Issue: West Coast Line* 13–14, 28.1–2 (1994): 5–6.

Miller, Nancy K. *Subject to Change: Reading Feminist Writing*. New York: Columbia UP, 1988.

Minh-ha, Trinh T. *When the Moon Waxes Red: Representation, Genre and Cultural Politics*. New York: Routledge, 1991.

Morgan, Robin, ed. *Sisterhood Is Powerful: An Anthology of Writings from the Women's Liberation Movement*. New York: Random House, 1970.

Morrell, Carol, ed. *Grammar of Dissent: Poetry and Prose by Claire Harris, M. Nourbese Philip, Dionne Brand*. Fredericton: Goose Lane, 1994.

Moses, Daniel David. *Delicate Bodies*. Toronto: Blew Ointment. 1980.

Moses, Daniel David, and Terry Goldie, eds. *An Anthology of Canadian Native Literature in English*. Toronto: Oxford UP, 1992.

———. "Preface: Two Voices." Moses and Goldie. xii–xxii.

Moss, John, ed. *Future Indicative: Literary Theory and Canadian Literature*. Ottawa: U of Ottawa P, 1987.

Mouré, Erin. "Acknowledging the Red Spades." Interview with Dennis Denisoff. *West Coast Line* 12, 27.2 (1993): 124–35.

———. *Domestic Fuel*. Toronto: Anansi, 1985.

———. *A Frame of the Book / The Frame of a Book*. Toronto: Anansi, 1999.

———. *Furious*. Toronto: Anansi, 1988.

———. *The Green Word: Selected Poems 1973–1992*. Toronto: Oxford UP, 1994.

———. Interview with Peter O'Brien. O'Brien, *So to Speak*. 230–49.

———. "It Remained Unheard." *dANDelion* 15.2 (1988): 79–85.

———. *O Cidadán*. Toronto: Anansi, 2002.

———. *Pillage Laud: cauterizations, vocabularies, catigas, topiary, prose: poems*. Toronto: Moveable Text, 1999.

———. *Sheepish Beauty, Civilian Love*. Montreal: Vehicule, 1992.

———. *Sheep's Vigil by a Fervent Person: A Translation of Alberto Caeiro/Fernando Pessoa's O guardador de rebanhos*. Toronto: Anansi, 2001.

———. *Visible Spectrum*. Vancouver: pomflit 1, 1992.

———. "Why Not Be Excessive?" Interview with Pauline Butling and Susan Rudy. Butling and Rudy, *Poets Talk*. 43–61.

———. *wsw (West South West)*. Montréal: Vehicule, 1989.

Nelson, Sharon. "Bemused, Branded, and Belittled: Women and Writing in Canada." *Fireweed* 15 (1982): 65–97.

Nelson, Linda, and Lise Weil. Preface. *Trivia: A Journal of Ideas* 13 (Fall 1998): 3-4.

Neuman, Shirley, and Smaro Kamboureli, eds. *A Mazing Space: Writing Canadian Women Writing*. Edmonton: NeWest, 1986.

New, W.H., ed. *Inside the Poem: Essays and Poems in Honour of Donald Stephens*. Toronto: Oxford UP, 1992.

Niagara Frontier Review. Ed. Charles Brover (1), Harvey Brown (2–3); Contributing Eds. Charles Olson, Jack Clarke, and Fred Wah (2–3). Buffalo, NY: 1964–1966.

Nichol, bp. *bp*. Boxed edition which includes a chapbook *Journeying & the returns*, flip book *Wild Thing*; envelope containing 13 poems on separate sheets ("Letters Home"), flexidisc recording of phonetic and sound poems ("Borders"), kinetic poem/sculpture ("Cold Mountain"), a visual poem/ envelope, an audio recording, and a single sheet "Statement: November 1966." Toronto: Coach House, 1967.

———. *bpNichol*. (aka *jouneying and the return*) Audiotape. High Barnet, 1972.

———. "A Contributed Editorial." *Open Letter* 3.9 (Fall, 1978): 5–6.

———. "Introduction to *The Last Blew Ointment Anthology Volume 2*." Miki, ed., *Meanwhile*. 417–21.

———. "Cutting Them All Up." Interview with George Bowering. *Alphabet* 18–19 (1971): 18–21.

———. "Dada Lama." Nichol, *An H in the Heart.* 33–37.

———. *Ear Rational: Solo Performances 1970–1980.* Audio tape. Milwaukee, WI: Membrane, 1982.

———. *Gifts: The Martyrology books[s] 7 & [Nichol's parenthesis].* Toronto: Coach House, 1990.

———. *An H in the Heart: bpNichol: A Reader.* Ed. Michael Ondaatje and George Bowering. Toronto: McClelland & Stewart, 1994.

———. Interview with Caroline Bayard and Jack David. Bayard and David, *Outposts.* 16–40.

———. Interview with Pierre Coupey, Dwight Gardener, Brian Fisher, Daphne Marlatt, and Gladys Hindmarch. *Capilano Review* 8–9 (Fall 1975, Spring 1976): 313–46. Rpt. and edited in Miki, *Meanwhile.* 146–59.

———. Interview with Ken Norris. *Essays on Canadian Writing* 12 (1978): 243–50.

———. Introduction. *Ganglia Press Index. grOnk* 8.7. Toronto: Ganglia Press, 1972: [5].

———. *Konfessions of an Elizabethan Fan Dancer.* London, UK: Writers' Forum Quartos. 3 January 1967.

———. *KonfessIonS of an ElizAbeThan Fan Dancer.* Toronto: Weed/Flower, 1973 [1974]. Rpt., Coach House Books, 2003.

———. "The Pata of Letter Feet, or, The English Written Character as a Medium for Poetry." *Open Letter* 6.1 (Spring 1985): 79–95.

———. "statement, november 1966." Miki, ed., *Meanwhile.* 18.

———. *Translating Translating Apollinaire: A Preliminary Report from A Book of Research.* Milwaukee and Toronto: Membrane, 1979.

———. *The True Eventual Story of Billy the Kid.* Toronto: Weed/Flower, 1970.

Nichol, bp, and Frank Davey. "The Book as a Unit of Composition." *Open Letter* 6.1 (Spring 1985): 39–46.

———. "The Prosody of Open Verse." *Open Letter* 5.2 (Summer 1982): 5–13.

Nichols, Miriam. "A/Politics of Contemporary Anglo-Canadian Poetries: The Toronto Research Group and the Kootenay School of Writing." Huk, *Assembling.* 66–85.

Niechoda, Irene, and Tim Hunter. "A Tishstory, edited by Irene Niechoda and Tim Hunter from an afternoon discussion at Simon Fraser University in 1985." Barbour, *Beyond TISH.* 83–98.

Norris, Ken. *The Little Magazine in Canada 1925–1980: Its Role in the Development of Modernism and Post-Modernism in Canadian Poetry.* Toronto: ECW, 1984.

O'Brien, Peter, ed. *So to Speak: Interviews with Contemporary Canadian Writers.* Montreal: Vehicule, 1987.

Olney, James, ed. *Autobiography: Essays Theoretical and Critical.* Princeton: Princeton UP, 1980.

——— . "Some Versions of Memory/Some Versions of *Bios*: The Ontology of Autobiography." Olney, *Autobiography* 236–67.

Olson, Charles. "Projective Verse." Allen, *New American Poetry*. 386–97.

——— . *Reading at Berkeley*. Transcribed by Zoe Brown. San Francisco: Coyote Books, 1966.

Ondaatje, Michael. *Sons of Captain Poetry* [Film 1970]. Rereleased on *The Films of Michael Ondaatje*. DVD. 2002.

——— , ed. *The Long Poem Anthology*. Toronto: Coach House, 1979.

O'Sullivan, Maggie, ed. *Out of Everywhere: Linguistically Innovative Poetry by Women in North America and the UK*. London: Reality Street, 1996.

Pacey, Desmond. "The Writer and His Public: 1920–1960." *The Literary History of Canada*. Part IV. Gen. Ed. Carl F. Klinck. Toronto: U of Toronto P. 477–95.

Parker, Alice. *Liminal Visions of Nicole Brossard*. New York: Peter Lang, 1998.

Parker, Alice, and Elizabeth Meese, eds. *Feminist Critical Negotiations*. Philadelphia: John Benjamin, 1992.

Perreault, Jeanne. *Writing Selves: Contemporary Feminist Autography*. Minnesota: U of Minnesota P, 1995.

Perreault, Jeanne, and Sylvia Vance, eds. *Writing the Circle: Native Women of Western Canada*. Edmonton: NeWest, 1990.

Persky, Stan, and Dennis Wheeler. "What We're Up To." *Georgia Straight Writing Supplement* 2 (18 January–4 February 1970): 39.

Philip, M. Nourbese. *Frontiers: Essays and Writings on Racism and Culture*. Toronto: Mercury, 1992.

——— . *A Genealogy of Resistance and Other Essays*. Stratford, ON: Mercury, 1997.

Pound, Ezra. "A Retrospect." Geddes, *Twentieth Century* (3rd ed.). 619–32.

——— . *Make It New*. New Haven: Yale UP. 1935.

Pratt, Mary Louise. *Imperial Eyes: Travel Writing and Transculturation*. New York: Routledge, 1992.

Preminger, Alex, and T.V.F. Brogan, eds. *The New Princeton Encyclopedia of Poetry and Poetics*. Princeton: Princeton UP, 1993.

Probyn, Elspeth. "Technologizing the Self: A Future Anterior for Cultural Studies." *Cultural Studies*. Ed. Laurence Grossberg, Cary Nelson, and Paula A. Treichler. New York: Routledge, 1992. 501–11.

Purdy, Al. *The Cariboo Horses*. Toronto: McClelland & Stewart, 1965.

Quan, Andy. Introduction. *Swallowing Clouds*. 7–10.

——— , and Jim Wong-Chu, eds. *Swallowing Clouds: An Anthology of Chinese Canadian Poetry*. Vancouver: Arsenal Pulp, 1999.

Read the Way He Writes: A Festschrift for bpNichol. Ed. Paul Dutton and Steven [Ross] Smith. *Open Letter* 6.5–6 (Summer–Fall 1986).

Reid, Dennis. "The Old Coach House Days." *Open Letter* 9.8 (Spring 1997): 23–25.

Reid, Jamie. Editorial. *TISH* 4 (December 14, 1961): 1. Rpt. in Davey, ed., *TISH No. 1–19*. 71.

Rice Paper. Editorial statement. 5.1 (1995): 2.

Rich, Adrienne. "Compulsory Heterosexuality and Lesbian Existence." *Blood, Bread and Poetry: Collected Poems 1979–1985*. New York: W.W. Norton, 1986. 23–75.

———. *Twenty-one Love Poems*. Emeryville, CA: Effie's Press, 1976.

Riley, Denise. *Selected Poems*. London: Reality Street, 2000.

Robertson, Lisa. *The Apothecary* [chapbook]. Vancouver: Tsunami, 1991.

———. *Debbie: An Epic*. Vancouver: New Star, 1997.

———. "How Pastoral: A Manifesto." Wallace and Marks. 21–26.

———. "How Pastoral: A Prologue." Robertson, *Xecolgue*. n.p.

———. "How Poems Work" column on "In 1970" by Denise Riley. *Globe and Mail* 8 September 2001: D14.

———. *Occasional Work and Seven Walks from the Office for Soft Architecture*. Astoria: Clear Cut, 2003.

———. *Soft Architecture: A Manifesto*. The Poetry Project at St. Mark's Church. 14 December 2000. <http://www.poetryproject.com/roberts .html>.

———. *The Weather*. Vancouver: New Star, 2001.

———. *Xeclogue*. Vancouver: Tsunami Editions, 1993. Rev. ed., Vancouver: New Star, 1999.

———, and Steve McCaffery. *PhillyTalks* 17 (3 October 2000). 17 May 2002. <http://www.english.upenn.edu/~wh/phillytalks/library.shtml> (Includes webcast reading.)

———, and Steve McCaffery. *PhillyTalks* 17 (3 October 2000). 24 November 2003. <http://www .english.upenn.edu/~wh/phillytalks>.

———, with Catriona Strang and Christine Stewart. *The Barscheit Horse*. Vancouver: The Berkeley Horse 49, 1993.

Robinson, Brad. "Before *TISH*: From *Oral History of Vancouver*." *Open Letter* 2:1 (Winter 1971–72): 30–36.

Rudy Dorscht, Susan, ed. *Wanting It Other/Wise: Race, Sexualities, Bodies, Texts*. Special issues of *Open Letter* 9.2 (Spring 1995) and *Open Letter* 9.3 (Summer 1995).

Salkey, Andrew. "Review of *Drawing Down a Daughter* by Claire Harris." *World Literature Today* 67 (1993): 435–36.

Samis, David, ed. *Love Poems for a Media Age*. Vancouver: Ripple Effect Press, 2001.

Sanders, Leslie. Introduction. *Daughters of the Sun, Women of the Moon: Poetry by Black Canadian Women*. Wallace, ed., *Daughters*. 10–13.

Sava, Sharla. "As If the Oceans were Lemonade." *Front* (The Western Front Society) 9.5 (1998): 24–27.

Schaub, Danielle, ed. *Mapping Canadian Cultural Space: Essays on Canadian Literature*. Jerusalem: Hebrew U Magnes P, 2000.

Scheier, Libby, Sarah Sheard, and Eleanor Wachtel, eds. *Language in Her Eye: Writing and Gender (Views by Canadian Women Writing in English)*. Toronto: Coach House, 1990.

Scobie, Stephen. *bpNichol: What History Teaches.* Vancouver: Talonbooks, 1984.

——— . "The Footnoted Text." Scobie, *Signature, Event, Cantext.* 70–89.

——— . *Signature Event Cantext.* The Writer as Critic: II. Gen. Ed., Smaro Kamboureli. Edmonton: NeWest, 1989.

Scream in High Park. January 2004. < http://www.thescream.ca >.

Scree. Ed. Fred Wah. Five Issues (March 1971–July 1972). South Slocan, BC.

Shaw, Nancy. "Expanded Consciousness and Company Types: Collaboration since Intermedia and the N.E. Thing Co." *Vancouver Anthology: The Institutional Politics of Art.* Ed. Stan Douglas. Vancouver: Talonbooks, 1991. 85–103.

Shakti's Words: An Anthology of South Asian Canadian Women's Poetry. Ed. Diane McGifford and Judith Kearns. Toronto: TSAR, 1990.

Shikatani, Gerry, and David Aylward, eds. *Paper Doors: An Anthology of Japanese Canadian Poetry.* Toronto: Coach House, 1981.

Siegler, Karl. "An 'Open Letter' to Members of ACCUTE." *ACCUTE Newsletter* (Fall 1995): n.p. [single page insert].

Silliman, Ron. Afterword. "*Who Speaks:* Ventriloquism and the Self in the Poetry Reading." Bernstein, ed., *Close Listening.* 360–78.

——— . *The New Sentence.* New York: Roof, 1987.

Silver. 25 Years of Artist-Run Culture. The New Gallery's Retrospective Catalogue: 1975–2000. Calgary: New Gallery, 2000.

Skarstedt, Sonja A. "Poetry and Feminism: The Requisite Duo." *Poetry Canada* 10.4 (1989–1990): 10–11.

Sloan, Mary Margaret, ed. *Moving Borders: Three Decades of Innovative Writings by Women.* Jersey City, NJ: Talisman House, 1998.

Souster, Raymond, ed. *New Wave Canada: The New Explosion in Canadian Poetry.* Toronto: Contact, 1966.

Sowton, Ian. "An Autobiography: Of Sorts (Reading Claire Harris, *Drawing Down a Daughter*)." *Open Letter* 9.3 (1995): 25–34.

Stake, Chuck. [Don Mabie.] "Correspondence Art. The First Ten: 1975–1985." *The Catalogue. Clouds 'n' Water Gallery / Off Centre Centre.* Calgary: Off Centre Centre, 1985. 110–116.

Stein, Gertrude. "Composition as Explanation." *Selected Writings of Gertrude Stein.* Ed. Carl Van Vechten. New York: Vintage, 1962. 511–23.

Sturrock, John. *The Language of Autobiography: Studies in the First Person Singular.* Cambridge, UK: Cambridge UP, 1993.

Suleiman, Susan. *Subversive Intent: Gender, Politics and the Avant-Garde.* Cambridge, MA: Harvard UP, 1990.

Sum. Ed. Fred Wah. Contributing editors: John Keys and Ron Loewinsohn. Seven Issues (December 1963–April 1965). Albuquerque, NM (to Issue no. 3) and Buffalo, NY.

Summer Poetry Course. University of British Columbia, Vancouver, 1963. Audiotape recordings. Contemporary Literature Collection, Simon Fraser University Library, Burnaby, BC and on-line at Slought Networks. <http://www. slought.net>.

Tallman, Warren. "'Some Consistent Quality of Intelligent Love': Open Letter to Phyllis Webb." *Vancouver Poetry Centre Newsletter* 18 (15 June 1979): 2.

Tator, Carol, Francis Henry, and Winston Mattis. *Challenging Racism in the Arts: Case Studies in Controversy and Conflict.* Toronto: U of Toronto P, 1998. 86–110.

——— . "The Writing Thru Race Conference." Tator et al. 86–110.

Thesen, Sharon, ed. *The New Long Poem Anthology.* Toronto: Coach House, 1991.

——— , ed. *The New Long Poem Anthology.* 2nd ed. Vancouver: Talonbooks, 2001.

Thomas, Audrey. *Latakia.* Vancouver: Talonbooks, 1979.

Thompson, Courtney, and derek beaulieu. "an editorial mapping." *filling Station* 16 (1999): n.p.

Thompson, Paul. "Believe It or Not: Rethinking the Historical Interpretation of Memory." *Memory and History: Essays on Recalling and Interpreting Experience.* Ed. Jaclyn Jeffrey and Glenace Edwell. New York: UP in America and the Institute for Oral History, 1994.

Thrall, William, and Addison Hibbard. *A Handbook to Literature.* New York: Odyssey, 1960.

Toronto Research Group [bpNichol and Steve McCaffery]. Introduction. *Canadian 'Pataphysics. Open Letter* 4.6 and 7 (Winter 1980–1981): 7–8.

——— . "Introduction: The Open Ladder Essay." McCaffery and Nichol, *Rational Geomancy.* 227.

Tratt, Grace, ed. *Checklist of Canadian Small Presses: English Language.* Halifax: School of Library and Information Sciences, 1974.

Turner, Victor W. "Liminality." Woodbridge and Anderson, 578–79.

Ubu Web Visual, Concrete, and Sound Poetry Website. <http://www.ubu.com>.

Vickery, Ann. *Leaving Lines of Gender: A Feminist Genealogy of Language Writing.* Hanover and London: Wesleyan UP, 2000.

Vidaver, Aaron. "Vancouver, 1963." *Minutes of the Charles Olson Society* 30 (April 1999): 2.

Wachtel, Eleanor. "Why bp into cc Won't Go." *Books in Canada* June–July (1979): 3–6.

Wah, Fred. AMONG. Toronto: Coach House, 1972.

——— . *Breathin' My Name with a Sigh.* Vancouver: Talonbooks, 1981.

——— . *Diamond Grill.* Edmonton: NeWest, 1996.

——— . "Don't Sit around Language: An Interview with Fred Wah." Interview with Lola Lemire Tostevin. *Poetry Canada Review* 9.1 (1987): 3–5.

——— . *Earth.* Canton, NY: Institute of Further Studies, 1974.

——— . "Editorial: A Sound Direction." *TISH* 3 (14 November 1961): 1. Rpt. in Davey, ed., *TISH* 1–19. 51.

———. "Faking It." *West Coast Line*, 10, 27.1 (1999): 30–33. Rpt. in Wah, *Faking It*. 11–16.

———. *Faking It: Poetics and Hybridity. Critical Writing 1984–1999*. The Writer as Critic VII. Gen. Ed. Smaro Kamboureli. Edmonton: NeWest, 2000.

———. "Five Ones for P." *Border Crossings* 10.1 (1991): 24.

———. "For the Western Gate." Wah, AMONG. 8.

———. "Fred Wah on Hybridity and Asianicity in Canada." Interview with Susan Rudy. Butling and Rudy, *Poets Talk*. 143–69.

———. "Half-Bred Poetics." *Absinthe* 9.2 (1996): 60–65. Rpt. in Wah, *Faking It*. 71–96.

———. "household." Calgary: Wrinke Press Broadside, 2003.

———. "If Yes Seismal." *Absinthe*. 5.1 (Summer 1992): 38.

———. Introduction. *Net Work: Selected Writing /Daphne Marlatt*. Marlatt, *Net Work*. 1–21.

———. *Lardeau: Selected First Poems*. Toronto: Island, 1965.

———. "Lardeau/Summer 1964." *Earth*. Rpt. in *Loki*: 36–37.

———. *Loki Is Buried at Smoky Creek: Selected Poems*. Ed. George Bowering. Vancouver: Talonbooks, 1980.

———. "Making Strange Poetics." *Open Letter* 6.2–3 (Summer–Fall 1985): 213–17.

———. "Margins into Lines: A Relationship." *TISH* 4 (14 December 1961): 5–6. Rpt. in Davey, *TISH* 1–19. 51–52.

———. "Mrs. Richard's Grey Cat." A discussion with Steve McCaffery. *Open Letter* 3.9 (Fall 1978): 53–63.

———. *Music at the Heart of Thinking*. Red Deer, AB: Red Deer College, 1987.

———. "Pauline's House" [written on the occasion of Fred and Pauline's 22nd wedding anniversary]. 1984. Reprinted as "Her House, Likewise Shining Words to Tell You I Love You." *Border Crossings* 10.1 (1991): 24.

———. *Pictograms from the Interior of BC*. Vancouver: Talonbooks, 1975.

———. "Poetics of the Potent." *Open Letter* 9.2 (Spring 1995): 75–87. Rpt. in Wah, *Faking It*. 194–208.

———, ed. *Scree*. Edited and published by Fred Wah, South Slocan, BC. (March/April 1971–July 1972).

———. *So Far*. Vancouver: Talonbooks, 1991.

———. "Transcreation: A Conversation with Fred Wah [with bpNichol and Pauline Butling]: T.R.G. Report One: Translation (Part 3)." *Open Letter* 3.9 (Fall 1978): 34–52.

———. *Tree*. Writing Series. Vol. 9. Vancouver: Vancouver Community Press, 1972.

———. *Waiting for Saskatchewan*. Winnipeg: Turnstone, 1985.

———. "Which at first seems to be a going back for origins: Notes on a reading of some American women writers." Neuman and Kamboureli, *A Mazing Space*. 374–79.

Wallace, Ann, ed. *Daughters of the Sun, Women of the Moon: Poetry by Black Canadian Women*. Stratford, ON: Williams Wallace, 1990.

Wallace, Mark, and Steven Marks, eds. *Telling It Slant: Avant-Garde Poetics of the 1990s*. Tuscaloosa: U of Alabama P, 2002.

Watts, Charles, and Edward Byrne, eds. *The Recovery of the Public World: Essays on Poetics in Honour of Robin Blaser*. Vancouver: Talonbooks, 1999.

Webb, Phyllis. *Hanging Fire*. Toronto: Coach House, 1990.

Wershler-Henry, Darren. *Free as in Speech and Beer: Open Source, Peer-to-Peer and the Economics of the Online Revolution*. Toronto: Prentice Hall, 2002.

——— . "'A New Medium Immediately': A Talk with Darren Wershler-Henry." *filling Station* 18 (2000): 10–12.

——— . *NICHOLODEON: a book of lowerglyphs*. Toronto: Coach House, 1997.

Wershler-Henry, Darren, and Mark Surman. *Common Space: Beyond Virtual Community*. Toronto: Prentice Hall, 2002.

Williamson, Janice. *Sounding Differences: Conversations with Seventeen Canadian Women Writers*. Toronto: U of Toronto P, 1993.

Wong, Rita. "The 'I' In Migrant." *West Coast Line* 30, 33.3 (Winter 2000): 105–108.

——— . Interview with Larissa Lai. *West Coast Line* 30, 33.3 (Winter 2000): 72–82.

——— . *monkeypuzzle*. Vancouver: Press Gang, 1998.

——— . "ricochet." Mathur, *Race Poetry, Eh?* 26–27.

Wong-Chu, Jim, and Andy Quan, eds. *Swallowing Clouds: An Anthology of Chinese-Canadian Poetry*. Vancouver: Arsenal Pulp, 1999.

Woodbridge, Linda, and Roland Anderson, eds. *Encyclopedia of Contemporary Literary Theory: Approaches, Scholars, Terms*. Ed. Irena R. Makaryk. Toronto: U of Toronto P, 1993. 578–80.

Woolf, Virginia. *A Room of One's Own*. London: Hogarth, 1929.

Yoon, Jin-Me, and Chick Rice. Untitled photographs. Concept by Jin-Me Yoon, Photography by Chick Rice. *Colour. An Issue. West Coast Line* 13–14, 28.1–2 (Spring–Fall, 1994): 297–301.

Young-Ing, Greg. "The Estrangement and Marginalization of Aboriginal Writers in Canada." *Paragraph* 15. 3–4 (Spring 1994): 23–27.

——— . "Traditional Aboriginal Voices." Armstrong, *Looking*. 178–87.

Zemans, Joyce. "Council's policy 'remains the same.'" *Globe and Mail* 4 April 1992: D7.

Canadian Government: Documents, Reports, and Statutes

Canada. An Act to Amend the Indian Act, SC 1985, c. 27 [formerly Bill C-31].

Canada Council. Advisory Committee for Racial Equality in the Arts. *Recommendations of the Advisory Committee to the Canada Council for Racial Equality in the Arts and the Response of the Canada Council*. Ottawa: The Council. 1992.

Canada Citizenship Act, SC 1946, c. 15 [came into effect January 1947].

Canadian Charter of Rights and Freedoms, Part 1 of the *Constitution Act*, 1982, being Schedule B to the Canada Act of 1982 (UK), 1982. c. 11.

Canadian Multiculturalism Act. SC 1988, c. 31 [formerly Bill C-93].

Constitution Act 1982, being Schedule B to the Canada Act 1982 (UK), 1982, c. 11.

Emergencies Act. SC 1988, c. 29.

Federal Cultural Policy Review Committee. *Report of the Federal Cultural Policy Review Committee*, by Louis Applebaum and Jacques Hébert. Ottawa: Department of Communications, Information Service, 1982.

The Indian Act, SC 1880, c. 28. Included in the *Revised Statutes of Canada 1886* as the Indian Act, RSC 1886, c. 43.

Royal Commission on Aboriginal Peoples. *Bridging the Cultural Divide: A Report on Aboriginal People and Criminal Justice in Canada*. Ottawa: The Commission, 1996.

Royal Commission on Bilingualism and Biculturalism. *Final Report of the Royal Commission on Bilingualism and Biculturalism, Volume 4*, by A. Davidson Dunton and André Laurendeau. Ottawa: Queen's Printer, 1970. Tabled in the Parliament of Canada, 8 October 1971.

Royal Commission on the Status of Women in Canada. *Report of the Royal Commission on the Status of Women in Canada*, by Florence Bird. Ottawa: Information Canada, 1970. Tabled in the Parliament of Canada in December, 1970.

Trudeau, Pierre Elliot. *The Federal Response* [to Volume 4 of the *Report of the Royal Commission on Bilingualism and Biculturalism*]. Appendix to Hansard, 8 October 1971. < http://www.canadahistory.com/sections/documents/trudeau_on_multiculturalism.htm > 5 March 2004. Known as *The White Paper*.

War Measures Act. SC 1914, c. 2 [included in subsequent *Revised Statues of Canada*: RSC 1927, c. 206; RSC 1952, c. 288; RSC 1970, c. W-2; RSC 1985, c. W-2].

■

Horner, Jan, 13

House of Anansi Press, 6, 32

housepress, 139

Howe, Susan, 46n9

Hryniuk, Angela, 9, 14, 131, 133

Hurtig, Annette, 15, 24

Hutcheon, Linda, 73

hybridity, 103–107, 111, 246

Hyde, Lewis, 63

Hyland, Gary, 11

identity politics: and poetics, 55. *See also* subjectivity.

image poetry (deep image), 17

Imago magazine, 3–4, 65

imperialism/anti-imperialism: and aesthetics, 89, 90, 91, 97, 100

Indian Act, 229, 230, 250n1

Inglish: Writing with an Accent conference, 136–37

Inkster, Tim and Elke, 12

innovation: as avant-garde, 17–20

Intermedia, 35

International Feminist Book Fair (third), 34, 80, 133–34, 239

International Festival of Sound Poetry, 13–14

internet: and poetics, 197–202, 243, 235

intertextuality, 175, 178

Interventing the Text conference, 136

Iron magazine, 5

IS magazine, 6

Island magazine, 4, 6, 38

Island: Vancouver Island's Quarterly Review of Poetry and Fiction, 9

It's a Cultural Thing conference, 137

Ito, Sally, 14

Itwaru, Arnold, 14

Jaeger, Peter, 134, 139

Jankola, Beth, 8

Japanese Canadian redress, 230

Jiles, Paulette, 6, 14, 130

Jirgens, Karl, 14, 128

Johanson, Reg, 138

Johnson, Dennis, 12

Johnsson, Tomas, 108

Jones, Daniel, 39, 42, 133

Jones, LeRoi [Amiri Baraka], 54

Joseph, Clifton, 68, 76n20

Kamboureli, Smaro, 42, 132, 230

Karasick, Adeena, 8, 129

Kattan, Naim, 144

Kearns, Lionel, 2, 6, 10, 52, 53, 58n2, 58n4; and *TISH*, 49; and concrete poetry, 66

Keeshig-Tobias, Lenore, 25, 132, 138, 232

Kemp, Penn, 73

Kerouac, Jack, 52

Kertzer, John, 42

Kirkwood, Hilda, 13

Kiyooka, Roy, 3, 8, 9, 13, 23; and performance 52; poetics, 91, 92

Klobucar, Andrew, 139, 242, 235

Knighton, Ryan, 138

Knister, Raymond, 17

Kootenay School of Writing (KSW), 35, 46n9, 127, 131, 133, 146; history of, 14, 130, 195, 227n2, 241–44

Kostash, Myrna, 147, 233

Kostelanetz, Richard, 18, 19

Kristeva, Julia, 36

Kroetsch, Robert, 10, 13, 115, 136; poetics of loss/absence, 116–21, 124; and subjectivity, 115–17, 120, 121; as theorist, 73, 118, 119, 147

Kwa, Lydia, 10, 13, 131

Kwakwaka'wakw, 95. *See also* potlatch.

La Fave, Kim, and Carol, 135

LaCapra, Dominick, 17, 27n5

Lai, Larissa, 26

Lambeck, Michael, 142, 148

Lane, Patrick, 8, 11

language: and the body, 116, 165, 167; centred poetry, 46n9, 47n12, 89, 195, 217, 226, 242; vs content, 50; and place, 89, 100, 101n1, 101n9, 115; and racism, 248; and subjectivity, 89, 167

Lanthier, Phil, 12

Laurence, Margaret, 118, 151

Lauterback, Ann, 39

Lavoie, Guy, 10

Lecker, Robert, 13, 44

Lee, Bennett, 235–37

Lee, David, 128

Lee, Dennis, 3, 6, 12, 23

LeHeup, Jason, 138

Leith, Linda, 12

lesbian: poetics, 186–94; as subject, 81–84, 194, 205–211, 215n1; racialized, 249, 250

Levertov, Denise, 51, 151, 159n15

Levy, Aaron, 139

levy, d.a., 5, 6

liberation rhetoric, 53, 55, 61
Line magazine, 127, 128
Lippert, Lora, 12
Livesay, Dorothy, 11, 17, 24
local/ism, 51, 55, 89, 90, 101n3, 195
Lockhead, Gordon. See Brian Fawcett.
Loewinson, Ron, 111
long poem, 31, 115, 137, 218
Long-liners Conference on the
  Canadian Long Poem, 131
lopes, damian, 13, 14, 134, 138, 244
Lowry, Glen, 135
Lundy, Randy, 239
Lusk, Dorothy Trujillo, 120, 133
Lynes, Jeannette, 130
lyric: and imperialism, 97; place in, 97,
  101n9; problems in, 96, 97, 100, 101n9;
  subversion of, 123, 175

●

Mabie, Don, 11
Mac Cormack, Karen, 13, 128, 139, 244
MacLeod, Dan, 58n3
MacLeod, Kathryn, 133, 134
Magazine of Further Studies, 108, 109,
  146
magazines, 17, 229, 240; and
  community, 37, 41, 51, 66, 68, 107, 108,
  110, 111, 146; editorial position of,
  38–41, 54, 107, 108, 111, 240; and
  feminist community, 153–56; and
  funding, 43, 44
Malahat Review, 7–8, 37
male/masculine aesthetic, 56, 60n21, 61,
  81
Mandel, Eli, 23, 51, 127
Manery, Rob, 135
Maracle, Lee, 31, 127, 133, 135
Marrelli, Simon and Nancy, 10
margin/alization: as subject position,
  50, 54, 55, 188; of artist, class-based,
  242, 243
Markotić, Nicole, 12, 131, 136, 139
Marlatt, Daphne, 8–10, 12, 13, 23–25, 72,
  133; erotics in, 186–94; influence of
  Merleau-Ponty on, 94, 101n5; as
  instructor, 132, 147; and language, 186,
  190–92; and place, 93–95, 186; poetics,
  91, 94, 95 185–193; publications, 8–10,
  12, 13, 132, 133; and subjectivity, 94, 95,
  185; and *TISH*, 49, 56, 58n3, 58n4,
  194n1; as translator of Brossard, 82
Marr, Lisa, 134
Marshall, John, 9

Martin, Stephanie, 131
masculine: as dominant subject, 142,
  150, 189, 214. *See also* male.
Massey commission *Report*, 41, 47n22
Mathur, Ashok, 72, 108, 130, 135, 136,
  138, 252n11
Matrix, 12
Matthews, Mike, 56
Matthews, Robin, 3
Mayne, Seymour, 54
Mayr, Suzette, 108, 136, 252n11
McBride, Jason, 138
McCaffery, Steve, 13, 14, 23, 24, 31, 33,
  47n9; collaboration with bpNichol,
  10, 69, 70; publications, 128, 138, 139;
  and sound poetry (Four Horsemen)
  67, 68; on writing as economy, 62,
  75n8
McCarthy, Cavan, 31, 65
McClure, Michael, 23, 66
McFadden, David, 4, 5, 14, 54, 127
McKay, Don, 10
McKay, Jean, 11
McKinnon, Barry, 9
mclennan, rob, 8, 136, 138
McPherson, Karen, 83
memory, 142
Mercury Press, 14
Merleau-Ponty, Maurice, 94, 101n5
Mezei, Kathy, 127, 131
Michelut, Dore, 31
Miki, Roy, 12, 26, 136; as editor, 128, 135,
  235, 239–41; and Writing Thru Race
  conference, 26, 233, 234
MillAr, Jay, 136, 138
Miller, Gene, 8
Ministry of Canadian Heritage, 231
minority: rights, 232–33; subject
  position, 19, 26, 172, 173, 231
Mitchell, Ken, 10
Mock, Irene, 130
modernism, 18, 43, 174
Moir, Rita, 130
Mondo Hunkamooga 39, 128
Moranga, Cherrie, 10
Morrisseau, Norval, 128
Moses, Daniel David, 25, 235, 238, 239
Moss, John, 73
Motel (magazine), 134
mother: and daughter subjectivity, 22,
  81, 162–68; in Kroetsch, 120
Mountain, 38
Mouré, Erin, 6, 205–214

Power, Nick, 39, 128, 133
Prairie Books Now, 37
Prairie Fire, 32, 37, 129
Pratt, Mary Louise, 89, 90
Press Gang, 8, 32
Press Porcepic 12
presses: as centralized, 46n6. *See* individual presses by name.
Prins, Marie, 14, 87
Prism International, 38
process-based poetics, 62, 108, 171
projective verse, 17, 30, 36, 183n9; and TISH, 59n17
prose poem, 193, 212, 218, 219
publishing, 31, 32, 65, 66; funding for, 75n6

Quan, Andy, 253n16
Quartermain, Meredith and Peter, 140
Queen Street Quarterly, 40, 138

R2B2, 35
Rabaté, Jean-Michel, 139
race/racialization: as discursive issue, 234, 239–41; and poetics, 72, 245, 248, 249; and subjectivity, 21, 104–106, 112n4, 162, 164, 169, 234, 244–50
racism: in fiction, 161, 164, 165, 169; and language, 248; legislated, 229, 230, 237, 250n1, 251n3
Raddle Moon magazine, 130
radical poetics: as contested, 57; and nationalism, 29; and radical lifestyle, 61, 75n4, 141, 171; and social relations, 141, 142. *See also* avant garde.
Radu, Kenneth, 12
Ragweed Press, 13
Rampike magazine, 128
Randall, Margaret, 147
Rashid, Ian Iqbal, 128, 137
reader: as feminist, 84, 213, 214, 216n4
reading: and community, 29, 34, 35, 37; and orality/voice, 35–37, 47n17, 59n14; as performance, 52, 67, 68; as research site 34
Reaney, James, 2, 65
Recovery of the Public World conference, 138
Red Deer College Press, 12, 32
Rees, Roberta, 136
regionalism, 32
Reid, Dennis, 4, 5
Reid, Gayla, 12

Reid, Jamie, 49, 58n4, 138
Reid, Monty, 7, 11, 12
Remski, Matthew, 137
renga, 31, 46
Repository magazine, and press, 9
representation: politics of, 236
Retzleff, Marjorie, 12
Rexroth, Marthe, and Kenneth, 59n11
rhizome model for poetic networks, 29, 30, 31
Rice Paper magazine, 40, 137–38
Rich, Adrienne, 15, 80, 151
rickey, r, 108, 137, 139
Riddell, John, 14, 67
rights: individual vs. minority group, 232, 233
Robertson, Lisa: influences on, 217, 218, 226n1; poetics, 217–26; and subjectivity, 218, 223
Robinson, David, 8
Rook, Constance, 7
Room 302, 14
Room of One's Own: A Feminist Journal of Literature and Criticism, 12
Ross, Stuart, 13, 39, 128, 133, 134
Royal Commission: on Bilingualism and Biculturalism, 41
Rungh magazine, 137

Samuels, Ian, 108, 139
Sapergia, Barbara, 11
Sarton, May, 14
Savoie, Paul, 31
Scobie, Stephen, 12, 15, 46n7, 68, 73
Scofield, Greg, 239
Scott, Barbara, 136
Scott, F.R., 17
Scott, Gail, 24, 131, 132, 134, 213
Scream in High Park festival, 137
Scree, 108, 110, 146
Seed, Debbie, 12
Seng, Goh Poh, 135
serial form, 171, 175
Serres, Michel, 177, 178
sexuality: and language, 186, 187, 190–94; lesbian, 205–14; and poetics, 171, 172, 180, 181, 185–94
Shaw, Nancy, 13, 244
Sheard, Charlene, 13
Sheard, Sarah, 5
Sherry, Charles, 109
Shikatani, Gerry, 14, 68
Shives, Arnie, 65